INDUSTRY AND LABOUR

INDUSTRY AND LABOUR

CLASS STRUGGLE AT WORK AND MONOPOLY CAPITALISM

Andrew L. Friedman

Lecturer in Economics
University of Bristol

First published 1977 by
THE MACMILLAN PRESS LTD
London and Basingstoke
Associated companies in Delhi Dublin
Hong Kong Johannesburg Lagos Melbourne
New York Singapore and Tokyo

Printed in Great Britain by
Lowe & Brydone Printers Limited, Thetford, Norfolk

British Library Cataloguing in Publication Data

Friedman, Andrew L
   Industry and labour.
   1.   Industrial relations – Great Britain
   I.   Title
   331'.0941   HD8391

   ISBN 0–333–23031–0
   ISBN 0–333–23032–9   Pbk

For Lola and Lloyd Friedman in Love

Contents

PART THREE

CENTRE–PERIPHERY RELATIONS

PART FOUR

NINETEENTH-CENTURY INDUSTRY-AREA STUDIES

PART FIVE

TWENTIETH-CENTURY INDUSTRY-AREA STUDY

PART SIX

ARGUMENT AND CONSEQUENCE

List of Graphs, Maps, Tables and Charts

Preface

Work on this book began in March 1974 when I was asked by John Bennington, then Director of the Coventry Community Development Project and now a member of Coventry Workshop, to carry out a study of the links between the industrial structure of Coventry and the socio-economic characteristics of Hillfields – Coventry C.D.P.'s project area. Though the study was completed in December 1974, my association with the Coventry C.D.P. and then Coventry Workshop has continued to influence my work. I am especially grateful to John Bennington for the stimulation and encouragement which he has given me as the manuscript progressed through many stages of revision and enlargement.

There are many others who have commented on versions of the manuscript, including those from Warwick University who acted as a reference group for the Coventry C.D.P. and the Bristol University Labour Process group. I would like to thank Sol Picciotto, Bob Fine, Theo Nichols, Miki David and Maralyn Porter in particular. Also I would especially like to thank Tony Brewer for applying his sharp critical eye to various versions of the work, thereby reducing the number of errors in the book considerably, and for his continual support since my arrival at Bristol.

Several people helped with the preparation of tables and gave other research assistance. I would like especially to thank Sylvia Fairbairn, Dominic Cornford, Margaret Bending and Annie Bednarska. More than a dozen people have typed sections of the manuscript. I would like in particular to thank Jan Nicholas for her diligence. I would also like to thank Janet Webb, Olive Santos and the denizens of 5 Harcourt Road for their forbearance, and especially Scarlet Friedman for showing me that there is more to life than academic success.

Bristol
January 1977

A. L. FRIEDMAN

PART ONE
INTRODUCTION

CHAPTER ONE

Background and Argument

This book arose out of two problems, one empirical and one theoretical. The empirical concern of the book is the problem of the persistence of areas of deprivation alongside areas of prosperity within cities or regions in spite of general prosperity in advanced capitalist countries from the late 1940s (at least until very recently), and in spite of government efforts to alleviate these disparities.

From the mid-1960s central government concern about the potential social and political disruption festering in areas of deprivation has encouraged considerable effort to be concentrated into discovering the reasons for areas of deprivation to exist, particularly in cities. Explanations which have guided public policy toward urban problems so far have been primarily psychological or sociological theories. Urban deprivation has been 'explained' as being due to:

(1) the personal characteristics of local residents,
(2) the administrative malfunctions of local government,
(3) the inequitable distribution of resources.

In the first view, areas of deprivation occur due to small concentrations of families with special defects (deviancy, apathy, inadequacy or ignorance) who should be helped to pull themselves up by their bootstraps and stand on their own feet again in order to prevent their weaknesses and abnormalities from being transmitted to the next generation. The solution is seen to lie in more self-help within the community, more co-ordinated social work help and better take-up of personal support services.[1]

The second view blames urban deprivation on the technical incompetence of the local authority – poor planning, unco-ordinated management, insensitive provision of services and inadequate public consultation. The Whitehall solution is to get civil servants, social scientists or private business consultants to prepare guidelines to help local authorities develop more 'total approaches' and 'comprehensive programmes' for tackling urban problems.[2]

The third view is tautological. It simply restates the problem. In its somewhat more sophisticated form it assumes that the cause of the problem is that governments have always given the urban poor and their environment a low priority because more affluent residents and businessmen have had the financial and, therefore, the political muscle to have their needs attended to first.[3] The solution to the problem is to bolster the political muscle of the urban poor – through lobbying parliamentarians (quietly or through demonstrations) to adopt positive discrimination policies. Again this simply restates the problem unless some reason for the initial inequitable distribution of resources is given.

In 1974 I was employed by the Coventry Community Development Project (Coventry C.D.P.) to carry out a study of the relation between Coventry industry and the plight of those living in an area of urban deprivation near Coventry's city centre, Hillfields.[4] The Coventry C.D.P. had tried 'solutions' based on each of the explanations listed above in turn, and each had failed miserably. They then began to look for more explicitly economic explanations for urban deprivation. This book in part arises from my attempt to provide them with such an explanation.

The theoretical problem out of which this book arose concerned my difficulty in finding a framework which allows the links between industrial development and the relative prosperity of small areas to be explored, particularly in the long run. Neo-classical economic theory is primarily concerned with the problem of optimal resource allocation in a static framework. Because neo-classical economic theory treats as exogenous technical development, initial property endowments and many other institutional relationships which would seem to me to be important for understanding the persistence of inequality (such as power relations which are implied by different property endowments) I have chosen to concentrate on the framework of Marxian political economy.[5]

The Marxian framework, while more suitable for dealing with long-run inequality, has remained primarily concerned with macroeconomic forces rather than small area patterns of development or the development of individual industries or firms. The strength of Marx's analysis has lain in its ability to deal clearly with the basic inequality between workers and capitalists and the reasons for their fundamental antagonism at the level of the capitalist mode of production as a whole. Any analysis of individual firms or industries or of small communities which claims to be Marxian must begin with these macroeconomic insights. But the theoretical exercise of using the Marxian framework for examining microeconomic problems is not one of simple application.

This is because Marx did not deal systematically with changes within the capitalist mode of production which are the outcome of class struggle. For Marx the importance of worker resistance lay in its potential for overthrowing capitalism. But worker resistance has clearly forced accommodating changes *within* the capitalist mode of production, particularly since Marx's day. This neglect of the power of worker resistance and its effect on the activities of capitalists and managers is particularly serious at the industry or firm level. I believe that it is impossible to understand changes in managerial behaviour and industrial organisation without explicitly taking struggle at the micro level into account. This is the major theoretical addition to Marx's framework which will allow the links between industrial development and the relative prosperity of small areas, the substance of my empirical problem, to be explored systematically.

While class divisions are at the centre of Marx's analysis of the capitalist mode of production, class struggle is not. In the first half of this book Marx's framework is amended at the general macroeconomic level by explicitly taking worker resistance (Chapters 4 and 5) and managerial counter-pressure (Chapters 6 and 7) into account.

In part the theoretical problem of amending Marx's framework involves incorporating features of capitalism which can be seen, with our twentieth-century perspective, to have been underemphasised by Marx; in part the problem is also to distinguish aspects of capitalism which have changed during the century since Marx wrote from aspects of capitalism which have remained the same. Chapters 2 and 3 attempt to deal with the latter problem.

In Chapter 2 Marx's framework is set out. His concepts of the capitalist mode of production and capitalist productive activity are examined. For Marx the capitalist mode of production defined the basic exchange relations which surround production. But for capital to be a process which accumulates, develops and ultimately destroys itself, a theory of the exchanges which initiate and sustain productive activity and which distribute its fruits is insufficient. A theory of how that productive activity itself develops is needed.

The mode of production (essentially the wage – labour relation under competitive conditions) defines the formal alienation of labour power and the formal possibility of exploitation. It is within the labour process that alienation from the product of workers' labour is extended to alienation from the organisation of work activity and therefore workers' labour time itself.

This extension of alienation and the attendant rise in exploitation are traced historically by Marx through the stages of Co-operation, Manufacture and Modern Industry.

Chapters 3 to 5 attempt to add further elements to Marx's framework as set out in Chapter 2. In Chapter 3 the rise of monopoly power is considered from the beginning of the Modern Industry period (1780s) to the present. Monopoly power is considered to allow top managers of large firms wider discretionary power over the strategies by which they may compete in product markets and maintain authority over workers. Top managers are not confined to *the* single short-run profit maximising product mix, price structure, organisation of work tasks, machinery set-up, or code of discipline, as is implied in both Marx's framework (Law of Value) and neo-classical models. This discretionary power has always been present to some degree. However, from the 1870s the degree of discretionary power enjoyed in certain firms, and the number of firms enjoying such power, increased such that a new stage of capitalism, Monopoly Capitalism, may be distinguished after Modern Industry. Monopoly Capitalism emerged during the 1870s to 1914 period in most advanced capitalist countries. My interpretation of the new stage of capitalism after Modern Industry is compared with those of Lenin (Imperialism) and Baran and Sweezy (Monopoly Capital) in Chapter 3, section 2.

Worker resistance is considered in Chapter 4. The strength of worker resistance has always been distributed unevenly among the working population and often the result of this resistance has been to shore up or even to augment differentials. The class often appears to be fighting among itself rather than for itself.

In Chapter 5 the development of worker resistance in the United Kingdom is examined from the 1780s to the present; some comparisons with other countries, particularly the United States, are also given. In each of the five time periods examined (1780s to 1840s, 1850s to 1870s, 1870s to 1914, 1914 to 1945, 1945 to 1970s) the different forms of resistance are indicated and the uneven development of organised resistance is demonstrated. The double-edged nature of resistance which challenges only aspects or symptoms of capitalist social relations (low wages or poor conditions), rather than the wage relation itself, is emphasised. While trade unions do redress some of the power imbalance within productive activity, they also reflect that imbalance. Because trade unions are concerned primarily with day-to-day struggles, where people continue to work under the capitalist mode of production, they must act as though capitalism were permanent for most of the time. Therefore employers, no longer powerful enough to destroy trade unions, are often able to use them to ensure the maintenance of their managerial authority.

Chapters 6, 7 and 8 present the key theoretical additions to the Marxian framework. The process of management is considered in Chapter 6. Given managerial discretion and worker resistance, management has a key role to play in the development of the capitalist mode of production.

Managerial functions include the co-ordination of the various activities undertaken by the firm and the exercise of managerial authority over labour power. Marx called labour power variable capital. This has a positive and a negative aspect for management. Labour power is, on the one hand, a potentially malleable commodity, but, on the other hand, it is also a commodity controlled ultimately by an independent and often hostile will.

In this chapter two basic managerial strategies are posed: Responsible Autonomy and Direct Control. The Responsible Autonomy strategy attempts to harness the adaptability of labour power by giving workers leeway and by encouraging them to adapt to changing situations in a manner beneficial to the firm. To do this, top managers give them status, autonomy and responsibility, and try to win their loyalty to the firm's ideals (the competitive struggle) ideologically. The Direct Control strategy tries to limit the scope for labour power to vary by close supervision and by minimising individual worker responsibility using Taylorist techniques. The first strategy attempts to capture the benefits of variable capital; the second tries to limit its harmful effects and to treat workers as machines.

Generally Marxists have treated the Direct Control strategy as *the* theory and practice of capitalist control over productive activity. This is a mistake. The mistake follows from a failure to appreciate the importance of worker resistance as a force provoking accommodating changes in the mode of production, and the mistake leads to a technological deterministic view of capitalist development. The most recent and important example of this is Braverman's work [1974], which is dealt with in detail in Chapter 6.

Because people *are not* machines and because labour power *is* alienated under the capitalist mode of production, each strategy, in its ultimate vision, is based on a contradiction. As either ultimate vision is approached that contradiction becomes more apparent.

In Chapter 7 the developing practice and theory of these managerial strategies is traced following the periodisation pattern suggested in Chapter 3.

While each managerial strategy is based on a fundamental contradiction this does not mean that either is impossible to carry out (except as an ultimate ideal). Contradiction rather implies the persistence of a fundamental tension generated from within. The contradiction may be suppressed, or disguised or bypassed, but its continued existence will regenerate tensions which will again threaten good order unless actively suppressed once more. The tensions appear during productive activity in the form of inflexibility generated by such types of managerial strategy.

In Chapter 8 one extremely important way top managers deal with these inflexibilities is examined in detail. This is to divide their workers in terms of the particular strategy used to maintain authority. Top managers will normally think of their workers as either central or peripheral. Central workers are those whom top managers consider to be essential to secure high long-run profits, particularly when product demand or general business conditions are depressed. Workers may be considered central *as individuals* because of their skills, their knowledge or their contribution to the exercise of managerial authority; or they may be those who, by the strength of their collective resistance, make themselves essential to top managers *as a group*. During times of adversity the employment positions of central workers will be protected while peripheral workers will be readily laid off. A significant earnings differential between the two groups will also exist. The division between groups will often follow sexual, racial or nationality lines, though this need not be so.

Within an industry *firms* may be considered central or peripheral on the basis of their relative monopoly power. This complements the centre – periphery pattern within each firm. Top managers of strong firms are able to give central status to a higher proportion of their workers because of their co-operative relations with weaker firms. These co-operative relations allow stronger firms greater flexibility over their own productive activity. When product demand falls strong firms are able to squeeze weaker ones through their co-operative relations, and co-operative relations may ensure steady supplies when internal productive activity is disrupted due to strikes or poor co-ordination. Subcontracting between central and peripheral firms, a particular form of co-operative relation, is examined formally in Chapter 8, Section 4.

In Chapter 9 the relatively privileged position of workers in capitalist countries is examined briefly within the context of struggle and centre – periphery relations.

The centre – periphery distinction serves as a link between the theoretical and macroeconomic discussion of managerial discretion, worker resistance and managerial counter-pressure in Part Two, and the microeconomic industry-area case studies in Parts Four and Five of the book. On the one hand the centre – periphery distinction contributes to the maintenance of managerial authority within capitalist society as a whole; on the other hand it represents the key to the persistence of areas of deprivation amid areas of prosperity.

Peripheral workers will earn lower wages and be laid off more frequently than central workers, as well as suffering the greater oppression engendered by direct control managerial strategies. They will only be able to afford to live in less desirable areas, and they will often be prejudiced against in the housing market if they are blacks or immigrants. More vulnerable to unemployment, peripheral workers will also be more likely to suffer the deskilling which often accompanies unemployment and re-employment. Moving location is difficult for all (except those newly entering employment) and the demoralisation and financial stress of unemployment will make movement in search of better job prospects even more difficult for peripheral workers. Such factors which connect the centre – periphery distinction to the prosperity or deprivation of small areas are discussed in Chapter 10. Long-run changes in centre – periphery relations are examined in Chapter 10. The particular groups of people enjoying central status or suffering peripheral status may change, though the centre – periphery distinction itself continues.

The centre – periphery pattern creates conditions which lead top managers eventually to try to destroy the pattern and re-create it elsewhere. Central workers' security, status and relatively high wages will probably prove to be an intolerable burden on top managers at some future date. Also central workers may lose their status after technical changes or shifts in product demand. In Chapter 10 this fragility of central worker status is examined briefly in relation to broad long-run shifts in the location of areas of relative prosperity in Britain as a whole.

The conclusion of the first half of the book in relation to the second half is that differences in the fortunes of areas are intimately tied to differences in the fortunes of particular groups of people as part of the normal working of the capitalist system. The problems of people living in small areas of deprivation (like Hillfields in Coventry) are not simply due to personal characteristics of the people who live there; not simply due to local authority incompetence or low priority given to the area. Rather the problems of areas like Hillfields must be understood as generated largely in the sphere of production.

In Parts Four and Five the categories and theoretical connections built up in the first parts of the book are applied in three industry-area case studies. In each case study monopoly power, worker resistance, managerial strategies and centre – periphery distinctions are examined historically to illuminate both the empirical industry-area links and to illustrate the power of the amended Marxian framework for examining microeconomic relations.

Though I have always kept in mind the problem of areas of deprivation continuing to exist near areas of prosperity in advanced capitalist countries, it is to my theoretical problem that I have devoted most space in the following chapters. Inequality in conditions of people distinguished by their location is but one symptom of the normal uneven development of capitalist societies. My central concern has been to provide a framework for analysing how uneven development is generated – a framework which is capable of illuminating concrete situations of people working in particular industries or living in particular areas.

In the normal running of capitalist societies most class struggle occurs at the micro or local level. Unfortunately almost all radical theoretical analyses of capitalist societies, particularly during the past fifty years, have been highly abstract – divorced not only from concrete local situations, but also from the concrete macro or national situations of particular countries.[6] The framework set up in Parts Two and Three is intended to provide a framework for micro analysis within the Marxian paradigm. This micro analysis is illustrated by the case studies in Parts Four and Five, though it is intended to be applicable to local situations in any society dominated by the capitalist mode of production.

CHAPTER TWO

Marx's Framework

1 Capitalist Mode of Production

It will be useful to begin with Marx's basic description or definition of the capitalist mode of production. The capitalist mode of production is peculiar to a limited period of history. It is distinguished from earlier modes of production[1] by the category of free labour. Labour is free under capitalism in two ways.

First, individual workers are free to sell and thus to *alienate* their capacity for labour or 'labour power' for a limited period of time in exchange with capitalists for money. Marx defines labour power as 'the aggregate of those bodily and mental capabilities existing in human beings, which he exercises whenever he produces a use-value[2] of any description' (*Capital*, vol. 1, p. 164). In feudalism serfs or vassals owe their lords so much of their labour power and the serfs are born into this relationship. There is no market where labourers may exercise proprietary rights over their own labour power. But under the capitalist mode of production people do have proprietary rights over their labour power and they are free to sell their labour power for *limited* periods of time.

The second way that labour is free in the capitalist mode of production is that the workers have nothing to sell but their labour power in order to gain the means by which they might subsist. They have no independent access to means of subsistence, such as through the produce of land-holdings, and they have no other commodities which they might exchange for means of subsistence.

In the pure capitalist mode of production[3] there are two clearly distinguishable classes. One, of people who own nothing but their labour power and who must sell that labour power to subsist – the workers. The second, of people who buy labour power and who use that commodity, combined with other commodities such as raw materials and tools or machines (what Marx calls the 'instruments of labour'), to produce commodities which they sell for money – the capitalists. With this money the capitalists acquire means of subsistence while retaining ownership of the means of production. 'He, who before was the money-owner, now strides in front as capitalist; the possessor of labour-power follows as his labourer. The one with an air of importance, smirking, intent on business; the other, timid and holding back, like one who is bringing his own hide to market and has nothing to expect but – a hiding' (*Capital*, vol. 1, p. 172).

Capital, the title of Marx's most developed treatise, is that process by which capitalists first exchange money for commodities by purchasing labour power and other means of production, then transform those commodities into new commodities (means of production and means of subsistence) in what Marx calls the 'labour process', and finally exchange those new commodities for money which enables them to start the process again. Capital, the process, is manifest in different entities at different stages – sometimes money, sometimes means of production and means of subsistence. But the process is based on the purchase and sale of labour power.

There is one other feature of the capitalist mode of production which Marx considers to be essential. Capital is not simply a process of endless alternation from money to commodities and then back to money. Capital is a *developing* process whose essential nature is that it expands; that capitalists *accumulate* more and more money representing more and more capital.

Why should this be so?

First, contained in the main features of the capitalist mode of production mentioned above are the potential ingredients for capital to expand. As a class the workers bring only their own hides to the market and as such they can only expect a hiding. But if the value of any commodity is taken to be the amount of labour time which is socially required to produce that thing, and if in return for their labour power the workers receive what is socially necessary to maintain them as proprietors of labour power (capable of making that labour power available to capitalists), then, in value terms, equivalents are exchanged. There is no exploitation. It is not in the exchange of labour power that the worker gets his hiding, but in the labour process which follows. Having sold his labour power to the capitalist for a period of time, the worker is now alienated from that labour power, and the capitalist may dispose of it as he wishes (within some bounds set by law and custom).[4] Labour power is a peculiar commodity in that it is possible for labour power to produce commodities, the value of which is greater than the value of the means of subsistence socially necessary to reproduce that labour power.[5] Not only has the worker become alienated from his labour power, but in so doing he has lost claim to the fruits of his labour. Surplus value created by labour power legally belongs to the capitalist and it is the form taken by exploitation in the capitalist mode of production.

What will the capitalist do with this surplus value?

The capitalist will consume part of it, but he will also plough part of it back into the process of capital in order to expand the value of his capital. Why should the capitalist abstain from immediate consumption?

First, the capitalist is driven by a desire for wealth as wealth, but second, the individual capitalist is driven to reinvest by the forces of competition. New investment embodies newer and more productive techniques for production. If an individual capitalist does not keep up with the most productive techniques his competitors will be able to sell their commodities more cheaply than him. Not only will the laggard capitalist fall behind in technique, but he will also be priced out of his commodity markets and destroyed as a capitalist. While the individual capitalist may have become a capitalist through avarice, continual abstinence is required of him due to the competitive nature of the mode of production. For Marx the character of the mode of production primarily shapes the psychology of the individuals rather than the other way around. I shall return to this theme in Section 2 below.

In the purchase and sale of labour power Marx demonstrates the *potential* for capital to expand. The purchase of labour power allows the capitalist to appropriate surplus value. In the forces of competition Marx provides a reason for that potential to be realised *continually*. This Marx calls the Law of Value, that capitalists are forced to extract surplus value from workers due to competition.

> The development of capitalist production makes it constantly necessary to keep increasing the amount of the capital laid out in a given industrial undertaking, and competition makes the *immanent* laws of capitalist production to be felt by each individual capitalist, as external coercive laws. It compels him to keep constantly extending his capital, in order to preserve it (*Capital*, vol. 1, p. 555).

The capitalist mode of production may therefore be defined by two features. First, labour is free in the double sense. The worker is free to sell his labour power, but because he is also free from the possession of other commodities which he might sell, he *must* sell his labour power to some capitalist.

Second, capitalists, while having a monopoly over the means of production as a class (and therefore not being required to sell their labour power), are not monopolists over sections of the means of production as individuals. They are subjected as individuals to forces of competition which *force* them to accumulate capital – though they *may* wish to accumulate anyway.

Marx's definition of the capitalist mode of production describes the exchange relations which surround production, rather than the capitalist method of production itself. The definition merely sets out the conditions which allow exploitation to occur; the conditions which allow one group of people to appropriate surplus product produced by another group. As such, it is capable of providing a theory to explain the distribution or allocation of wealth produced by the capitalist mode of production. Most Marxists, until very recently, have concentrated on Marx's theory as a theory of value, something similar to, though not quite the same as, the value theory of classical economists like Ricardo and the price theory of neo-classical economists today – a theory of resource allocation under certain initial assumptions. But for Marx the capitalist mode of production is an historically limited phenomenon. Not only is capital a process which grows, but the capitalist mode of production is a social system which develops, changes and ultimately will be destroyed because of changes which it has itself fostered as part of its development process.

To understand how the capitalist mode of production develops and changes Marx considers a theory of productive activity itself to be necessary along with a theory of the exchanges which initiate and sustain productive activity and which distribute its fruits.

2 The Capitalist Labour Process and the Valorisation Process

Productive activity for Marx is the unity of the labour process and the valorisation process (see note 5).

The labour process is not in itself peculiar to capitalism. It is a fundamental condition of human existence. The labour process in its most abstract aspect is 'human action with a view to the production of use-values, appropriation of natural substances to human requirements; it is the necessary condition for effecting exchange of matter between Man and Nature; it is the everlasting Nature-imposed condition of human existence, and therefore is independent of every social phase of that existence, or rather, is common to every such phase' (*Capital*, vol. 1, p. 179).

In this abstract definition the labour process is a relation between man and nature. But in any concrete stage of history the labour process is also a social process in which *people interact*. The particular form of the social aspect of the labour process will depend on the mode of production within which that labour process is situated.

For Marx what distinguishes the human labour process from that of other animals is that human labour is conscious and purposive rather than instinctive.

What distinguishes the worst architect from the best of bees is this, that the architect raises his structure in imagination before he erects it in reality. At the end of every labour-process, we get a result that already existed in the imagination of the labourer at its commencement. He not only effects a change of form in the material on which he works, but he also realises a purpose of his own that gives the law to his *modus operandi*, and to which he must subordinate his will. And this subordination is no mere momentary act. Besides the exertion of the bodily organs, the process demands that, during the whole operation, the workman's will be steadily in consonance with his purpose (*Capital*, vol. 1, p. 174).

In the abstract the labour process involves human imagination, human purpose and human will, but in a particular situation the people whose imagination, purpose and will direct the physical activity may be different from those who carry out that physical activity. This separation is increasingly incorporated into the labour process as the capitalist mode of production develops.

There are three elements to the abstract aspect of the labour process.

First, there is the work or labour itself—the personal activity of human beings.

Second, the subject of labour—nature's materials in their virgin state or worked up through previous labour into raw materials.

Third, the instruments of labour—the things which people use to mediate between themselves and the subject of their labour.

Under the capitalist mode of production the elements of the labour process are combined to produce surplus value as well as use-values. In the valorisation process commodities are used to produce other commodities, the value of which is greater than the constituent commodities. Marx calls the instruments of labour used up in the labour process (wear and tear or depreciation) and the materials used up in a given period of time *constant capital* (commonly labelled c). He calls the labour power used during that time *variable capital* (commonly labelled v). The capitalist buys the constant and variable capital at their values, at the amount of socially necessary labour time required to produce them, but labour power, v, creates commodities the value of which is greater than the value of the wages which are paid for labour power. The value which workers give to the commodities produced is therefore $v + s$, the value of variable capital plus *surplus value*. Constant capital, on the other hand, merely transfers its value to the commodities produced. Plant and equipment embody past live labour time so they have value, but it is only living labour which produces surplus value.

Therefore the value of commodities produced as part of the valorisation process equals $c + v + s$. The rate of exploitation is defined as s/v, while the rate of profit (assuming all constant capital which the capitalist purchases in one period is used up during that production period) is $s/c + v$ or surplus value as a proportion of total capital laid out.

Capitalist productive activity is a developing process which is both affected by the social relations which surround it and in turn also influences them. The effect of productive activity on the mode of production derives from Marx's view of human nature. For Marx, people's needs and abilities are not fixed. They change in the course of human activity and particularly in the course of work.

Productive activity is initiated by man 'in order to appropriate Nature's productions in a form adapted to his own wants', according to Marx. But he then goes on to say that man, 'by thus acting on the external world and changing it, . . . at the same time changes his own nature. He develops his slumbering powers and compels them to act in obedience to his sway' (*Capital*, vol. 1, p. 173).

Three characteristics or stages of capitalist productive activity are worth considering. First is what Marx calls *co-operation* — 'when numerous labourers work together side by side, whether in one and the same process, or in different connected processes' (*Capital*, vol. 1, p. 308). Co-operation is not peculiar to the capitalist mode of production, but it does distinguish capitalism in its earliest stages from the individual handicraft trades of the guilds.

While the category of free labour determines the legal possibility or potential for the extraction of surplus value, and while competition among capitalists provides the primary motivation for capitalists to try to realise that potential continuously, co-operation provides one of the main *technical* reasons which allows that *legal* opportunity for exploitation to be captured by the capitalist. To enable the capitalist to appropriate surplus value, commodities must be produced in the labour process whose value is greater than the commodities which went into it. What the capitalist pays the labourer is the cost of maintaining him for a fixed period of time, while what the capitalist receives is the labourer's capacity for working during that period of time. With co-operation a given expenditure of work by each individual labourer (a given degree of effort for a given amount of time) will produce more commodities than if those labourers were each working separately.[6] There are many reasons for this. For example, co-operation allows common use of means of production such as buildings; it allows a great deal of work to be carried out in a short space of time at critical moments such as during harvest time; and it allows a certain uniformity and continuity in commodities produced.

A second major characteristic of the labour process under the capitalist mode of production is the development of the *manufacturing division of labour* — the separation of tasks within a workshop or where a single final commodity is being produced.[7] This increases the productivity of labour beyond what is achieved under simple co-operation when everyone is doing the same things. The workers' dexterity at a simple operation increases with constant exercise and experience. Much of the time lost when workmen changed from one operation within the labour process to another is eliminated. Thus the amount of labour time required for the production of a fixed quantity of commodities falls. This means that commodities have fallen in value. Now if the amounts of commodities which the workers require as means of subsistence remain the same in physical terms, then the value of labour power falls. The labour time embodied in the means of subsistence required to maintain workers falls. If the amount of time the workers work stays the same, the proportion of that time representing surplus value and appropriated by the capitalist rises. This method of valorisation, increasing the rate of exploitation by cheapening commodities which enter into workers' consumption, Marx calls the 'production of relative surplus value'.

Marx considers the period when the capitalist mode of production was mainly characterised by the manufacturing division of labour as roughly from the middle of the sixteenth century to the last third of the eighteenth century (*Capital*, vol. 1, p. 318). Marx actually calls this period of capitalist development Manufacture.

During Manufacture, workers who had been trained as all-round craftsmen, often with a seven-year apprenticeship, came to be what Marx calls 'detail workers' and lose their all round craft skills.

This is one example of how the development of productive activity under capitalism can affect capitalist social relations, or the capitalist mode of production itself. The original condition which distinguished worker from capitalist, the lack of independent means of production (the lack of commodities other than his own labour power available for sale), is augmented by the degradation of workers' labour power. As the manufacturing division of labour proceeds within the labour process, the workers' general craft skills wither while their detail dexterity for a very specific operation is developed. Thus productive activity moulds a set of workers such that even if they could get access to some means of production they would no longer be able to produce entire commodities.

The manufacturing division of labour weakens the workers' position in another way. By splitting productive activity requiring general skills into component parts and filling those parts with different workers, manufacture 'develops a hierarchy of labour powers, to which there corresponds a scale of wages' (*Capital*, vol. 1, p. 330). As the individual components are simpler to master than the whole, the value of labour power is diminished. The training time required to reproduce labour power falls. There also arises a set of detail operations which require no skill at all. Manufacture 'also begins to make a speciality of the absence of all development' (*Capital*, vol. 1, p. 331). Workers are increasingly separated into skilled and unskilled. The cost of apprenticeship for unskilled workers employed is removed altogether.

As the position of the worker weakened in the market for labour power during this period, the position of the typical capitalist slowly improved. The manufacturing division of labour meant an increase in the minimum number of workers under the control of a single capitalist required for that capitalist's operation to be technically efficient. The rise in the minimum number of workmen also meant a rise in the quantity of tools and raw materials needed. So the amount of money which the capitalist must lay out to buy the labour power he needs (variable capital), and to buy the instruments of labour and raw materials (constant capital), rises. Each individual labourer's labour power represents a smaller and smaller proportion of the capital of the capitalist who purchases it.

A third major feature or stage of productive activity during capitalism is the use of *machinery*[8] to replace labour power and to increase the productivity of the workers who remain. Machinery acts like the manufacturing division of labour to reduce the labour time necessary to produce commodities and to increase the rate of exploitation by the production of relative surplus value. The widespread introduction of machinery into capitalist production began in the last third of the eighteenth century and Marx calls the stage of the capitalist mode of production from then up to his time Modern Industry.[9]

During this stage an equalisation or homogenisation of work activities by different workers occurs because now most workers are merely appendages to the machine rather than facets of a handicraft skill. Instead of a hierarchy of workers based on skills or tasks, most workers do unskilled work and the more important divisions within the labour force are based on age and sex.

Machines lessened both the brute strength and the level of skill required in productive activity. This allowed capitalists to employ more women and children. The employment of women and children meant that in order to produce labour power men did not have to be paid a family wage. Wages were actually reduced during this period, partly because of the pressure of women and children being added to the market as suppliers of labour power, and partly because the numbers of men looking for work was swollen due to men being thrown out of work when machines were introduced.

All productive activity is not mechanised immediately. The introduction of machinery into one labour process, by cheapening the value of labour power (production of relative surplus value), actually discourages the introduction of machinery into other labour processes. Machines have to be that much cheaper or they have to increase the productivity of the remaining workers by that much more if they are to replace cheapened workers.[10]

During the Modern Industry phase productive activity conducted on the basis of domestic industry and manufacture survives. But this productive activity is altered in that it comes to be affected crucially by the dominant Modern Industry sector made up of highly mechanised factories. Marx renames these less technically advanced sectors 'Modern Manufacture' and 'Modern Domestic Industry' during the Modern Industry stage.

First, conditions of work in these less technically advanced sectors deteriorate markedly. The widespread use of women and children is not confined to the Modern Industry sector during this period. While the lightened character of work in the mechanised Modern Industry sector first encouraged capitalists to employ women and children there, the consequent fall in wages also forced women and children into the less technically advanced sectors to make up the family wage. There the work was harder, often more dangerous because of poor sanitary conditions, hours were longer, and pay was often lower than in the more technically advanced sectors. This is because workers come to Modern Manufacture and Modern Domestic Industry after being thrown out of Modern Industry (and agriculture) in a desperate state, because these less technically advanced sectors could only compete with Modern Industry on the basis of cheap labour and hard conditions, and because workers' power to resist such conditions in the Modern Domestic Industry sector is weaker because the workers are so spread out.

Second, in many cases domestic industry or small workshops based on manufacturing division of labour become the outside branches of the mechanised factories. The same capitalist might control productive activity in all three sectors producing the same commodity. When demand for the commodity is high workers in the less technically advanced sectors will be put to work at an exhausting pace, but when demand falls off these workers will be the first to be laid off. This occurs because the capitalist will want to keep his modern factory running at a smooth continuous pace to gain the most from his machinery. He loses out when machines are idle because the machines deteriorate physically and because of obsolescence since continual improvements occur in new generations of machinery. Idle workers, laid off because of insufficient demand for the capitalist's commodities, cost the individual capitalist nothing.

Two further characteristics of labour processes under Modern Industry are worth noting.

The first is that while Modern Manufacture and Modern Domestic Industry survive for some time into this period, according to Marx these technically backward sectors eventually become mechanised. The cheapening of labour power and the miserably hard conditions of work in these sectors eventually meet with the natural barrier of human endurance.

'So soon as this point is at last reached – and it takes many years – the hour has struck for the introduction of machinery, and for the thenceforth rapid conversion of the scattered domestic industries and also of manufactures into factory industries' (*Capital*, vol. 1, p. 442). Another reason for the eventual disappearance of the non-mechanised sectors was the Factory Acts, which began to take effect during the 1830s. By limiting hours of work and regulating some of the most unhealthy conditions of work they weakened the competitive position of non-mechanised sectors relative to the mechanised ones.

The second characteristic of the Modern Industry stage is the continual change in methods of production which occurs even in labour processes where machines have already been introduced. Machines themselves are continually being improved, replacing more and more labour power. The production of relative surplus value – the cheapening of commodities by introducing technical improvements – grows in importance.

'Modern Industry never looks upon and treats the existing form of a process as final. The technical basis of that industry is therefore revolutionary, while all earlier modes of production were essentially conservative' (*Capital*, vol. 1, p. 457). Corresponding to these changes, the functions of the labourer and the social division of labour is continually changing; that is, changes in the particular tasks performed by workers within a single labour process and shifts in capital and labour from one branch of production to another are always occurring. But because the worker has sold his labour power to a capitalist these changes in technical conditions of production mean that workers often have to be thrown out of one labour process, have to return to the labour power market, in order to be regrouped around new manufacturing and social divisions of labour. This 'dispels all fixity and security in the situation of the labourer; . . . it constantly threatens, by taking away the instruments of labour, to snatch from his hands his means of subsistence, and by suppressing his detail function, to make him superfluous' (*Capital*, vol. 1, p. 457).

This continual technical change, which is primarily labour-saving according to Marx, perpetually creates and re-creates what Marx calls an 'industrial reserve army' of labour – a body of workers out of work, 'kept in misery in order to be always at the disposal of capital' (*Capital*, vol. 1, p. 457). Through the industrial reserve army, wages are kept down to near subsistence. [11]

The other important effect of technical change during the Modern Industry phase is that its labour power saving bias implies that the ratio of constant capital to variable capital (called by Marx the 'organic composition of capital') will rise. Because surplus value can only be extracted from labour power (constant capital merely gives up a part of its value as a commodity to the new commodities created by using up constant capital) the proportion of capital which yields surplus value will fall. If the rate of exploitation remains constant (the amount of surplus value appropriated from a given amount of labour time), then the ratio of surplus value to capital will fall. If we take this ratio as an indicator of the rate of profit generated within the system, we have Marx's law of the tendency of the rate of profit to fall. [12]

Co-operation, the manufacturing division of labour within a single labour process and the mechanisation of the labour process each dominate the labour process under the capitalist mode of production at different stages of its development, but during succeeding stages the main characteristic of earlier stages continues to characterise the labour process, though in a somewhat altered form. In the Modern Industry stage workers still perform detail tasks but they are now details of a machine process rather than of a handicraft.

To repeat the argument in favour of the Marxian framework as a starting point for investigating links between industrial development and area development, it is that Marx examined industrial production as a developing process: a process capable of changing itself and changing the exchange relations by which it is initiated and by which its fruits are distributed. While the links between industry and area are often exchange relations, unless we have some theory of how exchange relations develop, the relation between industry and area cannot be analysed historically.

PART TWO

MONOPOLY CAPITALISM, WORKER RESISTANCE AND MANAGEMENT

CHAPTER THREE

Monopoly Capitalism

The first step for altering Marx's framework concerns the power of competitive forces on firms and Marx's Law of Value. For Marx 'competition makes the immanent laws of capitalist production to be felt by each individual capitalist, as external coercive laws' (*Capital*, vol. 1, p. 555). But from the outset competitive pressures were not felt with the same force by all individual capitalists. Some firms were large and strong, some weak. For the weak firms the Law of Value (the need to squeeze as much surplus value as possible from their workers and to introduce the most productive techniques possible in the short run) was felt with vigour. But capitalists owning stronger firms were able to relax pressure on workers at times or to wait before introducing new machinery until it had been proved profitable. For them the Law of Value was less coercive. They enjoyed a margin of discretion over their policies.

This unevenness in the power of individual firms has become more pronounced since Marx's time. In all advanced capitalist countries there now exists a sector of huge corporations whose top managers exercise considerable discretion over their policies. We now live in the era of Monopoly Capitalism. This is not to say that competition no longer exists for these firms, simply that the coercive force of competition is at times relatively weak.

The size of larger firms and the proportion of individual markets they account for has been growing, at least since the beginning of the Modern Industry period. This has been a slow and very uneven process which is still going on. Nevertheless it is all too easy to see only the growth of large firms and to ignore small firms. In fact large firms derive much of their discretionary power from their relations with smaller ones. Finally, as will be shown more clearly later on in the book, relations between firms of unequal power represent one of the main factors helping to explain the existence of areas of deprivation beside areas of prosperity.

In this chapter Monopoly Power and Monopoly Capitalism are discussed more formally in Section 1. Previous Marxist attempts to deal with the era of Monopoly Capitalism are discussed in Section 2. In Section 3 the development of monopoly power is examined historically from the beginning of the

Modern Industry stage (1780s), with particular emphasis on the British experience.

1   Monopoly Power and Monopoly Capitalism

Around the end of the nineteenth century a new stage of the capitalist mode of production emerged in the most advanced capitalist countries. Following Baran and Sweezy (Baran [1957], Baran and Sweezy [1966]) I have labelled this stage 'Monopoly Capitalism'.[1] During Monopoly Capitalism a few large firms dominate productive activity in a large number of industries (Modern Industry was characterised by small-scale and highly competitive firms). These large firms are run by top managers, a group of people who generally do not own a majority interest or effective controlling interest in the firm, though they may do so.

Strong evidence of the separation of ownership from control of large companies emerged in the 1930s (Berle and Means [1932]), though Marx himself recognised this tendency in the 1870s (*Capital*, vol. 3, chap. 27). Certainly most are agreed that when *steady* average or even slightly below average profits are earned, shareholders exert very little control over the running of large corporations.

According to Galbraith control has passed to a large category of employees within large firms – the technostructure.[2] This is misguided. While the technostructure contributes information to group decisions, ultimately those decisions are taken by very few individuals, primarily the few directors and executives at the top. The important decisions – decisions about large-scale redundancies, new products, new technologies, prices, subcontracting, etc. – are taken by top managers. Certainly top managers often consult and receive information from many people to improve their decisions, but ultimately the decisions are taken by top managers alone.

The large firms of Monopoly Capitalism influence the activities of numerous smaller firms. Smaller suppliers, industrial purchasers, distributors and direct competitors are influenced through an intricate web of co-operative arrangements in which the larger firms generally hold the whip hand. Monopoly Capitalism as a stage is distinguished by the monopoly power which is enjoyed by a few large firms and which *the many smaller firms lack*. It is important to recognise that both groups of firms are part of Monopoly Capitalism.[3]

What does monopoly power mean for large firms?

Under Monopoly Capitalism large firms are more or less protected from competitive pressure because the scale of their operations acts as an entry barrier to limit the field of potential new entrants, and because their size and financial strength also enhance their power to retaliate against competitive initiatives from those already in the industry. Their monopoly power is based on their relative protection from competitive pressures and this monopoly power allows large firms a discretionary margin over their own activities. The top managers of firms with some measure of monopoly power are not forced to maximise short-run profits, as were the owners and managers of firms in the highly competitive markets of Marx's Modern Industry.

Top managers of firms with monopoly power do not have to choose the price and output combination, the level and type of mechanisation, the organisation of work tasks or the code of factory discipline which would maximise short-run profits in order to survive. Of course firms in highly competitive markets do not always make the correct profit-maximising choices, but if they do not choose policies which come close to short-run profit-maximisation, they would be underpriced by competitors and eventually forced out of markets. In Marx's highly competitive model of Modern Industry, as in the standard neo-classical model of perfect competition, cost structures, output levels and prices of firms are 'situationally determined' in that the discretion of decision-makers in firms is confined to something approaching a single-valued feasible set if they are to survive as decision-makers in those harsh market situations (Latsis [1972]). Under Monopoly Capitalism, on the other hand, top managers in many firms enjoy a margin of discretion over their decisions. For them the Law of Value is sometimes relaxed. Top managers in firms with monopoly power have the opportunity to realise more than average profits, or surplus-profits, over long periods (see Mandel [1975], chap. 3, for a discussion of surplus-profits).

The size and financial strength of these large firms have allowed them a measure of discretion in implementing new technology and, with advertising and co-operative arrangements, their relative insulation from competition has allowed large firms during Monopoly Capitalism some measure of stability in product demand. But monopoly power is a *relative* concept, and under capitalism the discretion enjoyed by even the largest firms is limited by potential competition, by stock market and financial institution constraints, by the limitations to the managing of consumer demand beyond which advertising is ineffective and of course by worker resistance.

Monopoly power does allow top managers of these firms the opportunity to make surplus-profits, but firms with monopoly power often do not appear to earn especially high profits. These top managers have the discretion to forgo some profit without immediate risk of financial ruin.

Several discretionary options are open to top managers of firms with monopoly power. First, they may choose to pursue goals other than profit-maximisation. They may choose to maximise growth, or sales, or staffs or some combination of these. Second, they may slack off or satisfice rather than maximise in the pursuit of their goals. Third, top managers can make mistakes, and go on making mistakes for a considerable period of time, while still surviving. And finally, it becomes possible for top managers to choose different routes to reach their goals. They may choose a strategy which sacrifices short-run profits in order to increase profitability later on.

Recent bourgeois theories of large firms have concentrated on the first two options, and primarily on the alternative goals option.[4] This emphasis is not particularly interesting for two reasons. First, the alternatives suggested require high profits. Growth, or higher sales, or staffs must be financed either through accumulated past profits or by appealing to financial markets and institutions which primarily consider profit prospects when allocating funds (Solow [1967]). Second, firms require substantial profits and particularly *steady* profits to maintain dividend flows and share prices. These are necessary to prevent shareholders from mobilising against incumbent top managers, and more important, to discourage take-over bids. Top managers in taken-over firms are often replaced or substantially reorganised (Singh [1971]).

The evidence cited above suggests that high profits are still important to top managers in large firms, though *steady* profits are more important. If steady profits are not maintained, managerial insulation from external financial interference will be threatened. If dividend flows and share prices are not maintained, the possibilities for shareholder interference and the risk of take-over will grow. Also, while evidence comparing profitability with the size of firms has shown no clear relation one way or the other, evidence for a clear positive relation between the size of firms and profit stability is strong (Singh and Whittington [1968]; Eatwell [1971]).

Thus it is not a change in the goals pursued by those in control of firms but rather a widening of the possible paths open to top managers leading to the achievement of high and steady profits which distinguishes Monopoly Capitalism. Therefore, for Monopoly Capitalism, analysis of industrial activity requires considerable attention to be paid to types of managerial strategies for dealing with suppliers, with customers, and particularly with workers whose organisational strength for resisting managerial initiatives increased significantly during the transition to Monopoly Capitalism. In the next four chapters worker resistance and managerial strategies for dealing with this resistance will be examined historically. In Chapter 8, and in Section 3 of this chapter, strategies for dealing with other firms will be discussed.

Finally it will be helpful to separate monopoly capitalism as an *analytical* concept – meaning the existence of a degree of monopoly power in the hands of top managers of some firms in a particular industry who enjoy a margin of discretion in their own activities and a degree of power over smaller firms in the industry – from Monopoly Capitalism as a *stage* of the capitalist mode of production – meaning the time when monopoly capitalism characterises most industries in a particular country.[5]

2   Marxist Interpretations of Monopoly Capitalism

From the early decades of the twentieth century Marxists have recognised that capitalism has changed since Marx's time. The best known interpretation of that change was Lenin's [1916]. For Lenin Imperialism, the highest stage of capitalism, was established at the turn of the century, when the German cartels of the 1890s survived the 1900–3 crisis (unlike those established in the 1880s which generally perished in the crisis of the early 1890s). Lenin's analysis of Imperialism merely consisted of five trends in capitalist development. According to Lenin these were discernible, but minor, in Marx's time. They had come to dominate the mode of production by 1900.

First, concentration of capital and production had developed to the point where cartels had become one of the foundations of economic life.

Second, because concentration in the financial sector proceeded more quickly than concentration in the industrial sector, banks had grown from humble middlemen into the directors of capitalist development through their monopoly hold on credit. At the top, on the boards of directors, the bankers and the industrialists fused under the rule of the bankers into what Lenin called the 'financial oligarchy'.

Third, capital exports became more important than commodity exports. The falling rate of profit had proceeded much further in developed countries than underdeveloped countries.[6] This sent capital flying to backward countries where profits were higher, where capital was relatively scarce and where land, wages and raw materials were comparatively cheap. For Lenin this accelerated capital accumulation in backward countries and retarded accumulation in advanced countries.

Fourth was the formation of international monopolies by agreements or the formation of multinational companies.

Fifth was the territorial division of the earth by the advanced capitalist nations.

Lenin's examination of Imperialism was descriptive. While he recognised the coming of Monopoly Capitalism ('imperialism is the monopoly stage of capitalism'), it did not imply any change in the behaviour of firms nor any changes in the fundamental laws of capitalist development for Lenin.

In particular workers and resources of an underdeveloped country coming into contact with capitalist enterprise during Imperialism would be affected as the developed countries were by capitalism during Manufacture and Modern Industry. Capital exports would accelerate the development of backward countries and retard that of advanced capitalist countries. In this Lenin agreed with Marx. The 'country that is more developed industrially only shows the less developed the image of its own future', wrote Marx (*Capital*, vol. 1, p. 19).

It is on this point that recent theories of Imperialism or Monopoly Capitalism have differed most sharply with Lenin. That the relation between advanced and underdeveloped countries is more complex than Lenin or Marx suggested has been shown by the rising economic gap between the two groups of countries, particularly during the 1950s and 1960s. This led recent theorists to examine monopoly capital more closely than Lenin, to see just how capital from developed countries affects underdeveloped countries, and in so doing, to see how monopoly capitalism behaves differently from modern industry within advanced countries.

The most influential theory of twentieth-century capitalism since Lenin has been that of Baran and Sweezy [1966].[7] According to them, 'Monopoly Capitalism is a system made up of giant corporations' (p. 62). They operate in an environment containing smaller firms, but the smaller firms exert no independent initiative, they simply react to initiatives from the giant companies. The crucial difference between Monopoly Capitalism and Competitive Capitalism is that the large firms of monopoly capitalism are price makers rather than price takers. Large firms are able to choose the prices they charge within wide limits. They are not confined to the externally given market price. Also large firms are not forced to maximise profits by equating marginal cost with marginal revenue, according to Baran and Sweezy. Nevertheless these firms are still anxious to make high profits because competition still occurs. The weapons of competition are now sales effort and cost reduction rather than price cutting, because the few large firms in each industry recognise that a price war will harm them all. High profits are necessary to sustain high sales effort, to allow for cost reducing, technologically advanced investments, and because more profitable firms are more able to dictate terms in all their financial dealings.

The general effect of monopoly capitalism is for the surplus enjoyed by firms to rise rather than for profits to fall when costs are reduced. Baran and Sweezy's major analytic change to Marx's framework is the replacement of the law of the tendency for the rate of profit to fall by the law of the tendency for the surplus to rise. What is the surplus? The economic surplus, for Baran and Sweezy, is the difference between what a society produces and the socially necessary costs of producing it (p. 117). It includes, as well as the traditional elements of Marx's surplus value (profits plus interest plus rent), wasteful expenses in business[8] and government expenses – both military and civilian.

The major economic problem for monopoly capitalism is how to absorb the rising economic surplus (which accrues to big business in the first instance) in ways which will provide demand for the particular commodities produced by monopoly capital. Otherwise the system will be thrown into depression, with idle commodities held by large corporations causing general unemployment and tempting firms to wage ruinous price wars.

There are a number of problems with this analysis. First there are the more technical problems of deciding what costs of production are socially necessary in any particular case. Actual costs are observed; socially necessary costs are not. What one considers to be 'necessary' will depend, to some extent, on how one thinks production *ought* to be organised. The problems of individual subjectivity are clear here. Nevertheless these problems are not insurmountable. Judgements can be made as to the size of economic surplus allowing some margin for error. A reasonable attempt at such measurement was made in the appendix to *Monopoly Capital*.

The second problem with Baran and Sweezy's analysis is their neglect of the relation between large corporations and small businesses. While they recognise the existence of the small business sector, they are concerned to show that this sector does not have effective power to counter initiatives from big business rather than to examine what those initiatives may be and the motives behind them. In order to link industrial development with area development these latter considerations must be examined thoroughly.

The third problem is the most serious one. Baran and Sweezy admit to neglecting the labour process (p. 22). Once they recognised that those running large firms have a wider margin of choice (over price) than small competitive firms, Baran and Sweezy were forced to discuss managerial motives and strategies. This makes the labour process even more important for under-standing Monopoly Capitalism than it was for understanding Modern Industry, unless the pressure of worker resistance on management has relaxed along with price competition. This, Baran and Sweezy do not believe. For them class struggle based in the labour process has become internationalised, but it has not disappeared, even in advanced capitalist countries. Nevertheless Baran and Sweezy have made a very strong assumption about the labour process which they do not back up.

They assume that the sales effort, business lawyers and accountants, government defence expenditure, government expenditure on police, unem-ployment benefit, old age pensions and expenditure on maintaining imperi-alist relations overseas – all these primarily serve to maintain effective demand, rather than to satisfy the need to quell worker resistance emanating primarily from the labour process. While some of these items clearly do have something to do with quelling worker resistance, there are many other items of capitalist expenditure which might well not be socially necessary. As marketing departments have grown considerably during the twentieth century, so have the numbers of foremen and supervisors, inspectors and testers.[9] Also personnel departments have grown considerably. Company recreational facilities and a whole range of status-indicating distinctions between white-and blue-collar workers and within each category have been established. Finally, and most important, there is the cost to the capitalist system of the high and rising real wages which are paid to unprivileged workers and the large pay differential between unionised and non-unionised workers, and between workers in large firms and those in small firms.

As mentioned above, deciding which items are 'socially necessary' and which are not is a difficult job. In one sense all items included in Baran and Sweezy's surplus as well as those suggested in the previous paragraph are socially necessary in that they all contribute to the smooth running of modern capitalist society.

Baran and Sweezy recognise that worker resistance may counter the theory of rising surplus if workers are able to capture increments of profits resulting from the combination of declining costs and monopoly pricing. They dismiss the argument because the workers' share of total income has not been rising. Baran and Sweezy conclude from this that the unions may be largely ignored because 'the actions and policies of the corporations play a far more important role than those of unions' (p. 85, fn. 1). But one does not have to say that unions are more powerful than corporations to argue that it is the interplay of worker resistance and managerial counter-pressure which primarily shapes the labour process and exchange relations under Monopoly Capitalism — just as one does not have to say that the slave is more important than the master to argue that the master's behaviour as a master of a slave depends primarily on the master — slave relationship. While workers' share of total income has remained constant until recently, the expectation from Marx's theory concerned the subsistence level of individual worker or individual family real wages. Real wages have been rising steadily throughout the twentieth century in advanced capitalist countries. They continued to rise in Britain during the 1930s despite mammoth levels of unemployment. Furthermore, significant differences in real wages exist within all countries depending on region, race, sex, country of origin and size of firms where people are employed, as well as tremendous differences in real incomes between countries. To presume that none of these persistent and systematic differentials imply that some groups of workers have been gaining more than 'socially necessary' wages is to equate socially necessary wages with actual wages and render the term redundant. These differences must be explained to understand contemporary capitalism. Differences in non-wage benefits such as hours of work, certain changes in conditions of work (health and safety), and government transfer payments must also be explained.

The first issue mentioned in the preceding paragraph will be dealt with in the following chapters of Part Two, while the second issue will be dealt with in Part Three.

3 Historical Development of Monopoly Power in Britain

A considerable portion of Part Two is devoted to the historical development of the part's three themes: Monopoly Capitalism, worker resistance and managerial strategy. I consider these sections important for understanding the themes as well as for separating those parts of Marx's framework which need amending from those which merely require updating. Also, *long-run* changes in the fortunes of particular areas and industries is one of my fundamental concerns as set out in Chapter 1.

In the historical sections of this part I have divided the time from the 1780s to the present into five periods or stages. The first two periods, the 1780s to 1840s and 1850 to the 1870s, roughly correspond to the transition to Modern,

Industry and the Modern Industry period proper. The period from the 1870s to 1914 represents the transition to Monopoly Capitalism and the period from 1945 to the 1970s represents Monopoly Capitalism proper. The period from 1914 to 1945, covering two world wars and the turbulent 1920s and 1930s, I have also treated as a transition period to Monopoly Capitalism in Britain.[10]

Dividing history into stages is an arbitrary exercise. Precisely when accumulating quantitative changes in the mode of production came to imply a qualitative change, a new stage, cannot be clearly marked.[11] For example, differences in the size and strength of firms within a single industry existed long before the end of the nineteenth century, and the concentration of industry has grown considerably throughout the twentieth century. Nevertheless there is evidence that monopoly power grew particularly quickly between the 1870s and 1914. The division has been made primarily to aid exposition. I am roughly following the division used by Hobsbawm [1968 and 1969]. While the exposition will refer primarily to the British experience, some reference to other countries, particularly the United States, will be made.

1780s to 1840s

According to Marx the transition to Modern Industry, or the industrial revolution, occurred when two technical conditions were satisfied. First, tools, formerly wielded by human hands, had to be fitted to a mechanism. Second, that mechanism had to be powered by a non-human force. Both these conditions were necessary.[12]

Together they required workers to be concentrated in a single place, the factory, and the factory became the visible mark of Modern Industry. For capitalists the factory meant increased size of investment necessary to finance the complex equipment, larger units of production to take advantage of the new economies of scale, and a leap in labour productivity if discipline could be maintained. For workers the factory meant the transformation of work from a process directed and paced by human judgement and whim into an activity subordinated to the requirements, pace and idiosyncrasies of machines of which they had comparatively little knowledge or control.

While this transition began in a significant way around the 1780s, it was a slow and a very uneven process across industries and areas. Long after 1850 most workers were not employed in factories.[13] Factories themselves were small by present standards, and the organisation of work in many factories often contained vestiges of workshop practices from the Domestic Industry and Manufacture periods. In the metal industries around the Birmingham area in particular, even in large factories, rent for shop-room and payments for power and light were deducted from wages (Allen [1929], pp. 159–60). Also the skilled worker in these factories, as in many other factories and workshops until late in the nineteenth century, was often an intermediate subcontractor and therefore an employer of labour. At blast-furnaces bridgestockers and stock-takers, paid by the ton, employed gangs to charge the furnace or control the casting. Butties contracted with management for the working of a stall and employed their own assistants in coal-mines. Women workers in button factories employed girl assistants. The master-roller in rolling mills and the overhand in brass foundries and chain factories were all paid by the piece and in turn employed others (Allen [1929], pp. 146, 160–5).

Much more important than the retention of vestiges of previous stages or modes of production in the early factories was the continued existence of those stages and modes of production themselves, long after factory production had become significant. They continued as the outwork departments of the factories themselves. While the number of power looms in England rose sharply, from a mere handful at the turn of the century to 2400 in 1813 and 55,000 in 1829, the number of hand-loom weavers also kept rising, to a maximum of about 250,000 in the 1820s (Hobsbawm [1969], p. 64).[14]

The factories themselves were generally small, but growing quickly. In the early 1830s average employment in textile mills was only 44.6 for wool, 93.3 for linen, 125.3 for silk and 175.5 for cotton (Clapham [1926], p. 196). But several of the larger factory owners employed many times more outworkers than factory hands. Also many firms controlled several mills. In cotton, for example, factory owners who originally simply controlled steam-powered spinning in their factory came also to control the organisation of both power-loom weaving and hand-loom weaving.

Cotton was the primary modern industry, particularly during the period up to the 1820s, and the industrial revolution in Britain was largely based on the technical revolution in cotton. During this period the size of cotton mills grew, particularly as they slowly embraced weaving as well as spinning. Until just after the Napoleonic wars many very small factory units crowded into cotton spinning, but during the next two decades these two-to-three person operations (mostly family operations) were slowly squeezed out by the larger spinning—weaving combined mills. In other industries the move to machine production and the growth of factory size occurred more slowly than in cotton, but the trends were visible enough in most cases.[15]

The transition to Modern Industry meant not only a rise in the number of large firms but also increased concentration of funds in the hands of men and institutions eager to invest it. By the 1820s vast sums had been accumulated, particularly in the textile areas. Some was invested in the textile industries themselves, but other outlets were being sought as well. The Bank Act of 1826 allowed joint-stock banks to be established in the industrialised areas, and during the 1820s loans were being provided for newly independent Latin American and Baltic governments. There had been a net capital outflow from Britain ever since the 1780s, but the normal pattern had been for the British to supply loans to allies in war and to prop up reactionary governments after wars (Hobsbawm [1969], p. 113). The loans provided to young and rather unreliable governments in the 1820s were evidence of the pressure for investment outlets. The early 1830s were marked by further outflows to American state-governments. During this period many foreign governments defaulted repayments or interest payments. After the mid-1830s it was to railway building at home that British investment flowed. With the technical, industrial and financial stimulus of British railway construction in the 1840s, the country entered its golden age.

Broadly, the war-torn period from the 1780s to 1815 was one of general business prosperity. Agricultural prices were generally quite high and the military demand for ships, clothes and arms stimulated industry – though selectively.

The peaceful period from 1815 to the 1840s was generally a troubled time for the British economy in spite of pockets of tremendous growth. The concentration of industry in the North and West meant industrial depression in the agriculturally rich South and East. While food prices were high, deprivation in the agricultural areas was masked. But with the fall of agricultural prices after the Napoleonic wars, distress in the South and East became acute. During the 1830s and 1840s rioting in agricultural areas was widespread.

The transition to Modern Industry was based on very few industries – primarily cotton, and other textiles to a lesser extent.[16] This slender base was a precarious one. The generally strong demand for textiles was tempered by wide fluctuations, particularly in foreign demand, which quickly brought disaster, especially to outworkers and smaller firms.

1850s to 1870s

The Modern Industry period itself was distinguished by its broader base. Textiles continued to expand during the third quarter of the nineteenth century (see Deane and Cole [1967], p. 187, Seward [1972], p. 42), but railway construction fuelled much faster growth in iron, steel, coal and all manner of metal working and engineering industries. It was upon this broader base that the British economy surged forward during the Modern Industry stage.

A combination of strong demand, particularly foreign demand, and the extension of the Factory Acts beyond the textile and allied industries in the mid-1860s encouraged mechanisation and a growth of factory size across a wide range of industries. Between the 1860s and 1880s the sewing machine led to the gradual transformation of the clothing industry from a domestic industry into a complex combination of factories and outworkers. Machines were also slowly expanding among the Birmingham and Black Country metal industries and the Sheffield cutlery industry. By 1871, in some metal working industries, establishment sizes had grown significantly, but compared with twentieth-century firm sizes they remained small (see Clapham [1934], pp. 117–19).

As Hobsbawm points out, in spite of the presence of large firms employing thousands of workers, what was notable during Modern Industry was

> the extremely decentralized and disintegrated business structure of the cotton industry, as indeed of most other British nineteenth century industries, the product of its emergence from the unplanned activities of small men. It emerged, as it remained, a complex of highly specialized firms of medium size (often highly localized) – merchants of various kinds, spinners, weavers, dyers, finishers, bleachers, printers, and so on, often specialized within their branches, linked with each other by a complex web of individual business transactions in 'the market' (Hobsbawm [1969], pp. 64–5).

Hobsbawm is right to qualify the term 'the market', though he does not pursue the point. In fact, in most industries, the complex web of business transactions (or co-operative relations) which linked firms to each other ranged from arm's length market transactions to the basically wage-labour relation of craftsmen to labourers employed in factories where some vestiges of the craftsman's former independence were retained. These co-operative relations at times represented the coming together of equals to derive some mutual benefit, such as the formation of cottage factories by domestic silk ribbon weavers in the 1850s and the formation of co-operative or company mills in the woollen industry from 1810 (Prest, [1960], pp. 96–135; Select Committee on Joint Stock Companies [1844], p. 348). More often they were relations between firms of widely unequal size where the larger firm generally took the initiative in starting and ending the relation, and derived the greater benefit from it.

Perhaps the clearest and most common example of this during the nineteenth century was the relation between factories and outworkers. Trade conditions fluctuated widely in all the nineteenth-century textile industries. During these swings Fay's analogy between outworkers and marginal land could be clearly seen (Fay [1920], pp. 174–6). During boom time in textile industries factory workers will be working to full capacity and outworkers in the towns who have been short of work will be employed. Soon work will be given out to villages surrounding the main textile centres, and as the boom continues the area covered will widen, often to the wives and children of farm workers or to the farm workers themselves.[17] These workers are paid less than factory workers or town outworkers, even during the boom. When the slump comes they are the first to be laid off. As the textile area contracts, the outworkers switch from marginal weavers back to marginal agricultural workers.

There are a number of themes relating to this pattern which will be taken up in detail in the industry – area studies below.

First, outworking, while certainly declining in importance after the 1820s and 1830s, has never been confined to weaving and a significant number of people are engaged in domestic outworking today.[18]

Second, while outworkers represent an easily visible, unequal co-operative relation between large and small producing units or between capital and labour (which can not be completely captured by classification as wage-labour), often the relations between large and small factory-working firms are of a similar type. These relations, far from declining after the 1820s, have grown in importance throughout the Modern Industry stage and generally characterise the organisation of industry during Monopoly Capitalism.

It is easy when considering outwork to see inefficient working at home, undisciplined and without power, as merely an outmoded remnant from a bygone age, hanging on desperately and bound to disappear in an age of modern industry. Similarly it is easy to consider small firms, using less than the most up-to-date equipment, merely as remnants which will soon disappear or change in an age of monopoly capitalism when huge automated factories employ tens of thousands of workers. But outworkers, workshops or small factories in times when industry is dominated by more mechanised or larger factories, are not simply resource bases out of which more 'modern' forms will grow. While particular forms of capitalist production have declined and almost disappeared, *capitalism has always been characterised by relations between more modern and less modern forms.*[19] Subcontracting between firms of unequal size as a particular form of co-operative relation, still common in contemporary Britain, is discussed in detail in Chapter 8.

Third, these co-operative relations in industry can have important conse-quences for the relation between areas of prosperity and areas of deprivation. The relation between the prosperity of towns compared with rural deprivation in the nineteenth century around textile manufacturing areas was clearly affected by the relation between town and village domestic weaving in the early years, and later by the relation between town factory workers and village outworkers. During the transition to Monopoly Capitalism the relation between large and small productive units comes to form the basis of the relation between outlying suburban or 'better' metropolitan areas on the one hand and slum areas near city centres or on council estates on the other hand.

1870s to 1914

Britain's monopoly of world industrialisation came to an end during the last quarter of the nineteenth century. While British exports to underdeveloped countries continued to grow, exports to America and the rest of Europe stagnated or declined as these countries changed from young industrialisers, eager to build with British capital goods, into mature rivals with large-scale and protected capital goods industries of their own.

Modern Industry does not simply involve the introduction of machinery into industrial establishments. As discussed in Chapter 2, during Modern Industry machines themselves are continually improved and the technical basis of industry is always being revolutionised.

The inventions of early Modern Industry were largely simple, relying on well-known sources of power and readily available knowledge of physical science. More important, the adaptations to major inventions which sustained early Modern Industry were the products of practical experience based on artisans' skills rather than systematic observation or sophisticated theory. Gradually, with increasing size of factories and growing complexity and scale of machinery on the one hand, and with the availability of important but unfamiliar raw materials (such as rubber and petroleum) due to the expansion of the world economy on the other, the importance of scientific theory for further discoveries and improvements grew.

By 1825 restrictions on emigration by British skilled artisans were lifted, partly in recognition of this change (though the change in legislation also reflected the gathering strength of British laissez-faire attitudes in general). Knowledge of electricity and chemistry required some formal instruction, and these fields were becoming increasingly important as the bases of new industries and for technical progress across a wide range of other industries. [20]

As more industrially useful discoveries came to emanate from university research laboratories, in Germany industrialists began to establish links with university science departments and polytechnic institutions (which were set up in the 1830s and 1840s) and to set up research laboratories themselves. [21]

American industrialists, slightly behind the Germans, were quickly catching up during the 1870s, 1880s and 1890s. German scientists were imported into American universities and industries. In 1876 Thomas Edison set up the first research organisation for the scientifically organised pursuit of industrially useful inventions. Before the First World War most huge American corporations had either set up their own research organisations, or dealt extensively with specialist research organisations (Braverman [1974], pp. 163-4).

These developments were of considerable importance in distinguishing Monopoly Capitalism from Modern Industry. During Modern Industry science was a generalised social property, only incidental to production, and technical progress was still based on the occasional appropriation of the fruits of science and on skilled workers' aptitudes. During Monopoly Capitalism much of science became capitalist property. Science became a conscious and purposive activity, often organised by capitalists – an internal balance sheet item rather than an external economy (Braverman [1974], chap. 7). Technical progress is now based on the scientific knowledge of a much smaller group of workers than the skill-based technical progress of Modern Industry. [22]

The incorporation of scientific theories and methods into the capitalist mode of production, like the mechanisation of capitalist industry, has been a continuously developing process rather than a series of acts. Science-based methods of product development, managerial co-ordination and managerial control over workers have been *continually* revolutionised during Monopoly Capitalism.

British capitalists were much slower than the Germans or the Americans in this transition to science. Often scientific breakthroughs pioneered in Britain were taken up elsewhere because capitalists in Britain could not or would not risk the funds necessary to develop them (see Hobsbawm [1969], p. 180). Along with British capital's slower incorporation of science, the growth in British firm and factory size and in the concentration of British industry proceeded more slowly than in American or German industry.

While the average size of *factories* was rising steadily but slowly throughout this period (much as it had risen in earlier periods both in Britain and abroad), after the 1870s a tremendous growth in *firm* size occurred. Vast firms (or loose administrative units) were created by the confederation or absorption of many smaller firms. The particular forms by which this concentration occurred varied considerably both between and within countries. Between the 1870s and the early years of the twentieth century Germany was covered by a vast network of cartels or agreements between firms to limit competition through some combination of market sharing, output restriction and price maintenance. The Kartell-Commission of 1905 reported about 400 cartels in Germany (Dobb [1963], p. 310). Agreements of this nature had been common throughout the history of the capitalist mode of production, but during the transition to Monopoly Capitalism, particularly in Germany, the number of these agreements qualitatively changed the degree of competition within the country.

Though competition was strong during Modern Industry in Britain the tradition of organisation among mercantile 'interests' to influence government policies from the eighteenth century was carried on by some of the larger industrialists. Along with combinations to influence government policies, less visible combinations existed to influence wages, output and prices. Adam Smith wrote in 1776,

> We rarely hear, it has been said, of the combination of masters, though frequently of those of workmen. But whoever imagines, upon this account, that masters rarely combine, is as ignorant of the world as of the subject. Masters are always and everywhere in a sort of tacit, but constant and uniform combination, not to raise the wages of labour above their actual rate. . . . We seldom, indeed, hear of this combination, because it is the usual, and one may say, the natural state of things, which nobody ever hears of (Smith [1974], p. 169).

These combinations often broke down because the number of firms supplying particular markets was too large to control and the average size of firm was too small to present a formidable entry barrier to new entrants. But these problems were gradually being overcome. The progress of mechanisation caused the technically most efficient minimum size required for several manufacturing operations to rise, limited liability and stock market quotation privileges were extended from banks and trading companies to manufacturing firms between 1844 and 1856, and institutions for promoting and underwriting new share issues were developed during the 1880s. Nevertheless during the 1880s industrialists were looking for a more secure and stable method for limiting competition than by loose or tacit agreement.

In America, where firm sizes and capital markets were growing quickly, the 1870s and 1880s marked the growth of trusts which concluded cartel agreements. These were broken up after 1890 by the Sherman Act which was directed against 'combination in restraint of trade'. German cartels in contrast had the blessing of the Government as well as tariff protection at home. Also German financial institutions played a larger role in German cartels and they encouraged rationalisation among the participating firms. The inefficiency of agreements in Britain and their illegality in America touched off the first great merger movements of the 1890s and early 1900s in these countries. Firms which could not be controlled by agreements to act together were now amalgamated or taken over.

Merger movements occurred at the same time in Britain and America, but the American movement was on a much larger scale and it left American industry much more concentrated. Between 1896 and 1905 the size of the hundred largest American companies quadrupled and by 1905 they controlled 40 per cent of America's industrial capital (Bunting and Barbour, [1971], p. 317). British concentration did not reach a comparable level until the inter-war years. Also British mergers affected a much smaller selection of industries. Textiles and brewing accounted for 47 per cent of all firms disappearing by merger between 1880 and 1909. Industries such as engineering, clothing, timber and furniture, leather goods and vehicles were hardly touched (Hannah [1974], p. 20).

In part, the British merger movement was smaller because alternative restrictive practices were still available to British firms. The government inquiry of 1918 reported more than 500 price-fixing associations in Britain (Clapham [1938], p. 316).

The British merger movement was limited too by the poor record of its merged firms. British mergers at the turn of the century, like contemporary American mergers, were often formed by the amalgamation of many small firms.[23] Unlike American firms, the fruits of most British mergers did not survive for long. One of the main reasons for this was that British mergers were, like British combinations and associations, collections of several firms without much inter-firm co-ordination because no one firm clearly dominated the merger. The dominant firms in early American mergers were often backed by strong financial resources from large American financial institutions (the House of Morgan in particular), and therefore they were able to buy outright rivals whose operations might have to be rationalised. Huge newly merged

American corporations were also protected by higher tariff barriers, in particular after the high McKinley Tariff of 1890.

Finally, the British merger movement was limited because British industrialists were able to turn to exports to underdeveloped countries, and because British financial interests were able to invest in foreign countries and continue to make good profits, particularly after the Great Depression ended in 1896. The value of British exports to Asia, Africa and Latin America grew quickly after 1896, though exports to Europe and North America continued to stagnate. By 1913 Argentina and India alone bought more British iron and steel than all of Europe. More important, British annual investments abroad began to exceed her net capital formation at home by 1870. Between 1902 and 1912 capital exports from the United Kingdom increased more than ten times over. From 1911 to 1913 twice as much was invested abroad as at home (Hobsbawm [1969], pp. 191–2). British capital was taking the *path of least resistance*. Modernisation and integration of British industry was a much more difficult task than making profits by foreign investment and export to semi-protected regions during the decades before the First World War.

While the British transition to Monopoly Capitalism occurred more slowly than the American and German transitions, the changes which took place between the 1870s and 1914 were significant. Though the combinations and merged companies were not always successful, the future path for British industry was clear. Britain's exploitation of foreign markets could not continue for ever in the increasingly competitive international economy while her home base remained relatively neglected.

The pre-war British associations and mergers were formed to keep prices up, rather than to rationalise and modernise British industry. Most mergers between 1886 and 1914 occurred at times when rising share prices corresponded with trade cycle recessions (Hannah [1974a], p. 9). That the merged firms did not integrate to take advantage of technical or managerial economies of scale highlighted a different reason for this growth in industrial concentration. The mergers, like the trade associations and combinations, reflected the old desire to defy the laws of capitalist competition.

During a recession prices generally fall suddenly, squeezing profit margins and causing the most inefficient firms to fail. Output is thereby reduced to what the most efficient firms can produce and these firms form the nucleus of the industry during the coming trade cycle boom. If prices can be stabilised and markets protected due to agreements and tariffs, then more firms may survive the recession. Output will fall due to reduced home demand, but the sudden and precipitous fall in prices which overshoots the mark and lays the foundation for the next boom may be avoided somewhat, allowing firms in the market time to adjust to the new conditions (often by increasing their exploitation of labour through increasing work speeds). Certainly mergers creating firms whose sales account for a high proportion of markets allow the possibility for rationalisations to occur during the slump, but they also allow firms the *discretion* of not making fundamental changes, for a time at least, due to the more stable market conditions which they can impose.

1914 to 1945

In the twenty-five years from 1914 the level of concentration of British industry increased faster than for most other advanced capitalist countries. The hundred largest firms controlled 24 per cent of manufacturing output in 1935 compared with only 15 per cent in 1909 (Hannah [1974b]). The change occurred because British export markets could no longer support her decaying traditional industries, because interest in home industry by the City financiers improved (especially after the collapse of world trade in 1929–33) and particularly because the State became actively involved in creating large and rationalised business units. While the magnitude of these three changes distinguished Britain's economic situation during the inter-war years from earlier periods, even by the late 1930s British industry's reliance on protected export markets, its isolation from the country's vast financial resources and the weakness of state intervention in the British economy at the level of the firm, each continued to distinguish British industry from its major rivals. British industry entered the Second World War with one of the highest concentration ratios based on formal ownership, but with large firms which were poorly rationalised and inadequately equipped, particularly compared with American, German and Japanese industry.

During the First World War the Government took control of major sectors of the economy including the coal-mines and the railways. The war was a good time for business, as are all wars. Behind strong import barriers, with heavy government purchasing, and the inflationary effects of war finance (through massive borrowing) enormous profits were made. The banking sector, recognising the high profits to be made at home, set up links with large British firms which had previously been ignored. At the end of the war the banks began to pull out of British industry, recognising the problems that lay ahead with the dismantling of import restrictions, tariffs and lucrative government contracts. They began to float companies on the Stock Exchange or water the capital as an alternative to encouraging modernisation (Foster [1976], p. 10).

Between 1918 and early 1920 the country enjoyed a huge inflationary boom, but the pound was suffering and London was losing her position as the financial hub of the world to New York. Between 1920 and 1925 the Government and the Bank of England prepared the country for a return to the gold standard at the unrealistically high rate of 4.86 dollars to the pound, under considerable pressure from the Americans to do so (Moggridge [1969]). The Bank of England encouraged the Treasury to restrict the money supply, the bank-rate was raised, and public expenditure was savagely cut in 1920, touching off a sharp recession. Between 1920 and 1923 prices fell by almost 30 per cent, but wages fell by almost 40 per cent. Unemployment soared to over two million by December 1921, or 18 per cent of all insured workers. Between 1921 and 1938 the unemployment rate never fell below 10 per cent.

In 1920 the Government could have chosen one of two policies to pursue. Either it could have encouraged the forging of close links between the City and large industrial firms, and fostered rationalisation, modernisation and concentration of home industry on the basis of low exchange rates, high tariffs, easy money, high government expenditure and strong state intervention at the micro level; or it could have encouraged the City to regain its paramount position in international finance with deflationary policies and a return to gold at a high exchange rate. The latter policy was chosen. By the mid-1920s British overseas investments earned more than ever before, as did her financial and insurance services. But with the simultaneous depression in all advanced capitalist countries which came in 1929 the policy collapsed.

After 1931 the Government at last moved to a strong protectionist policy for home and Empire markets. During the 1930s both the banks and the Government set about encouraging further concentration of British industry, price maintenance, output restriction and some rationalisation. Favoured firms or factories continued to work while unlucky (peripheral) factories, particularly in the North and West, were closed down leaving whole towns destitute.

In 1932 a giant cartel was established in the iron and steel industry in partnership with the Government through the Import Duties Advisory Committee.[24] The banks and most shipbuilding firms joined to form National Shipbuilders' Security Ltd. in 1930, to buy up and close down 'obsolete or redundant' shipyards out of a levy on those still in work. By 1934 40 per cent of the industry's berths had been purchased and scrapped. Similar associations were set up in the textile industry, though cut-throat competition and gradual attrition rather than planned and permanent closures of whole districts was the more prominent pattern in the cotton and wool industries. In 1936, by the Cotton Spindles Act, the Government forced spinning mills still at work to pay a levy to purchase and scrap redundant plant (Branson and Heinemann [1971], pp. 45–8).

While the 1930s marked a sharp shift toward home industry on the part of banks and governments, the policies pursued involved reducing productive capacity and increasing working speeds rather than large-scale modernisation or even integration of remaining capacity. The policy ensured that British industry would continue to falter relative to competitors after the Second World War.

1945 to 1970s

The growth of industrial concentration which marked the two earlier periods continued after the Second World War.

The growth of firm sizes has been particularly marked since the 1930s. In

1935 firms employing 10,000 people or more accounted for 13.7 per cent of employment and 14.8 per cent of net output in British manufacturing industries. In 1958 they accounted for 24.8 per cent of employment and 26.1 per cent of net output. Concentration ratios (proportion of activity accounted for by the three largest enterprises) increased in 27 out of 41 industries studied by Evely and Little (1960) and decreased in only 14 between 1935 and 1951. Of the 63 industries studied by Armstrong and Silberston [1967], concentration ratios increased in 36 and decreased in only 16 between 1951 and 1958.[25] The top 100 firms accounted for 47 per cent of total net assets of all quoted firms in 1948, 51 per cent in 1957 and 62 per cent in 1968 (George [1974], p. 37).

In spite of the tremendous growth in size of plants and firms and in concentration during the inter-war period and afterwards, a large number of small firms have remained. In 1935 76 per cent of firms in factory trades[26] employed 10 people or less. Also, 38 per cent of those working in manufacturing were employed in firms employing less than 200 people and those firms accounted for 35 per cent of all U.K. manufacturing net output. By 1963 firms employing less than 200 people still accounted for 20 per cent of people employed and 16 per cent of net output in U.K. manufacturing (Bolton [1971], pp. 58–9). While these numbers are substantial, the relative importance of small firms during the 1960s in the U.K. economy was far lower than for other advanced capitalist countries (see Bolton [1971], p. 69).

Why have so many small firms remained in spite of the trend toward concentration? As outworkers gave factory workers relative security and factory owners access to workers who could be paid less than factory workers, as well as flexibility in the textile industries during the first half of the nineteenth century, so small firms offer such advantages to those large firms which enjoy a significant degree of monopoly power today. Robson describes the forces shaping the form of the largest firms in the cotton industry which emerged during the 1920s and 1930s:

> More generally, some degree of integration gives the necessary flexibility to meet changing conditions of trade, since when trade is good integrated operations can be intensified and when trade declines more specialised operations can be conducted. Since, however, ownership cannot be initiated without considerable difficulty, integration has to be undertaken as a permanent policy and not just when the emergency arises. For this reason partial integration is once more the favoured device, especially in the form of tapered capacity, the converting section being larger than the weaving, weaving larger than spinning, and so on. Under these circumstances the converting section, for example, can buy more from outside weavers when trade is good and yet keep its own looms running when trade is bad.
>
> It is generally true that the most successful of the vertical firms in the cotton industry during the inter-war years had a structure of this kind. Present conditions of 'full employment' are such that long periods of trade

depression are unlikely and therefore a strongly tapered organisation is now perhaps less desirable (Robson [1957], p. 115).[27]

One feature characteristic of all major manufacturing industries is that there are several processes through which products must be taken before they reach the final consumer. While economies of scale have increased the minimum technically efficient size for several operations, a wide range of optimum sizes exist for the different processes involved in individual industries. A common pattern is for one or two processes to become highly concentrated and for the large firms in those sectors to begin extending forward and backward into other processes, often via take-overs. After some point these firms will refrain from further take-overs and several sectors will continue to be served by many small firms, dominated to a greater or lesser degree by large integrated firms whose own operations are often primarily concentrated in a different process. This has been the pattern followed in the motor vehicle industry with final assemblers integrating backward to suppliers and forward to distributors.

Whether the large-small firm relation works across different sectors within an industry (such as in the twentieth century motor industry), or mainly within a single sector (such as in the nineteenth century textile industries), the difference in wages, conditions and employment security between workers in the large firms compared with the small ones remains significant.

In 1973 skilled manual workers in British engineering firms employing 500 or more workers earned 26.8 per cent more than those working in firms employing only 25 to 99 workers (see Table 3.1). The difference in earnings for labourers was 23.0 per cent, and for semi-skilled workers (the majority in the larger firms) the difference was 28.8 per cent. These figures included the amounts earned while working overtime. The comparable figures excluding overtime pay were 29.1 per cent more for skilled workers, 24.1 per cent more for labourers and 29.6 per cent more for semi-skilled workers. Manual workers in smaller firms (particularly skilled workers) work more hours in order to receive smaller pay packets than those in the larger firms.

TABLE 3.1

Earnings of Manual Workers in the Engineering Industry, 1969–74
Firms employing 25–99 employees compared with firms employing 500 or more
(new pence per hour – annual average)

	Including overtime		Excluding overtime	
	25–99	*500 +*	*25–99*	*500 +*
1969				
Skilled	53.00	65.27	49.81	62.37
Semi-skilled	47.91	57.17	45.05	54.06
Labourer	38.84	44.47	36.20	41.37
1970				
Skilled	58.17	73.75	54.77	70.91
Semi-skilled	52.79	65.77	49.44	62.61
Labourer	43.01	51.18	39.76	48.08
1971				
Skilled	64.23	82.77	61.55	81.02
Semi-skilled	58.56	74.43	55.75	71.40
Labourer	47.69	57.41	44.79	54.55
1972				
Skilled	71.71	92.32	69.18	89.72
Semi-skilled	67.84	82.70	64.51	79.69
Labourer	53.46	65.24	50.66	62.39
1973				
Skilled	81.04	102.79	76.84	99.23
Semi-skilled	73.94	94.95	69.77	90.45
Labourer	61.17	75.21	57.42	71.26
1974				
Skilled	96.48	114.70	91.64	110.86
Semi-skilled	90.61	105.37	86.21	100.39
Labourer	76.07	85.02	71.29	80.42

SOURCE: Department of Employment *Labour Gazettes* (London: H.M.S.O., 1970–4).

CHAPTER FOUR

Worker Resistance– Argument

Struggle within the labour process over valorisation has occupied radicals throughout capitalism's history, but this struggle has been sorrowfully neglected by Marxist theoreticians. The schism between theory and practice concerning the daily struggle which occurs within productive activity has seriously weakened both. During the next four chapters this struggle is examined, concentrating on worker resistance first, and then on managerial counter-pressure. In this chapter the argument for incorporating worker resistance into a Marxian framework is put along with some discussion of its neglect. This is followed by an examination of some characteristics of worker resistance which will be examined historically in Chapter 5, and which will be used throughout the analysis in succeeding chapters.

1 Stages of Capitalist Productive Activity and Managerial Authority

For Marx the movement from one stage to another – from Co-operation to Manufacture to Modern Industry – was chiefly a technical matter, a development of the forces of production under the capitalist mode of production. Successive stages were technically more efficient in that relative surplus value rose. But each successive stage also involved a progressive removal of workers' ability to exercise independent judgement and authority over their labour power, thereby increasing managerial authority over productive activity.

Development of the manufacturing division of labour meant the over-development of individual worker's detail dexterity at the expense of his general craft skills. It tied these workers to the capitalist mode of production because the deterioration of workers' general craft skills meant they could not produce entire commodities themselves, even if they could acquire sufficient means of production to produce independently.

With the shift to Modern Industry, the deskilling of individual workers which characterised Manufacture became a decline of skills embodied in workers as a group. Previously top managers had to rely on workers' handicraft skills for guidance as to the best methods for carrying out particular tasks. Now machines are used as the basis around which work tasks are organised. Machines pace workers and define their particular tasks.

As capitalism progressed through these stages a gradual growth in managerial authority within the labour process occurred. In part this authority grew because of technical changes by which workers were deskilled. In part managerial authority grew because workers' power to resist authority was progressively weakened by the creation of more competitive labour power markets. During the handicraft period journeymen were protected by seven-year apprenticeships, by the power of many guilds to limit apprenticeship intake, and by customary lists of prices for their produce (set in part according to some notion of just prices). Also labour power markets were very localised.

The gradual shift to Modern Industry meant that workers no longer directly competed for jobs with those of the same craft alone. The continual introduction of labour-saving techniques meant too that large numbers of workers were being thrown onto the job market regularly. This increased the mobility of workers between industries and between areas, thereby increasing the size of the pool of workers directly competing for particular jobs. Marx notes the fall in real wages for men during the shift to Modern Industry which occurred largely because of this swollen industrial reserve army of labour. The swollen industrial reserve army also meant that the threat of being sacked came near to the threat of starvation. This caused managerial authority over the labour process to increase markedly. Throughout *Capital* Marx catalogues examples of the miserable conditions which workers were forced to put up with during the first half of the nineteenth century (vol. 1, chaps 10 and 15 in particular).

Marx concentrated on the progressive rise in managerial authority over the majority of workers which accompanied capitalist development. But during these stages of capitalist development significant differences between different groups of workers in levels of pay, working conditions and subjection to authority remained. In some cases these differences increased as the position of the unskilled deteriorated.

Marx did consider differences in conditions for different groups of workers, but he associated these differences primarily with differences in the technical development of various sectors of the economy. During the Modern Industry stage, Manufacture and Domestic Industry remain. Conditions for workers in these sectors degenerate even further than in the Modern Industry sectors. But as pointed out in Chapter 2, Marx regarded Modern Manufacture and Modern Domestic Industry as remnants which would eventually disappear. Presumably major differentials would also disappear. But significant differentials in working situations, even for people working for a single firm, have continued throughout the nineteenth and twentieth centuries.

The movement from Modern Industry to Monopoly Capitalism was also described primarily in technical terms in Chapter 3. It involved the growth of monopoly power among a few firms within most industries, and the incorporation of scientific theory and method directly into the operation of those firms. These two technical responses to the development of the forces of production also implied a progressive removal of workers' ability to exercise independent judgement and authority over their labour power. The incorporation of science meant further deskilling of skilled workers and their alienation from technical progress within the labour process. Monopoly power in theory increased employers' ability to withstand a strike due to greater financial resources, built-up brand loyalty and technical barriers to entry to the sector of the industry in which the large firms operate.

On the other hand the growth and complexity of machine equipment plus the growth of firm size and factory size during both Modern Industry and Monopoly Capitalism have *increased* the ability of workers *to resist managerial authority* through both individual acts of sabotage and organised collective forms of resistance. Also the tremendous growth of capitalist accumulation within developed countries, particularly from the mid-nineteenth century, has caused a drying-up of sources of labour power which previously fuelled the reserve army and weakened worker resistance. The active industrial reserve army rose during Modern Industry as deskilling and improved communications combined with widespread labour-saving mechanisation to increase the catchment space – from different industries and from different areas – from which displaced workers could press on particular local labour power markets. But the latent industrial reserve army was quickly being incorporated into industrial wage-labour or into the active industrial reserve army during Modern Industry and the years of transition to Monopoly Capitalism (see Table 5.1). This drying-up of the latent reserve army, along with the growth in factory size, formed the foundation for the growing strength of worker resistance among unskilled workers which emerged during the 1870s to 1914 period. Thus managerial authority did not always rise as much as might have been expected during the twentieth century from technical changes alone. Similarly the homogenisation of conditions and pay for different workers expected by Marx has not occurred since Marx's time, primarily because of differences in the strength of resistance among different groups of workers.

Differences in pay and conditions based on workers' skills, age, sex, race, country of origin or firm size have persisted from Modern Industry to the present day. The operation of these differentials has depended on a combination of custom, differences in the strength of the reserve army for that particular category of labour and differences in worker resistance. These three elements are interdependent. Differentials based on custom, without any support from active worker resistance to the erosion of those differentials, might not be expected to last long. Also the strength of the industrial reserve army can be manipulated somewhat by worker resistance through the maintenance of long apprenticeships, strict immigration policy and other forms of closed shops. Of course custom and the reserve army will affect the strength of worker resistance as well, but the active element in the combination is worker 'resistance. Thus to understand differences in pay, conditions and subjugation to managerial authority between different groups of workers, and ulimately to understand the pattern of prosperity and deprivation between different industrial sectors and different areas, the development of worker resistance must be examined.

2 Worker Resistance – Marx and Marxists

Of course Marx recognised the importance of worker resistance. It was through class struggle that the capitalist mode of production would ultimately be destroyed. For this the proletariat forms into a revolutionary class, 'a class for itself rather than simply in itself', a class which recognises itself as a class bereft of means of production and fights against its alienation from the means of production. For this to be achieved the class must first discover its unity. Its members must consciously act in solidarity with each other for the class to recognise its social position and realise its historical role. But the strength of worker resistance has always been distributed unevenly among the working population. Often the result of this resistance has been to shore up or even to augment differentials. The class often appears to be fighting among itself rather than for itself. A century after Marx and there has not yet been a single revolution in a country with a well-developed proletariat.

Therefore it is important to examine how the capitalist mode of production has accommodated itself to worker resistance, rather than simply how the capitalist mode of production might be overthrown through worker resistance.

Marx's analysis of the former issue is not well developed. Generalised worker resistance through strong worker organisations did not develop until after Marx's death.

Marx recognises that capitalists would act within the labour process to try to overcome worker resistance. 'As the number of the co-operating labours increases, so too does their resistance to the domination of capital, and with it, the necessity for capital to overcome this resistance by counter-pressure' (*Capital*, vol. 1, p. 313).

Just how the relation between worker resistance and counter-pressure works is not pursued thoroughly by Marx. There are scattered references to this counter-pressure in *Capital*. Marx mentions the introduction of piece-wage payment, by which capitalists replace direct superintendence of workers by a system of financial incentives for individual workers to work harder and longer (*Capital*, vol. 1, chap. 21). He describes the subcontracting of work, by which a group of middlemen arose whose gain consisted directly in the difference between the price for work paid by the capitalist and the part of that price which they actually gave the worker; people who therefore applied pressure to the workers instead of the capitalist himself and instead of at the direct order of the capitalist (*Capital*, vol. 1, pp. 435, 518–19). Marx also emphasises that the introduction of machinery itself accelerated after the limitation of the working day (resulting from pressure of worker resistance), and this meant that less technically advanced sectors of industry could not compete successfully on the basis of the lowest wage for the longest hours (*Capital*, vol. 1,pp. 442–50).

These examples have to be teased out of *Capital*. In general Marx describes the development of capitalist productive activity in terms of successive stages of social relations developing out of the technical progress of the forces of production once the initial basic mode of production is established. Given the establishment of free labour and capitalist competition, which provide the social framework for capitalist accumulation, the shifts from Co-operation to Manufacture to Modern Industry come as technical advances by which the mode of production progressively realises its potential to accumulate. Social relations within productive activity are shaped by these technical advances (managerial authority over individual workers grows, the working class as a whole becomes progressively deskilled, workers find themselves paced by machines and co-operating together in large numbers, etc.), but the technical advances themselves occur as part of an underlying social system – the capitalist mode of production – and they in turn are moulded by the logic of that system.

For Marx it is these underlying social relations, summarised by the term 'capitalist mode of production', which allow one to understand the nature of economic development. Ultimately this mode of production itself will give rise to technical and social changes which will lead to the overthrow of the mode of production. Ultimately the mode of production will be destroyed by contradictory or self-destructive forces which its technical and social development create.

What Marx did not study systematically was the possibility that technical and social changes might occur *under* the capitalist mode of production in response to the contradictory or self-destructive forces created by capitalist accumulation. He did not carefully examine the means by which *contradictions are accommodated*, by which the mode of production is sustained.

Worker resistance must be seen as a force (thrown up by the basic mode of production) which affects capitalist development, rather than simply a force which may eventually result in the destruction of the capitalist mode of production. This neglect, which was perhaps understandable in Marx's writing in the mid-nineteenth century, has become much more serious for Marxists of the twentieth century.[1]

Generally Marxists have followed Lenin's separation of worker resistance into two categories. The first is resistance which develops 'spontaneously' out of struggle directly between employers and workers within the labour process. This resistance is informed by what Lenin calls 'trade union consciousness'. The second is informed by 'socialist consciousness'. It does not develop spontaneously from experience in the labour process. Rather it develops from 'the sphere of the relations between *all* the various classes and strata and the state and government' (1937, p. 98).

While this distinction may be useful for guiding one's attitude toward different working class struggles, it has reinforced Marx's emphasis of worker resistance as a force for changing the mode of production, rather than a force which also causes accommodating changes within the mode of production. Despite differences in the relative desirability of these two effects, to treat worker resistance, which is informed by 'narrow' trade union consciousness and circumscribed by the particular factory or firm within which those workers are employed, as a secondary and primitive form of resistance because it is relatively ineffective for overthrowing capitalism, is to miss significant developments in capitalist productive activity during at least the past hundred years.

This attitude has contributed to an inevitablist view of technical and organisational changes within the capitalist labour process by Marxists since Marx. As Harry Braverman has recently reminded us, throughout the twentieth century Marxists have 'adapted to the view of the modern factory as an inevitable if perfectible form of the organisation of the labour process' (1974, p. 11). Lenin himself encouraged the imitation of capitalist technical and organisational methods in Soviet industry, including F. Taylor's scientific management techniques for controlling workers (1918, p. 259). But Braverman himself, while recognising that current technical and organisational methods of production are not inevitable to any future system, wrongly treats them as inevitable within the capitalist system. In so doing he misses the possibility of changes within the capitalist mode of production in response to worker resistance.[2]

3   Worker Resistance – Some Important Characteristics

In this section I will deal with three characteristics of worker resistance which are important for considering its impact on the development of capitalist productive activity. Distinguishing these characteristics now will help make the historical examination of worker resistance in Chapter 5 more meaningful. First, worker resistance may take on many different forms. Second, worker resistance is unevenly developed among different groups of workers. Third, the organisational strength of worker resistance may frustrate worker power (through managerial co-option) as well as enhance it.

Forms of Resistance

The method by which worker resistance is accommodated under capitalism will depend in part on the forms by which that resistance occurs. The various forms of worker resistance may be usefully categorised as either individualistic or collective, and collective resistance may be further divided into highly organised or institutionalised resistance compared with 'spontaneous' collective resistance.

Historically resistance to factory work by non-craftsmen was first manifest in individualistic forms. The 'habit of solidarity' takes time to learn and people came to the factories from much smaller scaled and geographically dispersed domestic production, manufactories or semi-feudal agriculture. Also until well into the nineteenth century collective forms of worker resistance were severely suppressed by the military and the courts.

Individualistic resistance appears to be concerned mainly with the loss of control over the workers' labour power for a fixed period of time and so a loss of control over their time for a fixed period. The maintenance of discipline has always been a problem for top managers. Resistance is expressed in terms of time by workers arriving after or leaving before the times specified in their employment contracts. Workers also gain free time by breaking machinery and various forms of deception by which foremen and supervisors may be led to believe that workers are busy when they are not. More important for top managers are absenteeism and voluntary quits. These expressions of resistance to work under capitalism are common when pressure from the reserve army is weak.

Refusing to carry out orders or carrying them out in a way which will harm top managers' interests are other common expressions of individual worker resistance. In a situation of powerlessness it may be relieving and amusing to cause the order-givers discomfort by disrupting work pace – by argument, or by causing equipment to break down. The effect of individual acts of sabotage will increase as the overall work process becomes more integrated. Finally the normal pace of work is often a matter of struggle between individual workers and their direct supervisors or foremen.

Collective worker resistance may take the same forms as individual resistance. Collectively workers may try to win back direct control over some of their time by establishing precedents for such work pace interruptions as tea-breaks, and by forewarning each other (and perhaps collectively deciding) when the machinery will break down. Workers may also 'cover' for each other to allow work breaks and to vary the pace of work. Workers may systematically resist particular orders by collectively arguing over issues through their stewards, via sabotage, via 'working to rule' or "going slow" or by unofficial strikes. It is in the cumulative effects of isolated worker resistance (through absenteeism or turnover) that individual resistance may harm top managers, but individual acts of collective resistance may themselves be very powerful weapons against managers.

One of the main problems during collective resistance is maintaining solidarity, and for a strike also keeping out blacklegs. This will involve establishing communication with comrades informally or via mass meetings, establishing pickets, and may also involve getting fellow trade unionists to stop handling goods going into the firm or coming from it and trying to invoke sympathy strikes elsewhere. Such forms of organised collective resistance have attracted most attention, primarily because they are the most public forms, but organised collective resistance does take other forms.

Though most strikes are about pay, specific factory conditions or particular redundancies, some are about setting precedents for work rules or procedures by which managerial authority (and particularly arbitrary elements of that authority) might be altered. These procedures or rules or customs themselves can represent an important form of worker resistance to alienation. Such arrangements are the embodiment of past struggles and can represent an alternative to overt resistance. Of course all those past struggles did not result in worker victories. Custom also embodies the compromises and the defeats of the past. Therefore it will often be something to be resisted in itself rather than a weapon of resistance.

Collective and individual forms of worker resistance often are both manifest in any particular capitalist firm. They are sometimes complementary, as individual dissatisfaction with an order may result in a collective expression of sympathy with the individual and concern with the type of order resisted, and this may in turn lead to official strike action. Often individual dismissals follow this pattern. Sometimes individual and collective forms of resistance are alternatives. Turner noted that the suppression of collective resistance by management in a particular car firm was associated with a dramatic rise in absenteeism, turnover and accidents (Turner [1967], p. 190).

Uneven Strength of Resistance

Worker resistance, particularly its organised form, is unevenly developed among different groups of workers. What determines the strength of organised worker resistance among any particular group is a complex question. A few general observations seem worth making.

First, it appears that workers in large plants, where many are working at similar and often boring tasks, tend to build strong local organisations or a high level of individual expressions of resistance. For example, modern large car factories have become the areas of highest worker resistance measured by organised and unorganised disruptions since the Second World War in most car-producing countries (Turner [1967]).

Second, it appears that worker resistance is high where workers live in a homogeneous community centred around a particular form of work such as mining or docking. In general high resistance appears in relation to the size and homogeneity of workers' situations and the closeness of their contacts. Evidence for this in several different situations has been found by Sayles [1958] and Lockwood [1958]. Workers are encouraged to verbalize complaints and to resist oppression if those around them reinforce their feelings, if those around them provide *resonance* by which those grievances are repeated and magnified. As Marx says, 'As the number of the co-operating labourers increases so too does their resistance to the domination of capital' (*Capital*, vol. 1, p. 313).

There are two ways in which heterogeneity of work experiences may weaken worker resistance. First, there is the difficulty of achieving resonance when work experiences are dissimilar and when workers are not in close contact with each other. Second, there is an additional problem if stratification accompanies heterogeneity. When groups are distinguished from others in the same plant or section of a plant according to some characteristic with which status and earnings differentials are associated, then sections of workers may become actively hostile to each other, rather than being simply unaware of or unconcerned with each others' grievances and frustrations. Many work disruptions reflect rivalries among different workers distinguished by differences in their skills, their union affiliations, the character of their work, their authority over others or other status levels created by management.

The effect of stratification in the work-place is complex. It will weaken overall solidarity and with it expressions of resistance common to the plant as a whole. On the other hand it may increase resistance by smaller groups within the factory which focuses on managerial organisation or supervision of those differentials. Stratification may encourage groups which are cohesive in themselves, particularly those with a measure of relative status or higher earnings which are threatened, to develop strong organisations for resisting the erosion of differentials. Therefore top managers may reduce overall resistance by maintaining or encouraging such differentials, but thereby increase sectional resistance.

As heterogeneity of worker experience *within* productive activity may weaken worker resistance, so heterogeneity of worker characteristics and experiences which are *brought to* productive activity may also weaken resistance. Differences in age, sex, race and nationality, and differences in working backgrounds may discourage resonance and encourage sectionalism, particularly when these sociological or demographic characteristics are matched by different working conditions, status and earnings levels within productive activity – when stratification accompanies social heterogeneity. In part this reflects the general racism and sexism of those societies. Top managers *do not create racism and sexism*, but they *do use these divisions* among workers to their advantage. Common work experiences can be, and at times are, great levelling influences against such prejudices. Without taking worker resistance and managerial strategy for dealing with that resistance into account, one would expect productive activity to act against such prejudices.

One might expect from Marx's analysis of the industrial reserve army of labour that top managers would use such disadvantaged groups to weaken the bargaining position of other workers and to lower wages generally. In fact top managers often isolate such categories of workers into low status and low and irregular wage jobs. In part this represents a means for encouraging stratification among its workers for reasons mentioned above; in part it occurs in deference to the pressure placed upon top managers by socially advantaged workers to insulate their jobs from reserve army pressures.

Some Forms of Resistance as Double-edged Swords

From the discussion of customs built up through past worker resistance and of sectional resistance among workers it should be clear that many forms of resistance are not unambiguously helpful for the working class as a whole, or even for those particular workers who are resisting. Building up a strong organisation can be crucial for maintaining solidarity during struggles, but it may also be manipulated to top managers' advantage. Also, because capitalism is a world system, a sectional aspect may be attributed to almost all forms of worker resistance, particularly those in the wealthier capitalist countries. This ambiguity stems from the equivocal nature of resistance to symptoms or aspects of capitalism which are only indirectly related to resistance to capitalism as such.

Power relations within productive activity are tempered by the wage relation, the social relation by which people enter that activity. Employers of labour power have the legal power to dispose of their employees' labour power as they choose. While worker resistance to this disposal within productive activity has grown and acquired institutional strength in the form of organised trade unions (and shop stewards' movements), this resistance has rarely challenged the basic wage relation itself. Worker resistance has challenged the realising of exploitation during the valorisation process, not the wage relation which gives rise to that potential for exploitation. The co-option of trade union leadership by employers reflects the continuing reality of employer power derived from the wage relation. While trade unions *do* redress *some* of the power imbalance within productive activity, they also reflect that imbalance. Because trade unions are concerned primarily with day-to-day struggles where labourers continue to work within the capitalist mode of production, they must act as though capitalism were permanent for most of the time. Therefore employers, no longer powerful enough to destroy trade unions, are nevertheless able, through those day-to-day struggles which do not directly challenge their existence as employers, to use those institutions of stable worker organisation to ensure the maintenance of their managerial authority.

The most powerful forms of worker resistance are double-edged swords. In challenging only aspects or symptoms of capitalist social relations, they allow the possibility for capitalism to accommodate such challenges by offering concessions and by co-opting institutions which were intended to marshal worker solidarity against aspects of managerial authority (to encourage predictability and to dampen worker resistance). In Chapters 6 and 7 I will examine managerial strategies for dealing with worker resistance which often make that resistance appear futile. But the futility is only appearance in most cases. Managerial counter-pressure is a reality of the modern capitalist labour process as is worker resistance. The continuity of the capitalist mode of production in all highly developed capitalist countries is the reality which must be understood.

CHAPTER FIVE

Worker Resistance – Historical Development

Workers have always resisted exploitation in the capitalist mode of production. This resistance has taken on many different forms, but both particular forms of resistance and general resistance itself have been unevenly distributed among different groups of workers throughout capitalism's history. During Modern Industry high skills and well-organised resistance were strongly correlated. With the spread of trade unionism among less skilled workers and continued deskilling during the transition to Monopoly Capitalism this correlation has been weakened. Two major changes in worker resistance have accompanied the coming of Monopoly Capitalism. First, workers' larger organisations for resistance have become centralised and have lost their militancy. This has encouraged the development of alternative, often antagonistic, local forms of resistance. Second, with the drying-up of the latent industrial reserve army in Britain and the growth of individual firm-size in relation to local labour power markets, as internal labour markets have grown in importance (see discussion in *1870s–1914* section below), worker resistance has been increasingly successful at winning real wage rises and improvements in working conditions.

1 1780s to 1840s

The dislocating effects of the transition to Modern Industry on domestic workers, agricultural workers and handwork artisans in workshops was masked during the years of prosperity from the 1780s to the end of the Napoleonic wars. This meant that worker revolt was all the more intense during the following decades when the veil of boom-time disappeared. The main expressions of worker resistance were machine breaking and riots (which often involved the destruction of many forms of property) on the one hand, and mass demonstrations and meetings on the other hand.

As Hobsbawm points out, machine breaking was connected only in part with hostility to new machinery (Hobsbawm [1968], chap. 2), just as strikes are connected only in part to worker displeasure with work itself. Wrecking machinery or tools, whether new or old, was also a major method for coercing employers to grant concessions regarding wages and conditions. The phenomenon was a serious business as early as the seventeenth century. Given that domestic work was dispersed among numerous houses and villages, given the weakness of trade union organisation and the absence of strike funds, blacklegging was a serious problem. The destruction of looms in the cloth industry, blast-furnaces in ironworks or winding gear at coal-pits effectively stopped work. When employers were small and capital scarce, the destruction of machines, tools, raw materials or even employers' own houses proved to be an effective weapon for worker resistance.

The productive activity of domestic industry was relatively flexible. It was very difficult for a few workers to disrupt production simply by withdrawing their labour when new workers in different houses could easily be employed. With geographical dispersion mitigating easy solidarity for a strike, the destruction of property provided the best weapon. Though domestic industry declined significantly during this period the workers who were attracted to the factories required time to adjust to this new labour process and time to discover new ways of dealing with their employers.

The other form of activity, the mass demonstration or meeting, more closely reflected discontent with general economic conditions (unemployment and high food prices) rather than sectional industrial bargaining. Mass demonstrations, which often led to riots and machine breaking, occurred in agitation for parliamentary reform (such as Peterloo, 1819; the riots of 1831–2 and Chartist riots of 1838–9, 1842 and 1848) or for specific legislative measures (such as the Ten Hours campaigns, 1830, 1833; and the anti-Poor Law campaigns of 1837).

The groups involved in these riots reflected the only partially formed nature of the British proletariat. Reform agitation in particular was a combined petty bourgeois and working-class effort. The timing of general activity also showed that it was not confined to the nascent industrial proletariat. According to Rostow's 'index of social tensions', between 1742 and 1850 maximum unrest coincided with a trough in the business cycle and these normally coincided with rising food prices (Rostow [1948], pt 2).[1] Business recession combined with high food prices meant great hardship for semi-independent artisans, domestic workers and small businessmen as well as unskilled factory workers. Many local riots were caused by high prices rather than particular wage rates (see Ashton and Sykes [1929], chap. 7; or Wadsworth and Mann [1931], p. 355).

British working people were severely divided in terms of forms and effectiveness of resistance pursued, as well as pay and conditions enjoyed. Effectiveness of resistance and economic situation were intimately connected. While hand-loom weavers and craftsmen producing consumer goods, such as tailors or furniture makers, suffered during this period from the rise of Modern Industry, other groups of skilled craftsmen, such as printers, metal workers and craft-producers of luxury goods, remained unscathed or even improved their position. For these trades the old distinction between craftsmen and labourer held. Craftsmen, by virtue of their skill and their craft union organisation, maintained seven-year apprenticeships which ensured closed shops. They thereby lived perpetually in conditions of near full employment. Labourers, on the other hand, were freely expendable. The rise of the industrial reserve army meant that they quickly suffered in depressed times. While other skilled workers were in intermediate positions between these two groups, a clear economic and social gulf between the well-organised craftsmen, or labour aristocracy, and unskilled labourers comprised the primary dividing principle among working people. These differences would become more pronounced during the second half of the nineteenth century and they have continued during the twentieth century, though in a somewhat altered form.

Privileged craftsmen also held back from violent agitations for reform, preferring peaceful negotiations which, for them, were effective. Their organisations were conservative and sectional. In the trades where factory working was not yet important disputes were settled by conciliation more often than by strikes (see Prest [1960]; J. L. and B. Hammond [1919]; Thompson [1968]). In the old domestic industries wages were paid to artisans according to lists of prices which were negotiated collectively at the community level by employers and employees. Wages were intended to enable artisans to live comfortably in accordance with their status. In the Nottingham and Leicester hosiery industries these amicable and ceremonious negotiations were strictly adhered to by employers in the entire area until the first two decades of the nineteenth century. In Coventry's silk ribbon trade the arrangement lasted until the 1850s. During these early years conciliation machinery set up between employers and employees would settle disputes. This included bringing pressure to bear on employers who paid less than the list price as well as on employees for embezzlement. The system broke down in all three areas during the nineteenth century with mechanisation. It was the employers who refused to be bound by the negotiated prices because their factory workers could produce more than domestic workers for similar or lower wages with the coming of modern industry.

Generally, in non-revolutionised crafts, skilled craftsmen would receive about twice as much as common labourers; 'a differential of great antiquity and persistence' as Hobsbawm points out (1968, p. 346). This customary wage calculation remained very important during the first half of the nineteenth century. Workers at the time had not been fully socialised into the bourgeois ethic. During the 1870s, iron-founders and engineers were in great demand, but their wage demands remained very moderate. In part this was due to the absence of strong unions. In part the demand for some of the extra price which they could have won was made in terms of better conditions. But in part moderation was due to the workers' customary notion of 'a fair day's work for a fair day's pay' (Hobsbawm [1969], pp. 348–9). Worker effort was governed by this ethic. Rather than charging what the market will bear or only working hard if either financial incentive is offered or coercion is applied, privileged workers' effort was influenced by a notion of fairness and pride in their work. This is shown by the similarity of output employers received whether skilled workers were employed on time-rates or piece-rates. Employers knew that piece-workers would not produce more than the standard output in fewer days. Among Coventry's silk ribbon weavers, along with most other craftsmen, the practice of taking off Saint Monday, and often Saint Tuesday as well, was widespread during the 1820s, 1830s and 1840s, even after they were forced into factories (Reports Commissions [1840], 24). Also the moral stigma against slacking while at work was still very strong among skilled workers.

Unskilled workers were not supported by the customary status afforded to craftsmen. They were not protected from the industrial reserve army by long apprenticeships. Forced to do extremely unpleasant work and with no established customary standards of work learned during years of training for the particular tasks they were required to perform, unskilled workers worked only as hard as they had to. With labour-saving mechanisation and frequent severe trade recessions swelling the reserve army for unskilled workers, their wages often fell below family subsistence wages. This, and the destitution of rural handicraft workers, meant that a flood of women and children were forced into factories and workshops to make up the family wage (see *Capital*, vol. 1, chap. 15).

Women and children were paid much less than men in the factories, partly because men performed those tasks which had not been severely deskilled and partly because of society's general prejudice against women workers. Women and children were paid less than men even when both did the same jobs, causing Marx to conclude that differentials formerly based on skill came to be based on age and sex with the coming of Modern Industry. Most important, women were generally excluded – by rule or by custom, by men or through their own socially shaped lack of trade union consciousness – from many skilled workers' organisations.[2]

Thus during the transition to Modern Industry a clear duality in strength and form of worker resistance developed between skilled male workers, who negotiated with employers from a position of organised strength based on custom and skill on the one hand, and, on the other hand, deskilled or unskilled men plus women and children, whose resistance at the point of production was poorly organised and who were much weaker at maintaining and improving their pay and conditions of work. Nevertheless outside productive activity, on the streets, the coalition of unskilled industrial workers, agricultural labourers, displaced domestic workers, near bankrupt petty commodity producers and small-scale employers provided a powerful force for legislative change as the early Factory Acts and the Ten Hours Act of 1847 showed. Not only were the forms of resistance different between skilled and unskilled, but also skilled workers often actively disapproved of the forms of unskilled radicalism (S. and B. Webb [1894], pp. 180–1.)

2   1850 to 1870s

As mentioned in Chapter 3, during this period Britain enjoyed the fruits of her world monopoly in industry. Real wages, which remained stable on average between 1830 and 1850 and fell for less skilled workers, generally rose for all groups of workers after 1850 (Mitchell and Deone [1971], p. 344). Between 1850 and 1874 average real wages rose by 33 per cent. In many areas working conditions also improved. With Peel's Factory Act of 1844 and the Ten Hours Act of 1847, and after a few years of struggle to get the laws enforced, the worst excesses of overwork for women and children in the textile industry diminished somewhat.[3] Relief was gradually extended to other industries after a succession of further factory and workshop acts which were passed during the next half century. Working-class rioting and mass demonstrations fell off drastically.

As the general level of prosperity rose and the proletariat became more clearly defined the basic division between sections of that proletariat also became clearer. The ranks of the unskilled were still swelling from further declines in domestic industry. Also more industries became mechanised and newer labour-saving machines were introduced into previously mechanised sectors.

Prosperous and inflationary times also meant that those groups of workers which were able to bargain hard achieved significant wage increases. Mechanisation often did not degrade all skilled work in an industry. For example, in the British cotton industry spinners' jobs remained relatively unmechanised in the mid-nineteenth century. The unskilled jobs were generally taken by women and this left skilled males in the industry even more prominent. Also many industries expanded by forms of subcontracting and here labour aristocracies could maintain themselves by specialising on high-grade work, though in the midst of an increasing mass of outworkers or depressed craftsmen (Hobsbawm [1968], p. 283).

Thus the gap between well-organised and non-degraded artisans, on the one hand, and the growing mass of less skilled and poorly organised workers, on the other hand, grew during the Modern Industry period. (See Hobsbawm [1969], pp. 293–5 for evidence.) Nevertheless, even for the most poorly paid and least organised group of workers – women – wages improved during this period as well as conditions of work, (Clapham, 1932, p. 450). This reflected

TABLE 5.1

Latent Industrial Reserve Army for Great Britain, 1801–1971

Date	Population 000s Great Britain	Population 000s Ireland	Percentage Agriculture 1	Percentage Domestic service 2	Percentage Self-employed 3	Total percentage 1+2+3	Percentage Unoccupied	Total Percentage 1+2+3 Unoccupied
1801	10,686	5,216	15.9	5.6	n.a.	21.5	n.a.	
1811	12,147	5,956	14.8	5.7	n.a.	20.5	n.a.	
1821	14,206	6,802	12.6	5.6	n.a.	18.2	n.a.	
1831	16,368	7,767	11.0	5.5	n.a.	16.5	n.a.	
1841	18,534	8,200	10.3	6.5	n.a.	16.8	n.a.	
1851	20,817	6,514	9.7	6.2	n.a.	15.9	41.9(b)	57.8
1861	23,128	5,788	8.4	4.9	n.a.	13.3	41.0	54.3
1871	26,072	5,398	6.8	5.0	n.a.	11.8	41.4	53.2
1881	29,710	5,146	5.5	4.8	n.a.	10.3(a)	43.6	53.9(a)
1891	33,029	4,680	4.5	4.9	2.1	11.5	43.8	55.3
1901	37,000	4,447	3.8	4.1	2.3	10.2	44.5	54.7
1911	40,831	4,381	3.7	3.4	2.3	9.4	44.5	53.9
1921	42,769	4,354	3.4	2.9	2.4	8.7	45.3	54.5
1931	44,795	4,229	3.0	3.1	2.6	8.7	45.8	54.0
1951	48,854	4,332	2.5	1.2	2.3	6.0	45.1	51.1
1961	51,284	4,245	1.7	—	1.8	3.5	45.5	49.0
1966	52,304	4,324	1.6	—	2.8	4.2	42.7	46.9
1971	53,821	—	1.2	—	3.4	4.6	42.4	47.0

NOTE: (a) Due to incomplete series on self-employed the final series are not continuous through 1881–91.
(b) The percentage figures for unoccupied pose many conceptual problems. They include landlords, wives, pensioners, students, etc. The figures were obtained by subtracting those occupied from total population. The chief difficulty arises from the social changes which have occurred over the period, which have diminished the age range over which a person can be occupied. The Education Act of the 1870s and the earlier retirement and increased longevity of 1950s and 60s both show up clearly as an increase in the percentage unoccupied.

SOURCE: Censuses of Population.

the coincidence of the drying-up of the latent industrial reserve army (see Table 5.1) and Britain's monopoly position in world trade.

One important reason for the persistence of social and material differentials between craftsmen and less skilled workers was the system of subcontracting. Subcontracting was a common way by which industries could expand quickly when little capital was available for expensive overheads, when sharp fluctuations in demand meant large overheads were likely to prove a burden, and when large economies of scale were not obviously realisable from increasing the size of factories or even the number of average-sized factories. Finally, the system provided incentives for several key groups of workers both to work hard themselves and to drive other workers to work harder. Though subcontracting was declining, the system was still 'widely prevalent in the iron and steel industry, iron shipbuilding, a part of coal mining (notably in the Midlands), all small-scale workshop or "sweated" trades, many transport trades such as dock-labour, in the period of rapid construction, in public works, railway and mine-construction and the like, and in several other trades' (Hobsbawm [1969], p. 299), including building, clothing and engineering throughout Modern Industry.

Generally a large employer would subcontract a major piece of work to a piece-master for a fixed price. The piece-master would then employ his own craftsmen out of that price and they, in turn, would hire and pay their own labourers. Sometimes piece-masters would also subcontract work to foremen, who would simply gather and supervise others.

The system meant that not only did craftsmen earn more than labourers, but they also had a direct profit incentive to exploit or to drive labourers. Not only were craftsmen and labourers employed through different labour power markets, but they also opposed each other across a single labour power market.[4]

The other difference between skilled and unskilled workers which continued during this period was the difference in earnings fluctuations. During slumps, unskilled workers' earnings fell faster than skilled workers' earnings. In rapidly expanding areas and in some booms unskilled workers' earnings rose faster. In Sheffield between 1850 and 1896 fluctuations in labourers' earnings were three to four times larger than those for skilled foundrymen, and two to three times larger than for skilled engineers (Pollard [1954], p. 62). That unskilled workers' earnings rose more quickly in some booms reflected a persistence of the 'fair day's work for a fair day's pay' attitude among craftsmen.

With the decline of mass demonstrations the major expression of worker resistance became the sectional craft-union organisations of the skilled workers. The major issues within productive activity concerned wages and conditions of the craftsmen involved and the maintenance of scarce markets for their labour power. In 1864 the International Working Men's Association was formed in London. Marx soon assumed the leadership. While some

British trade union leaders associated with the International, from 1867 onwards, as the revolutionary character of the continental sections became clearer, British leaders gradually disassociated themselves.

During the boom of 1870–3, trade union membership rose significantly in Britain. Membership in trade unions affiliated with the Trades Union Congress (T.U.C.) rose from 250,000 in 1869 to 509,000 in 1873. The trade union movement was aided by a series of legislative measures between 1867 and 1875. In 1867 the Reform Act enfranchised most of the male working population who would have joined friendly societies, co-ops and unions. The 1867 Master and Servant Act and the 1875 Employers and Workmen Act made it easier for workers to strike without being put in prison for breach of contract. The 1871 Trade Union Act helped secure the legal status of trade unions and the Conspiracy and Protection of Property Act of 1875 legalised peaceful picketing.

Much of trade union effort went into securing these legislative gains through lobbying candidates, putting up Labour candidates in the 1868 election, and lobbying members of the House of Commons thereafter.

According to Hobsbawm, in this period skilled workers began consciously to adjust to the rules of the capitalist game.

> Thus unions began in the 1840's to recognise the peculiar nature of the trade cycle in their provisions for unemployment, and a little later to develop the characteristic policies of the 'new model' unionism: restriction of entry, maximum labour mobility between areas of slack and full employment, emigration benefit, the systematic use of friendly benefits, and so on (Hobsbawm [1968], p. 350).

Unskilled workers, on the other hand, were not to form stable organisations until the 1880s. The long lag in organisation by unskilled workers was closely related to the size of production units. As long as they remained small compared with the size of local labour power markets the threat of a strike by unskilled workers was a weak weapon. As before unskilled workers only worked as hard as they had to. Incentives in the form of subcontracting or other piece-wage systems were not offered to the unskilled.

The result to the working class of this dual structure was that a minority of the working population, about 10 per cent according to Hobsbawm (1968, pp. 279–80), comprised entirely of skilled men (although not including all skilled men), successfully bargained for a share of the spoils which accrued to British capitalism during its era of world monopoly. The unskilled were not unaffected, but what they received was more like table crumbs.

What clearly emerged during this period was a dual labour power market. While Marx recognised its existence, he presumed the privileged position of the minority of labour aristocrats to depend on their craft skill rather than their organisation. While their organisation was far from a revolutionary force during this period, it did shore up their craft-based position. Later, the craft base would fall away for many labour aristocrats, but the importance of organisation for maintaining dualism among the labour force would remain.

3   1870s to 1914

This period marked the collapse of Britain's world economic leadership; a huge growth in the size of firms; the spread of unionism and the fruits of empire among workers other than skilled craftsmen alone; the in-stitutionalisation of valorisation process bargaining through conciliation, arbitration and trade union bureaucracy; and a significant shift in worker demands toward returns related to what the market will bear and to measure effort by payment if given the chance.

The period began with twenty years of generally high unemployment and a severe profit squeeze as British industry began to feel the effects of foreign competition. After 1896 British foreign investment and exports recovered. While the British share of the world market was falling, the size of that market during this classical era of imperialism was expanding rapidly.

As mechanisation proceeded a mass of semi-skilled labourers who worked machines came to occupy the gap between artisan and common labourer. As factory size grew, the proportion of old fetch-and-carry labourers as well as highly skilled craftsmen fell. With this more homogeneous set of workers and with the rise in size of factory units, which meant larger proportions of workers in a single industry working within easy communication distance of each other, the obstacles to stable organisations among non-craftsmen weakened.

Growth of Trade Unionism among the Less Skilled

During the 1880s and particularly in the relatively prosperous period from 1888 to 1892, trade union membership and the number of trade unions swelled. The major growth occurred among the less skilled workers.

The older trade unions were based on the philosophy that they could survive only by holding their members in times of depression by 'friendly benefits' such as sickness and burial insurance and pensions. The trouble was that such societies required high rates of contributions and so were limited to relatively well paid workers. Also this tying-up of funds discouraged strikes and pushed the organisations to rely on conciliation and arbitration. In the 1880s most of the new unions severed the traditional tie with friendly benefits and they built up funds for strikes, lock-outs and expenses of organising and administration. The leaders of old and new unions were somewhat hostile to each other, but during the late 1880s and 1890s they came together in area-based trades councils which quickly grew in number.

The new unions did not disappear when unemployment rose again after 1891, though their membership was greatly depleted. After the end of the Great Depression (1896) trade union membership in all unions rose once more. Again the major increases were among the less skilled workers. By 1914, 27 per cent of all industrial workers were trade unionists; the comparable figure in 1890 was only 8 per cent.

The new unionists, influenced by socialist parties which were set up in the early 1880s (Social Democratic Federation, Socialist League and Fabian Society), were much concerned with legislative issues. Their main demands were for an eight-hour day and a legal minimum wage. Between 1889 and 1893 they set up a number of parliamentary political parties, culminating in the formation of the Independent Labour Party by a conference of new unionists in 1893. Eventually the new unionists prevailed on the T.U.C. to set up a parliamentary party, and in 1900 the Labour Representation Committee was set up which in 1906 became the Labour Party.

In 1901 the Taff Vale Railway Company won a suit against the Amalgamated Society of Railway Servants for supporting a strike a year earlier which led to damage to the railway. The decision in effect used the civil courts to outlaw organised worker resistance. After years of struggle to end the persecution of organised worker resistance in the criminal courts, this decision was a great set-back. In the five years during which the decision was upheld strike activity was severely curtailed. Between 1893 and 1898 nearly eleven million days a year on average had been lost by strikes and lock-outs. Between 1900 and 1905 the average was less than three million days a year (Cole [1948], p. 484).

This contributed to the severe fall in money wages between 1900 and 1905. In 1902 a number of trade unions set up political funds to support the Labour Representation Committee in order to get the Taff Vale decision overturned by statute. In the 1906 election twenty-nine Labour candidates were successful. This, combined with the Liberal victory, led to the Trades Disputes Act of 1906, which protected trade unions and their funds from civil action.

The Liberals remained in power for the rest of the period. During this time they introduced an important series of social reforms. These reforms generally served to distribute a small share of the fruits acquired by the most prosperous society in the world at the time to its most disadvantaged members. It was the beginning of the Welfare State, though the benefits at first were minute.

Each reform in itself represented a gain for the working class: school meals, old-age pensions, an eight-hour day in the mines, workmen's compensation for a widened range of accidents and a few industrial diseases, relief works for the unemployed and moves to stop sweated labour. Nevertheless the way of compromise and parliamentary reform by which these benefits were achieved began to drain the vitality of the Labour movement. The problem became clear with the passage of the National Insurance Act in 1911. The act set up a system of insurance against some of the hardship of unemployment for certain trades, and against medical expenses due to sickness for most workers. The scheme was based on contributions from workmen, employers and the State, but the State's contribution was relatively small. As Cole says, the Liberal way of tackling problems of unemployment and sickness 'was on the lines of compulsory self-help. The duty of the State was not to provide for the worker, but, as far as practicable, to compel him to help in providing for himself' (Cole [1948], p. 308). This bill split the Labour Party. Most unionists, both new and old, favoured the bill for the real, though modest, gains it offered. Socialists and Radicals considered the bill to contradict the Labour Party's primary demand for the right to work. For the Socialists it was the duty of the community as a whole to provide work for all its members and to maintain their health. Given Marx's view of work as an activity by which humanity shapes itself (discussed in Chapter 2 above), it is easy to see how measures to mollify the unemployed without remedy would be opposed by Socialists as a measure likely to increase dehumanisation in the capitalist system.

As workers' resistance outside productive activity became more organised, more conciliatory, and more successful, so their resistance within the labour process came to acquire these features during the 1870s to 1914 period, though throughout the period, and particularly during its last few years, vigorous opposition to these developments flared up among several important groups of workers.

During the early years of the Great Depression, conscious and deliberate class collaboration by the old unions came into the open. The old labour aristocrats were relatively protected from the Great Depression, particularly as the cost of living was falling. They were generally opposed to the eight-hour day demand of the new unionists, in part because it would hurt the competitive prospects of their industries. During the 1880s the Boilermakers spent on average only 3.5 per cent of their funds on strikes. They would refund to their employers losses incurred due to unofficial strikes or bad workman-ship (Hobsbawm [1974], pp. 10–11). The old unions had settled to the task of protecting their own narrow position while accepting the system as a whole.

The new unions began in opposition to the sectional, skill-exclusive and conciliatory attitude of the old unions. But after a few decades they had shifted significantly toward the position of the old unions. In part this was due to the legal security and conciliation mechanisms established between 1867 and 1875. They made it easier for all unions to win substantial concessions within production without flexing muscles. After legislation on working conditions (such as the Factory Acts, minimum-wage legislation or anti-subcontracting legislation) had been passed, it required some struggle for employees to have the new laws enforced in the firms where they worked. These were struggles which were generally successful.

In part the shift was also due to the energy which the new unions threw into parliamentary battles. This tended to make them more centralised with attention focused on national agitation and national leaders. It encouraged neglect of local issues and struggles. Also, even though the trade union movement no longer represented a craft aristocracy alone, it represented only slightly more than one-quarter of the industrial working class by 1914. Members of the new trade unions might not directly exploit other workers as under subcontracting systems, but the better organisation of gas workers, dockers, miners and railway-men improved their wage rates relative to the unorganised majority of workers.

While some craftsmen were well protected from the ill effects of the depression, others were suffering from mechanisation and the threat of down-grading. The iron-founders were threatened by the rise of machine-moulding, the compositors by linotype and monotype machines and the boot and shoe makers by general mechanisation. In light engineering the proportion of semi-skilled workers rose sharply. They were generally paid on piece-wages and the differential between their wages and those of the skilled workers declined. These factors caused some old unions to move towards the more radical stance taken by the new unions.

While the differences between new and old unions were narrowing, the right-wing movement of the new unionists was more significant and widespread than the leftward movement of the old unions. By the late 1890s the Webbs stated,

> The mere extension of national agreements and factory legislation has already, in the most highly regulated trades . . . transformed the Trade Union official from a local strike leader to an expert industrial negotiator, with the cordial co-operation of the secretary of the Employers' Association and the Factory Inspector, in securing an exact observance of the Common Rules prescribed for the trade (1898, p. 825).

During the decade before the Great War, the leaders of old and new unions came under severe criticism from shop-floor workers, who were suffering from a decline in real wages which continued up to the war. Much as the socialists and new unionists criticised the craft unions during the 1880s and 1890s, so the trade union hierarchy was criticised now for conciliation in trade disputes and compromise in politics. As a section of the women's suffrage movement grew impatient with parliamentarism and turned to direct action under the Women's Social and Political Union (Rowbotham [1973]), so many shop-floor workers grew impatient with the procedures which tied up their demands in a knot of centralised bodies aiming for compromise. Unofficial and spontaneous strikes and syndicalist ideas grew among trade unionists, holding up the hope that the acceleration of strikes would eventually lead to a general strike by which capitalism might be overthrown.

The divergence in radicalism between the central hierarchy of most unions and their militant rank and file was recognised by employers. In 1897 The Engineering Employers' Federation viewed strengthening the engineering

unions' national leadership over its district committees as a major require-
ment for re-establishing managerial prerogatives. While the employers won a
procedural agreement which achieved this in official terms after the 1897–8
lock-out, the effect in practice was for the weakened local, official union
leadership to lose the initiative in local disputes to the shop stewards (see
Jeffreys [1945]; Wigham [1973]; and Chapter 14, Section 1, below).

Internal Labour Markets and External Labour Power Markets

As the size of factories and firms grew and as worker resistance also grew and
became organised and institutionalised, the pay and conditions of work of a
much larger proportion of workers came to depend on a process of bargaining
within firms rather than on demand and supply for labour power. To use
current terms from industrial relations and manpower analysis, as greater
numbers of workers became organised, the importance of internal labour
markets grew compared with external labour (power) markets. The external
labour power market is the market where labour power is bought and sold.
The internal labour market is where workers and managers bargain over the
terms of realisation of labour from labour power. Managers try to get workers
to perform particular tasks quickly and to their specifications, while workers
try to improve pay and conditions of work (see Doeringer and Piore [1971] for
an account expressed in different language but amounting to the same thing).

Systematic slacking as a means for increasing earnings was developed with
theoretical elegance by Tom Mann in *What is Ca' Canny?* in the 1890s.
Complaints about industrial sabotage (from the French *sabot* or to drag one's
shoes) were increasingly voiced by businessmen towards the end of the
nineteenth century, and there is some general evidence of slackening
individual productivity after 1900 (Hobsbawm [1968], pp. 350–1). Thus it
appears likely that as the initiative in internal labour market disputes came to
emanate more and more from the shop floor, groups of workers became more
inclined to consider their effort to be a negotiable aspect of the labour power
which they sold.

In earlier times, what distinguished artisan from common labourer was the
guild organisation by which journeymen were somewhat protected from
external labour power markets by seven-year apprenticeships. Masters were,
in theory, senior members of an organisation in a position to which apprentices
and journeymen might aspire. The gulf between journeymen and master
(as well as between small master and large master) grew as masters set up
factories and hired a greater proportion of unskilled or semi-skilled workers.
But hiring policies were still guided by the customary separation of artisan
from common labourer. The wage differential of something close to one
hundred per cent, and the protection of craftsmen's employment while laying
off non-craftsmen in droves when trade was depressed, continued throughout
most of the nineteenth century, except in more drastic cases of mechanisation.

The strength of craftsmen's organisation, combined with custom, ensured this protection from external labour power markets in spite of the fact that in many cases the work actually carried out by craftsmen no longer technically required extensive training. The Hammonds [1919] point to the ease with which women and children learned cotton and woollen handloom weaving, particularly during the Napoleonic wars. The facility with which dilution[5] was technically accomplished in British engineering industries during the world wars is also evidence for the organisation and custom basis for craftsmen's protection from external labour power markets.

During the 1870s to 1914 period this protection was extended to categories of semi-skilled and unskilled workers where their organisations were strong. Management came to prefer to grant concessions in internal labour market bargaining in return for stability of production and easy adjustment to changing organisation of work processes by the firm's existing labour force, rather than adjust to changes and weaken the position of existing workers by replacing many by fresh recruits. This occurred particularly in larger firms, where monopoly power allowed managers more discretion for dealing with workers, and where the size of firms' labour requirements was large compared with the size of the local reserve army of labour.

During the 1870s to 1914 period it became clear that level of skill was no longer the simple category which divided the labour force. In earlier times skill and worker organisation coincided to distinguish a labour aristocracy. Now the legal machinery for trade union organisation and conciliation, the growth in firm size and the rise in the proportion of semi-skilled machine operators made it easier for non-craftsmen to organise themselves into stable trade unions. As the period drew to a close the similarity of the new general or industrial unions with the old craft unions in their effects on productive activity and the level of worker resistance became clear.

This does not deny that the new unions represented an advance. Nevertheless they came to stifle local worker resistance. Also they did not directly represent the majority of workers. On the other hand they won significant wage rises for their members (particularly during the late 1880s and 1890s), as well as some general benefits for all working people in statutory reforms. In order to understand these apparently contradictory effects of organised worker resistance managerial response to resistance by workers must be considered (see Chapters 6 and 7).

4   1914 to 1945

From 1914, in spite of the wide contrasts of war and peace, severe depression and unparalleled prosperity (1919–20), the features of British worker resistance which emerged during the pre-World War I period remained and were strengthened.

With the continued concentration of British industry and the growing power of worker resistance (particularly during the 1914 to 1920 period), internal labour markets grew in strength relative to the reserve army of labour. Real wage-rates fell severely between 1920 and 1922 due to major worker defeats, but they rose steadily from 1922 to 1938, in spite of unemployment levels which never fell below 10 per cent and which rose to 20 per cent during the worst years. Money wage rates fell by a mere 6 per cent between 1929 and 1933, compared with falls of 6 per cent and 10 per cent during the far less depressed years of 1900–4 and 1853–5. Part of the reason for the decline in importance of the reserve army was the difference in location between expanding and declining industries. The old export industries were concentrated in the North and West, while the newer industries were expanding in the Midlands and the South-East. Wages would fall due to reserve army pressure only if a sizeable number of workers could be made available at the factory gates (see Chapter 10).[6]

During the 1914 to 1945 period the leaders of trade unions were drawn closer into collaboration with employers. Though collaboration with the Government to benefit British capitalism as a whole, rather than simply with their own employers to benefit their particular industries, became more important. As a result, unofficial worker resistance grew. The proportion of unofficial strikes and the importance of shop stewards in shop-floor agitation increased.

After the engineers' defeat in 1897–8 the initiative for resistance to mechanisation and scientific management techniques fell to the individual shops. Also, with the spread of piece-work, imposed by management, the scope for isolated shop-floor negotiations increased.[7] Wartime inflation and dilution meant sudden and arbitrary changes in wage differentials. But wartime demand for engineering products put the engineers in a very powerful position to resist.

The first general act of collaboration between the unions and the Government came during the war with the Treasury Agreement of 1915. The unions agreed to compulsory arbitration and 'the relaxation of the present trade practices' (the strike weapon in particular). This widened the gulf between local trade union leaderships and the rank and file, as well as between national leaders and their members. In the engineering industry in particular, conditions during the war favoured the growth of unofficial shop stewards' movements. The stewards were not afraid to become involved in strikes. In spite of their illegality there were 2427 recorded stoppages during 1916, 1917 and 1918.

As worker resistance from the shop floor rose during the war and in 1919 and 1920, union leaders were being pushed further to the left or pushed aside. The Russian Revolution encouraged shop stewards and other radicals, though at first sympathy for Russia was not widespread. British troops, along with their allies, invaded Russia in the spring of 1918. When they remained after the armistice in November 1918 and blockaded supplies to Russia opposition to the Government's policy swelled from a wide range of people. A national 'Hands off Russia' Committee was formed. From August 1920 local Councils of Action were set up, based on the local trade and labour councils,[8] to co-ordinate local activities against the Government's policy on Russia. The leaders of the Miners' Federation and the railway drivers' union (ASLEF) argued for direct action[9] at the Trades Union Congress in September 1919. Just after the war right-wing leaders of the Amalgamated Society of Engineers were replaced in the wave of radicalism.

This early post-war situation changed quickly during the next decade. With the coming of high unemployment trade unions went on the defensive. Trade union leaders accepted drastic wage cuts in the traditional industries.[10] Trade union membership plummeted from 8.3 million in 1920 to 5.6 million just two years later.

The trade union leadership responded to the recession by trying to moderate wage cuts while still accepting cuts in principle, in order to promote their industry's competitive position. Disaffection with this policy among the rank and file became increasingly apparent as trade union membership fell and as the National Minority Movement quickly gathered strength after its formation in 1927.[11]

In April 1921 the miners rejected a large wage cut and called upon the Triple Alliance to take strike action in their support.[12] The strike was called off at the last minute on Friday, April 15, as the leadership of the Triple Alliance lost their nerve. The rank and file were prepared to fight and this betrayal of the miners shook the trade union movement. After 'Black Friday' the Triple Alliance was destroyed.

The split between militant rank and file and conservative leadership was demonstrated again five years later during the General Strike of 1926. The General Council of the Trades Union Congress capitulated after nine days of unexpected solidarity among the rank and file. Workers returned with nothing to show for their efforts to face severe victimisation. Again workers left the unions. Membership fell from 5.5 million in 1925 to 4.9 million in 1927. With the Trades Disputes Act of 1927 general strikes and most sympathy strikes were outlawed. Also 1927 marked the beginning of bans and proscriptions against radicals in individual trade unions. In 1928 the Chairman of the T.U.C. General Council, Ben Turner, and the chairman of Imperial Chemical Industries, Sir Alfred Mond, began a series of talks which would be to the 'mutual advantage of both employers and union officials' and open trade-union collaboration at the national level during peacetime began.

Organisation among Less Skilled Workers

During this period the old coincidence between highly skilled and well-organised workers continued to break down. The Workers' Union was established in 1898 by Tom Mann, primarily for less skilled engineering workers. When it was taken over by the Transport and General Workers' Union (T.G.W.U.) in 1929 it had 100,000 members. The main unions to grow after the 1921 and 1926 defeats were general workers' unions. The T.G.W.U. was formed in 1922 by a merger of 23 separate unions (primarily transport workers other than railway-men). By 1937 it had 650,000 members and was the largest union in Britain. The other main general union was the National Union of General and Municipal Workers (N.U.G.M.W.), which grew quickly in the 1930s.[13] As they grew the general unions came to exercise a conservative influence on the whole trade union movement, though they originated in the more radical new unions of 1880s (dockers and gasworkers). With members in widely diverse industries, they provided no constitutional means for rank and file to repudiate the decisions of officials (unlike the more democratic craft unions). The officials increasingly viewed themselves as the brokers of 'business unionism'; they were in the business of selling labour (power) at as good a price as they could. Like other businessmen it was in their interests to remain on good terms with their customers.

Increased unionisation among less skilled workers, and the growth of mass production industries (vehicles, armaments and electrical goods), which primarily required semi-skilled workers, meant some closing of the gap between skilled and less skilled workers' wages.

During the war flat-rate awards based on the rising cost of living index were given to all grades of workers. Thus between July 1914 and April 1919 labourers' rates increased from 59 per cent to 76 per cent of the skilled rate (Bowley [1921], p. 125). During the long depression, with unemployment greater in unskilled than skilled work, the differential widened again, but it remained smaller than before the First World War.[14] Nevertheless the change in differentials was much smaller than the differentials themselves. Broadly, the age-old differential of labourers receiving half of artisan's wages had changed to unskilled workers receiving two-thirds of skilled workers' wages. Considering the change in organisational strength of unskilled workers,[15] and the decline of formal apprenticeships for skilled workers, the change has been remarkably low. Also the differential between men and women remained high in spite of the wartime influx of women into jobs formerly reserved for men. At the end of the war most women were encouraged, or forced, out of their wartime jobs. Women's average wages were 63 per cent of men's rates in 1913/14, 66 per cent in 1922/24 and 64 per cent in 1935/36. For skilled manual work their average wages changed from 44 per cent of men's rates in 1913/14 to 49 per cent in 1922/24 to 44 per cent in 1935/36 (Routh [1965], p. 107).

5   1945 to 1970s

Along with the drying up of the latent reserve army which has proceeded since the beginnings of Modern Industry, the period since 1945 has been marked until very recently by the drying-up of the active reserve army. During the 1921 to 1938 period annual unemployment never fell below 10 per cent of the insured population. From 1945 unemployment has never risen above 10 per cent. This situation of near full employment has characterised nearly all advanced capitalist countries since the war. To some extent the worker shortage has been alleviated by immigration and migrant workers, but this has only slowed down wage rises rather than reduce wages (Castles and Kosack [1973], pp. 377–8).

With the accession of Labour governments in 1945–51, collaboration between the trade union movement and the State reached a new level. The result, as with the early-twentieth-century Liberal Government, was a series of significant reforms benefiting working people (the National Insurance Scheme and the National Health Service) and in addition the nationalisation of several key, but generally faltering or largely publicly controlled, industries. The result was also a deeper commitment to 'nation' as opposed to 'class' among the centralised institutions created out of class struggle (Labour Party and T.U.C.), which has become clearer with each successive Labour government, (see Nairn [1973]). The deals for pay restraint between the Government and the major unions of 1975/77, the 'Social Contracts', would have been hard to imagine during the 1880s or in 1919–20.

After 1933 trade union membership rose steadily from 23 per cent of occupied workers to 43 per cent in 1946. Since then trade union membership has grown rather slowly and the proportion of the labour force belonging to trade unions has remained under 50 per cent.[16] One of the main reasons for this stagnation has been the lower proportion of women workers belonging to trade unions (plus the rise in the proportion of women in the labour force compared with men). In 1946 51.8 per cent of male workers, but only 24.5 per cent of female workers, were trade unionists. At that time the number of women employed was 47.2 per cent of the number of men employed. In 1968, with 42.5 per cent of the labour force in trade unions, 51.8 per cent of men and 26.6 per cent of women were members, while the number of women employed had reached 58.8 per cent of the number of men.

Men and Women

Why has the number of women trade unionists remained so low? One reason is because a high proportion of women take part-time work and office jobs, or work in smaller establishments. The growth of white-collar unionism among clerical and administrative workers has redressed some of this imbalance in recent years.

The other major reason for meagre progress has been the attitude of male trade unionists themselves. It is 'very natural for ladies to be impatient of restraint at any time', therefore the factory is an unsuitable place for them.

'Wives should be in their proper place at home' (Rowbotham [1973], p. 61). Thus spoke a prominent trade union leader in the 1870s – a statement which echoed the sentiments of artisans over the preceding century and which has reflected the attitude of many trade unionists during the following century.

From the beginnings of Modern Industry a pattern between women and men working side by side was established which has continued, basically unaltered, to the present day. In the Lancashire cotton mills, where women were comparatively well organised, they were excluded from the management of the union. Also figures from 1833 show that a differential between adult men and adult women's wages ranging from women's wage at 71 per cent of men's to women's wage at 39 per cent of men's, depending on age, was tolerated for workers *in the same factories* (Gardiner, [1974], p. 247).[17] Women entered the factories as weavers or spinners from domestic industry with the same skills as the men, but once in the factories men took on the more 'skilled' work as well as leadership of the unions.

During the First World War the unions accepted dilution and the suspension of other trade practices on the solemn guarantee by both Government and employers that trade practices would be restored at the end of the war. The Treasury Agreement of 1915 was amended at the trade unions' insistence in January 1916. The Amendment Act declared that unskilled workers employed in the place of skilled workers should receive the skilled men's rate of pay. This reflected skilled workers' desire to maintain their differentials rather than a desire to encourage higher pay for women and unskilled workers. As with women in the early nineteenth century cotton mills, the differential was primarily supported by a separation of women's jobs from men's jobs. If by some unusual circumstances women should be taken onto men's jobs, then they would receive men's rates. The differentials were maintained by excluding women from men's jobs rather than accepting unequal pay for equal work. At the end of the war government, employers and unions collaborated to redress dilution.

In fact, back in 1888, under the influence of the 'New Unions', the T.U.C. passed a resolution calling for equal pay for equal work. The problem with equal pay for equal work in 1888, as in 1976, is that what constitutes equal work (and work of equal value) is open to widely different interpretations.[18]

The differential between men's and women's earnings increased after the Second World War from women earning 53.9 per cent of men's earnings in 1946 to 49.1 per cent in 1968. Women have accounted for around 20 per cent of T.U.C. membership for decades, but only two of the 35 seats on the T.U.C. General Council are usually held by women, and those are specifically allocated to representatives of the women workers' group. Womens' membership in unions is also discouraged by the standard practice of having meetings in the evening when women are often putting children to bed or attending to other household 'duties'. Finally, and perhaps most important, male trade unionists' attitude towards women's work-place struggles has been notoriously unsupportive and often openly hostile. To cite only one example, in July 1973, the Associated Union of Engineering Workers (A.U.E.W.) convenor at the General Electric Company factory in Spon End at Coventry instructed his union members to break the picket lines of a strike by 200 women workers, though the women were also A.U.E.W. members (Edney and Phillips [1974], pp. 332–3).

Other Divisions

The attitude of male trade unionists toward women workers is paralleled by the traditional attitude of skilled trade unionists toward unskilled workers, and white native trade unionists toward blacks and immigrants.

The reluctance of skilled trade unionists to support unskilled workers' struggles or to accept them into their own unions was one of the major reasons for the tremendous growth of general workers' unions instead of industry-wide trade unions from the 1920s. The weakness of the workers' response to widespread lay-offs in the motor industry during the 1970s can be attributed, in part, to the fragmented nature of union representation in the industry (see Chapter 14). Artisans traditionally looked upon labourers or semi-skilled workers as social inferiors. Similarly the English looked upon the hundreds of thousands of Irish who poured into England and stayed from the 1820s as social inferiors. In part the attitude towards women, unskilled workers and immigrants reflects deep social prejudices, but in part it reflects a basic economic motive which has underlined much trade union activity. This is the attempt to escape from the pressure of the industrial reserve army of labour by setting up barriers to entry into one's own category of jobs. Along with 'skilled jobs' reflecting skilled workers' organisational strength, custom and years of training; organisational strength and custom have helped to create non-Irish jobs, white jobs, male jobs, English jobs (though they are generally called by some other name: traditionally, fitter, turner, ganger, smith or driver; more recently, grade A or B rather than grade C or D, trainee manager rather than shop assistant, section A or B rather than section C or D, or factory A or B rather than C or D).

Castles and Kosack [1973], have documented the attitudes of indigenous trade unionists towards the post-World War II influx of immigrant workers. Everywhere trade unionists have demanded that immigrants and indigenous workers should receive equal pay for equal work (p. 128). Generally trade unionists have then tried to exclude immigrants from certain categories of jobs. The main group of European immigrants to enter Britain came between 1945 and 1950. Collective agreements restricting these workers were concluded in nearly forty industries. These agreements often included clauses requiring foreign workers to be dismissed first in the event of redundancy and clauses restricting their promotion prospects (pp. 138–9). Union discrimination against Commonwealth immigrants has been less overt, but common at the local level (p. 143), with cases of Pakistanis being refused membership in skilled workers' unions (p. 149) and white unionist blacklegging and harassing pickets during struggles by Asians concerning differential pay or conditions (pp. 153–8; and Edney and Phillips [1974], pp. 342–3).

Of course sections of the labour force are not entirely hostile toward each other within any one country. References to hostility by privileged workers toward women, blacks, immigrants and unskilled workers can be supplemented by many instances of solidarity between different sections. Nevertheless the differences in pay, conditions and organisation remain.

CHAPTER SIX

Management – Preliminary Argument

1 Types of Managerial Strategies

Management[1] under the capitalist mode of production has always involved two rather different, but closely related functions.

First, there is the co-ordination of the various activities undertaken by the firm. Flows of input materials and instruments of labour must find their way to workers at well-timed intervals for each activity. Finances must be available from sales and borrowings to pay for labour power, materials and tools. The final output must be marketed. This job of co-ordination is part of any complicated economic process.

Second, there is the exercise of authority over workers. This second function of management is peculiar to productive activity in class-divided societies. Under capitalism, the capitalist buys labour power from the worker as he would buy any other commodity. But labour power is peculiar in that it is possible for labour power to create more value in the labour process than it costs to produce that labour power. When the capitalist buys labour power he buys the *possibility of exploitation*, because whatever is produced in the labour process legally belongs to the capitalist. Also, legally, the capitalist controls what the worker does in the labour process, within broad socially defined limits. As pointed out in Chapter 2, the capitalist is *encouraged to realise* this possibility as much as he can because of his avarice and because of competition. Marx described co-operation, division of labour and mechanisation as methods by which capitalists *might technically realise* the possibility for exploitation represented by the act of labour power purchase.

The final ingredient for exploitation is the theory and practice of exercising capitalist authority over labour power in the labour process. The capitalist or the manager may order the worker to do something, but how can he actually get the worker to do that thing, and to do it well and quickly? Certainly capitalists have often exercised their legal right to fire the worker who does not perform well, but the capitalist's problem would remain if the replacement worker also performed unsatisfactorily. Also many capitalists have considered the performance of all their employees to be unsatisfactory.

While the capitalist may turn to outside judicial or military power to discipline recalcitrant workers, even this may not achieve the obedience desired. To extend an old saying, you can lead a horse to water, you can even whip it for not drinking, but you still cannot force it to drink.

Marx emphasised this managerial problem under capitalism by calling labour power 'variable capital'. When the capitalist buys tools or raw materials he can determine their value in the labour process with a precision which is impossible when dealing with human beings. The capitalist knows that a certain portion of his outlay on constant capital will be transferred to each unit of production and he can account for this capital in terms of lay-out costs or depreciation. But when the capitalist buys labour power, he buys what is on the one hand a potentially malleable commodity, but what is on the other hand a commodity ultimately controlled by an independent and often hostile will. The exercise of managerial authority over labour power may be subdivided into two aspects. First, top managers try to mould labour power to fit in with changes in overall organisation or techniques more or less dictated by market conditions. Second, top managers try to subdue or limit workers' independent control over their actions once particular tasks have been assigned or general orders given.

These two aspects are closely related. It may be that top managers will try to reorganise the labour process in order to reduce workers' exercise of independent action, as well as simply to fit in with increasing relative surplus value as when machinery is introduced. Nevertheless it will be useful to separate worker resistance to reorganisations of the labour process planned by top managers from worker resistance to existing organisation. To put it another way, managerial attempts to realise more of the potential surplus value represented by their variable capital may be separated from attempts to retain the planned or expected value of that variable capital.

Broadly, there are two major types of strategies which top managers use to exercise authority over labour power – Responsible Autonomy and Direct Control. The Responsible Autonomy type of strategy attempts to harness the adaptability of labour power by giving workers leeway and encouraging them to adapt to changing situations in a manner beneficial to the firm. To do this top managers give workers status, authority and responsibility. Top managers try to win their loyalty, and co-opt their organisations to the firm's ideals (that is, the competitive struggle) ideologically. The Direct Control type of strategy tries to limit the scope for labour power to vary by coercive threats, close supervision and minimising individual worker responsibility. The first type of strategy attempts to capture benefits particular to variable capital, the second tries to limit its particularly harmful effects and treats workers as though they were machines.[2]

Both these types of strategies have characterised management throughout the history of capitalism, but generally the Responsible Autonomy type of strategy has been applied most consistently to privileged workers and the Direct Control type of strategy to the rest.

What has changed with the coming of Monopoly Capitalism? With the rising size and complexity of firms' operations, the rise of well-organised worker resistance among less skilled workers; and the incorporation of science directly into capitalist productive activity, management has become a more conscious, a better organised, and a more scientific activity. With the growth of monopoly power top managers have been able to experiment with new managerial techniques with less fear that failure will surely lead to financial ruin. Thus with Monopoly Capitalism came managerialism, meaning the proliferation of theories of how best to manage firms which have been based on some trace of scientific method.[3] Also, with the coming of Monopoly Capitalism, top managers have had to deal more specifically with *organised* worker resistance. This has meant a rise in relative importance of the Responsible Autonomy strategy, particularly increased use of techniques to co-opt worker organisations.

Marx concentrated on the pressure of the industrial reserve army, which allowed capitalists to maintain harsh disciplinary procedures to enforce managerial authority over the majority in factories. But given organised worker resistance among the less skilled, direct, harsh disciplinary methods may simply disrupt productive activity. Internal labour markets have grown in importance. Within these markets top managers have found co-option of certain groups and conciliation to be more effective than blanket coercion. Within large firms in particular, financial incentives and other concessions have been offered to encourage worker effort and to ensure compliance with changing managerial directives. Also systems by which managerial authority has been delegated have become increasingly complex. Hobsbawm stated, 'Capitalism in its early stages expands, and to some extent operates, not so much by directly subordinating large bodies of workers to employers, but by subcontracting exploitation and management' (1968, p. 297). But this delegation of managerial authority has continued long beyond capitalism's early stages. What was once carried out via quasi-market transactions in the form of subcontracting is now carried out through complex bureaucratic structures incorporating many layers of middle managers, and often several layers of trade union bureaucrats and a fat book on Procedure. (Of course the benefits top managers gain from union organisation and established Procedure arise from managerial adaptations to worker resistance, and therefore benefit can quickly turn to bane for top managers.)

A more detailed discussion of Direct Control and Responsible Autonomy strategies and their limitations may be found in Chapter 7, Sections 3 and 4, and Chapter 8, Section 1. These strategies are also discussed in Friedman [1977].

2 Management and Marxist Theory

Marxists have generally treated the Direct Control strategy as *the* theory and practice of capitalist control over the labour process. In fact Lenin argued for the introduction of Taylorian scientific management into Soviet organisation of production in 1918. He found in scientific management 'a number of the greatest scientific achievements in the field of analysing mechanical motions during work, the elimination of superfluous and awkward motions, the elaboration of correct methods of work, the introduction of the best system of accounting and control, etc' (1918, p. 259).

Recently, in an extremely important book, Harry Braverman [1974] has reminded us that Taylor's system was not a method for elaborating correct methods of work. It was a system for increasing the rate of exploitation of alienated labour and, one should add, of counteracting worker resistance.

Braverman correctly criticises Lenin for confusing social relations in productive activity specific to exploitation in the capitalist mode of production with technological factors or forces of production which are more independent of the mode of production (though they are shaped by the mode of production). Lenin confused authority during productive activity with co-ordination of complex processes. Both are managerial functions in the capitalist labour process, but only the latter is general to all modes of production. But Braverman too must be criticised for confusing one *particular strategy* for exercising managerial authority in the capitalist labour process with *managerial authority* itself.

Just as strict disciplinary rules were a particularly popular managerial strategy of top managers in the early years of the first industrial revolution, so strict work measurement and minute division of tasks have been popular managerial strategies, particularly during the first decades of the twentieth century. But Taylorian scientific management is not the only strategy available for exercising managerial authority, and given the reality of worker resistance, often it is not the most appropriate strategy from top managers' point of view (see Section 3 of the next chapter for a detailed discussion of Taylor's theory of scientific management).

Let us trace Braverman's arguments in detail. Braverman begins by distinguishing human from animal labour following Marx (*Capital*, vol. 1, pp. 173–4). Human labour is conscious and purposive, while other animal labour is instinctive. Human labour is guided by conceptual forethought. While human labour in the abstract involves both conception and execution, in its particular social form conception may be separated from execution. 'The conception must still precede and govern execution, but the idea as conceived by *one* may be executed by *another*' (Braverman [1974], p. 51). The unity of conception and execution, thus dissolved from the standpoint of the individual, would then be reasserted in the larger organisation or community which contained the individuals concerned. Braverman's major theme is that, as the capitalist labour process develops conception, is gradually separated from execution and conceptual activities are progressively concentrated among fewer and fewer people. Why should this occur?

Braverman notes the uncertainty and variability which labour power presents to the capitalist because ultimately it is controlled by the subjective state of the workers (p. 57). For Braverman the antagonism between worker and capitalist in the labour process is important primarily because of its exacerbation of this variability and uncertainty characterising labour power. For Braverman the problem of management is the problem of reducing this uncertainty by capturing control over the labour process.

The principal weapon by which management captures this control is to separate conception from execution through the division of labour and mechanisation. This progressively reduces the skill and imagination concerning individual tasks required of the mass of workers. This separation through deskilling, which was an unconscious tendency of capitalist production in early years, becomes a conscious and systematic strategy of management with the development of scientific management. With each worker performing only a simple task, conceptual activities and scientific development would be concentrated in the hands of managers (pp. 120–1). While scientific management seeks to increase managerial control by separating conception from execution, assuming a given technology, the technical development of machinery has also been shaped by this desire. As machines have become more automatic and more complex, the degree of judgement and control exercised by the machine operator over the labour process has declined. Knowledge of the machine becomes a specialised trait segregated from the actual machine operators. The pace at which the machine operates becomes a clearer managerial prerogative as control over that pace is centralised and often removed from the site of production to the planning office (pp. 187, 194–5).

For Braverman Taylorian scientific management *is* the fundamental practice of management in twentieth-century advanced capitalism.

> The popular notion that Taylorism has been 'superseded' by later schools of industrial psychology or 'human relations', that it 'failed' . . . represent[s] a woeful misreading of the actual dynamics of the development of management.
>
> Taylor dealt with the fundamentals of the organisation of the labour process and of control over it. The later schools of Hugo Münsterberg, Elton Mayo, and others of this type dealt primarily with the adjustment of the worker to the ongoing production process as that process was designed by the industrial engineer (p. 86).

Here Braverman's inadequate treatment of organised worker resistance is evident. First, labour power is variable both because individual human beings are intelligent and guided by subjective states, and because workers are alienated from the labour process and actively build organisations to resist managerial authority. These two aspects of labour power present top managers with two qualitatively different problems. Worker resistance does not simply make labour more uncertain, taking uncertainty to imply randomness. Top managers are often reasonably certain that if they were to do certain things (such as to dismiss someone for a reason which workers consider grossly unfair, or to change manning levels in some crucial way without prior negotiations) it would provoke a work stoppage. In a sense, the first sort of variability is so complex that employers cannot calculate probabilities as to its immediate prospect, while against the second sort of variability top managers can calculate reasonably good probabilities of occurrence. This is the distinction between uncertainty and risk made popular in economics literature by Frank Knight [1921]. The separation of conception from execution by division of labour, mechanisation or scientific management is not necessarily the best strategy for management in organising the labour process when confronted with worker resistance. Techniques which reduce managerial reliance on worker goodwill may not be most appropriate for insuring against the effects of determined worker resistance or for directly reducing expressions of that resistance.

Disadvantages of the Direct Control strategy are discussed in the next chapter. These disadvantages are particularly evident when demand is fluctuating widely (necessitating lay-offs), or when technical change is rapidly occurring.

Braverman suggests a strict division between design of the work process and selection, training, manipulation, pacification, and adjustment of the worker to fit that design. But management is not a two-tier process where work organisation designed by engineers is sacrosanct and primary, and the exercise of managerial counter-pressure to worker resistance is secondary. Both are managerial problems and are measured in terms of profits. If the costs of scientific management in terms of worker resistance or lost flexibility are too great, alternative strategies will be tried and these will involve changes in the organisation of work processes.

3   On Control

The word 'control' has caused confusion when applied to productive activity because it has been used both in an absolute sense, to identify those 'in control', and in a relative sense, to signify the degree of power which people have to direct work. This confusion has become particularly evident in discussions of workers' control. On the one hand, one wants to make clear that recent schemes for participation in the managerial decision-making apparatus or group technology do not confer workers' control in an absolute sense because the fundamental capitalist relations of production remain. Top managers are still 'in control' in that they, in their role as representatives of capital, continue to initiate changes in work arrangements and continue to exercise authority over the work activity of others. Also the products of workers' labour still belong to the capitalists. On the other hand, one wants to allow the possibility that changes in organisation of work or decisions about work may increase the power which workers may exercise to act within production according to their own judgement and their own will (over such things as their work pace, the particular tasks they do and the order in which they do that work). One wants to allow for shifts in the 'frontier of control', in spite of the continuation of the capitalist mode of production (Goodrich [1920]), and in spite of the continuation of managerial control in the absolute or identifying sense.

The notion of control by management in the absolute sense is further complicated by a possible confusion of control with creation. To control is to exercise restraint or direction upon the action of a force or thing. The force or thing, when referring to productive activity under the capitalist mode of production, is separate from its controller. It stands apart from the capitalists and the managers as well as the workers. People are not free to create their own history consciously, according to their needs and abilities, because capitalist society is class divided. The society, the mode of production and the associated labour process at any point in time, is created out of the dynamic of class conflict and the competitive struggle. Top managers are constrained in their power over productive activity by pressure to accumulate and the need to counteract worker resistance. While top managers are clearly those 'in control' of productive activity, their freedom to create and recreate this activity is severely limited by the relations of capitalist production.

If workers' control implies the possibility of those participating in productive activity exercising this creative sort of freedom, then workers' control could never be realised under the capitalist mode of production. Also its content would be very different from managerial control under capitalism. It could not mean a simple change in personnel 'in control'.

The notion of relative control is also complicated by the desire to identify 'progressive' changes from the workers' point of view. The difficulty is, of course, that workers sold their labour power out of economic necessity in the first place, rather than as part of a choice expressing their will and judgement. The overall organisation of work in capitalist enterprise is not a matter of worker choice. Nevertheless some changes are fought for and won by the workers and this means some increase in the power of workers to resist further managerial initiatives. On this point it may be useful to distinguish changes in work organisation and decision making which workers have fought for, and those which managers have initiated. Changes which top managers have initiated which increase workers' relative control over productive activity are likely to represent attempts to counteract, contain, or co-opt worker resistance, particularly when labour power markets are tight. Changes in work organisation in Swedish car factories may be viewed in this way. Faced with high labour turnover and absenteeism in Volvo and Saab car factories (encouraged by the scarcity of white male workers in Sweden's near full employment economy over the past few years), the car firms have made great publicity over their attempts to 'humanise' car assembly work. This has been 'achieved' by replacing long assembly lines with small working groups who assemble entire components or sub-assemblies together. Apparently these 'experiments' have been more limited in scope than the Swedish publicity implies.

At Fiat similar experiments were tried, but the impetus came from the workers and the changes were won only after long struggles. Eventually worker initiatives concerning work organisation within certain plants were superseded by initiatives concerning Fiat's overall investment policy and particularly its activity in southern Italy.

The different source of initiatives in the Swedish situation compared with the Italian one may be crucial in deciding whether the changes in relative control were progressive from the workers' point of view. The mere fact that the changes came out of victorious struggle in the Fiat case strengthens worker resistance and encourages further initiatives. Also changes conceived by the workers are more likely to be controlled by them in their detailed implementation. In the Fiat case managerial control over productive activity was weakened.

In both cases monotony was reduced and workers' relative control or autonomy over precisely what they do at any particular moment and the speed at which they do that work was increased. In the Swedish case, however, managerial control over productive activity as a whole was increased by loosening top managers' *direct* control over worker activity in order to reduce worker resistance. This conclusion makes sense only if one explicitly recognises the management of worker resistance to be an integral part of managerial control over productive activity.

Authority over workers, direction of worker activity and co-ordination of flows of materials, products and cash are all necessary aspects of managerial control over productive activity within the capitalist mode of production. If top managers decide to reduce their direct control over the direction of worker activity and the co-ordination of materials flows in order to increase their authority over workers, success in implementing this strategy will result in greater managerial control over productive activity as a whole, greater managerial control, given the reality of worker resistance. This will not occur if top managers have made a mistake. But mistakes, while possible, are a complication which may be ignored when speaking generally.[4]

So top managers may loosen direct control over work activity as part of a strategy for maintaining or augmenting managerial control over productive activity as a whole (Responsible Autonomy), or they may be forced to loosen direct control as part of a general shift in control over productive activity in favour of the workers. In this book I shall be focusing on the former situation because it has been the more common.

CHAPTER SEVEN

Management–Historical Development and Argument

Three major themes are demonstrated by the historical discussion of management which follows. First, the relative popularity of Direct Control or Responsible Autonomy strategies has changed markedly over the years. As with the strength of worker resistance, this has reflected conditions in both internal labour markets and external labour power markets. Second, different types of strategies have been used by top managers when dealing with different groups of workers. Differences in strategies applied have reflected differences in the strength of resistance by different groups of workers. Third, the coming of Monopoly Capitalism was marked by a great rise in theoretical development of strategies for maintaining authority over workers and in financial resources applied to the implementation of those strategies.[1]

1   1780s to 1840s

During this period a general fear of the revolutionary potential of the masses or the mob and a concern to keep the poor in their place coloured the attitude of factory owners toward their employees. Reaction to the French Revolution, particularly the Reign of Terror, and to the Nore Mutiny in 1797 was expressed in the Combination Acts (enforced from 1799 to 1824). To suppress anything which might lead to revolt, trade unions were outlawed. The Government sent spies, informers and even *agents provocateurs* into every working-class group which could be found. It also built up a powerful military force to deal with disturbances.

After 1825 workers were not prosecuted for forming trade unions as such, but because so many laws remained, confining the activities of organised groups of workers, prosecutions continued. The Poor Laws also reflected the unsympathetic attitude of the Government toward the labouring poor. Until

1834 paupers were hired out by the parish. The amount of this relief was very small and the existence of a pool of pauper labour kept wages generally down to a subsistence level. In 1834 the new Poor Law centralised responsibility for the poor out of parish hands. Now the unemployed were forced to labour in workhouses instead of outdoors on parish lands. Conditions in the workhouses were extremely harsh.

In capitalist production itself the operative principle of managerial authority was discipline backed by economic and non-economic coercion. Elaborate and severe systems of fines were imposed by employers on workers who arrived late or left early, and for faulty work (see various examples cited in *Capital*, vol. 1, pp. 400–1). If workers struck to protest against such employer-made laws, employers could take their workers to the criminal courts for breach of contract. A whole series of acts, from the Statute of Artificers of 1563 to the Master and Servant Act of 1824, made workers liable to imprisonment for breach of contract. Employers who broke contracts were only liable for money damages. Also an employer could give evidence against a worker to further his own cause, but a worker could not give evidence against his employer, or in his own defence.

Both discipline and mechanisation were the reasons for setting up factories. But to enforce discipline was the main reason at first. The rise of the factory system predated both the introduction of power to the labour process and any technical change in machine design or organisation of work for which factories were particularly suitable. In wool spinning, for example, the 'spinning jenny' was used without power in both factories and cottages during the last decades of the eighteenth century (Hammonds [1919], p. 146). A similar pattern prevailed where hand-looms were used in factories during the 1820s and 1830s in the cotton weaving trade, and in Coventry's silk ribbon-weaving trade (Prest [1960], p. 45).

In Domestic Industry workers would be given materials and have their finished products collected once a week by the merchant or his undertaker. During the week workers would work at their own pace. This often meant working long hard hours during the few days before collection in order to have time off during the rest of the week. Thus the quality of woven goods was often uneven. Factory discipline meant that labourers worked more regular hours and longer hours in all. Also in the domestic system workers could embezzle wool or silk, exchange poor quality material for good, conceal imperfections, or devise ways to make the finished material heavier (Marglin [1976], pp. 93–4).

It was this initial rise in output per cost of inputs to the capitalist offered by factory discipline which tempered managerial attitudes toward authority in the labour process. The problem of capturing this benefit occupied managerial effort during this period. Ure attributes Arkwright's successful spinning factory, compared with Watt's failure, to Arkwright's success at training human beings to renounce their desultory habits of work, and to identify themselves with the unvarying regularity of the complex automaton. To devise and administer a successful code of factory discipline, suited to the necessities of factory diligence was the Herculean enterprise, the noble achievement of Arkwright (Ure [1863], p. 15).

One effect of this emphasis was that not much attention was given to the organisation of work. ' *The Carding and Spinning Master's Assistant* of 1832 warned employers against rearranging their machinery once installed, even if they found the arrangement less than ideal, since the costs of reorganisation would probably exceed the savings' (p. 218, cited in Hobsbawm [1968], p. 354). This was a misapprehension, as employers were to discover toward the end of the nineteenth century.

Unskilled labour, dispossessed from the land due to the Enclosures movement and from Ireland, was cheap and readily available in the factory and mining districts to which they had come in search of work. Many of the new recruits to the factories were women and children, who could be paid far less than men anyway. Machinery and materials, on the other hand, were costly. Furthermore the benefits of introducing power and better machines into factories offered such great productivity advances that capitalists believed they could ignore any benefits from improved worker effort. Management concentrated on the second aspect of authority over labour power (p. 78 above)–to retain planned or expected value of labour power or planned effort for a given wage, rather than expanding that value or effort.

Unskilled workers were generally paid time-rates, and even when they were paid by results the system was conceived as a means of stopping productivity from falling below the norm when effective supervision was difficult, rather than a means of raising productivity (Hobsbawm [1968], p. 353). Beyond the employers' disciplinary code, managerial authority over unskilled workers was often maintained by close supervision through subcontracting arrangements.

What applied to unskilled workers did not apply to craftsmen unless they were being deskilled through mechanisation and at the same time were not effectively organised to resist. As mentioned in Chapter 5 skilled workers generally disciplined themselves and did not respond strongly to financial incentives. This was not true for subcontractors, but their position was something close to that of an entrepreneur. They had a direct interest in the exploitation of their associates and they set the pace of work for their assistants.

At this time the Responsible Autonomy approach was not an imposed strategy which managers applied to craftsmen. Rather, it took advantage of the much deeper attitude of craftsmen towards their work which characterised simple commodity production – self-respect, pride in certain standards of workmanship and customary rewards for different grades of skill. Responsible Autonomy is not simply a vestige of medieval days, but during the transition to Modern Industry it clearly obstructed mechanisation and subsequent deskilling. Loyalty to the firm, attention to good craftmanship, expectations of a 'just' wage or price were a hindrance to capitalists replacing major aspects of craftsmen's work with machines. This capitalists were anxious to carry out when the reserve army provided plenty of people to take on the deskilled work who were not in any position to expect justice or satisfaction in work.

In spite of the severe relative decline of Responsible Autonomy as a managerial strategy, both Responsible Autonomy and Direct Control strategies characterised management during this stage, though the Responsible Autonomy approach was reserved primarily for craftsmen in unrevolutionised trades.

Thus basic dualism in the labour process went far beyond wage differentials. Craftsmen, whether subcontractors or not, maintained greater autonomy over their own work pace and work methods. Furthermore their security of employment was much greater than for the unskilled. Under the subcontracting system piece-workers would be given larger or smaller subcontracts. They would keep busy themselves, but the number of assistants they would hire would vary with the size of the subcontract. Even if craftsmen were not also subcontractors, those who maintained restricted entry into apprenticeships were able to keep their labour power in short supply, even during depressed times.

The 'labour aristocrats' throughout the history of capitalism have been those who have maintained regular as well as high earnings.

2   1850 to 1870s

The general attitude towards workers during these decades of industrial peace began to change from fear and contempt towards a more accommodating view, particularly as the demand for labour power was rising. The Master and Servant Laws were abolished and legal restraints to trade unions were removed. The Poor Law began to offer relief rather than harsh discipline to the unemployed, particularly after 1867.

During this period hours of work were shortened, partly through legislation and partly through bargaining. This encouraged employers to try to raise labour productivity. Shorter hours encouraged mechanisation (see *Capital*, vol. 1, chap. 15), but also encouraged changes in wage payments systems.

Employers began introducing incentive payment systems to achieve what had been accomplished through harsh discipline and supervision for unskilled workers and by custom for craftsmen. The change in attitude was slow and uneven.

Perhaps the most noticeable feature of the period was the variety of experiences with payment by results systems. In some coal-fields most miners were paid by results (new fields in South Wales), while in other areas most were paid time-rates (older fields in the North-East). In some industries piece-rates were resisted and withdrawn (engineering), while in others they were accepted (railway construction) (Hobsbawm [1968], pp. 356–7).

While the discussion of managerial discretion in Chapter 3 was framed in terms of Monopoly Capitalism, monopoly power was considered as a relative concept. Even during this classical period of British small-scale competition many firms had some discretionary margin with which to experiment with different organisations of work processes and of managerial authority. What hampered this experimentation was only in part market discipline against mistakes. It was a long time before managers realised that experimentation with systems of organisation and authority might achieve significant productivity advances. This reflected the craftsmen's attitude towards effort which carried over from pre-capitalist times – that it was proper to give a fair day's work for a fair day's pay and that work was not simply a penalty or a disutility to be endured for reward, but rather work itself was a creative and dignified activity.

3   1870s to 1914

Falling profit rates during the Great Depression impelled managers to experiment further with methods of exercising managerial authority and organising work. Three features of this period mark the transition to Monopoly Capitalism: the growing inflexibility of large firms which accompanied growth in size, the rise of managerialism and the increased use of procedure to limit resistance by less skilled workers. These features reflected and contributed to the growing importance of internal labour markets discussed in Chapter 5.

Inflexibility

As firms grew in size more co-ordination was required. The job of management became much more complex as the work involved in keeping track of physical and financial flows multiplied, particularly after industrial firms began to take over marketing outputs and purchasing materials from merchants. The explosion of jobs for middle managers, clerical and secretarial workers, which has been so noticeable in recent years, began around the turn of the century. But as firms grew in size and complexity they also became more vulnerable to competitive pressures because of the size of their overheads and the integration of their processes. When increasing size went hand in hand with increasing productivity, market power, and opportunities to limit competition by agreements, this inflexibility was not a problem; but with rising competition from foreign rivals, who were also large and technically advanced, new methods for achieving higher productivity and greater flexibility were sought. In the short term this led to a desire to increase control over financial flows through better accounting methods, and direct control over labour power through systematic coercive methods. In the long run it encouraged managerialism in general and the use of procedure in particular.

Managerialism, Taylorism and the Limits of Direct Control Strategies

Along with the need for systematic forms of management, with the internalisation of science for technical change (research and development), employers, engineers and the Government became much more aware of the possibilities of using scientific methods in order to achieve more systematic forms of labour power management (see Report of Factory Inspectors for 1894, p. 213). The most visible aspect of managerialism during this period was the rise in methods which furthered managerial Direct Control over labour power. During this period, worker effort seriously declined as employees learned to treat their effort as a negotiable aspect of labour power (Ca'Canny) and as more unskilled workers organised (Hobsbawm [1968], pp. 360–5). In response employers began to experiment with new systems of incentive payments and with new systems for organising the work process.

At first, during the 1880s and 1890s, the major tool of managerialism was embodied in systems of piece-rate payment – systems by which payment was made automatically regressive, that is, the rate paid for successive increments of production declined. Often this feature of the systems was obscured by their complexity. But eventually managerialism and Taylorism (the ideas of F. W. Taylor) came to be thought of (mistakenly) as coincident. Taylor's ideas became very popular in America and soon spread to Europe.

The rise of Monopoly Capitalism in America proceeded more quickly than in Britain during the last quarter of the nineteenth century, and Taylor represented but one of the flock of engineers proposing systematic forms of management during the 1880s and 1890s. Their message was clearly stated in the *Engineering Magazine* (established in 1881), and the *Transactions of the American Society of Mechanical Engineers* (established in 1879). Effective management required systematic tabulation of financial flows on the one hand and physical flows on the other. Taylor was primarily concerned with co-ordination and the extension of managerial authority over labour power.

In Taylor's first book, *The Principles of Scientific Management* [1899], he distinguished between what he called ordinary management and scientific management. Under ordinary management the managers rely on the traditional skill of their workers. Workers' activities are controlled by general orders and managers try to induce 'each workman to use his best endeavours, his hardest work, all his traditional knowledge, his skill, his ingenuity and his goodwill – in a word, his "initiative", so as to yield the largest possible return to his employer' (p. 32).

Taylor clearly recognised that his methods were largely aimed at breaking down a particular form of worker resistance. It was 'systematic soldiering' which scientific management aimed at removing. Systematic soldiering was the deliberate and organised reduction of work pace by groups of workers. Workers would purposely slow down their pace of work because increments which they could earn on piece-rates due to working quickly would be followed by rate cuts after that pace became generalised.

What was scientific management? In theory scientific management was for management to achieve greater control over productive activity by controlling all decisions made in the course of work.

Taylor proposed three basic principles of scientific management:

(1) Management gathers and systemises all the workers' traditional knowledge.

(2) 'All possible brain work should be removed from the shop and centred in the planning or layout department' (1904, pp. 98–9).

(3) Management should specify work in complete detail, as well as the time allowed for the task, in advance and present this information as a written order to the worker. 'This task specifies not only what is to be done, but how it is to be done and the exact time allowed for doing it' (1899, p. 63).

Taylor's technique for gathering information about productive activity and keeping control over it was time study – the measurement of elapsed time for each component operation of a work process. Its principal instrument is the stop-watch.

Gradually managers and industrial engineers found time study too crude for their purposes. In time study managers were simply analysing production in terms of the actual daily practice of work. The other problem with time study was that it was tied to the particular forms of concrete work being studied. Information received was not about work in the abstract, but about some particular job like weaving silk or tanning hides.

To overcome these difficulties, one of Taylor's main followers, Frank Gilbreth, added motion study to time study. Motion study is the investigation and classification of the basic motions of the human body, regardless of the concrete form of the labour in which these motions are used. In time and motion study elementary movements are viewed as the building blocks of every work activity. Now motion pictures and stroboscopes are used and information can be gathered in research agencies rather than on the job. This has the great advantage of removing some direct antagonism between workers and work study engineers.

Taylorian scientific management can be seen as an advanced form of Direct Control via the division of labour. Marx distinguished between the social division of labour and the manufacturing division of labour. In the social division of labour the collection of different employments producing distinct commodities is divided among different producers. In the manufacturing division of labour the work process for producing a single commodity is subdivided among different workers. Finally, in scientific management, the individual workers' motions are subdivided and reallocated among different workers. Workers are now viewed as all-purpose machines made up of so many motion units per unit of time. For Marx, mechanisation in the Modern Industry stage meant workers came to be treated as appendages of machines. Now, with time and motion study, workers are viewed as human machines regardless of their proximity to physical machines.

Taylor's ideas spread very quickly within America and abroad. The extent to which his particular system was implemented is difficult to estimate, but it seems clear that the theoretical importance of Taylor's work outweighed the extent to which his pure system was used in practice (Calvert [1967], pp. 278–9).

The problems with Taylor's system reflect the problems with the Direct Control strategy in general, when pushed to its limits. Taylor began with a particular view of the worker – a view which closely resembles the *homo economus* used by bourgeois economists. For Taylor, workers were motivated by rational calculations of their individual self-interests. The disutility of work and the utility from commodities which could be purchased with wages were conceived as commensurable and measurable along a single-dimensioned index. The only difference from the standard bourgeois view was that utility for Taylor derived at least as much from workers' relative levels of consumption as their absolute levels. This view leads to a simple view of how to motivate workers (reduce resistance) scientifically. Along with prescribing all the details of tasks, pace and effort for first-class workers, those workers would be motivated to work in the 'first-class' manner by wages significantly higher than 'second-class' or 'ordinary' workers. While Taylor professed that practically everyone could be a first-class worker at some task, given sufficient training and the proper design of work (Rose [1975], p. 40), if everyone became first-class workers the relative earnings differential would disappear.

In fact this is what began to happen. Firms would begin to introduce time and motion studies and to delegate work tasks based on these studies. To induce workers to accept the loss of direct control over their work and the concomitant rise in boredom and monotony, firms at first offered much higher wages whether on a flat rate or on a differential piece-rate system as Taylor suggested.[2] But soon managers were tempted to cut wage-rates or piece-rates. Taylor complained bitterly about employers using only part of his system, but he neglected the law of value, which evaporated much of the monopoly gains to firms which first introduced scientific management once the system became more widespread among direct competitors. Nevertheless earnings differentials have remained between large firms using mass production techniques and smaller-scale or non-factory sectors of industry.

In general Taylor's attitude towards worker motivation was to concentrate workers' attention on higher earnings and to turn their minds off conceptual aspects of their work. Taylor believed that trade unions would become irrelevant if workers could be persuaded to sacrifice satisfaction at work and squabbles about their share of the pie in order to partake of a much larger pie. Individual workers were to become unconcerned with labour's share of the pie because 'first-class' workers would be earning far more than 'ordinary' workers. As long as workers behave as individuals this strategy makes sense, provided the overwhelming majority do not become first-class workers. But once workers become organised the system would become far less effective if ordinary and first-class workers united. Taylor's system was aimed against particular forms of worker resistance: individualistic and poorly organised. During the 1920s the Taylorian system came under attack from industrial psychologists. C. S. Myers, the most prominent British industrial psychologist at the time, criticised Taylorian methods from his British perspective by stating that the system would 'only survive where immigrant labour is cheap and unions weak' (Rose [1975], p. 98).

Taylor's system was also directed against resistance based on skills. Naturally, as workers became progressively deskilled, diminishing returns would set in. It became obvious during the First World War, and again in the 1930s, that worker resistance no longer simply reflected their skills. As a system for maintaining and augmenting managerial authority, scientific management generally fell from favour during the late 1930s after unionism spread quickly among unskilled workers in America.

In evaluating limitations to the Direct Control strategy it is important to take a historical perspective. It is the very success of the strategy which makes its limitations acute. Its contradictory nature is based on the impossibility of its ultimate vision. Ultimately the Direct Control strategy sees the majority of people working as machines manipulated by centralised planning departments. The problem is that people are not machines. They may sell their labour power but they cannot alienate their minds or their will. According to the Direct Control strategy, capital must continually subdue workers' independent and often hostile wills by appealing to their economic self-interest. But the will of workers is not guided simply by economic self-interest. There is a diminishing marginal utility to money in the sense that a starving person will risk death or dishonour in cases where money will not induce people in more secure positions. But part of the Direct Control strategy is that first-class workers will grow steadily more affluent.

These contradictions of the Direct Control strategy are manifest in the inflexibility which increasingly characterises productive activity as the Direct Control ideal is approached. By removing any intrinsic interest workers may have in the work activity they perform, worker dissatisfaction is increased. By reducing differences among workers based on skills, resonance is increased. By extending the division of labour and centralising control, the overall level of labour process integration is increased.

Individuals and small groups of workers are less able to disrupt the process by their absence if deskilling means that they are easily replaced. But technically the damage they may do to the whole process, both by sabotage or by the withdrawal of their labour if they are not easily replaced, is heightened. Organised worker resistance may make it difficult for top managers to replace workers who have withdrawn their labour. For thousands of workers to be laid off because of a strike by a small number of workers is a common occurrence in the British car industry, which is noted for its use of scientific management techniques.

Finally, there is the positive aspect of labour power which is forgone when people are treated as machines. With rapidly changing techniques top managers will often want a 'responsible' and responsive labour force. One cannot specify correct procedures or motions to operate a new machine in advance. New machinery will nearly always mean a period of 'teething troubles' (which can last throughout the useful life of the machine because old machines can be temperamental as well). In these cases top managers must rely on worker goodwill. The 'responsibility' on which top managers rely is evident from the drastic effects on production of a 'work to rule'. Similarly when demand falls suddenly the high overheads required to pursue the Direct Control strategy can become burdensome. In order to deal with the problems and contradictions of the Direct Control strategy (wrought by a century of mechanisation and several centuries of extending the division of labour as well as by more recent Taylorian techniques), a third major feature of Monopoly Capitalism emerged during the 1870s to 1914 period. During this period top managers came not only to accept trade unions as a common expression of worker resistance, rather than simply an expression of craft privileges, but also they came to regard the bureaucratic element of unions as a powerful means for preventing worker dissatisfaction from leading to work stoppages.

This is illustrated by the different aims of the engineering employers during the lock-out of 1897–8 compared with the previous lock-out of 1852. In 1852 the aim was to smash the newly formed Amalgamated Society of Engineers. In the end employees reluctantly agreed to sign a declaration that they were not union members and that they would not join a union. In 1897 employers wanted to stop unions from interfering in what the Employers' Federation considered to be managerial prerogatives (such as who should man new machines, how much overtime should be worked, etc.). Also employers wanted workers to accept a procedure by which matters under dispute would travel up union and managerial hierarchies before industrial action would be taken, (Wigham [1973], chaps 2 and 3). Stability sought by bureaucratic and procedural means for conciliation and arbitration meant a rise in the importance of internal labour markets. While Procedure was at first an innovation of employers to aid the smooth exercise of managerial authority, gradually it also came to be used as a protective device by workers, by forestalling arbitrary managerial changes in work practices. If management bypasses Procedure, often worker resistance will be provoked.

Procedure and Responsible Autonomy

Procedure is an *indirect* means for maintaining managerial authority via the Responsible Autonomy strategy. The essence of Procedure is to forestall a work stoppage while a lengthy process of negotiation occurs. But an equally important aspect of Procedure for employers, laid down after the 1897 lock-out, was that 'work shall proceed meantime on current conditions'. Employers intended this to mean conditions after the change which employees were challenging, not before it. But in practice the *status quo* came to be determined by shop-floor struggle. This struggle was reflected in subsequent modifications to Procedure. In 1914 the current conditions clause was left out. After the 1922 lock-out Procedure explicitly stated that 'General alterations in wages, alterations in working conditions which were the subject of agreements and alterations in the general work week were not to be given effect until the Procedure has been exhausted' (Wigham [1973], p. 124). This meant that employees were given some protection against certain rapid shifts in the exercise of managerial authority.

In Procedure, as in the rise of organised worker resistance itself, we may see a *general principle of power in action*. Power relations within productive activity are tempered by the wage relation, the social relation by which people enter productive activity. Employers of labour power have the legal power to dispose of their employees' labour power as they choose. While worker resistance to this disposal during productive activity has grown and acquired institutional strength in the form of organised trade unions (and shop stewards' movements), this resistance has rarely challenged the basic wage relation itself. Worker resistance has challenged the degree of exploitation achieved during productive activity, not the wage relation which gives rise to that potential for exploitation. The co-option of trade union leadership by employers reflects the continuing reality of employer power derived from the wage relation. While trade unions *do* redress *some* of the power imbalance within production, they also reflect that imbalance. Because trade unions are concerned primarily with day-to-day struggles where labourers continue to work within the capitalist mode of production, most of the time they must act as though capitalism were permanent. Therefore employers, no longer powerful enough to destroy trade unions, are nevertheless able, through those day-to-day struggles which do not directly challenge their existence as employers, to use those institutions of stable worker organisation to ensure the maintenance of their managerial authority.

What holds for employee resistance also holds for employer counter-pressure. Once employers have accommodated themselves to organised worker resistance, once they accept collective bargaining in internal labour markets, then institutions which they set up to limit the effects of worker resistance may also come to reflect the power of those very organisations of worker resistance.

Perhaps the most crucial development of the capitalist mode of production in Britain during the 1870s to 1914 period was the acceptance by many important employers of organised worker resistance as a permanent reality in their day-to-day dealings with workers. (American acceptance came somewhat later.) Organised worker resistance could no longer be viewed as a carry-over of protective medieval customs enjoyed by craftsmen. It would no longer go away simply by increasing the proportion of less skilled workers to craftsmen through mechanisation, though this might achieve other benefits for management, and, combined with other tactics, it might reduce the effects of worker resistance, as I shall discuss presently.

Thus Procedure, like the other forms of conciliation which were developed from the 1870s on, by trying to limit the effects of worker resistance while not challenging the reality of that resistance, came to be an institution by which the reality of worker resistance might be reflected. It came to be an institution through which workers might express their power.

The second two features of the transition to Monopoly Capitalism – the growth of managerialism and the development of procedural and conciliatory techniques – contributed to the first feature mentioned – the growing inflexibility of large firms. Advances in managerialism meant a rise in record keeping and supervisory personnel, and advances in Procedure and conciliation required more expensive and time consuming industrial relations apparatus. Because of these changes (as well as co-ordination problems accompanying the growth in firm sizes), Monopoly Capitalism has been marked by a huge rise in white-collar personnel: managers, professionals, and a mass of lower status functionaries from middle managers, supervisors, inspectors and testers to clerks, typists and office cleaners. The growth of office work may be clearly seen in the tremendous rise in clerical workers. In 1851 only 0.8 per cent of the labour force were classified as clerks. The proportion then rose quickly to 4 per cent in 1901 and 4.8 per cent in 1911 (Lockwood [1958]).

These workers have been viewed by top managers as more crucial to the working order of the firm, either because they contribute specialised knowledge which cannot be easily bought on the labour power market, or because they partake in the maintenance of managerial authority. During this period white-collar workers as a whole were primarily male, and for them Responsible Autonomy was clearly the approach taken by top managers.[3] Loyalty, accuracy and punctuality were required of them. Their employment security, rates of pay and working conditions were all far superior to those of manual workers. In the 1890s even the lower paid clerks were receiving £75 to £150 a year, a range of income achieved by only the top ten to fifteen per cent of the working class (Lockwood [1958], p. 28). Employment security and level of responsibility gave middle managers, professionals and clerks a social status which distanced them from other workers even farther than the artisan had been separated from the labourer.

4   1914 to 1945

Interest in managerialism grew, particularly during the depressed 1920s and 1930s. In 1926 Bedaux, an American company of consultants specialising in incentive systems and time and motion studies, guided hundreds of firms as they introduced Direct Control strategies. Bedaux (only the best known of many consulting firms) listed 240 firms operating their system by 1936 (Branson and Heinemann [1971], pp. 81–2). The new systems caused significant rises in output per worker where they were implemented, but they also provoked scores of strikes. Generally the systems succeeded in the more poorly organised factories, in spite of unexpected resistance (as among unorganised women workers at Lucas motor accessories in Birmingham). It was either not tried or quickly abandoned in many of the better organised firms, or where labour was scarce, such as at Rover Motors.

Another form of managerialism which complemented simple Taylorism was flow production. Introduced with great publicity by Henry Ford in America before the war, its impact on British industry came in the 1920s and 1930s. The Chief Factory Inspector noted the rapid introduction of conveyors into the Leeds clothing industry in 1935 (*Factory Inspectors' Report* [1935], p. 65). And during the 1920s and 1930s all the major car producers went over to flow production. Resistance to flow production was much weaker than to time and motion studies or incentive schemes. The immediate impact of flow production was to reduce human supervision and replace it by more subtle supervision from the line speed. Also flow production was often accompanied by very large wage rises. Taylorian systems increased absolute surplus value (increased the intensity of work under given technical conditions), while flow production increased relative surplus value (by changing the technique used—see p. 15 above). Work intensification with given techniques has generally been easier to resist because it is more visibly oppressive. Technical change is generally resisted only if it causes redundancies. In the motor industry technical changes during the 1920s and 1930s accompanied strong demand, and employment levels were generally maintained or augmented in spite of the switch to flow production techniques. Nevertheless flow production soon allowed top managers to increase absolute surplus value by line speed-ups and the application of Taylorian techniques to mass production. These actions provoked strong worker resistance when they were tried.

Top managers themselves, while attempting to implement Direct Control strategies, also continued to encourage co-option of top echelon trade unionists—epitomised by the Mond–Turner talks of 1928–9. Given the severe set-backs suffered by the trade union movement in 1921 and in 1926, and given the long years of high unemployment and squeezed profit margins, this combination of increasing Direct Control at the shop-floor level and attempts to co-opt trade union leaders to pressure workers to behave responsibly was understandable.

5 1945 to 1970s

The Direct Control – Responsible Autonomy mix of early Monopoly Capitalism became less effective with the drying-up of the active reserve army and the tremendous growth of British export markets during the first post-World War II decade. In tight labour power markets the effectiveness of trade union bureaucracies for encouraging workers to behave responsibly diminished. Localised forms of resistance could hit profits hard when demand was high.

Given the severe worker resistance to Direct Control strategies during the 1920s and 1930s, as well as the limitations mentioned above in Section 3, managerial theorists began to cast about for alternative strategies.

The Direct Control strategy is easily distinguished because of its primary standing in the 'progressive' or most developed sectors of the capitalist mode of production for so long (the movement from Domestic Industry to Manufacture to Modern Industry may be charted as progressive increases in managerial Direct Control over productive activity), and because Taylor was so forthright and clear. Its alternative, Responsible Autonomy, is more difficult to distinguish. Industrial psychology, industrial sociology and all other variant theories of managerial authority proposed since the 1920s have been groping for a clear statement of an alternative managerial strategy to Direct Control: a strategy by which the variable aspect of labour power is harnessed for managerial ends rather than subdued. A good summary of these theories may be found in M. Rose, *Industrial Behaviour* [1975].

It will be useful to begin with the view of worker motivation upon which these theories are based. In general they view people as creatures of instincts (industrial psychologists) or sentiments (human relations), where calculation of economic self-interest and therefore rationality (particularly for human relations school), are weak. It is easy to dismiss these theories as simply attempts to combat worker resistance on a purely ideological level by calling it irrational, rather than as guides for managerial practice. But the Responsible Autonomy strategy is based on a direct appeal by managers to these 'irrational' desires imputed to workers. The best known and most influential group of theorists was the human relations school of Harvard and Chicago, represented by Elton Mayo. According to human relations theory workers were obsessed with belongingness or sociability because the society as a whole, with its constant change and diversity, deprived people of intimacy, consistency and predictability (Rose [1975], pt 3). Workers sought to rectify this lack by informal contacts at work and through trade unionism. Social conflict was viewed as the product of individual maladjustment.

Taylor's solution to worker resistance was high relative financial rewards, based on his view of rational *homo economus*. The various psychological and sociological theorists have suggested a combination of: making the work itself more interesting (appealing to individual desires for sociability, security, challenge and variety); choosing workers who best fit in with the tasks required; and the sensitive and subtle exercise of managerial authority through the manipulation of sentiment – encouraging venom against competitors (particularly foreign), 'counselling' non-cooperative workers, and encouraging a feeling of team struggle through participatory and rewarded suggestion schemes, and the judicious payment of loyalty-inducing perks, such as company recreational facilities.

Some of these tactics are peripheral to the organisation of work – such as aptitude testing and company sports fields – but some imply substantial changes in the organisation of work. One notion which these theorists have had to contend with is Taylor's idea that 'One Best Way' to organise work existed at a given level of mechanisation or technology. The British Tavistock Institute of Human Relations in particular has emphasised the opportunity for management to choose different methods for organising work (Trist [1963]). According to A. K. Rice of the institute, the productive system has three key dimensions: the technological (rate of innovation introduction), the social (payments and other arrangements to reduce resistance), and the economic (short-run profit maximisation). Optimising along one of these alone will not produce optimal results for the sytem as a whole (Rice [1963]). The institute's message is misleadingly universal – they speak as though one can choose capitalism – but if judgement of their message is confined to the context of guiding managers operating in the capitalist mode of production then we can see that it is sensible.

Simple short-run profit maximisation is the only course open to management in highly competitive situations. In highly competitive markets top managers will not have the discretionary margin necessary to experiment with costly reorganisations of work to reduce resistance, just as they will not be able to resist introducing the latest technical improvements available (Law of Value). But once firms achieve a measure of monopoly power their degree of insulation from competitive pressures will allow them to take a long-term view. Monopoly power does not mean the absence of competition. Managers are still constrained by the need to make substantial profits, but in large firms it is *steady* substantial profits which are important. Thus organisational choice does exist for management, but it is limited.

Technical or mechanical details of productive activity are not independent of these strategies, though the effect of measures to reduce resistance on technical conditions will be limited. The movement towards group technology in large car firms is the best known example of major technical changes imposed to quell worker resistance and specifically to impose Responsible Autonomy. The Tavistock Institute's celebrated examination and recommendation of the switch from the standard flow production Longwell method of coal extraction to a more flexible system relying on small semi-self-regulating work teams in the 1950s (Trist [1963]) is another prominent example of the interdependence of the two managerial functions: coordination and exercising managerial authority.

The Responsible Autonomy strategy is designed to combat some of the undesirable effects of the Direct Control strategy. Setting up small work-teams which are able to make some of their own decisions over their direct work activity and increasing the variety of work tasks are intended to reduce resonance by encouraging stratification into small, partially competing groups. Also the technical disintegration of the labour process may reduce the power of small groups to disrupt the whole process through sabotage or strike action. Often teams will perform parallel tasks rather than tasks which feed into each other.

Thus the effectiveness of the Responsible Autonomy strategy must be seen in relation to Monopoly Capitalism. Before this stage responsible autonomy was viewed as an inefficient carry-over from feudal times. With the gathering force of the industrial reserve army and rapid mechanisation, employee loyalty and worker self-direction became less useful, or even burdensome, because they were less reliable than a machine or centralised internal record keeping. Also organised worker resistance was weak and heavily concentrated among craftsmen. These conditions have changed considerably in advanced capitalist countries with the drying-up of reserve armies and the rise of organised resistance among the less skilled.

Responsible Autonomy is impossible as an ultimate ideal as is Direct Control. Responsible Autonomy does not remove alienation and exploitation, it simply softens their operation or draws workers' attention away from them. Its ideal is to have workers behave *as though* they were participating in a process which reflected their own needs, abilities and wills, rather than a process aimed at accumulation and profits.

As the contradiction of the Direct Control strategy becomes more visible and more acute when its ideal is approached, so the contradiction of the Responsible Autonomy strategy becomes apparent when its ideal is approached and when the overall profit position of firms require them to cut back on loyalty or satisfaction payments. This is particularly clear when product demand suddenly falls or when general business conditions are depressed.

In order to deal with this double contradiction top managers split their labour force according to which type of strategy is used to maintain authority. The Responsible Autonomy strategy requires secure employment. It may be possible to persuade workers to behave responsibly while employed, but it is difficult to get those workers to behave 'responsibly' in accepting lay-offs without a struggle. When trade union apparatus is called on to help supervise redundancies this often weakens the union's credibility and provokes unofficial strikes.[4] Disruption lasting far beyond the redundancies themselves will be more likely when authority is based more on ideological maintenance of responsibility than on simple financial rewards and strict supervision. For this reason privileged groups – managerial, administrative and technical workers (except for the lower grades of clerical workers), male, white, skilled workers, or other workers who are particularly well organised – will be distinguished by far greater employment security as well as higher earnings. This line of argument is pursued in Part Three.

PART THREE
CENTRE–PERIPHERY RELATIONS

CHAPTER EIGHT

Firms and Workers

The five preceding chapters have demonstrated the importance of systematic differences among firms according to the degree of monopoly power they enjoy, and among workers according to the strength of their resistance and the pressure exerted on them by the reserve army. Marx recognised such differences, but he treated firms and workers as homogeneous categories for analytical purposes. The primary difference between Marx's analysis and the amended framework to be used here lies not in the recognition of these differences but in the analytic role played by the relation between firms of unequal monopoly power and between groups of workers of unequal strength and insulation from the reserve army. These differences allow top managers considerable flexibility for maintaining authority over all workers. Thus they represent an important means whereby the capitalist mode of production itself is maintained.

Firms and workers in widely different situations do not merely exist side by side. The steady profits of large firms and the steady, high wages of privileged workers depend on the instability of profits and wages of small firms and unprivileged workers in an unplanned system such as capitalism. Fluctuations in product demand, unplanned technical change and a massive latent reserve army all characterise this world capitalist system. Through the interaction of worker resistance and the strategic use of managerial counter-pressure those particular workers who may have been most likely to overthrow that system, those working in the largest firms whose organisations for resistance are strongest, have become somewhat insulated from the waves of insecurity thrown up by this unplanned system. Also they have largely escaped the heavy weight of the reserve army which pummels unprivileged workers in advanced capitalist countries and crushes unprivileged workers in underdeveloped countries.[1]

The limitations of the managerial strategies examined in the last two chapters are discussed in Section 1 below. Centre–periphery relations within firms as a method for overcoming some of those limitations are discussed in Section 2. General centre–periphery relations are examined in Section 3, and subcontracting relations, a particularly important form of the centre–periphery relation between firms, are analysed formally in Section 4. The chapter ends with a brief note on classes in Section 5.

1   Contradictions in Managerial Strategies and Flexibility

Both types of managerial strategies distinguished in the last chapter have serious limitations. These limitations stem from their common aim, to maintain and extend managerial authority over people who are essentially free and independent, but who have alienated their labour power. To treat workers as though they were machines, assuming they can be forced by financial circumstances or close supervision to give up direct control over what they do for most of their waking hours; or to treat workers as though they were not alienated from their labour power by trying to convince them that the aims of top managers are their own; both of these types of strategies involve a contradiction. People do have independent and often hostile wills which cannot be destroyed, and the aim of top managers ultimately is to make steady and high profits, rather than to tend to their workers' needs.

Though each strategy is based on a fundamental contradiction, the strategies are not impossible to carry out. Contradiction does not mean impossibility, rather it means the persistence of a fundamental tension generated from within. A contradiction may be suppressed, or disguised or bypassed, but its continued existence will regenerate tensions which will again threaten good order unless actively suppressed once more. These tensions will seem to emanate from the inadequacy of the means whereby the contradiction is suppressed, from the managerial strategies themselves. Tensions in productive activity appear in the form of inflexibility generated by each type of managerial strategy.

Management is an active process. To maintain stable and high profits requires continual reorganisation of lines of authority and tactics of management to deal with fresh worker resistance against the existing set-up and to get workers to fit in with changes required by the implementation of new technologies or the pursuit of new market opportunities. But once any type of managerial strategy is implemented it cannot be changed radically in a short period of time. Direct Control strategies require well-defined lines of authority and a high proportion of white-collar staff.

Responsible Autonomy strategies require an elaborate ideological apparatus for co-opting workers' leaders and the rank and file themselves as well as relative employment security. To switch suddenly from a strong Responsible Autonomy strategy to a Direct Control strategy or the other way round would cause severe disruption: many white-collar staff would have to be hired or fired, a complex ideological structure within the firm would have to be dismantled or erected, the organisation of work itself and the systems of payment would have to be altered somewhat. This may not pose so great a problem for top managers if workers were as machines, or if their aims coincided with those of top managers. But because of the contradictions of all managerial strategies under capitalism, such sudden changes in the labour process would generate severe worker resistance (in the case of a sudden move toward direct control) or severe problems of co-ordination (in the case of a sudden move toward responsible autonomy).

The history of struggles by craftsmen in the process of being deskilled gives ample evidence of disruption caused by a switch from Responsible Autonomy to Direct Control. Moves in the other direction have been less frequent and the disruption they cause is less public. Top managers have feared the total breakdown of authority which giving the majority of their workers more direct control over the labour process might generate. Besides undermining the authority of their own middle managers, planning staff and foremen, the old fear of rulers toward ruled, 'give them an inch and they will take a mile', has meant that Responsible Autonomy strategies have been implemented only under extreme pressure from workers (due to their collective demands or due to high absenteeism and turnover encouraged by tight labour power markets and good unemployment benefits). In Chapter 14 I shall discuss in detail a major *shift toward* Responsible Autonomy strategies.

Thus increasing direct control or increasing responsible autonomy must be viewed as two directions along which top managers may move, limited by whatever system of authority they have established already, rather than two fully blown systems of authority between which top managers may choose at will.

Besides the difficulty of changing strategies quickly, which presents a serious problem because top managers will often wish to do so in response to quickly changing product demand, technology or labour power markets, each type of managerial strategy appears to generate its own peculiar form of inflexibility. With a high degree of direct control, top managers will find it relatively difficult to move workers around factories or to change their work methods in response to machine faults, mistakes in co-ordination, changing techniques or changing product demand. Each change will require complex and time-consuming planning, communication and implementation of new detailed work tasks. With a high degree of responsible autonomy, top managers will find it relatively difficult to move workers in and out of the labour process itself, or to replace workers' skills and direct control with new machinery, without undermining the ideological structures upon which responsible autonomy is founded. Each of these peculiar forms of inflexibility is intensified the further top managers proceed along either strategic path.

From the discussion of the last few pages one would expect capitalist productive activity to be extremely difficult to manage. While changing competitive pressures and worker resistance force managers to try to alter managerial strategies from time to time, those changes will themselves generate tensions making further changes along the same direction more and more difficult and dangerous. Management *would* be this difficult if top managers applied the same types of strategies to all their workers. But they do not.

Splitting workers into various groups and applying different types of managerial strategies towards those groups represents a major method whereby flexibility is gained and the capitalist mode of production itself is maintained.

As mentioned in Chapter 7, encouraging divisions among workers often weakens overall worker resistance. But dividing workers according to managerial strategies applied also helps to counteract the inflexibility peculiar to each type of strategy. If the employment security of one group of workers is protected because top managers reduce costs by laying off members of another group first, then it will be easier to encourage responsible autonomy among the first group. Also, if workers in the second group are more easily laid off, and if the division between the two groups is widespread throughout the society, then the reserve army for the second group will be larger and it will be easier to impose greater direct control over the second group within the labour process.

Dividing workers into groups and applying different managerial strategies to each will make it easier for top managers to reverse directions with either group of workers as well as allowing them to pursue either strategy further for each group. The privileges of the group to which top managers apply Responsible Autonomy strategies may be more easily undermined if a mass of unprivileged workers are readily available. Also disruption arising from disputes with either group may be easily bypassed if the work they do could be done by the other. Of course this may itself generate further disputes. Dividing workers according to managerial strategy pursued (like the particular strategies themselves) does not eradicate the fundamental contradictions of the capitalist mode of production, it simply suppresses them. It allows top managers greater flexibility for a time, but it may also help generate further tensions. The use of one group of workers to bypass disruptions due to disputes by another may eventually encourage solidarity between the two groups and undermine the contribution of the division itself to the maintenance of managerial authority.

Unequal worker resistance and strategic managerial counterpressure in the labour process generate a pattern of disparity among workers which has been a fundamental feature of capitalism at least since the beginnings of Modern Industry. In the following sections this pattern of disparity will be examined.

2 Centre and Periphery within the Firm

In times of adversity whatever top managers consider to be essential to enable the firm to secure steady, high profits will be protected. Whatever they consider to be inessential to this objective, or whatever top managers fear is hindering steady, high profits, will be at risk. On this basis two groups of workers may be distinguished from top managers' point of view – central workers and peripheral workers.

Central workers are, on the one hand, those who through their skills or their contribution to the exercise of managerial authority are considered essential by top managers to secure high long-run profits. On the other hand, central workers are those who, by the strength of their resistance, collectively force top managers to regard them as essential. During recessions the employment positions of central workers will be protected, while peripheral workers will be readily laid off.

Top managers have come to regard their workers as either central or peripheral in part in response to the increasing inflexibility of capitalist productive activity. This has two aspects.

First, the progressive separation of conception from execution (via the manufacturing division of labour, mechanisation and Taylorian-type scientific management) has encouraged a hierarchy of workers in terms of their importance as individuals to top managers. The increasing complexity and integration of operations implied by these developments has meant that as skills have become concentrated into a smaller group of people, generally of white-collar technical staff, those skills themselves have become increasingly specialised within the technical staff group. This has made it more and more difficult for top managers to lay off their technical staff in precise proportion to the desired change in costs when product demand falls. To use common business language, technical workers' wages have come to be regarded as overhead costs rather than variable costs. In particular, given the level of mechanisation and the way work has been organised from Modern Industry (into integrated operations which feed into one another, rather than the duplication of many similar parallel operations), there is a level below which technical staff cannot be reduced without completely disrupting the flow of production.[2] This has pushed top managers to use a Responsible Autonomy strategy for these workers in order to discourage and to minimise the effects of turnover and absenteeism, and to encourage greater effort by building up their loyalty to the firm.

Similarly the size and complexity of operations combined with extreme division of labour has caused the maintenance of managerial authority to involve greater numbers of employees. Top managers must delegate their authority, and the loyalty of those workers who contribute directly to that authority must be won through a combination of Responsible Autonomy strategies and the maintenance of those workers' employment security.

Second, stability and relatively high earnings for groups of workers distinguished by the strength of their resistance, unconnected with skill or authority, have appeared with the coming of Monopoly Capitalism. In deference to the power to disrupt production which those workers wield (through both the strength of their organisations and the integrated nature of labour processes in large firms), top managers will try to co-opt the leaders of their organisations to establish procedures for staving off disputes, and to protect their employment when adjusting to short-run slumps in product demand by laying off poorly organised workers first. Top managers may attempt to introduce Responsible Autonomy strategies on the more individualised level for well-organised or particularly scarce less-skilled manual workers, such as the well-publicised group-technology systems which several car producers introduced in the late 1960s and early 1970s (particularly Volvo and Saab, but also British Leyland at its new Rover operations and Fiat[3]), or the gang system introduced into some Coventry car firms in the late 1940s and early 1950s (see Chapter 14). But individualised Responsible Autonomy strategies are usually reserved for workers with scarce skills or those who are closely associated with the maintenance of managerial authority.

In both cases top managers divide workers strategically into centre and periphery groups because technological or social factors have increased the inflexibility of their operations. In order to ensure that this inflexibility does not completely disrupt production and frustrate top managers' steady profit goal, they try to isolate the potentially most disruptive groups of workers and offer them security at the expense of peripheral workers. In this the central workers often collaborate (see Chapter 5).

What are the more important characteristics of peripheral or expendable workers? Expendability is really a continuum. Whether any particular worker or group of workers will be laid off depends on both *relative* expendability and *relative* severity of top managers' need to reduce costs. Nevertheless it is possible clearly to identify categories of workers which are significantly more at risk than others. Generally these will be workers who:

(1)   Perform work which can easily be carried out by the remaining workers,

(2)   Perform work which is not necessary for the output which top managers desire to be produced after demand has fallen, (i.e. work at jobs which are duplicated),

(3)   Perform work for which replacement workers are readily available when top managers want them,

(4)   Will not cause disruption among the remaining workers when laid off because of lack of solidarity with them,

(5)   Do not contribute to the maintenance of managerial authority.

While all workers considered in complete isolation would be expendable according to the first three criteria ('No-one is indispensable'), top managers have learned that in many instances even the laying off of a single worker can bring a whole factory to a halt if that factory is well organised and if the dismissal is considered to be unjust or to threaten the immediate security of others.

Nevertheless, when a firm is faced with a slump in demand, top managers do not wish to lay off workers one at a time. Top managers' main concern is not the expendability of each worker as an individual, isolated from the rest (though in some cases this will be important). They are concerned with groups of workers, often considered as a block, such as all the direct workers on track B, or even all of plant four.

As firms grow technological changes force top managers to consider expendability in terms of large numbers. But economies of large scale depend on integrating functions rather than duplicating them. While most production workers in a plant using flow production techniques are only semi-skilled (what they do could be learned by an unskilled labourer in a matter of months or even weeks), it is generally true that they each do something different and each job done is necessary for the completion of any one of the finished products produced. For example, when a multi-plant firm using flow production techniques wishes to reduce its labour force over all its plants by 1000, it will be difficult for the firm to lay off 200 men in each of its plants if each plant represents a single flow production process. If it employs 2000 workers in each plant it may have to stop production in an entire plant to reduce its labour force by anything more than a few hundred workers without disrupting production seriously in all five of its plants.

In this way technical changes since the beginning of Modern Industry have reduced managers' flexibility for varying their labour force. Top managers will wish to reduce their labour force smoothly, in step with falling output, but the technological constraints may force them to consider laying off only large sections of workers at a time, involving overshooting or undershooting the desired redundancies target.

Generally the groups of workers top managers consider to be peripheral will be unskilled and semi-skilled manual workers (and skilled manual workers to a lesser extent),[4] and lower level administrative staff such as clerical and secretarial staff, according to the first three criteria I have listed above. Unskilled and semi-skilled workers in large firms, through the strength of their organisations, may become central workers by criterion four. Also by category four one would expect women, blacks and immigrants to be peripheral workers considering differential worker resistance. Women, blacks and immigrants will generally be peripheral, largely because of the lack of solidarity with them on the part of male, white, native workers, reflecting general prejudice in society. Nevertheless the direct method by which these workers are treated as peripheral is by limiting their employment opportunities to peripheral jobs.

Clerical and secretarial staff may be treated as central workers if top managers believe them to be necessary for maintaining managerial loyalty or efficiency. This latter attitude has been very strong in the past. While the particular work performed by clerks and secretaries has been severely deskilled, and the availability of potential clerks and secretaries has grown considerably since they became 'women's' jobs (Braverman [1974], chap. 15), a division between white- and blue-collar jobs on the basis of relative employment security is still clearly discernible.

White-Collar and Manual Workers

White-collar unemployment received much publicity in the late 1950s and early 1960s when profits were generally squeezed in American firms after a decade of steady growth and high profits. But O. E. Williamson [1964] shows the *abnormality* of laying off white-collar employees at the time. The cost reduction programmes which resulted in white-collar lay-offs followed prolonged periods of profit decline (the programmes were implemented between 1958 and 1961, while profits were declining seriously after 1956 in all cases). Also they were preceded by either substantial reorganisations among top managers or the introduction of new budget review committees or systems. In one case, while the employment in support departments fell by 40 per cent due to the efforts of the cost review committee, the committee caused little reduction in employment in operating departments. But employment of direct production workers in operating departments *fell by 78 per cent.* The chief budgeting officer, commenting on this, said, 'Since the work of hourly employees is typically subjected to continuing analysis in an effort to improve standards and techniques, only modest cutbacks beyond those normally made were obtained within the hourly production group' (p. 102).

Generally the firms involved believed that cost controls over white-collar workers should be continuing rather than sporadic, but in practice, as profitability is restored, attention shifts away from cost control (p. 122).

Other Divisions

Evidence of higher rates of unemployment for unskilled manual workers compared with skilled manual workers, for manual workers in general compared with white-collar workers and for blacks and immigrants compared with white native workers is available.[5] Furthermore, the differentials generally grow during recessions. For example, in 1971 the general level of male unemployment in Great Britain increased sharply. The general rate rose from 3.6 per cent in October 1970 to 5.2 per cent in October 1971. In 1970 the rate for foremen and supervisors was 1.7 per cent, for skilled manual workers it was 2.5 per cent, for unskilled manual workers it was 9.3 per cent. By October 1971 the comparable figure for unskilled manual workers was 13.4 per cent (Hill [1973], Bosanquet and Standing [1972]). The rate for unskilled men in England's main peripheral region – the northern region – rose from 15.2 per cent to 21.6 per cent between 1970 and 1971.

This centre–periphery pattern may also be seen across racial lines. Davidson [1964] found that unemployment among black workers in Great Britain was four or five times higher than among white workers between

August 1961 and February 1963. Wright [1968] found a similar disparity and further concluded that 'during times of recession, unemployment amongst coloured workers has tended to rise more rapidly than amongst white workers and to go down more slowly again when trade recovers' (p. 85).

Castles and Kosack [1973] found a similar pattern considering the period from February 1963 to May 1968 and also mentioned that unemployment rates and fluctuations were greater for female black immigrants compared with the men (p. 91).

Thus top managers maintain their authority by dividing their strategies according to the expandability of workers. Responsible Autonomy will be encouraged among central workers, while Direct Control over peripheral workers will be deepened. This helps to counteract the contradiction of each type of managerial strategy. The alienation of central workers, which Responsible Autonomy strategies attempt to ignore or hide, may be masked by relative employment security which central workers will enjoy if top managers adjust to adverse competitive conditions by primarily laying off peripheral workers. The relatively larger active reserve army for peripheral workers' job categories will force them to submit to increasing Direct Control, and the relatively lower and more insecure wages which peripheral workers receive will encourage them to disregard deeper exploitation in response to financial incentives (will, that is, encourage the Taylorian *homo economus* in peripheral workers).[6]

Systematic divisions among workers according to the degree of status achieved during productive activity have been examined recently by several American radicals, notably under the heading 'Labor Segmentation' by Reich *et al*, [1973]; Gordon [1972]; Edwards *et al*, [1975] and Wachtel [1975]. While their work is very important, there are a few points I would like to take issue with here. According to their common position:

The evolution of capitalism, from its phase of modern industry to monopoly capitalism has been accompanied by a *qualitative* change in the working class, . . . *Homogenization* of the work force under modern industry has been supplanted by *stratification* under monopoly capitalism (Wachtel [1975], p. 104).

I believe this is a mistake. As I have shown in some detail in Chapters 5 and 7 above, stratification clearly existed throughout Modern Industry in Britain. I doubt that the American experience was very different, though evidence sufficient to allow such a judgement has not been revealed by the Americans.

Another problem is their overemphasis of stratification as the direct result of conscious managerial strategies, ' . . . employers turned to strategies designed to divide and conquer the work force' (Edwards *et al*, [1975], p. xiii). I do not think divisions among workers have been created in such a conspiratorial fashion by capitalists or top managers. Systematic divisions on the basis of sex, race, skill or other educational attributes not only predate Monopoly Capitalism, but also they predate capitalism. Certainly there was no golden age of harmony before capitalism among people from whom surplus product was extracted. That Marx was also aware of this is clear from the *Communist Manifesto*.

Top managers may encourage divisions among workers by establishing different status levels within productive activity during Monopoly Capitalism, (though at times they may discourage such divisions as during the early post-war years in the U.K. car industry – see Chapter 14, Section 3), but often top managers bow to demands for such divisions by workers (for example in the engineering industry when workers demanded the reversing of dilution after the world wars). The problem with the Labour Segmentation analysis, as with most other Marxist analyses, is its underemphasis of resistance as a *force throughout capitalist history*, which is *differentially* distributed among workers, and which capitalists and top managers often *accommodate* and attempt to co-opt.

3   Centre–Periphery Relations between Firms

As workers within a firm may be viewed as either central or peripheral on the basis of specialised knowledge, relation to authority or power of resistance, so firms in an industry may be considered central or peripheral on the basis of their relative monopoly power. These two dichotomies are connected. Large firms are able to bypass or forestall internal technical reorganisations to some extent when adjusting to changed product demand by increasing or decreasing their co-operative relations with smaller firms. Similarly they are able to bypass the disruptive consequences of central worker lay-offs by reducing co-operative relations in times of adversity. This is particularly important for large firms when top managers are faced with strong, organised resistance from the majority of their workers. Co-operative relations with smaller firms allow top managers in larger firms the luxury of treating a high proportion of their workers as central and to use Responsible Autonomy strategies when dealing with them. Of course the steady profits which co-operative relations allow top managers in larger firms and the security enjoyed by their workers have another side.

The flexibility which the large firms acquire from their co-operative relations means hardship and insecurity for workers in smaller supplier and distributing firms. Top managers in these firms are faced with much wider short-run fluctuations in demand than top managers in the larger firms. The proportion of workers that these smaller firms are able to consider central is relatively small. Also many of these smaller firms are eliminated altogether during a slump in demand for the industry's products. The unskilled and semi-skilled manual workers working for these firms are therefore peripheral workers on two counts. They are peripheral to these firms as are semi-skilled and unskilled workers in larger firms, but they are also employed in what might be considered peripheral firms.

A leading article in the *Financial Times* (15 October 1974, p. 15) clearly set out the difficulties facing small engineering firms even when their contracts were not actually cut during the 1974 slump in the British Motor and General Engineering industries. Small engineering firms were squeezed between large raw materials suppliers (such as British Steel Corporation and the oil companies) and large car and engineering firms. In 1974 British Steel Corporation was rationalising its operations and trying to increase profit margins. This was done at the expense of the smaller engineering firms. According to the *Financial Times* report:

> The large concern which supplies some of his [the small engineering firm's] raw materials is asking to be paid within 30 days rather than the 60 it has allowed for in years past. The supplier is carefully tending his own cash position and might indulge in a little polite blackmail to make sure that he is paid promptly – 'unless you pay on time we don't see how we can send out your next order'. The small engineer finds that his major customer is also carefully husbanding cash. It might mean that the customer delays payment for goods. But even if he does pay on time, he tends to haggle interminably about price increases which are desperately needed by the small supplier if he is to at least keep pace with the extra cost of replacing raw materials (p. 15).

Furthermore, in 1974, with the fall in property values, the small firms' assets were worth less. This meant that many could not secure bank loans to finance the gap between increased costs of raw materials, which had to be paid promptly, and revenues from their own output, which were delayed and often too low to cover the newly inflated costs. The article concluded that 'the smaller engineering company finds itself in a three-way squeeze: squeezed by customers, suppliers and the bank and with no certainty that it will escape before being crushed completely' (p. 15).

The small engineering firms are quick to feel such pressures whenever there is a general squeeze, and particularly when demand for the final products to which they contribute, such as cars, has fallen.

In good times, when motor and engineering industry product demand is high, when credit is loose, these peripheral firms expand and enjoy good profits. But with a slump in demand, especially when this coincides with tight money, these peripheral firms are squeezed first and squeezed hardest. They, in turn, squeeze their labour force to keep costs down. The workers that they consider peripheral go first. Then many of these firms go under altogether while the major car firms are just beginning to lay off their own peripheral workers. In these smaller peripheral firms worker resistance is generally weaker.

Thus workers in peripheral firms, who are peripheral to their own firms, are in effect, the first line in the defence of employment security of the best organised workers or those closest to managerial authority.

This pattern reflects a general managerial strategy to follow the path of least resistance. While top managers will often spend considerable effort directly counter-attacking worker resistance, they will also try to accommodate this resistance by pursuing policies which limit its effect. To co-opt union leaders, to maintain relations with small suppliers, to lay off poorly organised workers before well-organised ones; these strategies – as 'scientific' as Taylorian scientific management – largely reflect the reality of worker power within production in advanced capitalist countries, and top managers' recognition and accommodation of that reality.

So far I have been referring exclusively to centre – periphery patterns between firms within a single industry. O'Connor [1972] has explored the relation between what he calls competitive industries and monopolistic industries. The chief difference between these two industry groups for O'Connor is that firms in the monopolistic sector are able to pass wage increases on to consumers, while competitive firms cannot. In return for wage increases unions in the monopolistic sector (which are relatively strong) abstain from fighting productivity rises and help to maintain 'labor discipline' (p. 21). This results in the 'bifurcation of the workforce' (p. 20).

The main relationship between monopolistic and competitive sectors occurs *indirectly*, through labour power markets and through the State. Because of insufficient growth in demand and a labour-saving bias to technical change, there is a net flow of workers out of the monopolistic sector. This depresses wages and discourages technical progress in the competitive sector. Profits in the competitive sector are reduced by the lowering of entry barriers which accompany falling wages, and by the expansion of monopolistic firms into traditional competitive enclaves (p. 29). The competitive sector is maintained through state subsidies and the State also expands to take on workers thrown out of the monopolistic industries. Thus the stage is set for what O'Connor calls 'the fiscal crisis of the State' (pp. 33–5).

While O'Connor's analysis is very important, he is primarily concerned with analysis at the macro level, with the fiscal crisis of the State, rather than the situations of individual industries or groups of workers. He under-emphasises co-operative relations between monopolistic and competitive firms *within* industries and the bifurcation of workers both within industries and *within firms*.

Two points about centre–periphery relations in general ought to be emphasised.

First, the centre – periphery distinction arises out of struggle, out of a *combination* of differential worker resistance and managerial strategies for counter-pressure. It is not simply a function of attributes such as differences in race, sex, colour, nationality or skills. While the distinction will often follow such divisions, it need not.

Second, the different positions of central and peripheral workers during productive activity affect several aspects of their economic and social positions.

(a) Central workers will generally have more direct control over their labour in consequence of the Responsible Autonomy strategy.

(b) Central workers will generally be paid more than peripheral workers. While this may often simply reflect greater 'training costs' necessary for central workers to acquire skills, central workers are not treated as such simply on the basis of their skills.

(c) Central workers' employment security will be greater than that of peripheral workers.

Differences in employment security are particularly important for two reasons. First, in the short run, unemployment will mean loss of earnings,[7] loss of prestige and often loss of self-confidence. Second, unemployment often involves deskilling and general demotion of status. If the next job is taken with a different firm, status and earnings increments acquired through the internal labour market with the workers' old firm will generally be forfeited. If the next job taken is also in a different industry, the workers' skills will often be inappropriate and therefore unremunerated. Finally, the social and political shop-floor community in which the worker participated at the old job will be lost and the worker will have to fit into a new organisation. This will take time and he may never find the same cohesion as before.

Strong evidence for this deskilling via unemployment has been found by Hill [1973]. In the three towns studied by Hill he found that 21 per cent of the sample of unemployed male workers in Coventry, 19 per cent in Hammersmith and 33 per cent in Newcastle left unskilled jobs, but 36 per cent, 37 per cent and 63 per cent of the samples were 'registered' as unskilled by the Department of Employment (pp. 61–2).

Daniel [1974] found a similar pattern. Of his national sample, taken at a relatively prosperous time (October – November 1973, with unemployment at 2.3 per cent compared with 3.7 per cent during the previous year), 15 per cent of workers formerly in skilled jobs took unskilled jobs and 21 per cent took semi-skilled jobs. Meanwhile only 2 per cent of workers formerly in unskilled jobs took skilled jobs and 20 per cent took semi-skilled jobs. Of those formerly in semi-skilled jobs, 22 per cent found skilled jobs, but 28 per cent found unskilled jobs (1974, p. 99).

Daniel also reported workers' experience of unemployment itself. He concludes,

Nearly three quarters (72 per cent) of those concerned about being out of work spontaneously mentioned lack of money as the chief reason.

Psychological costs (such as boredom and inactivity, feelings of depression, apathy and listlessness) and social costs (a sense of being inadequate, useless, rejected and cut off from other people) were also widely mentioned. Indeed, one or other of these factors was mentioned by 58 per cent of respondents concerned about being out of work (pp. 149–50).

Also, over 'a third of those who had taken on credit loans while in work had not been able to make repayments and had found creditors inclined to be punitive,' that is, taking unemployed workers to court or repossessing goods (pp. 50, 150).

4 Subcontracting and Flexibility

Subcontracting relations between firms represent one of a species of inter-firm relations which are largely ignored by economic theory. Occupying a middle ground between arms' length market transactions between firms (regulated by the price system) and the direction of activities within firms (regulated by a fair measure of conscious planning), a wide range of relations based on co-operation or affiliation link firms with one another.

Co-operation in the form of price agreements and market sharing among firms in relation to a common market, co-operation representing something between competition and *horizontal* integration, is treated in standard textbooks as a method for restricting competition. Co-operation in the form of subcontracting, long-term contracts, and technical agreements among firms facing each other on opposite sides of a market, co-operation representing something between arms' length transactions and *vertical* integration, is commonly treated as business detail to be abstracted from.

Here I shall try to indicate the importance of co-operative relations of a centre–periphery type between firms facing each other on opposite sides of a market by concentrating on subcontracting relations in the U.K. motor industry. I shall deal with two questions in relation to subcontracting. Firms with broadly similar capabilities operating in the same industries often subcontract out very different proportions of their work. Why should this be so? And what might lead particular firms to alter the relative importance of their subcontracting relations?

In the U.K. motor industry there is a major difference in degree of vertical integration between the two largest manufacturers, Ford (UK) and British Leyland. British Leyland maintains subcontracting relations with about 4000 firms and about 65 per cent of the value of an average Leyland car represents 'bought out' parts and components. Ford, on the other hand, buys out about 50 per cent of the value of its cars on average (Rhys [1972]).

In Japan around 45 per cent of car value is bought out by car manufacturers and in Italy, Germany, France and the United States the proportions are from

25 per cent to 40 per cent. Furthermore, both Ford and the firms which make up Leyland were much less vertically integrated in the past. For example, before the war no major car manufacturer made its own car bodies.

Subcontracting or contracting out work is known to be widespread in a number of key industries in major industrialised countries. In 1969 information presented to a joint O.E.C.D./U.N.I.D.O. meeting indicated that 25 per cent of the value of production in the Swedish engineering industry and 30 per cent in the Japanese engineering industry represented subcontracted work (United Nations, 1970). Though accurate figures are not available for the United Kingdom, the value of production represented by subcontracting work in the U.K. engineering, motor vehicle, aerospace and construction industries is known to be high.

The diversity of contracting relations makes accurate estimates of their magnitude difficult to assess. Formally the term 'subcontracting' refers to a contract for work which comes from another contractor. Typically a large engineering firm which has won a large contract will farm out or subcontract some of that work to smaller engineering firms according to the larger firm's capabilities and convenience. When the contractor gives out a subcontract the subcontractor may receive the materials to carry out the work or he may have to purchase the materials himself. In the former case the subcontract is said to be 'free issue'. The distinction is not simple because the subcontractor may receive only a proportion of materials free issue and he may lease some of his equipment from the contractor.

The distinction between subcontracts and contracts is also vague, particularly in the motor industry. One would normally think of work done by direct suppliers of parts and components for one of the major motor vehicle manufacturers to represent either market transactions or contracted-out work – not subcontracted work. But the major motor vehicle manufacturers do not always sell vehicles on a single unit basis. Many commercial vehicles are sold in large blocks on contract to national and local governments, or to transport firms. A significant proportion of car production represents fleet sales to government agencies (such as police departments) or to large firms. Some export sales of cars or car kits are part of large block contracts with foreign governments. Amongst suppliers in the motor vehicle industry the term 'subcontracting' is often used to refer to relations with motor vehicle manufacturers which might properly be simply contracting-out relations.

As I shall be considering subcontracting primarily in relation to the motor vehicle industry, I shall use the term loosely to refer to situations when suppliers produce parts and components to specifications set out in advance by the large manufacturers, whether materials are issued or not, and whether the contract is directly with the large manufacturer or through some intermediary contract with another supplier.

Subcontracting and Centre–Periphery Relations between Firms in the U.K. Motor Industry

The major car producers are primarily assemblers. They mainly co-ordinate and execute the assembly of cars from castings, forgings, parts and components. Some of these they produce themselves from materials or similar parts, and some they buy out from a wide range of firms. In the United Kingdom about half the value of bought-out parts and components are purchased from six major firms which are similar in size to the car assembly firms.[8] The other half comes from several thousand firms which are very small compared with the car assemblers.

It is easy to see why the large car assemblers would be reluctant to take over one of the six major component manufacturers or to try to produce those components for themselves. These components manufacturers have achieved significant economies of scale precisely because they sell a wide range of products, many of which are highly standardised and are therefore easily sold to several different car assemblers both at home and abroad (see Rhys [1972], pp. 60–71). To take over one of these firms would be difficult financially and would involve a difficult burden of co-ordination, as the component firms' activities also involve supplying components to other industries. On the other hand, unable to achieve economies of scale in these components by servicing their own demand alone, the assemblers would be reluctant to make these components for themselves.

The smaller component manufacturers are a different matter. At first glance it is difficult to see why the large assemblers did not take over these firms, or the activities they perform, long ago. These firms perform activities which the assemblers could easily carry out themselves. In fact several of the sorts of components which are bought out from small suppliers are also produced by the assemblers themselves. Many of these component manufacturers are so small that they simply cannot afford to purchase the most up-to-date equipment, even though the advantage of such equipment is well known and the scale of particular component requirements by single assemblers which are purchased from small component firms might justify the implementation of this equipment (numerically controlled machine tools for example). The assemblers, by not taking over certain component firms or producing these components themselves, are actually supporting outdated technology. Furthermore many of the components which come from the small firms are specific to particular model ranges of the assemblers. When major model changes occur changes in components must be carried out in close co-operation with the assembler.

The major advantage of maintaining subcontracting relations with these relatively inefficient firms appears to be the lower wages which these smaller firms pay their workers. Evidence from various sources suggests that the differential is in the order of 25 per cent to 50 per cent (see Chapter 15). This is primarily because worker organisation is much weaker in the small supplier firms. If the assembler took over the low-wage supplier, it is likely that the workers in the smaller firm would begin to demand parity of wages and conditions with their new fellow workers in other plants of the large assembler. The history of labour relations in the motor industry is filled with parity disputes following mergers, take-overs and setting-up of new facilities in this country (see Chapter 14).

In spite of the wage differential it is difficult to see why assemblers maintain such seemingly archaic co-operative relations, given the transport costs, the difficulties of achieving well co-ordinated quantity and quality control over these components, the capabilities of the assemblers and the possibilities for technical advance if the work was consolidated.

The Value of Flexibility

This difficulty is removed once one looks beyond static costs and benefits. In general terms the primary benefit accruing to assemblers from their myriad subcontracting relations is flexibility.

Flexibility from subcontracting relations is reflected in several common situations which the assemblers face.

First, the demand for cars before the Second World War was characterised by both a high seasonal component and wide cyclical fluctuations. Since the war the seasonal component has been ironed out by export demand, but the cyclical component has remained, partly due to successive governments' stop—go policies which involved changes in hire-purchase conditions and luxury-goods taxes. The advantage of having subcontracting arrangements during depressed times is that the responsibility for idle overheads is borne by the smaller subcontracting firms.

Second, given the unequal power relation between subcontracting partners, it is easy for the large assemblers to squeeze their subcontractors during hard times by simply not paying their bills on time (see Chapter 14).

Third, it is easier for small subcontractors to lay off workers. Workers in large car firms are well known for their strong shop-floor organisation. It is difficult for car firms to lay off sections of their labour force quickly because of established procedures, and laying-off some workers sours industrial relations with those who remain.

Fourth, if the assemblers have subcontracting relations with more than one firm for obtaining the same or very similar components, or if they currently produce these components in small amounts themselves, they will not be too bothered if a few of their suppliers go bankrupt.

In boom times it is not difficult for a large car firm to convince a small general engineering firm to carry out subcontracted work for them. Generally when the demand for cars has grown it has grown very quickly. Assembly firms would not be able to build up the capacity to produce many components themselves quickly enough. Furthermore they may not wish to extend their capacity for some time even after a time of high demand. Past experience may lead the assemblers to prefer to leave it for others to accept as much of the risk of a sudden slump as possible.

The prices assemblers pay to subcontractors must be sufficient to induce them to do the work. If the work requires substantial setting-up costs, this may be reflected in the price as well. On individual contracts subcontractors may be given prices which contain some margin for risk and setting up costs. The size of this margin will depend on custom, the relative sizes and numbers of assemblers versus potential suppliers and the strength of demand for vehicles. As long as expansion occurs these small suppliers may enjoy a degree of surplus profit. But it is likely that some of the inducement for subcontractors to undertake the work comes from the promise, often not backed by a written long-term contract, that further work will be ordered. This promise is limited by the assumption of normal (good) times.

Fifth, alternative sources of supply represent the assurance of some inflow of components when interruptions (usually due to management–labour troubles but also due to problems of mismanagement or poor co-ordination) occur in the stream of components coming from any one supplier, or even from component-producing sections within the assembler's own organisation. Multiple sourcing is common in the car industry, and with the growth in labour militancy during the 1960s the advantages of what might appear to encourage small and technically inefficient supply units from a static viewpoint have grown.

To summarise, the value of flexibility via subcontracting may be considered to comprise two main elements.

First, alternative sources of supply will make it easier for firms to maintain a desired output level when faced with difficulties of labour relations or mistakes in co-ordination.

Second, alternative centres of responsibility for certain overheads, and a fragmented labour force, make it easier for firms to adjust desired output when faced with fluctuations in final product demand.

This second element of flexibility becomes particularly important when selling in an oligopolistic industry where firms will be reluctant to alter prices because of uncertainty concerning the reaction of competitors and because of the damaging effects which retaliatory reactions might have.

The Decision to Subcontract Work

Let me return to the first question I posed above – why is it that firms with broadly similar capabilities, operating in the same industries, often have very different proportions of subcontracting relations? Concentrating on subcontracting relations between partners of clearly unequal size, with the larger firm giving out the subcontract, such as between car assembly firms and their suppliers, one may view the decision by a large assembler to take over a small supplier as a strategic decision over which top managers in the car assembly firm normally exercise considerable discretion.

As was shown above, the decision to take over a small supplier is not an easy one to make. Broadly, the decision-maker faces the following strategic choice. Do I opt for flexibility on the assumption that supply and demand will be unstable in the future? Or do I opt for integration, which involves more direct control over the production process but also more responsibility for overheads — assuming that demand will be stable (or at least predictable well in advance), and assuming that my control and co-ordination over the production process will ensure a smooth output flow?

This strategic choice may be illustrated with the help of some simple diagrams. In Graph 8.1 curve C^A shows how total costs vary with output in the short run if the firm continues to maintain subcontracting relations with many suppliers. Curve C^B shows the short-run total cost curve which would describe the firm if it took over some of its small suppliers. Curve R represents the total revenue curve. I will assume output price is expected to remain constant in the short run.[9]

Assuming that the firm was producing Q_t units initially, if output remained at that level, top managers would be better off to integrate vertically. They would also be better off as long as the desired level of output did not fall below Q^1_{t+1} or rise above Q^2_{t+1}. Costs do not fall so quickly when top managers wish to reduce output along C^B because of increased overheads and decreased flexibility in dealing with labour. (Also costs may rise more quickly if top managers wish to increase output in the B situation because it would take longer for the vertically integrated firm to expand capacity or to set up subcontracting relations than it would take for the less integrated firm to increase its orders from secondary suppliers.) If top managers in the car assembly firm believe the likelihood is high that demand conditions will change such that they will be able to sell no more than Q^1_{t+1} (and that they will be able to sell more than Q^2_{t+1}), then they will not wish to undertake the added capital investment required to take over their supplier or the activities carried out by that supplier.

The decision is more complicated than this. Not only must top managers form some view of the likely stability of demand in the future, but they must also form a view of the likely smoothness of flow of parts, components and sub-assemblies from existing suppliers and from within their own operations.

In Graph 8.2 this further problem is illustrated. In the first situation it was *desired* or *planned* output which changed given changed demand conditions. Now the problem is that output may fall below planned levels.

In Graph 8.2 on the abscissa the proportion of actual output which comes from the firm through expected channels is shown, that is, where value is added by the firm itself or through planned suppliers. If constant prices are

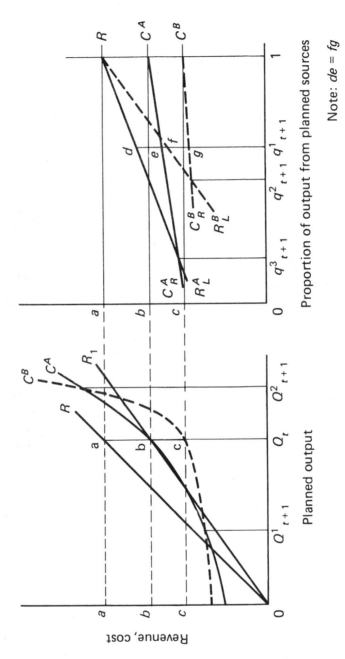

GRAPH 8.2

Note: *de = fg*

GRAPH 8.1

assumed throughout the production process in the short run, constructing this index should be no problem. At the full proportion, actual output coming from planned sources is at the planned level and profits will be either ab or ac, depending on whether the firm maintains its subcontracting relations (curve C^A in Figure 1), or not (curve C^B).

When the production flow is disrupted because of lack of supplies from some external or internal source, two things will occur.

First, revenue will fall because of lost output. But the fall in revenue will not be as great as the fall in the value of output from planned sources because stocks of final goods may be run down in the short run. Similarly the fall in value of output from planned sources will not be as great as the fall in value of supplies because stocks of components may also be run down. Some of the lost output and lost supplies may be made up by overtime working and some may be made up by switching to alternative sources of supplies. But there is a big difference between switching to alternative supplies which may quickly bypass the bottleneck, and working that much harder after the bottleneck is cleared up. The longer time output is held up and the more retail stocks are run down, the more likely will be customer switching to other firms. If you cannot get a fire-engine red Vauxhall VX – 490 within the next two months you may decide to buy a fire-engine red Ford Granada rather than wait, or rather than buy a sienna brown VX – 490. Thus the advantage of alternative sources of supply is that revenue will fall by a smaller amount when a disruption occurs. This is illustrated in Graph 8.2 by the revenue-loss curve in situation A being less steep than the revenue-loss curve for situation B ($R_L{}^A$ less steep than $R_L{}^B$).

Second, costs will fall. Costs to the firm with greater subcontracting arrangements for cutting back on supplies of components which are temporarily unnecessary will be less than the costs to the firm with less subcontracting arrangements for laying off sections of its labour force while still paying some overheads. Top managers in the smaller subcontracting firms will find it easier to lay off workers because of weaker worker organisation within those firms. Thus in Graph 8.2 the cost-reduction curve will be more steep in situation A than for situation B ($C_R{}^A$ more steep than $C_R{}^B$).

Because the revenue-loss curve is more steep and the cost-reduction curve is less steep in situation B, the profit differential bc will dissipate if the proportion of output from planned sources falls below $q^1{}_{t+1}$. As the proportion falls below $q^2{}_{t+1}$, the firm in situation B will be making a loss while in situation A the firm will remain in profit unless the proportion falls below $q^3{}_{t+1}$.

Given the importance of *estimated* future stability of demand and supply conditions on the decision to take over a supplier, and because of the difficulty of estimating these magnitudes, it is not hard to see why firms may choose very different mixes of flexibility and control when they have the power to choose over a wide range of such mixes.

The decision will become simpler if the firm does not have much scope for discretionary strategic decisions. If competitive pressures on output prices cause the revenue curve to fall from R to R_1, the scope for deciding on flexibility narrows considerably. Firms will be pressed to integrate vertically if they can. Not all firms will be able to afford the higher initial expenditure (perhaps they will do it by integrating first and then undercutting competitors), and the traditional method of adjusting supply to adverse demand conditions – by the exit of less efficient firms – will occur.

On the other hand, if top managers of large firms come to view their internal production processes as inflexible, they will be tempted to insure against the adverse effects of this inflexibility by multiplying alternative sources of supply for various parts of their own operations (as long as the costs of lost scale economies and greater coordination between firms are not too high). One might expect differences in the degree of subcontracting relations not only between firms in the same industry, but also in different countries, when differences in the security of employment and the likelihood of strikes are great.

The well-known security of employment enjoyed by Japanese workers in large firms is not shared by workers in very small firms. This may account for the higher proportion of subcontracting relations in the Japanese motor industry compared with the industry in other major manufacturing countries. Similarly the high incidence of strikes in the U.K. motor industry may account in part for the relatively high proportion of subcontracting in the U.K. industry. Of course this will depend on the relationship between strike incidence and its effect on materials from suppliers compared with the major car firms.

Finally, where wage differentials between large firms and small firms in the same industry are greater, one would expect subcontracting relations to be more widespread.

Here is a crude answer to the second question posed above – why should firms alter the relative importance of their subcontracting relations? When top managers face widespread price competition one would expect them to integrate vertically. If competitive pressures are light, one would expect a range of subcontracting relations when the industry suffers from wide, but short-lived, fluctuations in demand. One would also expect subcontracting relations to grow when wage differentials and differentials in employment security and strike incidence develop and grow between large and small firms in the industry.

Subcontracting and Flexibility: Evidence

A number of testable hypotheses follow from the analysis outlined above, concerning changes in subcontracting relations over time for a single firm or comparisons concerning changes of strength of subcontracting between firms and across industries. But the analysis would be most convincing if one could show empirically that subcontracting relations do in fact provide large firms with flexibility. Do large firms which subcontract out work cut their contracts with outside suppliers before they cut their own internal costs when product demand falls, and subcontract out work before incurring internal costs when demand rises?

Partly because subcontracting has been ignored theoretically, partly because of definitional problems mentioned above, and partly because cooperative relations between firms are highly protected by confidentiality granted by law, sufficient data to test directly any of the hypotheses mentioned above is not available. Nevertheless it is possible to test the hypothesis mentioned in this section indirectly for the U.K. motor industry.

Annual figures on numbers employed, separated into males and females, per minimum list heading from 1951 to 1973, were available for Coventry County Borough from national insurance returns. In Coventry MLH 381 (Motor Vehicle Manufacturers) covers primarily British Leyland and Chrysler factories, about 74 per cent of employment in 1971, while MLH 342/349 (Other Mechanical Engineering), MLH 332/333 (Machine Tools and Pumps, Valves and Compressors) and MLH 399 (Other Metal Goods), primarily cover smaller firms. For example, of those in MLH 381 in 1971 almost half worked in factories employing over 10,000 people in Coventry while none covered by the other MLHs worked in such large factories. While only 5 per cent worked in factories employing under 1000 people in MLH 381, 15 per cent did in MLH 332, 63 per cent in MLH 349, and 100 per cent in MLH 399. According to the national input – output tables from the Census of Production 1968, 6 per cent of commodities entering MLH 381 come from these MLHs. This represented 15 per cent of commodities other than those from MLH 381 itself, primary inputs, or iron and steel. In Coventry in 1971 MLH 381 accounted for 25 per cent of the occupied population and 33 per cent of occupied males, while these supplier MLHs accounted for 10 per cent of the occupied population and 11 per cent of occupied males.

It is also known from a survey carried out in Coventry in 1974 that a significant number of firms in these supplier MLHs in Coventry carried out subcontract work. [10]

Given this background information, the theory that large firms use subcontracting relations to gain flexibility may be tested by the hypothesis that in Coventry changes in employment in MLH 381 will be correlated with *earlier* changes in employment in MLH 332/333, 342/349 and 399, rather than changes in employment in the latter MLHs during the same year. One would expect the lag between cuts in subcontracts and lay-offs among car firm workers to be quite short. When the demand for cars fell between 1951 and 1973 it fell for one year only or for only two years consecutively (see Graph 13.2). Though car demand expanded for several years at a stretch, because no new major car factories were built in Coventry during the period, the lag

TABLE 8.1

Regression Results for Males in Coventry's Motor-vehicle and Supplier Industries

$\Delta M V_t = 1.15 + 0.190 \Delta S_{t-1}$ $R^2 = .36$ $\bar{R}^2 = .33$
         (3.30) $DW = 1.72$
                                $Df = 19$

$\Delta M V_t = 2.24 - 0.0326 \Delta S_t$ $R^2 = .01$ $\bar{R}^2 = -.04$
         (0.45) $DW = 2.36$
                                $Df = 19$

$\Delta M V_t = 1.27 + 0.149 \Delta X_{t-1} + 0.314 \Delta Y_{t-1} + 0.148 \Delta Z_{t-1}$
              (0.74)   (1.55)   (1.61)
                           $R^2 = .38$ $\bar{R}^2 = .27$
                              $D W = 1.73$
                              $Df = 17$

$\Delta M V_t = 1.59 - 0.330 \Delta X_t - 0.134 \Delta Y_t + 0.137 \Delta Z_t$
              (1.54)   (0.59)   (1.37)
                           $R^2 = .26$ $\bar{R}^2 = .13$
                              $D W = 2.45$
                              $Df = 17$

NOTE: t scores in parentheses below coefficients. With 19 degrees of freedom, t scores above 2.53 are significant at the 1 per cent level. Those above 1.73 are significant at the 5 per cent level.

$M V$ = MLH 381
X = MLH 332/333
Y = MLH 342/349
Z = MLH 399
S = MLH 332/333 + MLH 342/349 + MLH399

between the time when car firms would have given out new subcontracts and when they would have hired more workers would have been short as well. Thus a one-period lag was tested on the annual data though a shorter lag would have been tested if appropriate data had been available.

The results are shown on Table 8.1. The regressions were tried for all employees as well as for men alone. The all-employee results were not so clear as those for the men alone because of the strong upward trend in women workers which in all industries, though especially in the car firms, was impervious to short-run conditions. This reflects the growth in managerial and administrative activity within firms in the motor industry as they have grown in size and as problems of coordination and the maintenance of managerial authority have grown during the past few decades (see Chapter 14).

The results were much better for the three MLHs used as lagged independent variables when added together than when run as a multiple regression because of more likely intrusion of other factors including shifts in employment among the 'explanatory' MLHs and conditions specific to the demand for products from each MLH, unconnected with the car industry.

The regressions on lagged variables all have the right sign while those on the unlagged variables usually have the wrong sign. The coefficient of the lagged regression with MLHs added together was significant at the 1 per cent level while the unlagged regression was not significant and of the wrong sign.

5   On Classes

It may be thought that my distinction between central and peripheral workers suggests that central workers are not part of 'the working class'. This was not intended. I have been thinking of both groups of workers as working class. Nevertheless in trying to distinguish the working class more clearly, I think the framework does suggest one group of central workers who would be excluded. That is, those people who are considered central to top managers because of their contribution to the exercise of managerial authority. This group cuts across some categories of people who are normally thought of as working class – such as foremen and supervisors. I am thinking of class structure rather than class position here (see Poulantzas [1975]). It is quite possible for foremen to side with 'the lads' in a dispute, or for foremen to resist managerial authority over themselves, but in the nature of their labour process activity I think the exercise of managerial authority engenders a 'habit of mind' which would normally lead foremen to side with top managers, particularly if struggle became acute. While those who contribute to the exercise of managerial authority directly contribute to exploitation of the working class, central workers as a whole do not exploit peripheral workers, even though they enjoy better wages and conditions, and even though top managers play one group off against the other. The relation between central and peripheral workers is that central workers are able to exclude others from certain tasks; they are able to protect themselves, in the short run, from the reserve army of labour; they are able (with managerial encouragement), to divide the working class into non-competing groups.

CHAPTER NINE

The State and Relations between Countries

The subjects of this chapter are worked out in a very preliminary fashion. They have been included primarily because it is at the level of international relations that most Marxist analysis of unequal fortunes of different groups of workers is pitched (see Baran [1957]; Frank [1967]; Emmanuel [1972]; Wallerstein [1974]). I believe all these analyses suffer from a neglect of struggle within productive activity in each country.[1]

In Section 1 social formations and the state are discussed very briefly, and in Section 2 disparity between countries is examined.

1 Social Formations and the State

Within any country all economic activity does not strictly occur under the capitalist mode of production. A country is a complex social formation made up of economic activity under different modes of production. In any country there are simple commodity producers, such as small shopkeepers, artisans and small-scale farmers. There are also many independent professionals offering services. If these do not hire wage-workers or work for a wage themselves, their productive activity is not technically capitalist. Similarly, in underdeveloped countries, there are many forms of agricultural production which are technically feudal. Nevertheless today all non-Communist societies (some would say all societies; Wallerstein [1974]) are capitalist in that their social formation is dominated by capitalist productive relations.

As I have been dealing with productive activity in advanced capitalist societies, where a very high proportion of economic activity is carried on under the capitalist mode of production, I have not distinguished the capitalist mode of production from capitalist social formations. There is one large group of people in all capitalist societies whose working activity is not technically part of the capitalist mode of production; that is, many categories of people working for the State. I do not propose to deal with the class position of these people at all. Nor will I deal with the effect of their activity on value relations or on labour process development within the capitalist mode of production, except for one aspect – the importance of state activity for managerial strategies.

The State has been important as a direct buttress to managerial authority in capitalist productive activity from the outset. During the transition to the Modern Industry period direct control strategies were supported by the Combination Acts and active government enforcement of the acts in the form of spies, informers and *agents provocateurs*. More directly, employers could always rely on the military to intervene when worker resistance got 'out of hand'.

Perhaps the most visible change in the State's role in buttressing managerial authority is the greater sympathy of the State toward responsible autonomy strategies, particularly from the Modern Industry period. According to Marx and Engels the 'executive of the modern State is but a committee for managing the common affairs of the whole bourgeoisie' (*Manifesto of the Communist Party*, p. 49). Policies most effective for managing the *common* affairs of the bourgeoisie may not coincide with those which are most effective for managing the productive activity of the *average* capitalist or top manager. The State must be sensitive to resistance to authority in the social formation as a whole. Challenges which may spread are most anxiously headed off or broken down. Thus the State, especially during the twentieth century, has been particularly active in co-opting trade union leaders formally through state institutions (such as conciliation boards and the Labour Party), and in co-opting lower-level worker organisation during times of crisis (such as the shop stewards' movement during wartime: see Chapter 14).

2 Disparity between Countries

How have workers in advanced capitalist societies managed to raise the value of their labour power? The possibility for this gain came with insulation from the reserve army. Central workers had always gained wages above the value of labour power because they have insulated their job categories from competition in labour power markets. This possibility grew in importance for peripheral workers too, with the drying-up of the latent reserve army, with the growth of internal labour markets, and with the growth of organised worker resistance from the late nineteenth century.

The growth of internal labour markets and the decline of external labour power markets are intimately related. As shown in Chapters 4 and 5 a major aim of worker resistance has been to protect workers from reserve army pressures. Internal labour markets, as islands of relative security, have more chance to remain secure if they are surrounded by a more shallow reserve army. Also the growth in size, number and different categories of these islands of security reduces the depth of the reserve army surrounding any one of them, assuming small, stable, population growth and low net immigration. This occurs because external labour power markets become localised and stratified according to skill, race, sex, etc., once internal labour markets grow in significance within the national economy.

Capitalism is marked by continual technical change. Productivity increases from technical change will either accrue to customers from declining prices and rising quantities produced, or they will accrue to workers and capitalists in the form of higher wages and profits. For the latter to occur worker resistance must be strong, competition from new capitalists must be limited by monopoly power and the ability or desire of existing capitalists to expand in those markets must be limited. Generally these conditions were satisfied for several advanced capitalist countries (Britain, Germany, America and France) from the late nineteenth century. They had enclosed their manufacturing industries within protective tariffs (except for Britain) and competition from within was limited for several industries by the barriers to entry which large firm size provides. On the other hand a large proportion of their trade was with their colonies or spheres of influence. In the colonies the former situation existed because of unlimited supplies of labour power.[2] The late nineteenth century in developed countries was a period of falling prices and rising working-class standards of living. It was working-class consumer goods, primarily wheatstuffs, which were falling in price most quickly. Capitalists in developed countries were unable to keep money wages down to match the falling prices, in part because of strong worker resistance.

This combination of areas with high wages trading with low-wage areas (assuming workers to be relatively immobile between areas) represents conditions of unequal exchange if the higher surplus value created in the low-wage countries is spread over the whole system by equalising profit rates; that is, by lowering prices and therefore profits in low-wage areas.[3] This lowering of commodity prices from underdeveloped countries compared with those from developed countries has continued in broad terms throughout the twentieth century (until recently). Taking 1938 as 100, the terms of trade of primary products against manufactured goods in world trade were 147 in 1876–80, and 137 in 1913. For the United Kingdom, taking 1938 as 100, the terms of trade (import prices divided by export prices) were 163 in 1876–80 and 137 in 1913 (Emmanuel [1972], p. xi).[4]

Workers in advanced capitalist countries are able to raise the value of their labour power in their own country more easily, because surplus value is transferred from underdeveloped countries to developed countries via unequal exchange.

Workers in a developed country *could* raise the value of their labour power by considering that country as a closed system. They *may* bargain for increased real wages at the expense of profits at any time, depending on class forces. Also the possibility of success at raising real wages will be increased if technical change takes place with a severely limited latent reserve army. This way profit rates do not have to fall when real wages rise.

Also one *could* argue that if technical change is sufficiently labour saving, then the system will be able to expand with constant real wages and a constant population. While technical change has been labour-saving by and large, there is no reason to expect that it should be sufficiently so to allow capital to accumulate as fast as it is able without requiring additional labour power. Historically capital accumulation has always involved increasing the labour power available to capitalists and raising real wages when labour power has become scarce.

When dealing with value theory separate from any consideration of labour process struggles, there is often a temptation to consider only the *possibilities* of accumulation at certain rates, or in certain forms, rather than the *probabilities* of such developments occurring. One can imagine capital accumulation with constant real wages in countries with low latent reserve armies, just as one can imagine rising real wages in advanced countries cut off from links with underdeveloped countries. Nevertheless in reality capital takes the path of least resistance. If stores of labour power are available in underdeveloped countries, then capital will take advantage of them in its search for profits and expansion. If workers in developed countries put up determined resistance to exploitation, they may well be bought off, if that is viewed as the least disruptive method of carrying on. The ease with which this co-option can occur will be facilitated by transferring surplus value to developed countries by exchanging commodities of unequal value with underdeveloped countries. If this method of extending accumulation and buying off disruptions is suddenly cut off, the theoretical possibility of capitalist accumulation without it will remain. Even so the danger of disastrous disruption during the period of readjustment presents a real threat to the survival of a system based on alienation and exploitation.

The effects of instability in developed countries are cushioned somewhat by wider fluctuations in prices of primary products compared with typical export products from most developed countries. Prices of minerals and agricultural products are particularly sensitive to conditions of demand in developed countries. This makes it easier for firms in developed countries to cut costs during a recession without laying off workers, and for employed workers to maintain real wages during times of high unemployment. On the other hand this may increase the instability of employment for workers in the under-developed countries.[5] In the absence of strong trade unions it is easier to lay off native workers in those countries. In a sense, therefore, one can separate central and peripheral countries as well as central and peripheral firms and workers on the basis of relative strengths of organised worker resistance and reserve armies. While capitalists and capitalist nation-states have been particularly concerned about revolution in underdeveloped countries, until recently the general approach has invariably been coercion of native people rather than co-option.[6]

The problem has been, 'How can we keep the natives down?' rather than, 'How much do we have to give them, or their leaders, to prevent them from going on strike or to prevent general rebellion?' This attitude reminds one of the early nineteenth century attitude of capitalists and politicians towards non-craftsmen in England (see Chapter 5, Section 1).

While I believe this attitude has characterised relations in production within underdeveloped countries within colonial or native-run enterprises (primarily because of huge, readily available reserve armies and small firm size resulting in weak worker resistance), one might expect this to change somewhat in the long run when large multinational companies set up large-scale factories in these countries. Nevertheless I imagine multinationals would, in the first instance, import the most sophisticated Direct Control strategies, developed elsewhere, against native workers, as Direct Control strategies represented the initial development of management after the growth of Modern Industry in developed countries. I doubt that very much of the difference in wages between developed and underdeveloped countries reflects lower intensity of work in underdeveloped countries. Evidence on car firms setting up facilities in underdeveloped countries suggested that for the particular processes set up, these factories are at least as capital intensive as those in developed countries; that is, that the difference in wage-rates does not reflect differences in productivity in those duplicated facilities (see Chapter 16).

It is important to note that unequal exchange depends on the under-developed country producing products which do not directly compete with those of the developed countries. If they produce competing products, the price advantage from underdeveloped countries would swamp products produced where high wages must be paid. To say that if developed countries produced the same products using more capital-intensive techniques they would still be able to compete, ignores one important fact. It is generally multinational companies (often in conjunction with the governments of underdeveloped countries) which set up directly competing facilities, if they are set up at all, in underdeveloped countries. They are not capital-poor and therefore they are able to set up the most up-to-date, capital-intensive plants in underdeveloped countries.[7]

Generally, developed countries have protected themselves against such competition (particularly since the 1870s) by a combination of low tariffs against non-competing commodities and high tariffs against competing ones. This can remove price advantage due to low wages. It will discourage production of competing commodities in underdeveloped countries altogether, considering the enormous time necessary for a new industry in any country to attain competitive levels of productivity (especially in an under-developed country with low external economies such as communications infrastructure). Nevertheless, with the growth of multinational companies removing the capital-scarcity problem, with the relative political stability attained in certain underdeveloped countries, and with the lowering of tariffs since the 1930s against selected underdeveloped countries (such as those of Mediterranean Europe), directly competing commodities from under-developed countries have grown in significance. In spite of this capitalists in developed countries have managed to protect themselves by shifting to different branches within industries. As Emmanuel notes:

> Britain exchanged her cotton goods for Indian cotton and gained from this exchange the means of paying high wages to her workers. The day when India took up weaving . . . Britain changed her approach. She began to exchange her cotton yarn for Indian cotton and Indian fabrics. Then India started to produce her own yarn. So now Britain exchanges her looms and spindles for Indian fabrics, still obtaining the wherewithal to pay her workers their high wages. If India were to begin tomorrow to make her own looms and spindles, Britain would . . . send out machine tools for making these spindles and looms. . . . It is not even necessary for Britain to climb upstream in the production process every time. . . . If India were to specialize one day in metallurgy and engineering, to the neglect of her textile production, Britain would find no difficulty in taking up the latter branch again (1972, p. 146).

Movement up or down stream in an industry and shifts to new industries have occurred in Britain, particularly during the inter-war years, but the movement was *not* the simple, smooth process suggested by Emmanuel. When India began producing her own fabrics and yarn the British cotton industry did not suddenly disappear with all the capitalists and workers formerly in cotton rushing into the textile machinery industry. Instead capitalists were forced to integrate facilities, reduce capacity and labour force, lower wages and intensify work practices (Chapter 3). The formerly high-wage and labour-power-drawing northern regions of the country became a depressed area (Chapter 10). Capitalists received tariff protection which allowed wages to remain relatively high compared with underdeveloped countries, and eventu-ally the Government was forced to supply 'aid' to these areas in terms of 'unearned' unemployment insurance and poor relief.

Why?

Because it was, by and large, *other* firms which took advantage of the capital goods requirements for foreign textile industries, and workers in *other* areas who gained from the higher wages and improved conditions bred by high product demand in tight labour power markets. Some Lancashire textile workers moved to the West Midlands and the South-East, but generally it was their sons and daughters who moved and who continue to move out of the North.

Furthermore Emmanuel's argument applies most clearly to the developed countries as a block, which maintain higher wages than the underdeveloped countries they deal with. Just as inter-industry and intra-industry shifts need not occur within single firms or within a single region of a country, they need not occur within any one particular developed country. The degree to which the cotton textile industry of all developed countries was concentrated in Britain has not been matched by the degree to which the developed world's textile machinery industry is concentrated in Britain.

What seems to have occurred is a slow shift in Lancashire workers' position in the world cotton textile industry from a central to a much more peripheral position. The proportion of workers which top managers of British textile firms can afford to treat as central has diminished considerably. This has coincided with a rising proportion of women and immigrants being taken into the mills, with long-run, higher than average levels of unemployment in Lancashire (in spite of net emigration from the area), with levels of unemployment which rise more quickly during generally depressed times, and with increasing use of Direct Control strategies to deal with workers. A similar pattern may be seen in the British motor vehicle industry during the past ten years. This is examined in detail in Part Five.

CHAPTER TEN

Long-run Patterns
for Industries and Areas

Centre–periphery patterns distinguished in the previous two chapters are related in Section 1 to the persistence of areas of deprivation alongside areas of prosperity. In Section 2 the fragility of central workers' status in the long run is discussed, along with the consequences of this fragility for area patterns. While centre–periphery patterns have always marked capitalist societies, the particular groups of workers with central status have been changing continually. The broad long-run pattern of relative prosperity for areas within Britain reflecting this fragility is briefly examined in Section 3.

1 Centre–Periphery within Productive Activity and Area Patterns

Centre–periphery patterns demonstrate the fundamental inequality among workers which is generated through struggle as part of the *normal* development of capitalist societies.

Within a small region areas of deprivation existing alongside areas of prosperity will reflect centre–periphery patterns within and between firms of a single industry. People in jobs peripheral to a single industry will find it difficult to move to areas where their chances of central jobs might be higher. Also workers in peripheral jobs are often marked as peripheral workers by social characteristics which they cannot change by a simple shift in location or by training (sex, colour or race). Peripheral workers will generally live in less pleasant areas. They cannot afford to keep up their neighbourhood. They cannot afford to move to a 'better' neighbourhood. Local authorities are prejudiced against spending a lot of money on such areas (except to make way for commercial usage). Privileged workers are prejudiced against moving into neighbourhoods where peripheral workers live (particularly if the distinction is clearly racial), and against having peripheral workers move into their own neighbourhood. Also most housing stock is clearly stratified by price from the outset, because it is easier to build houses all within a limited design range within a single small area, and because as towns have expanded areas have become clearly stratified by age of houses.

Thus peripheral workers remain in areas of deprivation in spite of especially high rates of unemployment during trade recessions. There they form a pool of cheap labour, readily available to top managers when trade revives. This location pattern is clearly demonstrated in the industry-area studies of Parts Four and Five.

2 The Fragility of Central Workers' Status

In the long run, changes in techniques, changes in labour power market conditions and changes in product demand all represent potential threats to central workers' privileged condition. The coming of modern industry could involve a shift in geographic area and often meant a change in the sorts of skills needed. Workers in previously privileged areas or with skills which enabled them to secure privileges through their organisations in the early nineteenth century often became peripheral outworkers around modern factories with the move to modern industry (Chapter 11). Similarly changes in competitive conditions at any time in any industry may result in a shift in the locus of that industry's new investment to new areas, leaving previously privileged workers in a vulnerable position (Chapters 14 and 16). When major technical changes or changes in competitive conditions occur, the prosperity of entire areas (towns, cities or even larger regions) is threatened.

Why should the prosperity of areas be so tied to the vagaries of technical change and product demand for a single industry? First, a single small area will usually be dominated by one or two industries which directly employ a high proportion of the population. Usually each industry supports another large segment of the population indirectly, through supplier and distributor firms located in the area, through retail and wholesale outlets for consumer goods dependent on the industry's workers, and through local authority contributions from the industry and its workers gathered by local forms of taxation.

Second, when workers fall from a central to a peripheral position in an industry, it is unlikely that they will move to the areas or acquire the skills around which the industry's centre is reforming, and be re-hired as central workers. There are many reasons for this. It takes a long time before workers recognise that the fall in their position reflects a permanent shift in the industry rather than a temporary adjustment, especially if the industry is normally subject to short-run fluctuations. Often worker organisation will be strong enough to slow down the shift or limit its effects.[1] This will also cloud workers' awareness of the danger. Even once it has become obvious that prosperity will not return in the short run, workers will find it difficult to learn new skills or to move to new areas. The facilities available, especially to older people, for learning new skills are very poor and the possibility of a long period of training with little money coming in is daunting, especially for someone with a family. Also there is no guarantee that the outcome will be a good job. Similarly moving location is difficult, expensive and often a traumatic prospect for people long established in a certain area. Again there is no guarantee that a good job is waiting for the migrant, particularly if he or she is older.

Eventually people do move out of a depressed area, but those who move out are usually younger. Their training and employment prospects are greater in the areas to which they move and their ties with the older areas are less strong. It is their parents who have made the ties and younger people are often anxious to make their own way. This leaves the depressed areas with an ageing population which is more vulnerable to the process of deskilling by unemployment described in Chapter 8 Section 3.

What are the chances of individual workers losing their central status? Deskilling is a strong possibility for all unemployed workers.[2] Even if the centre–periphery distinctions according to occupational classification or monopoly power of the firm worked for remain stable, any person may easily fall from central to peripheral category (usually replaced by a younger new entrant into the labour power market). But the categories themselves often change in status in the long run. Changing technology, changing market conditions and changing political climates all reduce the permanence of any group of workers' central position.

The stability of large firms will depend, in the short run, on their ability to find peripheral means to absorb fluctuations, but in the long run, in order to survive, these firms will have to be able to *shift their centres*. The centre – periphery distinction itself is not disturbed, rather the expendability of particular workers defined by skill, sex, race or geographical location will change. This was demonstrated for the case of Lancashire textile workers at the end of Chapter 9.

The very nature of the centre–periphery pattern creates conditions which lead top managers eventually to try to destroy the pattern and recreate it elsewhere. The security, status and relatively high wages won by central workers and strategically conceded to them by top managers (given the existence of a peripheral cushion), will probably prove to be an intolerable burden on top managers at some future date. While competition is somewhat reduced during Monopoly Capitalism, it is certainly not removed altogether. Stable centre–periphery distinctions can still be upset by the appearance of major technical changes which can not easily be absorbed by existing industrial organisations (such as the shift to electrical power), or by capital moving to take advantage of cheap and relatively docile workers elsewhere. All it takes is for one large firm to take advantage of a major technical breakthrough or of hitherto peripheral workers, and other firms will be forced to follow suit. Furthermore, the expanding size and financial strength of large firms and their increasingly global perspective since the Second World War (not merely for export or for financial investment, but for their own productive facilities – the multinationals as opposed to the transnationals) intensify the possibility of significant geographical movement of work processes *within* the firm (Chapters 14 and 16).

Much of the history of worker resistance has been concerned with struggles by central workers, usually craftsmen, trying to defend their status as a combination of machinery and peripheral categories of workers have been undermining their central status. Similarly large companies, particularly in the past few decades, have been shifting their new investments to where they can take advantage of immigrant workers: to less developed regions of developed countries, or to less developed countries. There wages are lower, workers are poorly organised and often the local state offers to bolster Direct Control strategies with coercive labour laws.[3] The foundation for the central status of workers in developed countries, their inexpendability to top managers, may then be undermined. Often these new facilities will represent parallel processes to those carried out in traditional locations. As workers in traditional centres struggle against the tightening of direct control which accompanies a fall from central status, top managers will be able to bypass disruptions they cause by using their parallel facilities (Chapters 14, 15 and 16).

Thus the comfort and security of any one small group of workers, any one region's workers, or even any one country's workers, is never assured in an unplanned system based on profit.[4]

3 Long-run Patterns of Relative Prosperity between Regions in Britain

From the 1780s there have been two broad shifts in industrial growth from one section of the country to another, and a third seems to be emerging. During the eighteenth century the prosperous areas of the country were primarily around London and the good agricultural lands of the South and East. With the transition to Modern Industry the locus of economic activity shifted to the North and West for technical reasons (availability of fuel and raw materials), and because of the availability of abundant cheap labour power.[5]

Both industry and population come to concentrate around the coalfields (the line on Map 10.1 dividing England into high-wage North from low-wage South corresponded to the limit of the coalfields). Coal was the only domestic fuel available in quantity after the woodlands had been stripped in the seventeenth and early eighteenth centuries and coal was the source of power for steam-raising. In part it was the relative poverty of agriculture in the North which encouraged industry to move there in the late eighteenth century. At

MAP 10.1 *Broad Areas of Relative Prosperity in England, 1850*

SOURCE: Clapham [1926], p. 437.

that time labour power was cheaper in the North due to greater rural depopulation.

From the late eighteenth century to the early twentieth century it was the North and West which attracted the growing industries and eventually attracted migrants from the South and East, and particularly from Ireland. In part because of the tight labour power markets thereby encouraged, many groups of workers in those areas attained central status within their industries. Wages in towns and cities in the industrialised North were generally higher than those in the South (Clapham [1926], pp. 466–7).

In the early twentieth century a second major shift in the locus of British industrial activity occurred, primarily due to changed competitive conditions rather than technical changes.

The main industries in decline – textiles, shipbuilding, iron and steel and coal – were those traditional industries upon which British prosperity during the Modern Industry periods was based. Just before the war some of these industries were producing more for export than for home demand.[6] The return to gold policy of the early 1920s was disastrous for them.

Between 1920 and 1924 real wages fell markedly in those traditional industries which had become highly dependent on exports. Real wages in coal, iron and steel, shipbuilding and cotton fell by 26 per cent, 20 per cent, 14 per cent and 11 per cent respectively. In industries which were working for the home market, such as public utilities, transport and communications and the distributive trades, real wages rose markedly, by 10 per cent, 17 per cent and 14 per cent respectively (Mitchell and Deane [1971], pp. 352–3). Employment in the traditional industries was particularly hit after world trade collapsed in 1929–33, and the Government's policy of closing down capacity in whole districts for these industries, rather than gradually running them down or working short-time, meant mass unemployment in certain areas.

During the 1920s several new industries were expanding, particularly motor vehicles, electrical apparatus, and artificial silk. With the switch from steam power to electricity in homes as well as factories from the beginning of the century these industries were freed from the need to locate near coalfields. Increasingly they congregated near the largest market–London (and Birmingham to a lesser extent). Between 1923 and 1929 the insured working population rose by 8 per cent, but in London it rose by 13.6 per cent. In the south-eastern region around London it rose by 22 per cent, reflecting the growth in size of factories which could no longer be accommodated in central London, and the bicycle and motor vehicle age which allowed factories to gather workers from a wider area.

The Government has been concerned about this regional imbalance since the new pattern emerged in the 1920s. Unemployed workers in the North and West could not relieve tight labour power markets (reduce wages) in the South-East and Midlands, and the unemployed were a huge burden on state relief (Branson [1975], pp. 70–81). The Industrial Transference Board was set up in 1928 to alleviate the problem by transferring people from areas of high unemployment to areas where industry needed more workers.

While a steady movement from the depressed regions was taking place, it was a very slow process. There were good reasons for people staying in their traditional communities in spite of the vagaries of capitalist industrial location. Close contacts with family and friends, particularly in times of personal tragedy, are extremely important. To be laid off is just one of those times.

Community feelings and mutual aid were particularly important in the towns where unemployment reached mammoth proportions, such as Jarrow or in the Rhondda valleys of South Wales. Leaving one's family and friends, perhaps one's relatively cheap colliery house (and later on one's relatively cheap council house) to look for work in a strange place among strangers is a difficult and traumatic step.

Industrial Transference was a failure. Of 90,000 men transferred under Ministry of Labour schemes between 1930 and 1937, over 49,000 were known to have returned home, though they faced certain unemployment (Political and Economic Planning [1939]).

Gradually the Government lost faith in its policy of encouraging industrial rationalisations which caused high unemployment in depressed areas combined with industrial transfer. But no serious moves towards directing industry to depressed areas was made until after the Second World War.

During the past few years, in part due to the Government's regional policy and the discovery of North Sea oil, but also due to the availability of cheap labour power in Scotland and the North and West of England, the locus of new investment seems to be shifting to the 'depressed areas' of the twentieth century. This is reflected in the greater uniformity of the rise in unemployment during the 1975–6 recession compared with previous recessions in which the differential in unemployment rates between depressed areas and the relatively prosperous South-East and West Midlands had widened severely. (This regional shift within Great Britain, however, appears to be overshadowed by a shift in economic activity to other countries).

Certain features of these patterns are worth noting. First, they are long-run patterns. Depressed areas remain depressed for a long time. It takes time for workers' strong organisations, which were built up during periods of prosperity, to be destroyed. It takes time for an area's normal relative wages to fall significantly, and for property values and rates to fall. In Britain the process had normally taken at least a few generations and often a century. Second, for reasons mentioned above, though people do move out of an area, depressed areas have rarely been totally abandoned. Thus the country is normally scarred with large numbers of people living in areas previously thriving but now depressed, even though the precise location of these areas has changed over the centuries.

The case studies which follow demonstrate both the fragility of central workers' status in the long run and the long-run availability of peripheral workers to firms in the silk ribbon, hosiery and car industries during both good and bad times. They show that the pool of peripheral workers move in and out of employment, but remain in the areas where the industries need them.

PART FOUR

NINETEENTH-CENTURY INDUSTRY-AREA STUDIES

CHAPTER ELEVEN

The Silk Ribbon-Weaving Trade in Hillfields and Coventry Region

1 Historical Background

In 1451 Henry VI raised Coventry and the villages neighbouring it to the status of a county, (see Maps 11.1 and 11.2). For centuries the city and adjacent villages had formed a cohesive and largely self-sufficient economic unit. A cohesive unit, but not a homogeneous one. The villagers were far less prosperous than the inhabitants of Coventry city. Politically the villagers were barred from the corporate privileges of the city and in parliamentary elections they were unable to vote either in the city, where the franchise was confined to freemen, or in the northern division of the county of Warwickshire because of Henry VI's decree.

The silk ribbon-weaving trade was established in Conventry early in the eighteenth century. Almost all the ribbons were woven in the homes of the weavers. By the Census of 1851, at the height of the trade's strength in Coventry, 46 per cent of Coventry's total labour force were engaged in the ribbon trade.

Early in the nineteenth century, after the Napoleonic wars, the silk ribbon trade was particularly prosperous. The supply of weavers in both England and France had been depleted from the fighting. Strong demand for luxury adornments was released after being pent up during the wars. In this boom situation it became relatively easy for journeymen to buy their own looms.

As well as the trade spreading further out among the neighbouring villages conditions within the city were becoming cramped. In 1828 the building of a new suburb just outside the city wall began. The suburb was first called New Town, but later it came to be known as Hillfields. Hillfields houses were purpose-built for weavers, with specially large windows lighting workshops on the top floor. It was the first-hand journeymen who moved there (skilled weavers who owned their own looms). The houses were well built. They were

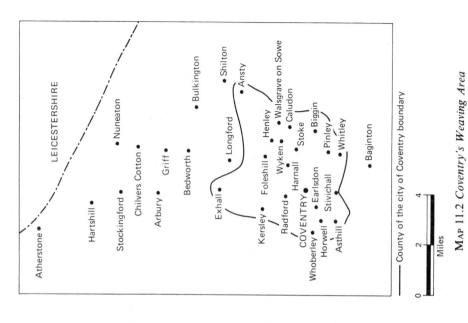

MAP 11.2 *Coventry's Weaving Area*

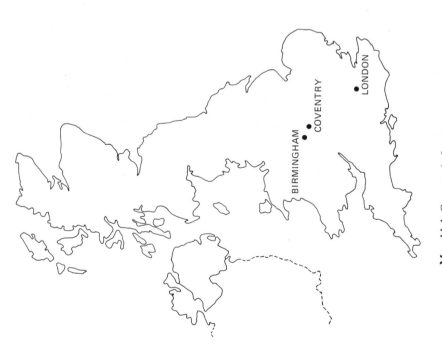

MAP 11.1 *Coventry's Location*

well lit and the air was good around them; there were gardens and allotments and a chance to see the countryside. Most of the weavers who remained in the city were journeymen's journeymen (who rented looms from masters or first-hand journeymen) or factory hands.[1] While the standard of living of those who could move to Hillfields improved, conditions for those who remained in the city centre deteriorated due to overcrowding and foul air.

The fortunes of the ribbon trade fluctuated widely. During the seasonal lull in the summer weavers were often faced with two months unemployment. Also the trade had undergone severe cycles of prosperity and depression since its establishment in Coventry. But throughout the eighteenth century and the first half of the nineteenth century, the long-run trend was upward.

The peak selling season for ribbons in the shops was the spring so that the ribbons could be worn in summer. Summer was the period when old stocks were sold and new designs were prepared for the next year. Therefore summer was often a hard time for the weavers. Being a luxury product, ribbons were sensitive both to the general state of the economy and to the vagaries of fashion.

During boom periods the ribbon weaving gradually spread to Coventry's neighbouring villages, especially among the wives of colliers in the villages to the north and north-east of the city. On Map 11.2 the extent of the ribbon weaving area by the 1830s is shown. By that time the trade extended to the Leicestershire area of stocking knitting which was also carried out at home in villages. If one trade was more brisk than the other, the frontier between the two trades would temporarily shift, but a normal frontier corresponding to the county boundary remained the equilibrium position to which the frontier always returned in 'normal' business times throughout the nineteenth century.

2 Monopoly Power

At the end of the eighteenth century there were 10 to 12 merchant manufacturers enjoying collective monopoly power in the trade. They kept warehouses in London and in Coventry and had undertakers who would collect and distribute work between the weavers and the Coventry warehouses. The capital required to set up such an operation was sufficient to ensure the monopoly position of these merchant manufacturers for two decades. But with the huge demand for ribbons which burst forth as the Napoleonic wars came to an end, wholesalers in London changed their old trade practice of buying from merchant-manufacturers' warehouses in London and came up to Coventry to deal for ribbons with the undertakers directly. The London merchants also extended five months' credit for silk and this enabled many Coventry first-hand journeyman weavers to become small masters. By 1838 there were about 117 masters in Coventry, 70 employing less than 10 looms each, 35 employing between 10 and 100 looms, and the 12 'old' masters employing over 100 looms each.[2]

Furthermore the 1,868 first-hand journeymen owned 4007 looms which were worked by themselves and members of their families, or by journeymen's journeymen (See Table 11.1).

TABLE 11.1

Social Distribution of Coventry Families in the Ribbon Weaving Trade (including Hillfields), 1838

	Number	Per cent
Manufacturers	117	3
First-hand journeymen		
of whom in business on own account	40	1
of whom working for manufacturer	1828	52
	1868	53
Journeymen's journeymen		
of whom working for first-hand journeymen	852	24
of whom working in factories	373	11
	1225	35
Factory hands	300	9
Total	3510	100

NOTE: Therefore 4 per cent worked for themselves; approximately 25 per cent employed people outside their own family; 56 per cent owned their own machines.

These 3510 families accounted for about 45 per cent of the total population of Coventry at the time (30,000 people).

A much higher proportion of Hillfields families were first-hand journeymen.

First-hand journeymen worked at home and owned their own looms, together the 1868 first-hand journeymen owned 4007 looms which were worked by members of their own families or the 852 journeymen's journeymen.

Journeymen's journeymen did not own their looms. In good times they worked for first-hand journeymen and in bad times they worked in factories.

SOURCE: Prest [1960], pp. 50–3.

There was, during the 1820s and 1830s, a considerable division of interest among the masters. The old masters wished for stability and wanted to pursue Responsible Autonomy strategies toward their Coventry weavers.[3] This was partly because of their attachment to custom and feelings of responsibility for the good order of the whole town; partly because they could afford to do so, particularly (as will be discussed in Section 5) because of the periphery which the larger masters' operations allowed in the form of the village weavers; and partly because of the collective strength of the weavers themselves. Smaller masters, on the other hand, were anxious to pay as low a price as possible for the ribbons woven for them. This meant paying rates below the 'list of prices' in Coventry, particularly during recessions. Smaller masters were also anxious to band together to build workshops and factories.

Though competition within Coventry increased significantly during the 1820s and 1830s, Coventry itself enjoyed a virtual monopoly in fancy silk ribbons. The only other town in England where a similar product was produced was Derby. But Derby masters concentrated on plain ribbons and masters in the different towns generally let each other be. Also the importation of foreign ribbons was prohibited until 1826 and remained heavily protected (25 per cent tariff) until 1846.

3 Worker Resistance

Given the strength of Coventry's monopoly power, weavers were somewhat justified in claiming that sales of ribbons depended more on fashion than on prices (i.e. the elasticity of demand for Coventry ribbons was very low and likely to be of little consequence in relation to shifts in tastes). Coventry's monopoly power was one reason for the unusually long period during which weavers' rates of earnings in Coventry were relatively immune to economic fluctuations. Weavers in Coventry were paid according to a list of prices for ribbons which was set at a level which would enable weavers to live comfortably without requiring them to go to the parish for relief. The list remained in force in Coventry until 1860, though this medieval custom of wages based on 'just' prices had disappeared for domestic weavers forty years earlier in nearby areas.[4] The other reason for the long life of the list of prices was the strength of the Coventry weavers' collective resistance to its demise.

After serving their seven-year apprenticeships Coventry's medieval tradition allowed the weavers to become freemen of the city and to vote. Also freemen held rights of pasture over lands that completely encircled the city (except for the north-east corner where Hillfields was built). To enclose these lands would have required an act of Parliament which members for Coventry would have to speak to. But none would do this because the freemen held a majority of the franchise (at least until 1868, after the Second Reform Bill of 1867).[5]

The importance of these lands was far greater than the direct benefit of pasture rights. The ring of common lands also limited the growth of the town. Weaver power could not be overcome by bringing workers (usually Irish) in from outside, as was done in Lancashire cities and elsewhere during the first half of the nineteenth century.

Bottling up the town made it easy for weavers to organise as well as hard for masters to swamp them with the large latent reserve army of labour available in England at the time. The weavers represented 45 per cent of Coventry's families in 1838. As Prest says, 'the constables could catch the individual thief, but they were powerless, at elections and at meetings of unemployed weavers, to control a riot' (1960, p. 33).

The weavers' organisation was strong. The moment a dispute arose, often concerning an individual master paying below the list of prices, a meeting of the weavers would be held in a pub. Almost always it was decided that the weavers employed by the offending master should strike. The others would contribute money to support them and to keep them off the parish relief list. Otherwise, if freemen, they would lose their voting rights. Weavers would also go round the town to collect subscriptions to support the strike. In this they were usually successful. In fact weaving masters often contributed to these strike funds because many of them considered paying below the list as dishonourable (masters paying below the list would be at an 'unfair' advantage).

Weaver resistance also meant steam power was late in coming to Coventry's workshops. No-one even attempted to set up a steam factory until 1831. The one erected in 1831 was burnt down by the weavers. Its owner was set on a donkey with his face to the tail and paraded through the streets. Meanwhile steam power was spreading among manufacturers in Derby, and they began to enter the fancy ribbon trade. Eventually, in 1837, the first permanent steam factory was built in Coventry by a syndicate of Coventry masters.

The strength of worker resistance and the privilege of relatively high earnings ended at the town boundary. The village weavers were primarily women and children (75 per cent of them), mainly the families of men who worked in the collieries to the north of Coventry or farmed the land. They could not become freemen. They had no rights of pasturage. No strong cohesive organisation was possible among the women, tied to the home and widely scattered. Each village formed a reserve army for the others, forced by poverty to take work whenever it was offered and at low prices. Coventry weavers did not support the villagers. In fact Coventry male weavers effectively kept most village weavers at a technical disadvantage by insisting that women only be allowed to work simple hand-looms.

4 Management

Until the late 1830s workshops were set up by some masters before the advantages of steam power could be tapped because of their desire for greater direct control over the weavers.[6] Weavers who worked at home were often in dispute with their employers about the embezzlement of silk and the quality of silk given out. A great advantage of the trade from the weavers' point of view was the degree of direct control which they exercised over their hours and pace of work. The silk was given out and the ribbons collected on Saturdays. The weavers then worked towards completing a certain number of ribbons by the end of the week. They often took Mondays and sometimes Tuesdays off and then worked very long hours towards the end of the week to make up their quotas. Other workers, such as brickmakers and colliers in the villages, were envious of the weavers' relative freedom. In 1838 they said to the Commissioner, 'it was very hard on them to be turned out at early hours every day, instead of being able to take what hours they please, like the ribbon weaver: and like him, take *Saint* Monday and *Saint* Tuesday too, if they choose' (Reports Commissioners [1840], pp. 301–2).

With steam the economic advantages of the factory, where looms could be powered cheaply from a central source, became even more compelling. During the 1840s and 1850s more and larger steam run factories were built. In 1859 there were 15 large factories with 1250 power looms in Coventry.

The first-hand journeymen of Hillfields looked down upon the factory hands in the city centre. Besides having much more freedom in their hours and work pace, and living in a much more pleasant area, their earnings were higher. While the first-hand journeyman in Hillfields working on his own account could average 15 shillings and sixpence a week, factory hands at the highest paying factories in Coventry averaged 13 shillings a week up to the 1850s.

Eventually, with steam and experience, factories became more efficient and factory hands' wages rose. They therefore became less dependent on the list of prices for their standard of living, while weavers working at home became more and more dependent on the list. This was exacerbated because home weavers worked with less efficient equipment. The majority had no steam power and many were using older design looms. Several of the simplest, 'single-hand' looms were still in use in Coventry in 1838. At that time there were also 3504 Dutch engine looms (introduced around 1770) in use, but only 1678 of the latest (introduced after 1795) Jacquard looms (Reports Commissioners [1840], p. 67). The smaller masters in particular began squeezing their domestic workers by paying below the list of prices and by employing women on the Dutch engine loom. Previously this had been confined to men at the weavers' insistence.

Nevertheless the speed with which Coventry's domestic weavers were pressed into workshops and factories, with which steam power was introduced, with which women were brought onto the more advanced machinery, with which the list of prices was challenged, and with which Coventry weavers were left with no work when trade was slack; all these marks of rising direct control were slowed down in Coventry because masters were able to cut costs, by paying village weavers less and by reducing work given out to villagers first when trade was slack. (Direct Control strategies were also slowed down by the strength of Coventry masters' collective monopoly power and the strength of Coventry weavers' resistance.)

5   Centre–Periphery Pattern

Most factory owners also gave out work to Coventry and village domestic weavers, and masters who had no factories gave out work to both Coventry and village weavers. A clear centre–periphery pattern had been long established between the two groups of domestic weavers. Because silk ribbon weaving was a simple process, the centre–periphery pattern existed within firms, rather than between firms. Firms competed for the same market rather than supplying different parts of a complex process.

As Fay emphasised (1920, p. 176), weavers in the countryside were treated like marginal land in the theories of classical economists.

The area of weaver employment around Coventry expanded and contracted according to the demand for silk ribbons, protecting Hillfields and Coventry at the centre, just as the area of land cultivation expanded and contracted at the margin according to demand.

As emphasised above, the fortunes of the silk ribbon trade as a whole fluctuated widely – both seasonally and with longer period trade cycles. In such conditions it was essential for masters to be able to draw on nearby labour when times were good and to be able to shed labour easily when times were bad. This required laying off many workers at times, but it was also advantageous to the master to lay off workers in step with sales losses and therefore to have several lay off times with only a few workers going each time. Thus it was essential to be able to lay off workers often and in small numbers without disrupting the work which continued. Workers who were least well organised, workers who were working in isolated and parallel processes, that is processes which were not integrated with the rest of the work such as weavers working in the villages, were the first to go. Their earnings were also lower than the rest.

The following rough guide for evaluating standards of living of artisans was commonly used in the nineteenth century: 'If an artisan could afford no bacon, he was badly off. If he could afford bacon, but no meat, then he was doing middling well. If he could afford butcher's meat, and had a clock in the house, then he was very well off indeed' (Prest [1960], p. 75).

According to Prest, during the first half of the nineteenth century Coventry's first-hand journeyman weavers (concentrated in Hillfields from the 1830s), enjoyed life in the third category – very well off indeed. Table 11.1 shows the social distribution of Coventry families in the ribbon weaving trade. In 1838, 56 per cent of Coventry families in the trade were at least 'very well off indeed'. Journeymen's journeymen and factory hands in Coventry were in the second category – doing middling well. But weavers in the villages were badly off; worse, they were often starving. Earnings in the countryside were lower than in Coventry both because prices were lower and because of lower output per loom. Of the village weavers, 75 per cent were women and children and therefore barred by custom from working the more efficient, newer sorts of looms. Village weavers had no list of prices. Journeymen's journeymen in the countryside were getting slightly more than *half* the earnings of journeymen's journeymen in Coventry per week. They worked fewer weeks in the year as well.

A high proportion of the children in the countryside were set to work at early ages for miserably low wages to supplement the family earnings. Children began working at eight to ten years of age. They usually earned only about one shilling a week, (compared with five shillings per week for adult country journeymen). In Coventry children often attended dame or charity school for a year of two before starting work.

The pattern in Coventry's region was slightly more complicated than this simple centre–periphery structure. Some journeymen in Bedworth and Nuneaton (see Map 11.2) were organised under masters independent from Coventry masters. Also these two small towns represented secondary centres with parts of their neighbouring countryside containing weavers subordinate to masters in the two towns. The Commissioners to the Commission on Unemployed Handloom Weavers (1840), thought the villages of Hartshill and Chilvers Coton to be subordinate to Nuneaton, and Bulkington was thought to be subordinate to Bedworth (pp. 30, 51).

While Coventry represented the main centre of the area, these other two towns represented mini-centres with their own peripheries, though they, in turn, were part of the Coventry periphery.

The centre–periphery relation was crucial for understanding the condition of the outlying villages. Prest states,

These villages were an essential, but the least regarded part of the weaving trade. They were given work only when the city had more orders than it could manage, and they were the first to be laid off when there was a recession. Last in, first out, they lived in almost complete subjection to the city which exploited them, and kept them permanently on the margin of employment (1960, p. 45).[7]

6 Shift in the Centre of the Silk Ribbon Trade

During the 1840s and 1850s weavers' struggles to maintain the list of prices became more acrimonious and more protracted. Meanwhile factory hands' wages rose as new and more efficient factories were built. Between 1853 and 1858 weekly wages in the factories rose from 12 or 13 shillings to 17 to 19 shillings (Prest [1960], p. 113). From 1847 some home weavers tried to keep up with the factories by converting their houses to working by power and by having new Hillfields houses built with steam power in mind. They built steam-engines at the ends of rows of weavers' houses and passed a steam shaft through the whole top floor of the terraced row of houses. By the late 1850s these *cottage factories* represented a serious alternative to the factory. In 1859 there were about 1000 power looms in 300 cottage factories in Coventry along with the 1250 power looms in Coventry's 15 large factories (Reports Commissioners [1860], p. 452). Although this response to the factory challenge by the weavers was valiant, they could not keep up with the increasingly more efficient and larger factories. Nevertheless by 1859 most of Coventry's weaving was still carried out in small and relatively inefficient units compared with silk ribbon weaving elsewhere.

The prohibition on imported silk ribbons was lifted in 1826 and a 25 per cent tariff imposed. After a slack period when the French and Swiss captured a large share of the English market for fancy ribbons, the Coventry trade recovered. In 1846 the protective duties were reduced by Peel to 15 per cent and once again Coventry weavers quickly recovered from the blow. From the 1830s factory work spread much more quickly in other silk weaving areas than in Coventry. In 1860 the Cobden Treaty was concluded under Gladstone's Chancellorship, allowing French ribbons into England free of duty while English ribbons were still to be taxed entering France. This time Coventry weavers did not recover from the increased competition.

By April 1860 unemployment was already widespread among Coventry weavers. Three months later the manufacturers decided to overthrow the list of prices for good. The weavers responded with a general strike which stopped every loom in Coventry. The strike lasted six months. At its end the list was broken. So was the Coventry weaving industry. The weavers lost the strike, but both weavers and employers lost out.

In the city it was the Hillfields weavers who suffered the most. The relative inefficiency of home workers and Hillfields cottage factories could be tolerated while the trade was booming and demand was high. They were the first to go during the depression. The cottage factories in Hillfields were more efficient than home workers without power, but in spite of using steam and more up-to-date looms, they could not take full advantage of the economies to be had from centrally organised factories. Cottage factories were, for the most part, identical processes carried out side by side in the top floors or top shops of each of the cottages in a terrace.

Weavers had to do more than simply weave the silk. They had to prepare it. They had to wind it around a drum to get even tension. They had to fit the warps to the loom, that is, the threads which formed the length of the ribbon. And they had to 'fill the quills', that is, fill the shuttle which was passed backward and forward between the lengthwise warps on the loom to weave the cross strands of silk into the lengthwise threads. In the cottage factories, as in ordinary domestic weavers' workshops, these preparatory tasks were carried out by the weaver or by women and children on a casual basis. In the factories these jobs were separated more clearly, allowing for the development of greater dexterity in each.

Some additional constraint was placed on the weavers' time in the cottage factory because the steam being used for one loom was generated for all, and the weaver whose loom remained idle while the others worked still had to pay rent for his share of the steam. But the custom of taking Saint Monday off and working long hours toward the end of the week remained as the custom was widespread and it was therefore easy for all the weavers in the terrace to take off time at the same time. The resulting uneven pace of work meant uneven quality in the ribbon woven as well as some ruined ribbons woven on Friday nights. The close supervision of the factory, where steam power running times and pace were controlled by the employers and not by the weavers, meant more ribbons per weaver on average throughout the week. Finally, the larger factories allowed transport costs to be cut significantly.

The cottage factory combined much of the relative inefficiency of domestic work with some of the relative inflexibility of the large factory. When the steam power was on, the full cost-saving advantages of power could be captured only when all the looms in the block of cottages were running. When some weavers in the block were out of work and the rest were working, they all had to pay rent for the steam which turned the shafting in all their workshops. From the recession beginning in 1860, with many of the weavers in cottage factories often out of work, many of the cottage factories reverted to hand power. In March 1861 the factory inspector noted that well over one-sixth of Coventry's 383 cottage factories (situated mainly in Hillfields), had reverted to hand power. The looms were then turned by young boys often working very long hours on a Friday.

In the 1860s and 1870s the entire Coventry region was in a wretched state. Besides the Cobden Treaty with the French, the Americans introduced the Morrell tariff during the Civil War, destroying that market for British silk. Also fashion in decoration for ladies' dress began to change from ribbons to feathers. Hillfields' first-hand journeymen, once proud and prosperous, now sold their furniture and pawned their Sunday clothes. Many went out to the commons each day to work for sixpence and a loaf of bread. A national fund was set up to relieve Coventry in 1860 and 1861 to which the Queen subscribed. But as time went on and the trade remained depressed the weavers began the long process of adjustment to declining industry. Besides reverting to hand power, many of the cottage factories were converted into proper factories by knocking down the partition walls and introducing factory hours and supervision. Others were closed down. The Hillfields weavers who remained in work had to journey into the city centre, into the despised factories, joining the factory hands whom they had looked down upon in years past. The trade rationalised into fewer, larger and more efficient units.

Gradually the weavers began to leave the trade and to leave Coventry altogether. They began to apprentice their sons to watch-makers. Between 1861 and 1871 the proportion of Coventry's labour force in the silk trade fell from 46 per cent to 34 per cent, by 1891 the figure was only 14 per cent and in

1901, less than 10 per cent (Census of Population). The population of Coventry fell from 41,546 in 1861 to 39,991 in 1871, a decline of almost 4 per cent at a time when the populations of other Midlands towns were growing very quickly. Between 1861 and 1871 the population of Birmingham increased by 16 per cent, Leicester's population increased by 40 per cent and Leamington's increased by 20 per cent.

While the Hillfields weavers suffered more than other weavers in the city, weavers in the neighbouring villages suffered more than Hillfields' journeymen. At least for Hillfields' weavers there were nearby factories and a few other trades to turn to. The village weavers had nothing. The population of Foleshill fell by 18 per cent between 1861 and 1871. Stoke's population fell by 20 per cent, Sowe's by 16 per cent, Exhall's by 6 per cent, Bedworth's by 9 per cent and in the Nuneaton area the population fell by 5 per cent.[8] While the centre of the weaving trade within the area had shifted from Hillfields to the factories, in fact the whole area had become peripheral to the European trade. Differences within the region drastically paled in significance compared with this shift.

For the next twenty to thirty years Coventry's population stagnated. Then, with the bicycle industry during the late 1880s and 90s, and later the car industry, people began moving into Coventry and Hillfields. But now the people who came to Hillfields were not the most skilled. The people already living in Hillfields had inappropriate skills for the new industries. Engineering skills were needed for most Coventry industries after the 1880s. The main exception was the move to Coventry by Courtaulds in 1905. But Courtaulds came to Coventry primarily because of the plentiful supply of unemployed women available in Hillfields and the northern villages (Allen, [1929], p. 312). The skills required in making artificial silk are very different from weaving skills. It was the lack of competition for these female workers (and therefore the relatively low wages which they could be paid) rather than their skills which attracted Courtaulds to Coventry some forty years after the ribbon weaving industry began its dramatic decline. In Chapter 16 the development of Hillfields and Coventry will be continued from the end of the nineteenth century to the 1970s.

CHAPTER TWELVE

The Hosiery Industry in Leicester in the Late Nineteenth Century

1 Leicester and Coventry during the Nineteenth Century

Like Coventry, Leicester was the centre of a thriving industry during the eighteenth and nineteenth centuries. But the difference in conditions between Leicester's domestic hosiery knitters and those of the surrounding villages, while noticeable, was not nearly so great as the difference in conditions between weavers in Coventry and its surrounding villages. This was due to the relatively poor conditions of knitters in Leicester rather than prosperity in Leicestershire villages.

There were several reasons for this. First, Leicester was not hemmed in by a belt of common lands and this allowed the supply of labour power to increase quickly to meet rising demand for workers. Second, the villages surrounding Leicester were more heavily populated with people who had little alternative employment prospects. Thus villagers acted as a strong reserve army pressing on Leicester labour power markets, either directly, through migration into Leicester, or indirectly, as a pool of cheap workers to whom work was taken by subcontractors and factory owners in order to escape relatively high wages or better working conditions won by workers in Leicester. Also the normal size of firms remained very small in the hosiery industry. This hampered the organisation of worker resistance.

As in ribbon weaving, the distinction between town and countryside weavers roughly coincided with a distinction between male and female workers. During the second half of the nineteenth century average wages were held down when demand was high and when real wages were rising in the country at large, by the progressive replacement of men by women in the hosiery industry. Often this was achieved by shifting location to where women were traditionally more readily available and men more poorly organised.

The vast majority of hosiery workers never attained a position of centrality within the industry during the nineteenth century. By 1906 19 per cent of men employed in hosiery factories would have been earning enough to put them into the group which Hobsbawm calls labour aristocrats (earning 40 shillings or more a week – 33 per cent of the men were earning twenty-five shillings and less). While this proportion of males as labour aristocrats was quite high compared with other industries listed by Hobsbawm (ninth out of 24 listed; [1964], p. 286), the 19 per cent of men represented less than 5 per cent of all 51,000 hosiery factory workers (1907 Census). Hobsbawm estimates those to be earning forty shillings and over to account for about 15 per cent of all workers in the country. Considering the 25,000 female outworkers and another 1000 male outworkers working for hosiery firms in 1907 (Wells [1935], p. 191) who were certainly earning less than forty shillings a week, only about 3 per cent of all hosiery workers were 'labour aristocrats'.

Also in many factories as late as the 1890s workers had to bribe employers in order to get work, hours of work often exceeded legal limits, factory and workshop conditions were extremely unsanitary and unsafe, and in the villages around Leicester trade unionism was actively suppressed (Royal Commission [1892], pp. 46–83).

A combination of highly competitive conditions facing Leicester firms in product markets, plus highly competitive conditions facing Leicester workers in labour power markets, contributed to the prevalence of direct control strategies pursued in the hosiery trade in Leicester and the surrounding villages throughout the nineteenth century (except for a brief period from the mid-1860s to the mid-1880s). The main difference between prosperous and stagnant product demand was in numbers of workers employed rather than in average wages and working conditions.

2 Historical Background to the Hosiery Trade

The history of the British hosiery trade properly begins with the invention of the knitting-frame in 1589. Though the frame was invented near Nottingham, the framework knitting trade was based mainly in London during the seventeenth century.[1] Knitted stockings were luxury products made of silk. Proximity to the main market in London was important because fashions changed quickly and because the supply of raw silk came to London first.

The London Company of Framework Knitters was incorporated and chartered as a proper guild in 1657. To ensure 'proper' prices for stockingers' work, the company tried to prevent the export of frames and to restrict the numbers of apprentices to two or three. The company failed at both endeavours. Frames made their way to the Continent, particularly to France, and later to Germany, and masters evaded the apprenticeship limitation by moving out of London. Most moved to Leicestershire, Nottinghamshire, or Derbyshire.[2] They moved there for two reasons. Knitted stockings made from wool or cotton for non-aristocrats were becoming more popular and the East Midlands was a major wool producing area. But the most important reason was the plentiful supply of workers who had no alternative employment after agriculture, (Nelson [1930], p. 469; Wells [1935], p. 54).

Thus from the earliest years hosiery masters in the East Midlands pursued harsh strategies towards their workers in order to retain the price advantage to be had from relatively cheap labour power (rather than from better machines or greater division of labour). Masters employed as many as fifty apprentices who, when they came of age, were discharged to make room for younger charges. The displaced journeymen wandered about seeking work. They often accepted prices below the customary amount and this generally drove earnings down. The company tried to enforce its rules in the East Midlands, but the wide area over which hosiery knitting was pursued made negotiation through deputies from London impossible. Evasion of the company also

MAP 12.1 Distribution of the Hosiery Industry in Great Britain, 1844

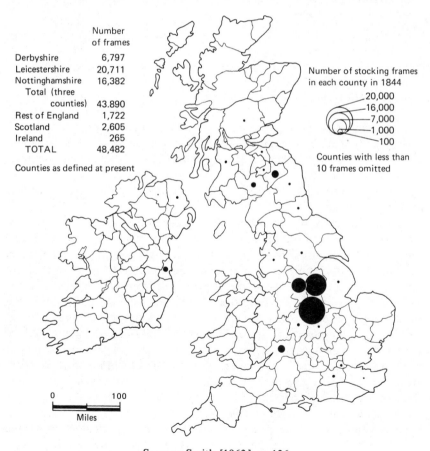

	Number of frames
Derbyshire	6,797
Leicestershire	20,711
Nottinghamshire	16,382
Total (three counties)	43.890
Rest of England	1,722
Scotland	2,605
Ireland	265
TOTAL	48,482

Counties as defined at present

Number of stocking frames in each county in 1844

20,000
16,000
7,000
1,000
100

Counties with less than 10 frames omitted

0   100
Miles

SOURCE: Smith [1963], p. 126.

encouraged dispersal of hosiery knitting within the Midland counties. The two major centres, Leicester and Nottingham, employed only 900 frames in 1727 out of 4650 in the three counties.

By the end of the eighteenth century the movement to the East Midlands from London had been completed. The distribution of frames in England by 1812 is shown in Table 12.1.[3]

TABLE 12.1

Distribution of Knitting-frames in England, 1812

Place	No. of frames	
London	20	
Suburbs of London	137	
Leicestershire	11,233	
Of which in Leicester		1,650
Nottinghamshire	9,285	
Of which in Nottingham		2,600
Derbyshire	4,800	
Of which in Derby		500
Elsewhere in England	4,107	
Total	29,582	

SOURCE: Nelson [1930], p. 470.

Notice that the Leicestershire hosiery trade was not heavily concentrated in Leicester. In fact there were less frames per head in Leicester than in Leicestershire. Leicester had only 14.7 per cent of the frames in Leicestershire, while Leicester's population in 1811 was 23,453, representing 15.6 per cent of that of all Leicestershire (see Map 12.2 for the distribution of frames within the East Midlands in 1844).

The manufacture of hosiery was somewhat more complex than that of ribbons. In Leicester and the larger Leicestershire villages such as Hinckley and Loughborough master hosiers often put out only single processes to stockingers' (journeymen's) homes; one would only do legs, another tops, another feet. The materials would be given out from a warehouse and the stockingers would return the finished articles to that warehouse. There the hosier would inspect the work and pay the stockingers. The master-hosier would often have a room in his warehouse in which women would be employed on seaming and other finishing operations, or he would also put out this work. In addition there were preparatory tasks for framework knitting, such as winding the yarn and keeping the shuttles filled, which were usually done by stockingers' children.

As well as putting out materials, master-hosiers also put out frames and charged frame-rent. The practice of frame renting began early in the seventeenth century, but spread very quickly during the eighteenth century.

MAP 12.2 Distribution of the Hosiery Industry in the East Midlands, 1844

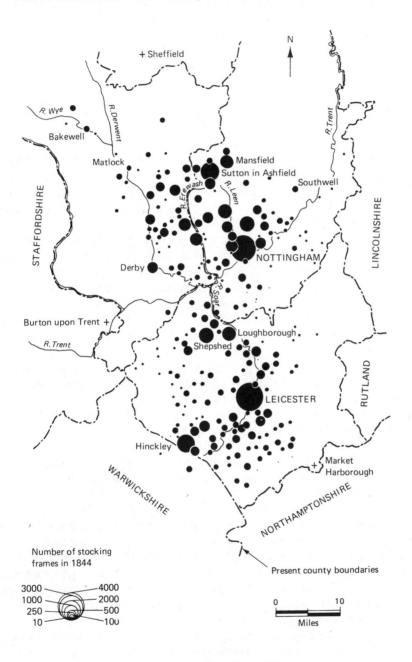

SOURCE: Smith [1963], p. 130.

By the end of the century it was rare for a stockinger to own his own frame (Wells [1935], pp. 74–5). As late as 1835 60 per cent of Coventry journeymen weavers owned their own looms (see Table 11.1). The growth of frame renting in part reflected the increasing poverty of the stockingers. It also reflected the preference of hosiers for putting out work to those stockingers to whom they rented frames rather than to independent stockingers.[4] Frame-rents often had to be paid whether stockingers were working for the master who supplied the frame or not.[5] This secured a steady return for the hosiers in spite of wide fluctuations in product demand, and in consequence threw the burden of some overhead costs during periods of slack demand onto the stockingers.

Frame-rents did not fall in the late eighteenth century in spite of the declining cost of producing frames and the wide availability of second-hand frames.[6] It appears that rents actually rose between 1780 and 1840. To some hosiers the profit from the hire of frames was greater than that from the hosiery itself (Wells [1935], p. 28), and many capitalists invested in frame letting on its own.

This contributed to the extreme wretchedness of stockingers when trade stagnated from 1819 to 1850. The Commissioner on Framework Knitters reported the extremely depressing state of stockingers in 1845. For example, 'in Hinckley demoralisation is fearfully extending itself; hunger and distress are fast destroying all honesty in one sex and all chastity and decency in the other' (1845, p. 54), or, one can always tell stockingers by their appearance; 'there is a paleness and a certain degree of emaciation and thinness about them' (1845, p. 108).

Miserable as conditions were during the first half of the nineteenth century for stockingers in the large towns of the East Midlands, conditions in the surrounding villages were still worse.

In these villages the hosiery industry depended largely upon a middleman called 'bagman' or 'bag-hosier'. Originally an independent journeyman who carried his finished work to town in a large canvas bag slung over his shoulder, he had become a middleman between other village stockingers and town hosiers. The bagman lived on the difference in price paid to village and country stockingers for their work compared with those in town. The scattered location of those working for the bagman and their ignorance of town rates made them easy prey for price cutting by bagmen.[7] Also the payment of frame-rent to town hosiers was made through the bagmen who sublet frames to villagers at a higher rent than that paid to the actual frame owner. During the depressed first half of the nineteenth century bagmen were hard pressed for cash and had to go into debt to the hosiers for frames and materials. This encouraged the bagman to pay his stockingers in truck (in food or supplies). Truck provided yet another technical means whereby village stockingers were oppressed because the bagman controlled the prices of provisions (see Map 12.3 for the village areas to which work was put out from each East Midland centre).

Map 12.3 Organisation of the Domestic System in the East Midlands Hosiery Industry, 1844

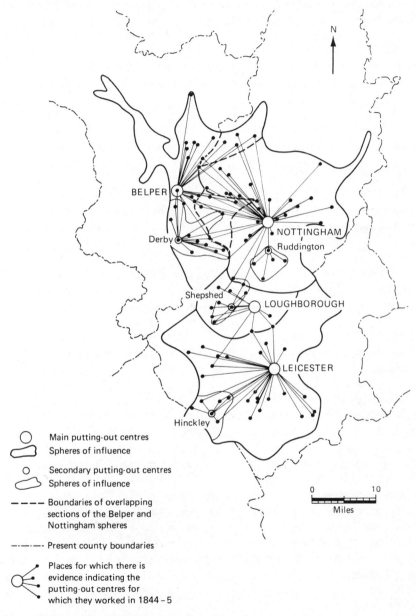

Main putting-out centres
Spheres of influence

Secondary putting-out centres
Spheres of influence

— — — — Boundaries of overlapping sections of the Belper and Nottingham spheres

—·—·— Present county boundaries

Places for which there is evidence indicating the putting-out centres for which they worked in 1844 – 5

NOTE: For the sake of clarity, a number of less important places putting out work locally have been omitted.

SOURCE: Smith [1963], pp. 134–5.

The application of power to framework knitting was slow in coming. In part this reflected the greater complexity of knitting machines compared with those for spinning or weaving. In part it reflected the steady, relatively certain return to be had from renting hand machines compared with the large capital investment required to set up a factory and the uncertainty of adequate profits.[8] In part it reflected the resistance of the stockingers to workshop discipline. The 'main obstacle to change, however, was still to be found in the conditions of the labour market, where supplies remained plentiful and cheap.' (Wells [1935], p. 146).

The feasibility of factories had been demonstrated in the 1840s, but hardly any had been set up until the 1860s and 1870s. During the 1860s factory production was still limited to the main towns – Leicester, Nottingham, Belper, Loughborough and Hinckley. In 1862, out of about 120,000 employed in the industry, only 4063 came under the Factory Acts, (Wells [1935], p. 179). Instead competition from the few factories encouraged the setting up of workshops to gain greater productivity through increased discipline. In spite of the Workshops Act of 1867, which limited child employment and hours of work and prohibited some of the most unsanitary conditions, conditions remained poor because it was much more difficult to enforce the Workshops Act. Workshops were very small and located in backstreets and alleys of towns or in the out-of-the-way villages. The inspectorate was hardly adequate to cope with the factories; the workshops were impossible.

It was only in the 1870s that factory production expanded quickly. The Education Act of 1870 made provision for elementary education and the Act of 1876 made school attendance compulsory between the ages of five and fourteen. This was a tremendous blow to domestic work, which relied on the work of the entire family to remain competitive. In 1851, according to the Census, about 13 per cent of hosiery workers were under fifteen years of age, by 1881 only five per cent were under fifteen. Because the Census appears to have seriously underestimated those employed in the hosiery trade for the early years, particularly by missing many part-time workers, the proportion of children working in the industry in 1851 was probably much more than 13 per cent (Wells [1935], p. 157).

Mechanisation was also encouraged from the 1870s by the growing shortage of cheap adult labour power. This was due to a combination of tremendous growth in hosiery demand, stimulated by the general prosperity of the Modern Industry period in Britain, and the competing demand for labour power from the boot and shoe industry. This industry was originally attracted to Leicestershire because of plentiful cheap labour power in the 1850s, and it grew tremendously in the area throughout the second half of the nineteenth century.[9]

Also the Truck Act of 1874 made frame-rent and other fixed charges, deductions, and commissions illegal as well as truck. While the system continued surreptitiously, the act did eventually mean the disappearance of the small bagman.

The 1860s and early 1870s were very prosperous for hosiers as well as for hosiery workers, particularly those in the factories. But in the 1880s and particularly the 1890s a falling-off of exports due to growing German competition and the American McKinley Tariff (1891) brought hardship once again to hosiery workers. In the following sections I will examine the hosiery industry in Leicester, primarily during the last quarter of the nineteenth century.

3 Monopoly Power

The hosiery industry throughout its history had been highly competitive and in the last quarter of the nineteenth century competition intensified yet further. The capital required for setting up factories fell after the first wave of innovation in the third quarter of the century, largely because of the increasing practice of letting out factory rooms with power supplies. Some entered the trade after purchasing machinery at bankrupts' auctions and others brought machinery on credit from local machine builders.[10] Small manufacturers increasingly set up factories in the smaller towns and villages, often renting space in a larger manufacturer's building. They increasingly took over the old bagman's role and many bagmen became small manufacturers. By taking advantage of poorly organised workers and often employing members of their own family, they improved their competitive position. The division of labour remained relatively primitive in the hosiery trade (with only the half-dozen or so different tasks outlined in the previous section), allowing these firms to survive, at least in prosperous times, in spite of their use of less up-to-date machinery. Also the small manufacturer was sustained by spinners allowing manufacturers credit or yarn until nine months after delivery. The spinner made up the cost of this long credit in the price of yarn. This made sense for the spinner, who faced a higher elasticity of demand with respect to credit rather than price of yarn because small manufacturers (and shopkeepers, who were also given long credit) were tempted to place larger orders than they could handle (Wells [1935], p. 173). As a result bankruptcies among small firms, even during short-lived recessions, were common.

Besides high competition within Leicester and between Leicester and other Leicestershire areas, Leicester hosiers competed with hosiers in Nottinghamshire and Derbyshire (as well as with some in Scotland). Generally each Midland county concentrated on hosiery of different materials, Leicestershire, wool and worsted; Nottinghamshire, cotton; and Derbyshire, silk. But these divisions were never rigid and strong German competition in the cottons caused most of Nottingham's hosiers to switch to woollens between 1891 and 1895.

Foreign competition had always been a major problem for hosiers. The bad years between the end of the Napoleonic wars and 1850 were marked by a drastic fall in exports.[11] In the 1880s and 1890s strong competition both in export markets and at home came from German hosiers in particular.

Finally, there was one other major group of producers with whom Leicester's hosiers competed: the consumers themselves. Wool stockings were commonly knitted by hand from wool spun at home at the beginning of the nineteenth century. During the nineteenth century, when poorer families were pressed, some money could easily be saved by knitting many clothes at home from pre-spun wool or from wool spun at home. Stockings were the easiest and therefore the most common item to be knitted at home.

The hosiery industry was subject to wide fluctuations of demand when fashions changed, when military requirements changed and during general national fluctuations in prosperity.

In these conditions of strong competition and widely fluctuating demand, exit from the industry was common. According to Wells, between 1863 and 1891 out of 105 firms which had begun in the hosiery trade 27 had been declared bankrupt, 27 simply closed down, 13 had transferred their business and about 21 there was no information. Only 17 were still in business (1935, p. 176).

4 Worker Resistance

Traditionally worker resistance had been weak in Leicester. Hosiers moved to the East Midlands largely to escape the Company of Framework Knitters, which allowed traditional protection of craftsmen to stockingers in London. While an agreed list of prices had been established in Leicester, it never worked as well as the list in Coventry. After 1807 it was largely abandoned by hosiers who then bargained individual stockingers down to as low a price as they thought they could get.

During a recession in the 1770s stockingers formed an Association of Framework Knitters to petition Parliament to fix wages at the current level. Parliament rejected the plea in 1779. This resulted in widespread rioting (primarily in Nottingham), which was put down by the military and the association was destroyed. Later attempts at organisation in the first decades of the nineteenth century (the Luddites), while successful at first, also ended in crushing defeat for the stockingers. The main obstacle to stable organisations for worker resistance in the early nineteenth century, as in the late nineteenth century, was the difficulty of organising workers who were so widely scattered. Besides sprawling over the three Midland counties, the majority of stockingers within Leicestershire never lived in Leicester (see Maps 12.2 and 12.4 and Table 12.2).

MAP 12.4 Leicestershire – Bag-hosiers and Hosiery Manufacturers, 1851–1900. Hosiery Firms, 1932

SOURCE: Parker [1955], p. 17.

The other problem was the abundance of workers who had little alternative means of employment. As long as some work was available people were unwilling to move out of their villages. Along with the oversupply of journeymen due to the system of over-employing apprentices in the early

TABLE 12.2

Number of People Returned as Occupied in Hosiery Manufacture, Leicester and Leicestershire, 1851–1901

	1851		1861		1871		1881		1891		1901	
	Male	Female	Male	Female	Male	Female	Male	Female	Male	Female	Male	Female
Leicester	5,758	2,891	4,153	2,449	3,037	1,886	3,391	5,308	4,286	8,381	3,282	9,107
Leicestershire minus Leicester	11,002	10,723	7,714	8,449	5,890	5,022	6,013	8,913	5,212	7,685	4,239	9,230
Leicester as a percentage of all Leicestershire	34.4	21.2	35.0	22.5	34.0	27.3	36.1	37.3	45.1	52.2	43.6	47.1

NOTE: 1851, 1861, 1881 all ages; 1871 only those 20 years of age and over; 1891, 1901 ages 10 and over.
SOURCE: Censuses of Population.

years, the system of frame-rents encouraged bagmen and master hosiers to distribute frames as widely as possible, ensuring only that each stockinger got enough work to be able to pay his or her frame-rent. In spite of the possibility of higher wages and shorter hours in town factories during the 1850s, 1860s and 1870s, most stockingers preferred the greater direct control they had when working in their own homes and the social benefits of remaining in the villages where they were born. (As early as 1845 a wage differential of two to three shillings a week was established between factory hands and domestic workers; Ashworth [1958], p. 311).

From the late 1850s, with increasing demand for hosiery due to rapidly rising real wages in Britain, and with the rapid growth of the boot and shoe industry in Leicestershire, the traditionally abundant cheap labour power available in Leicester and its region dried up. Trade union activity grew, especially in the new factories. For a very brief period, from the late 1850s to the early 1860s, the industry was marked by widespread and often successful strikes. Major improvements were won, particularly in factory wages and conditions.[12] Frame-rents were reduced for domestic and workshop workers and they were nearly abolished from factories well before the 1874 Truck Act (Church [1966], p. 260). Wages continued to rise during the prosperous 1860s and early 1870s, though rises generally were far greater for men than for women. In Leicester a man and a woman working two power frames between them would earn 12s (shillings) to 15s and 9s a week respectively in 1862 (Wells, [1935], p. 148). By 1890 men were getting 25s 4d (pence) a week on average (though with wide variations – 15s to 35s – depending on the sorts of work and the sophistication of the machines they used). 'In nearly all cases women's earnings were less than half those of the men' (Wells [1935], pp. 198–9). Average wages for women were 11s 6d, while average wages for boys were 9s 6d and for girls 8s 3d (average weekly wages for a sample between 1886 and 1891; Ashworth [1958], p. 311).

The years of prosperity during the 1860s and 1870s did not leave Leicester hosiery-workers with strong trade unions. While wages and conditions improved, much of the edge was taken off worker resistance by the Board of Conciliation and Arbitration set up in Leicester in 1866.[13] During the late 1860s and early 1870s the board's influence was strong because employers were willing to make concessions. By the late 1870s and early 1880s, with increasing competition from Germany, concessions from employers were no longer forthcoming. Also the workers themselves were severely divided. Therefore the board, intended for orderly negotiation between two united but opposing groups, was hardly used after the mid-1870s. In 1884 the board ceased to operate.

Divisions among the workers were always a severe limitation to organised worker resistance in Leicestershire. These divisions were exacerbated during the stagnant last quarter of the nineteenth century when employers would play off one group against the other. The main divisions were between town and countryside workers, between men and women, and between factory workers and outworkers. These divisions generally overlapped; a high proportion of outwork was carried out by women in the small villages.

In 1885 the Leicester and Leicestershire Amalgamated Hosiery Union (L.L.A.H.U.) was established. Its membership grew slowly until 1893 and then fell off seriously. At its peak in 1893 it claimed only 3860 members. The old divisions soon reasserted themselves. In 1890 a separate Women's Hosiery Union was established, though its peak membership during the 1890s was a mere 300 in 1894 (Board of Trade [1900], pp. 58, 59, 132, 133). Representatives of the Midland Counties' Hosiery Federation[14] complained to the Commission on Labour in 1892 about married women accepting wage reductions in the factories.

In the entire Midlands Federation there were only about 4500 members in 1892 out of at least 30,000 people employed throughout the districts. Only 1500 of these were women, though women outnumbered men in factories by about three to one by this time (Royal Commission [1892], p. 63; and Census [1891]). While it was generally agreed that getting women to join trade unions was difficult, a representative of the Nottingham and Derby Union admitted to the commissioners in 1892 that little attempt had been made by their union to organise women (p. 66). This undoubtedly contributed to the formation of the Women's Hosiery Union in 1890. Women remained largely unorganised. In 1934, while almost 40 per cent of adult men in the hosiery industry belonged to trade unions, only 20 per cent of adult women belonged. In the 1930s women outnumbered men in the hosiery industry by about four to one, (Wells [1935], pp. 231, 239–40).

The strength of trade unionism was also very uneven between larger centres and their surrounding districts. This was not simply because of the greater prevalence of domestic workers and workshops in the villages, because from the mid-1870s top managers set up new factories in the villages and often moved factories from cities to villages in order to take advantage of their lower wages and the absence of trade unions (Wells [1975], p. 195). The relative weakness of worker resistance in the villages was due to the higher proportion of women employed in them, higher general levels of unemployment due to the lack of alternative employment, smaller size of factories set up there and the animosity of trade unionists in the towns. Outside Nottingham and Leicester unions were still fighting for recognition in the 1880s and 1890s. Employers were still able to choose not to employ any trade unionists in villages in 1892 (Royal Commission [1892], pp. 89–101).

One of the difficulties unions faced in their half-hearted attempts at securing standard rates for women, (in order to stop the movement of work away from men and the cities), was the competition from domestic workers. These women, often married and tied to the home with children to look after, were willing to accept extremely low wages (Wells, [1935] p. 194). In 1866, in the whole country there were an estimated 100,000 domestic menders, seamers, winders, cutters, finishers and makers-up and about 50,000 frameworkers in the hosiery industry. Only about 5000 of these were employed in factories. By 1907 there were still 25,000 women outworkers along with 51,000 men and women in factories (women outnumbered men in the factories by three to one). There were also about 1000 old men making army pants on hand frames (Wells [1935], pp. 187, 189, 191).

Thus worker resistance among Leicester workers, while stronger than that in the surrounding areas, was weak and poorly organised relative to other industries during the last quarter of the nineteenth century.

5 Management

While geographic, sexual and technical divisions among workers weakened their resistance, animosity between groups of workers was actively fostered by the manufacturers. The story of managerial strategy within the East Midlands hosiery industry was from the outset one of active search for cheap and easily coerced workers. This was carried out either directly, through increasing direct control over workers (by the system of frame-rents and other deductions, truck payments, setting up workshops and using these levers to force wage deductions and faster work pace), or indirectly by moving to areas where direct control could be managed more easily (the move to the East Midlands in the first place to escape the Company of Framework Knitters, and moves towards the villages where a high proportion of women could be employed at particularly low wages, escaping male-dominated trade unions in Leicester).

Only for a very brief period, between 1866 and the mid-1870s, did employers in Leicester's hosiery industry move towards a Responsible Autonomy strategy. Then, conditions of high product demand, scarce labour power and a growing number of strikes encouraged employers to try to co-opt worker organisation through the Leicester Board of Arbitration. The strategy behind the Board in Leicester may be seen from the better-known board in Nottingham on which it was modelled. In Nottingham, after a series of strikes and lockouts in 1860 and widespread wage rises, three of the *largest* manufacturers, Mundella, Lee and Ashwell, decided to set up the board. [15] As Church reports:

> Mundella and Lee maintained that competition from Germany made it impossible to pay higher wages and Mundella suggested that a council should be formed to check the practices of 'bad employers and middlemen' and, on behalf of the manufacturers, offered to pay the passage of a workman's delegation to Germany to investigate the extent of German competition (1966, pp. 269–70).

While there had been joint bodies to regulate wages over all Leicester in the past (the old list of prices), they were never particularly successful. The boards set up in Nottingham and Leicester in the 1860s were successful largely because the temptations of 'bad employers and middlemen' to cut wages had already been removed by rapidly expanding demand and labour power shortages. To convince workers' representatives to moderate their wage demands, to act 'responsibly' in the face of German competition, at a time when worker resistance was particularly strong, was the aim of the boards. In this they appear to have largely succeeded. It was precisely when demand stopped growing so quickly and plentiful cheap labour-power was again available that the boards fell into disuse. During the last quarter of the century when manufacturers were really suffering from German competition, it was the unions who wanted the board revived, not the employers. In 1891 a representative of the Nottingham and Derby Union asked employers if they would consider reviving the famous Nottingham Board. Of fifty manufacturers circulated in Nottinghamshire and Derbyshire, only nine replied; only one of these was definitely in favour and four others in favour only under certain conditions (Royal Commission [1892], p. 66).

In the last quarter of the nineteenth century manufacturers reverted back to Direct Control strategies. Pushed by increased competition and the desire for closer supervision, and encouraged by the availability of rentable power, rentable factory space and long-term credit, the old middlemen were fast becoming small manufacturers (gathering those to whom they had put out work from their homes into small factories). These small manufacturers often led the way in direct coercion of their workers because their relatively poor equipment and weak bargaining position with wholesalers (see Section 7 below) meant that their competitive strength lay in the lower wages they paid and the lower outlays on working conditions they made.

In spite of the Truck Act of 1874, several manufacturers managed to lower their wage costs by forcing deductions on their workers. Workers were still generally paid by the piece. *Within factories* workers in the 1880s often competed for work. Employers would tacitly arrange with their workpeople to leave money on the table after wages were paid in order to get a good amount of work the next day.

Small manufacturers also used government military contracts, representing particularly good runs of work, to bargain workers' rates down. These contracts were used to discriminate against trade unionists as well (Royal Commission [1892], pp. 56–8). Also small manufacturers in particular often broke the Factory Acts by forcing workers to work long hours and late at night. Wholesalers placed their orders with small manufacturers as late as possible and were able to demand early delivery, knowing that small manufacturers could get their workers to work at an exhausting pace (and a dangerous one due to gas fumes at night before electric lighting) when the work was available. Evidence to the Royal Commission shows that the

Factory Acts offered little protection to workers because of the greater number of small factories compared with the number of factory inspectors, as well as a lack of zeal on the part of the inspectorate for making prosecutions.

These coercive strategies were easily pursued against country and women workers. But male workers in Leicester were always under the threat of employers moving their factories if they resisted managerial initiatives too strenuously. The 1890s in particular marked an exodus of factories from Leicester to villages where a higher proportion of women were employed, (see Table 12.2). Also within Leicester the proportion of women employed in the trade rose dramatically from the mid-1870s. In 1861, 31.1 per cent of Leicester's hosiery workers were women; by 1881, 61 per cent were women and by 1901, 73.5 per cent.

6   Centre–Periphery Patterns within Firms

The main centre–periphery pattern within firms in the last quarter of the nineteenth century was between men and women. As men won better wages and conditions hosiery manufacture became primarily a 'women's' industry.[16] As the centre became more pronounced, employers busily extended the proportion of peripheral to central workers. Employers were stimulated to do this by strong competitive conditions; they were able to do it because of the wide availability of women willing to work for low wages and relatively weak resistance by the men. Given social conditions, it was easy for men to maintain a high wage differential above women, as this differential was widespread throughout the society.

The centre–periphery pattern between men and women dates back to the outset of the trade when most framework knitters were men. Referring to the situation of domestic workers in the first half of the nineteenth century Nelson states:

> The knitter's wife was always one of his greatest industrial assets. When he worked on fancies and completed the whole article, she seamed and finished it. After he became a specialist at a single process on the frame, she supervised and assisted the younger children in winding the yarn and keeping the shuttles filled; and she had, of course, her regular household duties to perform. Occasionally women worked on the frame, but usually as an emergency measure, although after the 'long depression' many women kept their husband's frame busy far into the night in order to eke out the husband's income (1930, pp. 478–9).

It is clear from this passage that the difference in situation between men and women in domestic work was normally paralleled by the different tasks they performed. The men normally worked the frames; the more capital intensive and status-laden task. This did not reflect greater strength or skill on the part of the men, as during hard times the women did work the frame while the men slept (that is, women did the status work only when the men physically could not). Most putters-out considered the work of women equal in quality to that of the men and paid them equal rates during the first half of the nineteenth century if they were in the same location (Nelson [1930], p. 479).

The centre—periphery pattern between men and women became clearer when they both entered factories. Then women were paid much less than men. Also the majority of women continued to perform subsidiary tasks (winding, seaming, making-up, etc.). Those who worked frames generally did so under the supervision of a male overlooker.

The men were not strong enough to prevent women from working frames in the factories, nor were they strong enough to demand that women doing similar work to men should be paid at the same rate (as engineers managed during the two world wars, see Chapter 14). Women on frames earned similar wages to women sewing-machinists, winders and menders, reflecting the general convention concerning what women 'ought to earn' (Wells [1935], p. 199).[17]

Before the Education Acts, children also occupied an important peripheral position in the hosiery trade, particularly at home and in workshops. From the beginning in the Midlands apprentices were employed in great numbers as a means of securing cheap labour power rather than to provide sound training for entrance into a privileged craft. After having served their apprenticeships, young journeymen were laid off to make room for a new crop of apprentices. In the home of their stockinger fathers children often began work at under eight years of age, generally on subsidiary tasks such as stitching, winding, or carrying work to the bagman or hosier (Wells [1935], p. 151).

During the last quarter of the nineteenth century young children disappeared as a major periphery in the hosiery industry, but their mothers working at home continued to play this role. Long after the introduction of power machinery women at home were able to compete successfully against factory workers for linking, stitching and seaming work. The spread of sewing machines and similar treadle-driven machines (such as linking machines) after the 1870s gave outwork new life. These machines were not drastically improved by the use of power. Some homes had steam power anyway – run in along the top floor of a row of houses like the Coventry cottage factories of the 1850s (Royal Commission [1892], p. 55). The machines were put out to women's homes along with materials. Factory workers complained that women outworkers would 'work for less on the quiet' resulting in a general tendency for wage reductions in the factories (Royal Commission [1892], pp. 55–6).

While the vast majority of outworkers were women, there also remained a hard core of male hand-frame knitters during the last quarter of the nineteenth century. In 1892 there were an estimated 5000 in the Midland Counties (Royal Commission [1892], p. 77). They survived primarily because of government military contracts which specified handknitted pants, and because they were willing to work for less than those in the factories.

The male/female and factory/outwork distinctions were largely reinforced by a town/village distinction. Not only were employers shifting factory production from town to country, but they would also play town-workers off against country-workers in order to reduce wages for both. As one worker representative stated to the Commissioners in 1892:

> He, [a manufacturer] has taken the work into the country, and helped to starve the men in the town, and then when he has started the men in the town at a reduction, he has told the men in the country they have got to work for a bit less, or else he shall have it done in the town. This is how it has been for years, shuttlecock and battledore (p. 57).[18]

7 Centre–Periphery Pattern between Firms

The rise in competition among small manufacturers due to fallen entry costs from the 1870s allowed wholesale dealers to play off manufacturers against each other. Merchants used to seek manufacturers to give their orders, but by the 1870s the merchants were in a position to require the manufacturer to produce and submit samples priced according to the manufacturer's estimate of the market. Wholesalers often submitted those samples to another firm with a request for a lower quotation. As demand was slacking off from the late 1870s, the second firm often complied (Wells [1935], p. 175). The inequality in power between wholesaler and manufacturer was so great that wholesalers could ask for a reduced price in response to a fall in the price of yarn after an order had been half filled by the manufacturer. If he refused, the wholesaler could then cancel the order and find someone who had been buying yarn at the lower price to fill it more cheaply. To sue the wholesaler for breach of contract was open to the manufacturer, but rarely taken up for fear of losing a customer and perhaps victimisation by other wholesalers (Wells [1935], pp. 175–6). Of course the loss of an order by the manufacturer meant immediate short-time or unemployment for his workers.

Therefore, looking at the industry as a whole, those working for smaller manufacturers were working for peripheral firms; firms which could ill afford a large proportion of central workers within them. In 1851, 53 per cent of Leicester firms employed less than 10 men and 94 per cent employed less than 100 men. In England and Wales as late as 1930, 37 per cent of firms employed less than 10 people, 81 per cent of firms employed less than 100 people and 91 per cent employed less than 200.[19] Firms employing under 200 workers accounted for 41 per cent of employment in the industry.

8   The Hosiery Industry and Leicester

A centre–periphery pattern between Leicester hosiery workers, who were primarily male factory workers, and Leicestershire countryside workers, among whom there was a far higher proportion of women and domestic or workshop workers, allowed Leicester workers the sorts of advantages from the 1850s to the 1880s which Coventry ribbon weavers enjoyed up to the late 1850s – higher wages, greater employment security, better working conditions.[20] But while there were significant differences in conditions between town and countryside as well as between men and women and between factory workers and outworkers throughout the second half of the nineteenth century, these were not non-competing groups. Therefore the differences between central and peripheral workers was limited.

Improvements for Leicester workers were somewhat mediated by the shift in workers from countryside into Leicester, and by the replacement of men by women (as well as the general shift from domestic to factory work), between the 1850s and 1880s. Coventry and particularly Hillfields ribbon weavers, on the other hand, were protected from the reserve army available around the city, and from women workers, by the belt of commons and by their strong organisation.[21] When the hosiery trade fell off after the 1870s the flow of countryside workers and women moving into Leicester factories was counteracted by a flow of factories moving out to the countryside to take advantage of relatively cheap female labour. Such movements, and the threat of moving, undermined the resistance of Leicester hosiery workers and resulted in a deterioration of their working conditions.[22]

This decentralising tendency is somewhat masked in the figures on Table 12.2. Firms moving factories out of Leicester often did not move to the Leicestershire countryside. For example, in 1886 the firm of Pool, Lorrimer and Tabberer, employing about 800 workers in Leicester, moved their factory to Foleshill, near Coventry, leaving only 400 people employed in Leicester at their warehouse.[23]

Firms were able to move out of Leicester because they were small and their machinery was easily transported. They were tempted to move out of Leicester because of the wage differential between Leicester and countryside industries, which had widened during the years of prosperity.[24] And they were impelled to move out of Leicester because of harsh competitive conditions and the fall in hosiery demand.

The number of Leicester workers in the hosiery trade, stagnated between 1891 and 1901, rose slightly by 1911 and then fell off drastically by 1921. This, along with stagnation in the boot and shoe industry, meant that for Leicester the period from 1891 to 1921, a generally prosperous period for the country at large, was one of stagnation and depopulation, particularly from the late 1890s. Between 1901 and 1921 Leicester's population rose from 211, 579 to 234,143, a mere 10.7 per cent increase over twenty years. Given a natural rate of increase of about 9 per cent during the first decade of the twentieth century and about 7 per cent during the second decade,[25] Leicester suffered a net loss of population through migration of about 6 per cent during those twenty years.

PART FIVE

TWENTIETH-CENTURY
INDUSTRY-AREA STUDY

CHAPTER THIRTEEN

The Motor-Car Product Cycle, Coventry and the Law of Value

1 The Motor-car Product Cycle and Coventry

Coventry's industry-area long-run pattern may be usefully described by examining the pattern of new car registrations in the United Kingdom. In spite of the sudden rise in British car exports between 1945 and 1950 and the sudden rise in car imports after 1968, the basic health of the industry in Britain may be inferred from the long-run pattern of new car registrations in the United Kingdom (curve *D* on Graph 13.1).[1] New car registrations may be divided into five distinguishable elements:

(1) first car purchases by private households,
(2) replacement car purchases by private households,
(3) second car or further car purchases by private households,
(4) initial car purchases by businesses,
(5) replacement car purchases by businesses.

The particularly rapid growth of new registrations from the early 1930s until the mid-1960s (labelled 'Peak Period' on Graph 13.1), was due primarily to the first element, the diffusion of car ownership among private households. Once saturation of British households is approached, new car purchases will level off. Purchases may remain high because of replacement demand, and they may grow somewhat due to multicar purchases and new initial business purchases.[2] But these purchases will be tied closely to general economic conditions. Considered as luxury purchases more than initial car purchases by private households, they are easily put off and are therefore more unstable in the short run. A very substantial and sudden change in attitudes or economic conditions would be required to stimulate another long boom in car sales such as occurred during the U.K. car industry's peak period.[3] Thus the long-run pattern of first car purchases by private households might be expected to look like curve *C* on Graph 13.1. The long-run pattern of all new registrations

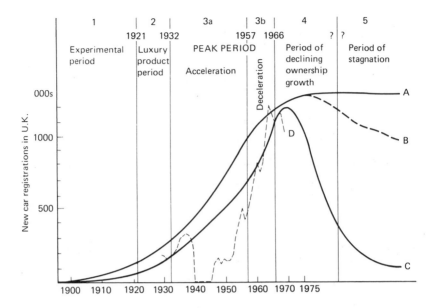

GRAPH 13.1   Product Cycle for Cars in the United Kingdom
SOURCE: Society of Motor Manufacturers and Traders

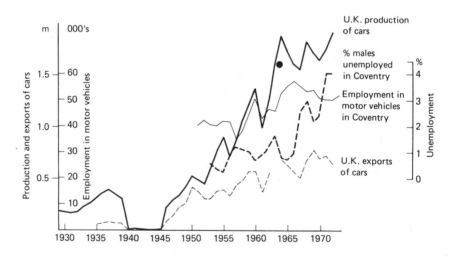

GRAPH 13.2 U.K. Car Production and Coventry Employment, 1929–72
SOURCE: Society of Motor Manufacturers and Traders; Coventry Employment
        Exchange

might be expected to take on an S-shape such as Curve *A*, or even Curve *B* if environmentalists grow in strength and if public transport is improved.[4]

This pattern is similar to that of many new products in an unplanned social formation such as that dominated by the capitalist mode of production. It is known as the *product cycle*. The product cycle pattern is distinguished by a period of extremely rapid growth in demand and production, preceded and succeeded by periods of very slow growth (and sometimes decline in the latter case). During the initial slow-growth experimental period, design of the product and production methods are unstable and not well known. During the rapid accumulation phase, product design and production methods are perfected, allowing prices to fall. Demand is also stimulated because potential consumers are now more certain about what they are in fact buying and because they are stimulated by seeing their friends and neighbours successfully using the product. Eventually demand for the new product stabilises or even declines as the market becomes saturated. The industry, basing new investment on immediate past demand growth, soon suffers from overcapacity and a period of heightened competition and contraction ensues. On Graph 13.1 I have divided the car product cycle into the following periods:

Experimental Period	1896–1921
Luxury Product Period	1921–1932
Peak Period	
Acceleration Part	1932–1957
Deceleration Part	1957–1966
Period of Declining Ownership Growth	1966– ?
Period of Stagnation	?

The timing of these periods is rather arbitrary, but they will be helpful for exposition purposes. They broadly help to distinguish changes in competitive conditions facing the U.K. car industry. While changing competitive conditions do not, in themselves, create changes in monopoly power, worker resistance or managerial strategies, they do represent the background against which such changes occur.

The importance of the car industry for Coventry may be seen from Graph 13.2. The car industry has been heavily concentrated in Coventry since its inception at the end of the nineteenth century. In 1911 there were 6838 male workers in Coventry's motor vehicle industry. The next most important centre for car workers was Birmingham, with 5400 male workers. In 1911 the motor vehicle industry accounted for 18.5 per cent of Coventry's occupied male population and 1.5 per cent of its occupied females. By 1921 Coventry's motor vehicle firms employed 36.8 per cent of Coventry's occupied males and 10.6 per cent of its occupied females.[5] The motor vehicles industry has continued to account for a high proportion of Coventry's rapidly growing occupied population. In 1961 30.9 per cent of males and 9.7 per cent of females were so employed while the number of occupied males had grown from 44,855 in 1921 to 119, 180 in 1961 and females from 15,929 in 1921 to 50,820 in 1961. In 1971 32.9 per cent of Coventry's 128,702 occupied males and 10.7 percent of 61,488 occupied females were employed in the motor vehicle industry.[6]

These figures severely underestimate the importance of the motor industry to Coventry's economy. A substantial proportion of the work carried out by Coventry's mechanical engineering and other metal-working firms is destined for the car industry (see Chapter 8, Section 4). In 1971 these industries, (Standard Industrial Classification Numbers 6, 7 and 12), accounted for 16.1 per cent of Coventry's occupied males and 10.6 per cent of occupied females. Thus the car industry directly or indirectly affects almost half Coventry's male workers and over one-fifth of female workers.[7] The close relation between fluctuations in car production and fluctuations in Coventry's male unemployment figures (clearly shown in Graph 13.2), indicates Coventry's heavy dependence on favourable conditions for the U.K. car industry.

It is worth pointing out that all the major car firms are not represented in Coventry. The majority of Chrysler's workers (at the Stoke and Ryton plants) and a high proportion of British Leyland's workers (at some seven different factories including Jaguar and Standard Triumph), work in Coventry. Ford and Vauxhall have no manufacturing facilities in Coventry.

2   The Product Cycle and the Law of Value

Competitive pressure to increase absolute and relative surplus value, Marx's Law of Value, has always acted with unequal force on different firms. Larger and stronger firms have always enjoyed a wider margin of discretion than smaller and weaker ones. This difference in the force by which the Law of Value coerces different firms grew with the coming of Monopoly Capitalism (see Chapter 3 above).

But competitive pressures on individual firms (whether strong or weak), do not usually remain constant for long periods of time. Sometimes product demand is very high. Sometimes barriers to entry are particularly strong. During these times firms enjoy a wider margin of discretion than they normally do. The product cycle pattern is used in the next chapter merely to illustrate when car firms in the United Kingdom had wide or narrow discretionary margins, when resources around the motor industry were likely to be allocated more or less strictly according to the Law of Value, when top managers were more likely to move towards Responsible Autonomy strategies and when towards Direct Control strategies. All these things are related, and I do *not* wish to imply a simple uni-directional causality running from the product cycle or changes in competitive conditions to types of managerial strategies. The strength and character of worker resistance will also affect managerial behaviour, though competitive conditions in product markets will also encourage or discourage worker resistance. Finally, struggle within productive activity will affect both managerial discretion and competitive positions.

In the next two chapters I will try to show how these elements have related to one another throughout the history of the U.K. motor industry looking particularly at those firms which have been heavily concentrated in Coventry – Chrysler and British Leyland.

CHAPTER FOURTEEN

Historical Development of the Car Industry in Coventry: Monopoly Power and Struggle

In this chapter monopoly power, worker resistance and managerial counter-pressure are examined as they developed during the history of the car industry in Coventry. The product cycle pattern set up in Chapter 13 is used to distinguish phases with different competitive conditions.

1 Experimental Period 1896–1921

U.K. Car Industry

In Britain before 1896 the speed limit for a potential motor-car was fixed by the speed of a man walking in front of the machine carrying a red flag. The rule did not particularly encourage the production of red flags. It also removed from the motor-car the potential for its most important attribute – sustained speed. Meanwhile thousands of cars were being produced in the 1880s and 1890s, mainly in Germany and also in France.[1] In 1896 the thirty-one-year old 'red flag' rule was abolished and a speed limit of fourteen miles per hour was imposed.

In 1896 the Daimler plant was set up in Coventry and the British motor industry began. The country's first cars were produced in an old cotton mill in the north end of Coventry. In 1897 the leading concerns working on Continental patents were all to be found on various floors of that old Coventry mill (Allen [1929], p. 297). By 1900 major car factories had been set up in Birmingham and Wolverhampton as well, though in 1911 Coventry still employed more people in the motor industry than Birmingham and Wolverhampton combined. Throughout its experimental period the British motor industry remained almost totally a West Midlands industry.

Many of Coventry's bicycle manufacturers moved into the new industry after the slump in bicycle demand in 1898. The bicycle makers had the advantage of assembly experience with a similar product over most of the hopefuls who entered with only an idea, personal engineering experience, a bit of cash and much enthusiasm (see pp. 190–1 below).

Monopoly Power

The Daimler plant was set up as a subsidiary of the British Motor Syndicate under Coventry's super-financier of the bicycle industry – Henry Lawson. Lawson floated the Daimler Motor Company with a public issue of £100,000. The public, whose imagination was fired by the prospects for horseless carriages, oversubscribed to the issue. In the main the money was not used to produce cars in the Coventry mill. It was used to buy up patents so that the syndicate could acquire monopoly control over the entire industry and extract royalties from every British car manufacturer, importer or owner. Very few cars were produced between 1896 and 1901 from the Coventry group as the syndicate appeared to be succeeding in its monopolising aim. But in 1901 the courts finally decided decisively against the syndicate and from then the industry, already populated by many small firms, was flooded with new entrants. As George Maxcy put it:

> Lawson undoubtedly realized that, at this early stage in the development of the industry, it was ideas and not firms that were of value and in his bid for monopoly control he bought up patents, not firms. . . . What Lawson could not see was that his attempt to corner the market in ideas was bound to fail. The rate of progress was so rapid that no patent was of value for any length of time (1958, p. 358).

During the Experimental Period of a new product, particularly a complex product such as a car, a television or a bicycle, the design is unstable. This uncertainty, which lasted a very long time in the car industry, lured many recruits to the young industry with new ideas from widely different industrial backgrounds. It also meant that many followed up ideas which did not work out. There was considerable confusion about the power source. As late as 1912 several steam cars and a number of electric cars were exhibited at the Motor Show. Significant improvements in engine performance and in body design occurred every year. Up to 1913 nearly 200 different makes of cars had been put onto the British market. More than half had disappeared by 1913 (Political and Economic Planning [1948], p. 18).

Firms were small. Before the First World War the largest firms never produced more than a few thousand cars in a year, while the vast majority produced only a few hundred or less. Many firms operated on a kind of domestic system in that production was carried out in the same premises as the producer lived. Nevertheless a domestic system such as dominated Coventry's ribbon-weaving trade, where merchants or their undertakers brought work to the weavers and collected the ribbons weekly, never characterised the motor industry.

Even when firms were successful they grew very slowly because of the poor quality of parts and components available before the Great War. Many firms tried to expand by making their own components, but this was very costly. After the British Motor Syndicate affair, the public, the bankers and large firms from outside the industry were not anxious to sink money into what was recognised as a highly risky industry. High fixed capital expenditures on equipment and space to make parts left little working capital left over to finance inventories. With demand narrow and fickle, overextension was often disastrous. Ford, with output in 1913 almost as great as the output of the five other large producers combined, was able to remain an assembler because parts and components were shipped from Detroit.

In 1913, the peak pre-World War I year, around 25,000 cars were produced by the British car industry. In that same year, 45,000 cars were produced in France and 462,000 in the United States. During the 1914–18 war private car production and development work halted in Britain. Munitions and military vehicle production expanded greatly, particularly in Coventry. In 1915 the McKenna duty of 33.3 per cent *ad valorem*, on the landed cost of imported cars was imposed. The tariff remained at this high level until 1956, leaving British manufacturers virtually free from foreign competition in their home market for over 40 years. After the Armistice the pent-up demand for private cars was matched by another wave of hopeful experimenters. In 1919 and 1920 alone, forty new motor manufacturing firms were formed in England (Rhys [1972], p. 19). During the war parts and components specialists became significant so most of the new post-war entrants were merely assemblers. The foundations were laid for mass production, though it was still possible to enter the industry with very little capital.

Background to Coventry's Car Industry

Coventry's metal-working industries remained 'new' from the 1870s until well into the twentieth century. The watch-making trade was established in Coventry during the seventeenth century, but remained small until the early nineteenth century. Between 1830 and 1860 the trade expanded tremendously and by 1861 it employed 2704 people, representing Coventry's second largest source of employment after silk ribbon weaving.[2] The trade continued to grow during the 1860s and 1870s, but its rate of expansion declined considerably. As with the silk ribbon weavers during this time, though on a much smaller scale, Coventry's watch-makers were beginning to feel the pinch from foreign competition. The trend was to continue throughout the rest of the century, though it was not until the late 1880s that the industry became seriously depressed. At that time the Victorian fashion for ornate gold watches was ending. Swiss and American watches – machine-made, cheaper and more simple – captured much of the British market. Between 1891 and 1911 the proportion of Coventry's labour force employed in watch-making fell from 13.2 per cent to 2.9 per cent, (from 3,565 workers to 1,486).

Meanwhile, in 1869 the Coventry Sewing Machine Company (established in 1863 near Coventry's main watch-making district), began to make the first bicycles to be produced in England. The bicycle industry went through its 'Experimental Period' during the 1870s. During the 1880s and early 1890s the bicycle industry was expanding very quickly with the main growth in Coventry. In 1881 400 of Coventry's workers were employed in the bicycle industry. By 1891 4054 were employed and by 1901, 6042, or 18.5 per cent of Coventry's labour force, worked in Coventry's bicycle industry.[3] The bicycle industry drew many of Coventry's depressed watch-makers as well as agricultural labourers from the surrounding countryside and from depressed areas in the South. Between 1891 and 1911 Coventry's occupied population almost doubled (26,949 to 50,382) and its occupied male population more than doubled (16,948 to 37,322).

During the main boom period for Coventry's bicycle industry (from 1887 to 1897) a few firms grew quite large. These firms were able to expand quickly by using the new limited liability laws and flotation procedures. The industry quickly became overcapitalised and oversupplied during the late 1890s, and in 1898 Coventry was suddenly plunged into a deep, though short-lived, trade recession.

The larger firms survived the slump while many smaller ones were eliminated,[4] but many firms saw the writing on the wall as foreign competition was also beginning to choke off bicycle export markets by this time (Derksen and Rombouts [1937]). During the 1890s some Coventry bicycle manufacturers began turning to motor cycles. After 1898 this switching increased as well as a gradual switch to motor-cars. Switching from bicycles and motor cycles to cars continued among Coventry firms until the 1920s. During the first decade of the twentieth century the main centre for bicycle manufacture moved to Birmingham as Coventry's firms switched more quickly to motor vehicles. In 1911 Coventry had around 6000 bicycle workers and 7000 car workers, while Birmingham had 9000 bicycle workers and 5000 car workers.[5]

Worker Resistance

From the 1850s developments in engineering technology had made a variety of new machine tools available to the metal-working industries. In spite of the rapid growth of metal-working industries from the mid-nineteenth century and the accompanying demand for skilled metal-workers, the position of craftsmen in these industries was being steadily undermined by mechanisation. New machines often could be operated by people with only a few months' training or less.

Nevertheless the process was very piecemeal as the number of hand tools used by skilled engineers was vast and a new machine never suddenly eliminated all skilled work necessary for the process it performed. The machines required setting-up and maintenance, and work often required hand rectifying to reach the specifications necessary (Rowe [1928]). This, combined with the growth in demand for metal-working industry products, put craftsmen in the engineering trades in a particularly strong position. The principle of craft exclusiveness, limiting the supply of skilled workers, was consolidated during the 1850s and 1860s.[6] Craftsmen were represented by several union organisations. The most important of these was the Amalgamated Society of Engineers (A.S.E.) formed in 1851.[7] Before the twentieth century semi-skilled workers and labourers in the engineering industry remained largely unrepresented by union organisations.

A.S.E. policy toward mechanisation was to claim that all jobs traditionally performed by craftsmen should continue to be paid at the craft rate and performed only by 'legal men', even when machinery had eliminated most of the skill required for the job (Jefferys [1946], pp. 103, 142). Even when machines and semi-skilled work were introduced craftsmen were often able to win special consideration from employers for displaced craftsmen (Jefferys [1946], p. 134).

The high financial cost of introducing the new machines, the disruptive effects of mechanisation, and the excess payment required to keep deskilled craftsmen employed on those machines all slowed down the rate of mechanisation, particularly in the northern centres. In Coventry, on the other hand, growth of new industries allowed much easier introduction of the latest machinery. Skilled watch-makers were not deskilled by machines directly; they went through a process of deskilling by unemployment and shifting trades (see Chapter 8, Section 3). Similarly agricultural labourers took up semi-skilled and unskilled work in the bicycle firms from an immediate state of destitution, rather than proud craft organisation within the bicycle industry. The shift to cars would have *increased* the proportion of skilled to semi-skilled workers necessary compared with bicycle production, though only temporarily.[8] The vast numbers of semi-skilled workers necessary to produce cars when individual firms grew large enough to carry out batch production rather than individual vehicle production, and when bicycle firms shifted to cars, were already available *as semi-skilled workers* in the bicycle firms or as unemployed emigrants from depressed areas of the country or from the watch-making trade.[9]

By 1911 Coventry's engineering skill distribution looked considerably different from that of other British engineering centres, as is indicated in Table 14.1.

In consequence it was in Coventry (and Birmingham) that the Workers'

TABLE 14.1

Composition of Labour Force in General Engineering, 1911

	Sheffield	Glasgow	Coventry	National
Percentage of Skilled and labourers	84	81	55	82
Percentage of Semi-skilled	16	19	45	18

SOURCE: Hinton [1973], p. 218.

Union (W.U.), which came to cater primarily for less skilled engineering workers, achieved its greatest success.[10] In other engineering centres it was generally known that whenever craftsmen went on strike, whatever the outcome, they would eventually be re-employed by their old employers. This was not true at all for labourers, and it was far less true for semi-skilled workers (Hyman [1971], p. 176). In Coventry, with continuously tight external labour power markets from the mid-1880s onwards and a high proportion of those markets for less skilled workers, this old distinction did not hold. The Workers' Union was established in Coventry in 1913 when they won a rise in the hourly rate for labourers from $4\frac{1}{2}d$ to $6d$ after a one-week strike at Coventry's largest firms (Daimler, Humber and the Coventry Ordinance Works). The victory was soon followed by rises for semi-skilled workers. Thus in 1913 labourers' wage-rates were raised to 71 per cent of the Coventry district rate negotiated by the A.S.E. for craftsmen (compared with 50 per cent to 60 per cent of the district rate in other areas), and 'many of the higher grades of semi-skilled workers were already receiving the full district rate' (Hinton [1973], p. 219).

One important reason for the success of the W.U. in 1913 was the support given to the strike by skilled workers. While the A.S.E. wanted to maintain a differential between skilled and less skilled rates, it did not want that differential to become so wide as to encourage the substitution of craftsmen by less skilled workers 'unduly'. In 1899 a short-lived attempt to organise the W.U. among Coventry's bicycle workers and corporation employees in order to get the labourers' rate raised to $6d$ was conducted by an A.S.E. member. Nevertheless, while the A.S.E. wanted less skilled workers organised,[11] it still did not want less skilled workers operating machines claimed for skilled workers. The machine issue clearly separated the interests of the A.S.E. and the W.U.

The relative strength of semi-skilled workers compared with craftsmen in Coventry helps to explain the rather different character of the shop stewards' movement in Coventry during World War I. During the war Coventry's shop steward movement was moved more by the militancy of semi-skilled workers attempting to grasp the opportunities for improving their wages and conditions presented by the extremely tight labour market than by the militancy of craftsmen attempting to preserve their privileges against the threat of dilution (Hinton [1973], p. 333). Dilution, which came suddenly to northern engineering centres in 1915–16, had occurred more gradually and earlier in Coventry, and it had occurred through massive expansion of *new* industries rather than direct deskilling within traditional industries.

The relative strength of semi-skilled workers in Coventry and the relative militancy of the W.U. also help to explain the greater formal success of the shop stewards' movement in Coventry (compared with the movement in northern engineering centres), and the different attitude towards it taken by trade union officials and top managers.

Management and Worker Resistance

In 1896 the A.S.E. rules allowed for the appointment of shop stewards. Originally the functions of these unofficial union members were limited to recruiting new arrivals and making sure that all union decisions were observed. But the nature of technical change in engineering industries and managerial strategies for taking advantage of new machines ensured that the role of the shop steward would eventually be extended. The variety and complexity of new machines encouraged negotiations concerning manning to be conducted at the shop-floor level. Also the extension of piece-working systems, and particularly Taylorian Premium Bonus systems from the 1890s, enhanced the potential role for shop stewards because employers insisted on the principle of mutuality in the 1898 Terms of Settlement after the engineering lock-out.

Mutuality means that 'the prices to be paid for piece-work shall be fixed by mutual arrangement between the employer and the workman or workmen' (Terms of Settlement [1898], p. 286). Agreement to this in 1898 meant that the A.S.E. in effect gave up any official role in what was to become an extremely important source of concern of their rank and file.

Target rates for jobs were already being measured by 'experts'; 'speed and feed' men, progress chasers, rate-fixers, or operational inspectors, against whom the unions were already protesting in 1897 (Wigham [1973], p. 73). Collective action against things individual workers were ill-equipped to resist increasingly centred around the shop stewards.

With the Treasury Agreement of 1915 most forms of overt collective resistance fell to the unofficial workshop committees of shop stewards. In April 1917 a strike at the Hotchkiss machine-gun works in Coventry[12] for recognition of their shop committee led the firm and the Coventry Engineering Joint Committee (C.E.J.C.) of union representatives to set up a representative shop stewards' committee under strict trade union control.

Both the firm and the C.E.J.C. were opposed to the strike. The new shop stewards' committee was formed only at the insistence of the Ministry of Munitions, but after it was boycotted by the militants it became acceptable to both managers and union representatives. Thus the local officials in Coventry managed to undermine the local workers' committee by co-opting shop-floor organisation rather than by opposing it.

In October 1917, after a strike at White and Poppe in Coventry for shop stewards' recognition, the C.E.J.C. put themselves at the head of agitation for recognition by launching a firm-by-firm battle for recognition. The success of this strategy, and a one-week city-wide strike at the end of November, led to an agreement by the end of the year between the Engineering Employers' Federation and all major engineering unions (*except the A.S.E.*). In the agreement the shop stewards' right to negotiate on behalf of individual workmen or groups of workmen on issues previously negotiated under strict mutuality was recognised (Hinton [1973], p. 225). In pushing for this the A.S.E.'s local officials in Coventry represented on the C.E.J.C. were clearly at variance with their own union's policy.

During the war it was the Ministry of Munitions which was particularly anxious to use a strategy of co-option, to get trade union officials at the local level to encourage Coventry's skilled and semi-skilled rank and file to behave 'responsibly'. Local firms gave into these wishes after relatively weak protest. Later top managers in the firms themselves would be anxious to use the same strategies in order to smooth technical changes with both semi-skilled and skilled workers, and to ensure relatively smooth supply when demand appeared insatiable.

2 Luxury Product Period 1921–1932

Monopoly Power

The motor industry quickly recovered from the 1921 slump. During the 1920s output increased more than five-fold – from around 35,000 cars produced in 1920 to 182,000 produced in 1929. In the Experimental Period much of the growth of output was due to more firms coming into the industry rather than growth of existing firms. This was reversed during the Luxury Product Period. As before, a large number of new firms entered the industry between 1921 and 1925, but between those years many more were eliminated. More than 150 motor-vehicle producing companies were wound up between 1921 and 1925 (Rhys [1972], p. 11). According to Maxcy the number of car producers fell from 88 in 1922 to 31 in 1929 (1958, p. 365).

The primary reason for this change was the stabilisation of car design, which allowed some firms to replace batch production with flow production (moving assembly line production) techniques. This led to tremendous savings in costs per car as production increased. According to the 1947 report of the National Advisory Council for the Motor Manufacturing Industry:

> In batch production, to step up the rate of output from 1,000 a year to 2,000 a year may well lead to a saving of, say, $7\frac{1}{2}$ per cent in the cost per unit. But in flow production, an increase in the rate from 1,000 a week to 2,000 a week may well give savings of 15 per cent in the cost per unit (Maxcy [1958], p. 366).

This in turn led to a fall in car prices. Between 1924 and 1929 the Society of Motor Manufacturers and Traders Retail car prices index fell by 25 per cent (S.M.M.T. [1939], p. 46). This severe price competition from the successful initiators of mass production (first Morris and then Austin) caused the elimination of many small firms, financially or technically unable to follow suit.

With stable car designs it was possible for specialist producers of particular car parts and components to grow. During the 1920s such large-scale specialists as Joseph Lucas (supplying electrical components and strongly based in Coventry) became part of the industry. While the components industry developed through independent firms, Morris began taking over many of his suppliers. In 1923 alone he took over three Coventry parts manufacturers – Hotchkiss et Cie SA (France), making engines, Hollick & Pratt Ltd, making bodies and Osberton Radiators Ltd. Although almost all expansion of actual car output occurred internally, Morris also took over the ailing Wolseley Company in 1927.

Chart 14.1 summarises the development of British Leyland and Chrysler via mergers and take-overs. The chart indicates that mergers and take-overs primarily occurred during three time-spans: 1923–7, 1931–7, and 1959–68. The first of these time-spans corresponds roughly with the product cycle Luxury Product Period for cars. This period marks the rise of the Morris conglomeration (during the second period the Rootes empire was formed and during the third the Leyland empire).

The degree of monopoly power enjoyed by the top few firms producing cars increased significantly during the 1920s. In 1913 the top four firms accounted for 43 per cent of car output, in 1929 they accounted for 79 per cent.[13]

Ford introduced flow production in a very small way at Trafford Park back in 1911. During the 1920s only Morris, Austin and Singer introduced flow production, and only on a rather small and primitive scale compared with producers in America at the time. In 1923 Ford produced more than two million cars in America. Morris, the largest British firm, produced 63,000 in 1929 (and only 3,000 in 1921). Firms the size of Joseph Lucas were still rare in the components industry. Most of the car firms' bought-out parts and components came from small engineering firms, many still backyard businesses. In Coventry these small firms came to be very dependent on

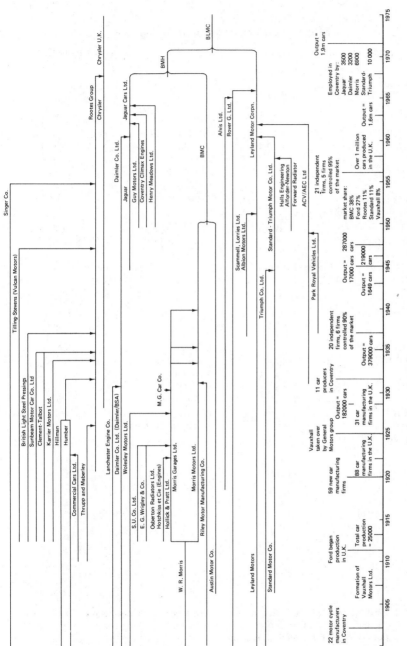

CHART 14.1 Take-overs and Mergers in the U.K. Car Industry
SOURCE: Various books and pamplets on the car industry.

TABLE 14.2

*Shares of Car Output of Major Car Firms, 1913–75, and
Shares of U.K. New Registrations for 1975*

Experimental period (1913)

Firm	Market share per cent	
Ford	24	⎫
Wolseley	10	⎬ 43
Morris	5	⎪
Austin	4	⎭
Singer	4	
Rover	4	
Others (about 42 firms)	49	
	100	
Total output	25,000	

Luxury product period (1929)

Firm	Market share per cent	
Morris	35	⎫
Austin	25	⎬ 79
Singer	15	⎪
Ford	4	⎭
Standard	3	
Others (about 26 firms)	12	
	100	
Total output	182,000	

Peak period acceleration (1955)

Firm	Market share per cent	
B.M.C. (Austin-Nuffield)	39	⎫
Ford	27	⎬ 87
Rootes	11	⎪
Standard	10	⎭
Vauxhall	9	
Others (about 12 firms)	4	
	100	
Total output	898,000	

Peak period deceleration (1965)

Firm	Market share per cent	
B.M.C.	38	⎫
Ford	$29\frac{1}{2}$	⎬ $91\frac{1}{2}$
Vauxhall	13	⎪
Rootes	11	⎭
Standard	$6\frac{1}{2}$	
Others (about 10 firms)	2	
	100	
Total output	1,722,000	

NOTE: Imports negligible before 1968, in 1968 imports 9 per cent of new registrations, in 1966 6 per cent, in 1972 24 per cent in 1974 28 per cent.
SOURCE: Society of Motor Manufacturers and Traders

Peak period acceleration
(1938)

Firm	Market share per cent	
Morris	24 ⎤	
Austin	20 ⎬ 72	
Ford	17 ⎟	
Vauxhall	11 ⎦	
Rootes	10	
Standard	10	
Others (about 16 firms)	8	
	100	
Total output	341,000	

Peak period acceleration
(1947)

Firm	Market share per cent	
Nuffield (Morris)	20 ⎤	
Austin	19 ⎬ 67	
Ford	15 ⎟	
Standard	13 ⎦	
Vauxhall	$10\frac{1}{2}$	
Rootes	$10\frac{1}{2}$	
Others (about 15 firms)	12	
	100	
Total output	287,000	

Period of declining ownership
(1975)

Firm	Market share per cent	
U.K. Car Production		
British Leyland	$47\frac{3}{4}$ ⎤	
Ford	26 ⎬ $99\frac{1}{2}$	
Chrysler	18 ⎟	
Vauxhall	$7\frac{3}{4}$ ⎦	
Other British (about 9 firms)	$\frac{1}{2}$	
	100	
Total production	1,267,695	
Total sales	1,194,000	

U.K. New registrations

Firm	Market share per cent
B.L.M.C.	31
Ford	22
Vauxhall	7
Chrysler	7
Other British	(less than $\frac{1}{2}$)
Total British	67
Datsun	5
Renault	5
V.W./Audi/N.S.U.	4
Fiat	3
Other foreign	16
Total Foreign	33

subcontracted work from the car firms, who were mainly assemblers, as they had been on bicycle firms earlier.

Worker Resistance and Managerial Strategy

During the war the grip of the Engineering Employers' Federation (E.E.F.) and of the firms themselves over the labour process was loosened by government intervention and the growing power of workshop organisation. The post-war inflationary boom, which lasted until late 1920, meant engineering workers remained in a strong position. Large wage increases were won at local levels.

During the war a number of workers in Coventry's Daimler works were beginning to operate a team or 'gang' system 'surreptitiously'.[14] The company was operating individual piece-work systems in accordance with the mutuality clause of the 1898 Terms of Settlement. It was against company rules for one worker to have anything to do with another worker's earnings. But small groups of workers were pooling some proportion of their earnings and sharing out some jobs among themselves. This earnings pool represented a strong weapon against victimisation because one of the main methods of managerial exercise of discipline against individuals on piece-work systems was to stop or slow down work coming to them. This would not disrupt production, but such disciplinary action against a whole gang would. In 1919 top managers tried to reimpose individual piece-working and this led to a three-month go-slow which was solid among 6000 Daimler workers (Drayton [1972], p. 7). Top managers gave in to the workers' demands for the gang system in 1919, but with the 1922 national engineering lock-out individual piece-working systems at Daimler and general workshop practices imposed by the 1898 Terms of Settlement throughout British engineering industries were reimposed. (The A.S.E. repudiated the 1898 terms just before the war and the W.U. was not a signatory in the first place.)

The lock-out arose over whether top managers had the *sole* right to decide when overtime would be worked, but the E.E.F. (and particularly its chairman, Allen Smith) fought against the broader issue of allowing the unions to be brought into joint bodies or consulted on any issues. The E.E.F. was, in effect, asserting its right and its intention to pursue Direct Control strategies rather than continue further along the Responsible Autonomy road. While it was impossible for engineering employers to smash the unions in 1922, or even to destroy shop stewards as a representative force, the E.E.F. was retreating from the Ministry of Munitions' position of increasing trade union involvement in what were formerly considered to be solely managerial functions. Overtime was but one of a host of issues which included manning, premium bonus systems and apprenticeship control.

On the issue of trade union co-option or Direct Control strategies the engineering employers were not entirely united, though their disunity would become clearer long after 1922. During the lock-out thirty-seven member firms were expelled from the E.E.F. for failing to post lockout conditions notices. After 1922 firms began leaving the E.E.F. in droves, particularly in the Midlands (Wigham [1973], chap. 6). They left because they feared that E.E.F. policy might lead to another serious lock-out at a time when some engineering industries were recovering quickly.

In the early 1920s the engineering industry was becoming clearly divided into a stagnant or declining main sector of old industries and a smaller, vigorously growing new sector. [15] In 1923 general engineering, engineers' iron and steel founding, and marine engineering accounted for 73 per cent of engineering employment, while electrical engineering and motor vehicles, bicycles and aircraft accounted for 25 per cent. By 1929 the older group had hardly grown in employment at all and accounted for only 64 per cent of the industry, while the new industries now accounted for 33 per cent. [16] Both groups were hit hard by the 1921–2 recession, but the new industries recovered quickly. Unemployment rates in 1923 were more than 20 per cent for the old industries and less than 10 per cent for the new ones. Unemployment rates in the old industries continued at about double the rates for the new ones until 1927. The depression of the early 1930s hit the new industries much less hard and they recovered much earlier.

A difference in types of managerial strategies pursued corresponding to this division of industries became clearer with the Mond–Turner talks. As Wigham states:

Though the Federation was hostile, a number of well-known engineering employers were in the Mond group, including heads of *big* companies in the expanding motor manufacturing and electrical sectors of the industry (1973, pp. 131–2; emphasis added).

As well as being more anxious (and able) to co-opt trade union leaders in order to ensure secure supplies, the larger firms paid far more than the smaller ones and employed far fewer women (see Chapter 15).

Coventry and the Car Industry

Coventry's economic position during this period reflected the basic strength of the car industry compared with most other industries. Though Coventry had both car assembly and car components industries, the proportion of Coventry workers in car assembly was higher than in other motor industry areas. In 1921 6.4 per cent of those working in Coventry's motor vehicle and bicycle industries were employed in motor and bicycle accessories, while for all England and Wales 10.1 per cent were so employed. Weekly earnings for fitters were 22 per cent higher in Coventry than in other engineering centres in 1923 and 28 per cent higher in 1929. Labourers in Coventry's engineering industry received 13 per cent more than those in other centres in 1923 and 19 per cent more in 1929 (Hart and Mackay [1975] pp. 20–4).[17] Unemployment rates in Coventry remained well below the national average (see Graph 14.1).

GRAPH 14.1 Percentage of Insured Workers Unemployed in Coventry as Compared with that of Great Britain, 1928–38

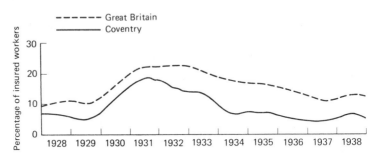

SOURCE: *West Midlands Plan.*

Table 14.3 shows the skill distribution of Coventry's occupied population compared with that of England and Wales for 1921 and 1931. Though Coventry has been heavily concentrated in manufacturing industries compared with service industries (as the lower proportion of professionals, managers and administrators in Coventry reflects) it had an extremely high proportion of women clerical workers (15.65 per cent in 1921 and 16.03 per cent in 1931, compared with 8.58 per cent and 10.42 per cent respectively for England and Wales). This reflects the large-scale and relatively modern techniques both for managerial co-ordination *and* for the maintenance of managerial authority used in Coventry car firms.[18] This is further demonstrated by the higher proportion of foremen, inspectors and supervisors in Coventry compared with England and Wales (1.98 per cent compared with 1.69 per cent in 1921 and 2.26 per cent compared with 1.63 per cent in 1931).

While top managers in some large motor manufacturing firms were anxious to co-opt trade union leaders at the national level, the engineering unions' defeat of 1922, the general working-class defeat of 1926 and high rates of unemployment made it relatively easy for employers to deal with workers individually at the factory level, and to extend piece-work payment systems which involved measured target output rates. Thus the number of foremen, inspectors and testers rose very quickly in Coventry during the 1920s. Top managers in some large car firms (notably Ford, but also some Coventry firms such as Standard Motors), did not negotiate with unions at all for most of their workers (Melman [1958], p. 30).

Work in the car industry before the Second World War was highly seasonal. Car workers were generally laid off for a few months during the summer, (see

TABLE 14.3

Percentage of Persons Employed in Each Occupational Group, England and Wales, Coventry C.B., 1921 and 1931

		1921			1931		
		Male	Female	Total	Male	Female	Total
England and Wales							
Higher professionals	1A	1.36	0.17	1.01	1.51	0.30	1.15
Lower professionals	1B	2.00	7.46	3.61	1.98	7.20	3.59
Employers and proprietors	2A	6.52	5.98	6.36	5.96	4.99	5.67
Managers and administrators	2B	5.04	2.06	4.16	4.61	0.82	3.48
Clerical workers	3	5.42	8.58	6.35	6.96	10.42	7.99
Foremen, inspectors and supervisors	4	2.25	0.36	1.69	2.12	0.49	1.63
Skilled manual	5	36.21	24.14	32.65	34.10	22.64	30.69
Semi-skilled manual	6	32.61	47.39	36.97	24.77	46.10	31.11
Unskilled manual	7	8.59	3.86	7.20	17.91	7.03	14.68
		100.00	100.00	100.00	100.00	100.00	100.00
Total		12,061,853	5,041,853	17,103,706	13,195,046	5,581,002	18,776,048
Coventry C.B.							
Higher professionals	1A	0.87	0.06	0.66	0.97	0.07	0.72
Lower professionals	1B	2.04	6.28	3.15	2.31	5.83	3.27
Employers and proprietors	2A	3.79	7.58	4.78	3.73	6.19	4.40
Managers and administrators	2B	3.58	1.58	3.06	3.07	0.44	2.35
Clerical workers	3	4.76	15.65	7.61	5.94	16.03	8.71
Foremen, inspectors and supervisors	4	2.48	0.58	1.98	2.72	1.04	2.26
Skilled manual	5	53.37	32.03	47.79	53.04	34.04	47.82
Semi-skilled manual	6	24.00	32.45	26.21	14.83	28.95	18.71
Unkilled manual	7	5.11	3.79	4.76	13.39	7.40	11.74
		100.00	100.00	100.00	100.00	100.00	100.00
Total		44,724	15,843	60,567	60,787	23,019	83,806

SOURCE: Relevant *Censuses of Population*; Occupational Classification following Routh [1965].

Graph 14.2). This severely curtailed collective organisation among car workers. The particularly high weekly earnings in Coventry's engineering industries in part reflects this seasonality as well as the relatively tight external labour power market.

GRAPH 14.2 Seasonal Unemployment in Coventry Compared with that of Great Britain, 1928–38

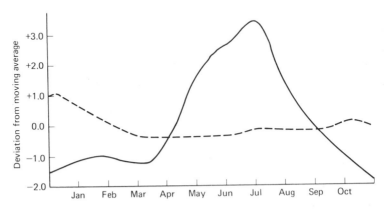

SOURCE: *West Midlands Plan*

Coventry had a far higher proportion of skilled manual workers compared with semi-skilled workers than the rest of England and Wales. This appears to contradict the evidence from Table 14.1 above, which distinguished Coventry for the opposite reason. It appears that Coventry's proportion of semi-skilled manual workers as a percentage of all manual workers *fell* from 45 per cent in 1911 to 33 per cent in 1921, and then to 24 per cent in 1931.[19] The solution to this apparent contradiction lies in the fact that many semi-skilled workers (that is, those who only required a few months' training at the most to perform their tasks), managed to gain skilled status in Coventry. To be classifed as skilled in Coventry's car industry came simply to distinguish those workers who were being paid the district skilled rate. Increasingly workers achieved this rate on account of their individual bargaining power rather than their skills.

The motor industry was relatively free from strikes during the 1920s and early 1930s, and *none* were recorded for Coventry's motor industry in the Ministry of Labour Gazette until 1934. This reflected the weakness of collective worker resistance and the strength of individual resistance in Coventry at this time. Most motor industry strikes were about wage reductions (as at Birmingham in 1929 and in Scotland during 1931). Coventry's wages remained well above those in other centres.

3 Peak Period-Acceleration Part 1932–1957

During the Peak Period the larger car firms enjoyed a high degree of monopoly power by virtue of their size, their relative protection from foreign competition and the very strong demand for British cars. The wide discretionary margins which this fortunate set of circumstances allowed top managers are clear from their model policies, their avoidance of uncomfortable rationalisation after mergers, their dividend policies and, particularly from the 1940s, their strategies for maintaining authority over their workers. This loosening of competitive pressures (loosening of the law of value) was a temporary phenomenon. But the strength of worker resistance built up among 'central' car workers (particularly in Coventry), and the entrenchment of policies and strategies which top managers could afford to pursue during the Peak Period, meant that the adjustments required of top managers when Ownership Growth began to decelerate, and to reverse, were late in coming and extremely disruptive.

Monopoly Power and Discretion

During the 1930s Morris and Austin failed to consolidate the position of market dominance which they achieved by the late 1920s. The full cost-reducing potential offered by flow production was not realised during the 1930s because manufacturers began to put more and more models onto the market. The ten largest manufacturers offered 46 different models at the 1929 Motor Show. In 1932 they offered 64. Of 40 different engine types produced by the six largest firms in 1938, 26 had sales of less than 5000 units, which was reckoned as an uneconomic level in the 'popular' class.

Part of the model explosion was caused by a shift in demand to smaller cars. This was due to the depression of the early 1930s and heavy taxation which was assessed on horsepower from 1910. Morris and Austin were slow to adjust to the new situation. It was not until 1934 that Morris introduced a new small car (the Morris Eight), which was completely redesigned to fit the new production methods adopted by the firm. Ford introduced the Ford Eight in 1931.

The other side of Morris and Austin's decline was the rise of Ford, Vauxhall, Rootes and Standard (see Table 14.2). The other side of the failure of Morris and Austin to capitalise on their head start with flow production was the ability of the other four to introduce mass production successfully. The 1930s saw the large-scale intervention of two large American firms into the British market. In 1928 General Motors gained a foothold by taking over Vauxhall, which was on the verge of bankruptcy. Vauxhall's share rose steadily, though unspectacularly, during the 1930s. By 1938 their market share had doubled. Ford and Vauxhall accounted for 28 per cent of the British market in 1938 (compared with only 5 per cent in 1929), both having expanded entirely internally.

The Rootes empire, heavily concentrated in Coventry, arose through a series of mergers and take-overs (Chart 14.1). Rootes Brothers were sales agents and distributors until they took over Thrupp & Maberly in 1926. In 1932 they took over Coventry's Humber, Hillman, Commer group and in 1934 and 1935 they took over several more ailing car firms. Always they bought firms which were in severe financial difficulties. They rationalised and integrated them and succeeded in capturing 10 per cent of the car market by 1938.

Standard (entirely in Coventry), particularly benefited from the shift to small cars. Standard, with Hillman, was the first company to have a car in the newly popular 9–10 h.p. field. As a result, Standard's share of the market doubled in a single year. As more firms introduced flow production in the early 1930s costs fell further. Between 1929 and 1932 retail car prices fell by about a third after falling by about a quarter in the late 1920s (Political and Economic Planning [1948], p. 19).

The American industry was far more concentrated than the British. The top three manufacturers, General Motors, Ford and Chrysler, accounted for about 90 per cent of the market in the late 1930s compared with only about 60 per cent for the top three British firms. The Americans made slightly fewer models and used many more standardised parts and components. In foreign markets the British were unable to compete successfully, especially with the Americans. In 1938 only 44,000 private cars were exported and of the these 33,000 were sold in Imperial Preference markets. The home market was protected by the 33.3 per cent McKenna tariff. Therefore about 97 per cent of the 341,000 British cars produced in 1938 were sold in protected markets.

While the industry's output rose from 171,000 to 390,000 units between 1932 and 1937, car prices remained stable.[20] The models boom not only harmed Morris and Austin's competitive position, it also hurt the whole industry. New models and frequent model changes cut short the long production runs which were necessary to reap the benefits of flow production. Each new model required considerable re-tooling and re-organisation of assembly lines. This initial lay-out occurred no matter how many cars were produced. The expense was only justified if more than a certain number of cars were produced. During the mid-1930s output of the major firms did rise to allow output per week to climb from 1000 units per week to 2000 units. Prices could well have fallen. However, due to the wasteful proliferation of models, they did not. The British motor industry, technically out of the Luxury Product Period, was behaving as though it was still servicing an individually stylised market.

According to Political and Economic Planning (PEP), at car prices and running costs prevailing before the war, people with incomes below £250 a year could not afford a car. This left a potential market of only 2.5 million earners at the outside (1948, p. 19). As the number of cars in use jumped from 1,149,000 in 1932 to 1,834,000 in 1937, with the potential market three-quarters saturated, the market would have entered the Declining Ownership Growth Period. In fact the annual increase in number of vehicles in use reached a peak in 1935 (171,000). It had already fallen significantly by the peak pre-war sales year of 1937 (159,000). Therefore a significant shift in the character of car demand from new owner purchases to replacement purchases occurred in the mid-1930s, long before the war disturbed the market. By extending their model ranges rather than their production runs in the early 1930s, car firms effectively traded an expanding industry for the hope of increasing market shares.

During the war the production of private cars in Britain was suspended. Car firms made service vehicles, tanks and aeroplanes, marine engines and a wide range of arms and equipment. Coventry in particular became the home of shadow factories attached to the car firms producing arms and planes. The capacity of the industry increased during the war as car firms prospered on government military contracts. As the PEP put it, 'considerable liquid assets were accumulated.' The War Office did try to spread the contracts around and smaller firms also benefited.

While the capacity of the British motor industry expanded during the war, the production capacity of major competitors (except for the United States) was largely destroyed. For a decade after the war demand for cars provided no limit to car output, but supply conditions did. Along with the vast export potential created by wartime destruction on the continent, the British market had been starved for cars for six years. The stock of passenger cars in use in the United Kingdom fell from two million to 1.5 million between 1939 and 1945, (Maxcy and Silberston [1959], p. 225). On the other hand wartime shortages of raw materials and labour persisted until around 1954. With the steel shortages it was also difficult for car firms to replace old and inefficient equipment.

In this temporary post-war situation of high demand, high liquidity from wartime contracts and raw materials temporarily in short supply to the industry, but fairly evenly available to all firms in the industry, small firms flourished and the trend towards concentration was temporarily checked. The relative share of Morris and Austin continued to decline – from a combined share of 60 per cent in 1929 to 39 per cent in 1947, while the share of small producers returned to the 1929 level of 12 per cent (see Table 14.2).

Firms eventually recognised that the problem would be production rather than sales for some time to come. Following from this the car manufacturers began to buy up their suppliers, particularly their suppliers of car bodies, to ensure steady supplies as best they could. Major absorptions occurred in 1953 when Ford took over Briggs Motor Bodies and British Motor Corporation (Austin–Morris) took over Fisher and Ludlow Ltd.

After the war the Government gave each firm in the industry an export target and began to allocate steel on the basis of export performance. In 1937, the peak pre-war export year, Britain exported 20 per cent by number of the vehicles and chassis it produced (18 per cent of the private cars by value which were produced in 1937 were exported). The Commonwealth took 76 per cent of motor exports by value, Europe took 15 per cent. In 1938 Britain's share of world car exports was only 13 per cent by number.

The situation was completely altered after the war. Between 1948 and 1952 the proportion of British car production which was exported varied between 62 per cent and 77 per cent (Rhys [1972], p. 382). By 1950 the United Kingdom was the world's largest car exporter, accounting for 55 per cent of world car exports (by number of cars and car chassis). After 1950 the British share of world exports fell as the German, French and Italian motor industries recovered. After 1952 the share of British production sold abroad also declined, but it remained roughly between 40 per cent and 50 per cent. Similarly, though the decline in the British share of the world market was steady, the United Kingdom still accounted for 29 per cent of the world car export market in 1957.

Pre-war British car exports were sold primarily in protected markets. After the war the United Kingdom still exported most of its cars to Commonwealth countries, especially Australia and New Zealand during the late 1940s and early 1950s, but export sales to Europe, and especially to America, began to rise (particularly after import restrictions on cars were imposed by Australia in late 1951). In 1956 23 per cent of British car exports went to the United States. The country's all-out drive to produce cars for world markets, to earn the foreign exchange needed to finance post-war growth, meant that the quality of British car exports suffered.

Coventry and Car Firm Prosperity

The dash for high production also meant that firms competed for raw materials and labour rather than car buyers. Wages and raw materials costs began to leapfrog as firms tried to stretch their profits into higher immediate production figures. The competition for workers was especially fierce in Coventry, where several large car firms competed in the same labour power market. In 1945 Standard Motors withdrew from the Coventry Engineering Employer's Association because the E.E.F. tried to limit wage competition.

Other Coventry car firms, and later non-Coventry car firms, soon followed Standard's high-wage leadership. According to Turner, 'by 1947 earnings in the different car plants seem to have been back in line, other firms having presumably caught up with Standard' (1967, p. 141). At the end of 1948 Standard Motors again increased wages so that average hourly pay was now 20 per cent above the pay of other motor firms, but 'by the early 1950s other Coventry plants – especially, Rootes, . . . had already (also) begun to pull away from the generality of car firms in terms of wages paid per hour' (Turner [1967], p. 141). The range between car firms narrowed appreciably between 1953 and 1957, and wage increases generally accelerated. Ford, the lowest paying firm, increased wages steeply during this period and particularly in 1956–7.

People had been pouring into Coventry for well over 50 years. The city's population grew from 70,000 in 1901 to 168,000 in 1931. During the Acceleration part of the Peak Period in the motor-car's product cycle, Coventry's population grew to 267,300 (1956). Much of the increase in Coventry's labour force during this later period was also due to the growth of the aircraft, electrical engineering and mechanical engineering industries in the city, but these were all in some way connected with cars. Between 1946 and 1956 unemployment in the country as a whole remained quite low, between 1 per cent and 2 per cent of the labour force, but in Coventry unemployment was always below 1 per cent and often as low as 0.2 per cent.[21] Only in 1956 and 1957 did the level of Coventry's unemployment exceed the average level for Great Britain between 1946 and 1961. With a very high demand for skilled and semi-skilled engineers from many general engineering, car and aircraft firms competing in Coventry, wages in Coventry's engineering industries shot up to 35–40 per cent above wages for comparable engineering labour in the rest of the country (Knowles and Robinson [1969], p. 2). This percentage differential was maintained throughout the 1950s and 1960s (in 1969 the differential was 36 per cent), (Brown [1971], pp. 7–8).

While Coventry workers emerged during the war as the main central workers within the U.K. motor industry, two changes in market structure during the 1950s would augur poorly for Coventry's future position within the U.K. motor industry. The first was the dramatic rise in Ford's market share, Ford being the major non-Coventry car firm.

Most of Ford's increased market share came at the expense of the small producers. In the early 1950s small producers left the industry because their small orders with outside suppliers put them at the end of the queue for materials and components, especially car bodies. Greater integration by the big firms cut off supplies to the smaller ones. Jowett, Singer (a Coventry firm) and Lea Francis left the car market primarily because they were outpriced by Ford in the popular car market.

The second major change in market structure was the Nuffield – Austin merger in February 1952 forming the British Motor Corporation (B.M.C.). This was the largest merger in the history of the industry and the first time a horizontal merger had occurred between two prosperous companies. It reflected the firms' recognition of the competitive edge of the two American firms.

The merger was not a success. Maxcy (1958, p. 380), sums up the problem of the two major British firms' management strategy as well as that of the new mammoth car firm by relating the following incident:

From the end of the war up to the time of the BMC merger, Ford and Vauxhall had been investing large sums in new plant and equipment, and huge expansion schemes were then under consideration. It was subsequently disclosed that these plans involved a capital expenditure of £65 million for Ford and £36 million for Vauxhall. Sir Leonard Lord, chairman of the new British Motor Corporation, replied . . . that he was not prepared to 'bandy millions' with the Americans, who were preparing to use production in this country as a 'spring board for the Commonwealth markets'. . . . He concluded by saying, 'We expect keen competition, but we have a few shillings in the bank and friends who will lend us money. We are feeling pretty comfortable' (from an article in the *Financial Times*, 28 September 1954).

B.M.C. were certainly feeling pretty comfortable. Between 1949 and 1954 U.K. car production jumped from 442,000 to 769,000. In 1949 Austin and Morris made £4 million net profits before tax.[22] In the year before the merger they made £16 million and in 1954 B.M.C. made £18 million. Though Sir Leonard was not prepared to 'bandy millions' with the Americans, he certainly had millions to bandy. Even with tax rates at 50 per cent, during the five years between 1950 and 1954 they could have accumulated something like £35 million in the bank, if not for dividends.[23] In 1955 alone B.M.C. made over £20 million net profits before tax.

The first post-war decade was a very prosperous time for all major car firms in the UK. While Ford had never made more than £1 million in any year before 1939, Ford's profits jumped from £4 million in 1947 to £10 million by 1950. In 1957 Ford made £21 million. Rootes earned £3 million a year every year from 1950 to 1955, Standard £1 million to £3 million per year and Vauxhall, which had been earning roughly between £2 million and £3 million a year from 1947 to 1951, made £5 million in 1952, and between £10 million and £12 million between 1953 and 1955 (Maxcy and Silberston [1959], p. 229).

Most of these profits were reinvested in the firms to increase output, but 27 per cent of net profits of the major firms were distributed as dividends between 1947 and 1956 (amounting to some £36 million over the 10 years). While Ford was distributing 21 per cent and Vauxhall 26 per cent of their profits in dividends, B.M.C. distributed 32 per cent, and before the merger Morris distributed 61 per cent of their profits in dividends (Maxcy and Silberston [1959], pp. 176–7).

Automation and Insecurity among Car Workers

After the war top managers in the major car firms began to introduce what has been called 'automation'. Automation essentially means the setting of machines to do several tasks in succession. This can be divided into two aspects. First, machines do certain operations several times without requiring resetting. Second, machines may be used to transfer materials from one production point to another. What was called automation was the joining of these two aspects of machine use.

As the numbers of cars produced by an individual firm increase, the extra costs of introducing expensive machinery comes to be justified by the savings in costs per car which the machines allow. At first, as the size of a firm's output of single models rises to a few hundred cars a year, cars can be produced in batches. It becomes economical to leave a machine to do a single task many times.

As the output of firms reached many thousands of cars per year in the 1920s (the Luxury Product Period), the second aspect of automation was introduced, that is, the use of machines to move parts and components from one production point to another. Flow production replaced batch production. Until the late 1940s these two aspects of automation remained separate. Assembly lines carried parts and components between workers doing specific tasks. At other places in the factories large machines stamped or pressed or machined individual types of parts many times.

In the late 1940s and in the 1950s firms began to introduce 'automation' in the form of automatic transfer machines. These machines are automatic flow-production lines with machines at the production points, all synchronised to work in step with the pace of the whole production line. The advantages of automation are similar to the advantages of any form of mechanisation. Working stocks required and product handling are reduced, allowing greater consistency in quality. Of course, the major saving to the firm is in direct labour.

Automation in the first post-war decade did not cause unemployment, because of the greatly expanded demand for cars. The long-run trend in car employment as with car output, was upward. Nevertheless the fear of redundancy from automation added to workers' feelings of insecurity in the motor industry. As with bicycles and silk ribbons before, even in the most prosperous period, the Peak Period, Coventry car workers were often unemployed. Before the Second World War, car workers were regularly laid off during the winter lull in sales (Graph 14.2). After the war export demand in Australia and New Zealand helped to smooth seasonal fluctuations, but periodic recessions still occurred. Thousands of workers were laid off in 1953 and 1956. It was of little comfort to the men being laid off to discover that the cause of this redundancy was a short-run recession (short-run in 1953 and 1956 meaning up to two years), rather than an automatic transfer machine.

Turner summed up the workers' logical reaction to this insecurity:

Their anxiety over security has led many workers to reason that since they have no way of knowing how long either their high boom-time earnings or their jobs will last, their best policy is simply to go all out for what they can get while the company's profits are high. In our view, this outlook has been a circumstance of fundamental relevance to the car firms' dispute-proneness, and the contribution of automation to the industry's strike record is largely dependent on the part it has played in developing it (1967, p. 83).

Fluctuations in motor industry employment have particularly affected Coventry. By the end of 1956 over 2000 more men were unemployed than at the end of 1955 (Coventry Employment Exchange). This was largely due to Standard sacking 3500 men in 1956 in Coventry, though in 1956 most car firms were laying off workers (especially B.M.C., which laid off one in eight of its workers).

Worker Resistance, Management and the Gang System in Coventry

During the 1940s and early 1950s the shop stewards' movement in Coventry's engineering industry became very powerful. The Government pushed engineering firms toward Responsible Autonomy strategies during the Second World War, particularly through the co-option of trade union leaders, as it had during the First World War. Trade unions became registered agents of the Ministry of Labour for paying out unemployment benefits and for the disbursement of workers to individual firms. If a trade union officer sent a man to a firm and the managers turned him down, the trade union could cause an official inquiry to be made. This considerably changed management–union relations in the car industry, where many firms had acquired a reputation for dismissing active trade union supporters during the off-season (Turner et al. [1967], pp. 193–4).

While skilled men continued to be represented by several craft unions,[24] less skilled workers were almost exclusively represented by the Transport and General Workers Union (T.G.W.U.), into which the W.U. had amalgamated in 1928.[25] During the 1940s all unions made strong headway with recruitment (especially the T.G.W.U.) due to government encouragement and the end of wide seasonal fluctuations in employment. It was only in 1943 and 1944 that Vauxhall and Ford finally recognised trade unions. During the 1940s the attitude of British-owned firms toward the unions softened further.

A few years before the war workers at Coventry's Armstrong Whitworth aeroplane factory began to form gangs. That top managers at Armstrong Whitworth readily tolerated the gang system reflected both the tightening external labour power market in Coventry and rapid technical change in the aircraft industry. Drayton, who worked in Armstrong Whitworth at the time, says:

The all-metal aircraft of today were then just emerging and entirely new techniques were evolving almost every job being a 'problem', . . . nearly all daywork shops tended to be 'stagnant', lacking in incentive, so most jobs were put on piecework. *Individual* piecework. The result was thousands of jobs being timed or estimated, and therefore thousands of arguments between men and rate-fixers (who were in short supply) and there was more argument than working (1972, p. 8).

The gang system represented a solution to top managers' need for an extremely flexible and 'responsible' labour force, when new materials and new tasks had to be incorporated quickly into productive activity. The gang system also increased workers' direct control over productive activity, increased their job security, increased their security against other forms of disciplinary action and improved their working relations with each other. Nevertheless the switch to the gang system *reflected* the strong position of workers and helped solve top managers' technical predicament.

During the war, as car firms switched to aircraft and munitions production, workers from Armstrong and Whitworth were assigned to other major Coventry firms. With them the gang system followed as car firms faced similar labour power market and technical conditions.

Under the gang system the gang leader or 'ganger' would negotiate a 'contract' (usually unwritten) with top managers to produce a given output. The ganger would then keep track of work and money to try to ensure that each gang member kept up his work-load. The major difference between the gang system and the old subcontracting system within firms which was common during the nineteenth century was that the ganger was generally elected by the gang and responsible to its members.[26] Often the gang would distribute work and discipline members collectively. Drayton points out that the contract 'was not between the firm and the ganger, but between the firm and the gang as an entity' (1972, p. 9).

The gang payment system was also much more favourable than most individual piece-work systems. Taylor's system and the premium bonus system emphasised penalties for not achieving the target rate and limited the excess payment to be gained for exceeding the target. Under the gang system wages were arranged from a base rate which would allow what was considered a 'decent' wage. Generous incentive bonuses were also available for output above the contracted amount. This system was encouraged by cost-plus contracts given to the firms for wartime work. The role of supervisors or foremen also changed. They became more concerned with co-ordination of production flows than with the maintenance of managerial authority. Thus the need for supervisors and foremen declined significantly.

After the war the gang system was continued in several of Coventry's car firms, but it was most widespread at Standard Motors. (Standard was then the second largest employer in Coventry after Rootes.) As a result Standard became known for high wages, more pleasant working conditions and faster work pace. Standard also required significantly fewer administrative, technical and clerical workers. In 1939, 16.5 per cent of Standard's workers were from the administrative groups, which was comparable to the rest of the motor vehicle industry (15.6 per cent for the whole industry in 1937). Between 1948 and 1954 the percentage rose from 19.5 per cent to 22.2 per cent for the whole motor industry. It varied between 15.3 per cent and 17.8 per cent at Standard (Melman [1958], pp. 123–4).

Standard, and other Coventry car firms to a lesser extent, were considerably at variance with the E.E.F. over 'appropriate' wage levels and general managerial strategies. Standard withdrew from the Coventry branch of the E.E.F. in 1945. Car firms which were not concentrated in Coventry reacted to the immediate post-war conditions of full employment and high demand by recognising the advantages of co-opting trade union leaders, primarily at the *national* level, Standard and other Coventry firms reacted by moving to Responsible Autonomy strategies which encouraged small groups of *shop-floor workers* to behave responsibly through loosening direct control. What they gained was flexibility within the workshop while introducing complex and continual changes due to automation. Drayton points out, 'no written rules were made, consequently there were no "orthodoxies", everything being left as fluid as possible' (1922, p. 9).

Gang sizes were largest at Standard. By 1953 all workers at the main car plant were in fifteen gangs and all 3000 workers in Standard's tractor plant in Coventry formed a single gang (Melman [1958],pp. 12–13). In most other major Coventry plants gangs were of five to a hundred workers and gangs represented only a minority of workers (Higgs [1969], pp. 116–19).

While the Responsible Autonomy strategy gives top managers wide flexibility for getting workers to fit in with changes required for technical reasons,[27] it increases inflexibility concerning the relative difficulty of discharging workers when labour-saving machines are introduced, or when market demand conditions impel top managers to reduce labour costs.

Up to the mid-1950s the shop stewards of Standard, '– partly because of the semi-managerial role that the firm had conceded them – were . . . undoubtedly the most tightly-organised in the motor industry' (Turner [1967], p. 213). Turner then notes with surprise that this was a period of comparative industrial peace at Standard (p. 213). Surely this is to be expected considering the managerial strategy pursued. Then in 1956 as Standard began to lay off workers due to the general slump in car demand, 11,000 workers at Standard went on strike for two weeks over the failure of the company to help work out short-time schemes to deal with the slump. This strike accounted for almost one-half of the 270,000 striker days in the motor industry in 1956, in spite of the generality of the slump and the common experience of lay-offs for most firms. While Standard laid off 3500 workers in 1956, some 20,000 were laid off throughout the industry in that year, (N.E.D.O. [1969], p. 37). The strike did not spread to other Coventry firms during 1956, because it primarily reflected the breakdown of Standard's somewhat distinctive managerial strategy. In the late 1950s Standard became one of the most strike-prone of car firms, in sharp contrast to a record of almost ten strike-free years from the end of the war. In 1961 the ailing company was taken over by Leyland after a run of loss-making years, due in part to persistent industrial relations difficulties. While the gang system continued at the Standard factory until the end of the decade, the credibility of the managerial strategy it represented had been undermined.

The major switch away from Responsible Autonomy strategies in other car firms would come later, when market conditions had deteriorated further.

4   Peak Period – Deceleration Part 1957–1966

During the Deceleration Part of the Peak Period, as competitive pressures began to intensify, the burden of high dividends, low past investment, strong worker resistance and increasingly inappropriate Responsible Autonomy strategies began to tell on the major car firms. When top managers tried to intensify work, reduce manning levels or discipline workers, they encountered strong resistance. It was during this period that the car industry achieved its reputation for strike-proneness.

Table 14.4 indicates the tremendous growth of strike activity from 1956.

TABLE 14.4

Industrial Disputes in Car Firms, 1947–64

Annual averages of 3-year period	Number of separate strikes	Workers directly and indirectly involved	'Working days lost'
1947–49	10	9,000	25,000
1950–52	14	25,000	131,000
1953–55	14	42,000	137,000
1956–58	31	82,000	322,000
1959–61	75	116,000	307,000
1962–64	86	141,000	321,000

NOTE: Workers involved in more than one strike are counted more than once.
SOURCE: Turner [1967], p. 23.

While competitive pressures were as yet relatively weak and profits still high, work intensification and rationalisation occurred piecemeal. Only later, during the Period of Declining Ownership Growth, would the car industry's problems come to occupy the centre stage of the British Government's industrial policy.

Changing Competitive Conditions

The dividing line between the acceleration and deceleration parts of the Peak Period is rather arbitrary. Certainly the years between 1956 and 1964 were very good ones, as can be seen from Graph 13.2. But signs of weakness in the demand for cars and in the firms producing cars were appearing. Periodic slumps in demand continued with increased severity. In 1956 car production fell by 140,000, in 1961 car production fell by 349,000, and between 1964 and 1967 car production fell by 316,000. The industry came to service the home market more and more as Britain lost her export edge. Between 1953 and 1964 U.K. producers exported about 47 per cent of the cars they produced. By 1966 only 35 per cent of U.K. cars were produced for export. World car exports during this period grew very quickly, but the U.K. share of this trade fell from 29 per cent in 1957 to 17 per cent in 1966. Nevertheless the number of new registrations at home grew tremendously during the second post-war decade (Graph 13.1).

Responses to Altering Competitive Conditions

It was during the Peak Period – Deceleration Part of the bicycle product cycle (around 1901–14) that most of Coventry's bicycle producers were turning to motor cycles and motor-cars, at least on an experimental basis. Without this new product to take up the slack which was developing in the bicycle industry many bicycle firms would not have survived past the 1920s and Coventry would have become a depressed area as in the 1860s and 1870s. But the car firms have not turned to new products, though they were generally operating at less than 80 per cent capacity after 1964 (Rhys [1972], p. 359).[28]

   Given that firms were not moving toward new products, the recognition of excess capacity and the erosion of export markets could have led U.K. car firms to another strategy. They could have rationalised their facilities to produce fewer models with larger production runs per model. This would have required further mergers among the major producers and further capital investments. This they did not do. During the second post-war decade five major car-producing firms serviced markets which never exceeded two million cars per year. According to Maxcy and Silberston, in 1959 individual firms should have been producing about one million units of a single model to take full advantage of the economies of large-scale production available at that time (1959, chap. 6). In the year of highest car production the country's biggest producer, B.M.C., made only 719,000 of all its models combined.

   B.M.C. itself was an uneasy amalgamation of Morris's and Austin's empires. Before the merger the two companies were both essentially one-man operations which had outgrown their founders (Turner [1971], p. 88). When the companies came together in 1952 the two continued to compete. 'The companies kept separate boards of directors and separated books right up until 1966, and cars assembled partly in one company's plants and partly in the others – (as with Morris cars assembled at Longbridge) – were sold from one company to the other, and sometimes back again' (Counter Information Services [1974], p. 10). B.M.C.'s co-ordination problems were listed in an article in *Car* magazine of October 1967.

> Firstly, there is the added complication in the factories of building cars with varying specification which require additional ordering, stocking, and even machining operations. Secondly – and probably of even greater importance – there is the loss of impact in trying to promote six brand names instead of one or two on what must inevitably be a finite budget. And thirdly, there is the problem of stocking thousands of not-quite-similar spares in out-of-the-way distributorships.

But the problem was not simply that B.M.C. was not integrated between Austin and Morris, just as the problem now is not simply the lack of integration of British Leyland. The real problem is that the U.K. motor industry is not integrated between Ford, Vauxhall, Chrysler and British Leyland. This is of course all the more difficult because three of the four firms are not owned in this country.

The car firms also reinvested relatively little of their profits in their firms. Between 1947 and 1956 the major firms distributed 27 per cent of their net profits in dividends. But between 1959 and 1965 they distributed some 44 per cent. In 1966 profits after taxes of the major companies fell drastically, from £56 million in 1965 to *£30 million*, but the major car firms distributed *£33 million* in dividends and as a result they made a *net loss* after tax and dividends of £3 million (N.E.D.O. [1969], pp. 33–5).

This underinvestment, especially in B.M.C., meant that British firms were less capital intensive, less mechanised and less able to take advantage of economies of scale. In 1956–66, 'BMC produced 8.5 cars per man per year compared with 9.7 at Ford, 10.6 at Vauxhall and *16* at Volkswagen' (Rhys [1972], p. 369). The productivity of large Continental firms such as Volkswagen and Renault was much higher than U.K. firms, partly because they produced a smaller range of cars and changed models less often. Also in other countries the largest firms generally supplied a larger share of the market and were consequently larger than the largest British firm even when the total home market was smaller. In 1967 Volkswagen accounted for 47 per cent of German production, Renault 40 per cent of French production, General Motors 56 per cent of American production, Toyota 39 per cent of Japanese production and Fiat 86 per cent of Italian production, while B.M.H. accounted for only 36 per cent of U.K. production. Whether *all* these companies were large enough at that time to take full advantage of economies of scale (except perhaps General Motors, which was almost four times larger than any of the rest) is doubtful. Only Fiat, Volkswagen and the three

American giants produced more than one million cars in any one country.

The British home market had been highly protected for a long time. The 33.3 per cent tariff on cars remained until 1956 when the rate was reduced to 30 per cent. Further reductions in 1962 and 1963 brought the rate down to 25.5 per cent and in 1968 the rate was reduced to 22 per cent. These changes were part of the general tariff reductions in Europe during the 1960s. Imports as a percentage of new car registrations in the United Kingdom remained low throughout the 1950s and early 1960s, but the percentage increased from 5 per cent to 6 per cent in 1966 and then to 8 per cent in 1967. This began a trend of increased imports which has continued to the present.

The relative market shares of car firms hardly altered between the mid-1950s and the mid-1960s (Table 14.2). Ford and Vauxhall's advance continued, mainly at the expense of Standard. In 1966 British Motor Corporation (Holdings) was formed as B.M.C. merged with the newly-formed Jaguar empire (see Chart 14.1) and with Pressed Steel.

The 1960s also saw the rise of the Leyland empire (Chart 14.1). In 1961 Leyland, a commercial vehicles producer, entered the passenger car market in a major way by taking over Standard Triumph (Standard took over Triumph in 1945). In 1962 Leyland absorbed Associated Commercial Vehicles and in 1967 Leyland took over Rover (which had absorbed Alvis the year before). In 1968 Leyland Motor Corporation took over B.M.H. to form British Leyland Motor Corporation. B.L.M.C's share of the 1968 market was 45 per cent.

Leyland, like B.M.C., was the master of a poorly integrated empire. Leyland in the 1950s was 'run as a loose collection of lorry companies, often competing with each other and with only a certain degree of commonality of parts and marketing, with, in effect, one man at the centre co-ordinating them – Donald Stokes.' (Counter Information Services [1974], p. 21). When B.M.H. and Leyland merged, the result, British Leyland, was an even larger collection of poorly co-ordinated factories.

Worker Resistance and Management

Throughout the 1950s and 1960s workers in Coventry's engineering industries persistently maintained a high earnings differential over car and engineering workers in the rest of the country (35–40 per cent from 1957 to 1966). This was due in part to the tight external labour power market in Coventry, but it was also due to strong shop-floor organisation particularly among Coventry's car workers (who continued to be wage leaders within Coventry). In common with other car factories the power of Coventry shop stewards derived from several factors; first, the importance of locally negotiated overtime and bonus rates; second, the technical changes which required transferring workers around factories and working with new machines and which could only be negotiated at local levels; and third, the fact that problems peculiar to the car industry could not be adequately dealt with by officials of the major car-

worker unions because the bulk of the A.E.U. and the T.G.W.U.'s membership were not working for car firms. In addition it was top managers' policy to
deal with individual workers at the shop-floor level rather than groups
(mutuality). From 1922 individual shop stewards were allowed to negotiate
for individual workers with managers' representatives.

This mutuality principle was particularly important in Coventry, where
piece-work payment was more common than elsewhere.[29] In Coventry the
traditional method of piece-work payment was money piece-work rather than
time piece-work. Under money piece-work, which was appropriate for the
gang system, production workers are paid at a price per piece directly
proportionate to output of the individual or the gang. Under time piece-work
(Taylorian, premium bonus or Bedaux-type systems), workers are paid bonus
earnings over the basic rate in relation to time saved against time allowed, and
they are penalised for not working within the time allowed. The latter system
involves elaborate measurement and specification of *how* work *ought* to be
done, as well as how much should be produced. The latter system involves
much greater direct control by managers.

Money piece-work reflected Responsible Autonomy strategies pursued by
car firms in Coventry (until the late 1960s). The basis of the E.E.F. strategy in
1897 and in 1922 when pushing for mutuality was to be able to pay low rates to
workers in relatively weak bargaining positions without having to pay those
rates generally throughout firms. The strength of this strategy lay in work
measurement by experts (time piece-work system), which would make it
difficult for workers to argue with managers' representatives over appropriate
rates *and* make it difficult to compare one worker's earnings with another as a
bargaining counter. In Coventry the level of earnings considered 'decent' by
workers rather than the time 'scientifically' required for a particular task
became the issue of negotiation between managers and stewards at the shop-
floor level. Thus the stewards, by acquiring some knowledge of earnings levels
throughout the factory, were able to bargain more effectively for workers in
Coventry, whether workers were in gangs or not.

With money piece-work, top managers might have thought they were
trading a loosening of direct control over workers for a reduction in
supervision costs, higher output per man and the ability to discriminate
earnings levels easily on the basis of individual workers' productivity and
bargaining power. In fact, through the strength of shop-floor organisation,
the loosening of direct control over costs and authority over workers was
accompanied by continuous shop-floor struggle over earnings and increasing
bitterness over rather arbitrary variations in final earnings achieved.

Comparability of earnings levels was enhanced by the Coventry Toolroom
Agreement. During the war the acute shortage of craftsmen in Coventry led to
a wage spiral. The Coventry and District Engineering Employers' Association
(C.D.E.E.A.), in order to stop individual employers from poaching craftsmen
from one another, concluded an agreement in January 1941 that toolroom

workers in Coventry should earn no less than the average earnings of the skilled production workers in federated firms in the district. The C.D.E.E.A. then compiled and published a list of earnings of skilled production workers (skilled fitters, turners and skilled machinists) in the district. Essentially 'skilled' *production* workers were Coventry's semi-skilled (by training necessary) engineering workers, whose earnings were rising much faster than craftsmen in internal labour markets both because of their bargaining power and because their earnings were tied more closely to fast-rising output per man. The effect of this agreement, which continued in force until 1971, was to increase shop-floor knowledge of how their earnings compared with others in Coventry. This exacerbated wage-structure negotiations from top managers' point of view. Gradually, with the growing strength and sophistication of the stewards throughout the motor industry, the Coventry Toolroom rate came to be used in wage negotiations by stewards in other Midlands factories and eventually in car factories elsewhere in the United Kingdom.

As can be seen from Table 14.5 wage structure and work loads were the main reason for the rise in strikes after the early 1950s.

TABLE 14.5

Percentage Striker-days in Car Firms by Cause, 1946–64

	1946–55	1956–60	1961–4
Straight wage-increase demands	22.3	10.1	9.2
Wage-structure and work loads	18.1	32.2	39.0
Working hours and conditions	–	4.0	3.3
Trade union relations	36.1	16.3	13.4
Individual dismissals	4.3	5.3	14.6
Redundancy, short-time	16.0	28.6	9.3
Management questions	3.2	3.5	10.6
	100.0	100.0	100.0
Number of striker-days (000s)	94	227	246

NOTE: General engineering stoppages are excluded.
SOURCE: Turner [1967], pp. 66, 67; though see all of Chapter 2 for details of this classification scheme.

Rising shop-floor strength meant more than high labour costs and high negotiation costs for top managers (high negotiation costs particularly in terms of *time lost* during negotiation and during small disputes which could indirectly involve many workers). It also provided a disincentive for top managers to introduce new models or invest in new machines. When car firms faced weak competition in product markets as from 1946 to 1956, they could afford to buy off worker resistance. However as product markets became more competitive top managers began to try to re-establish direct control on the one hand,[30] and, on the other, to isolate and limit the importance of well-organised workers in their major factories by shifting new investments to areas of high unemployment within the country and abroad.

Centre–Periphery within Car Firms

Within car firms during the 1940s and early 1950s the vast majority of workers were treated as central workers with Responsible Autonomy strategies.[31] As competitive conditions changed, setting up new factories far away from the firms' main central workers held out the possibility of an effective centre–periphery relation within car firms, strongly based on location rather than race, sex or skill. During the early 1960s all the major car firms set up major new factories or large factory extensions in areas of high unemployment, primarily around Liverpool and in Scotland.

Certainly the Government's policy for moving industry to depressed regions, which became more intense with the 1960 and 1963 Local Employment Acts,[32] affected top managers' decision to set up new factories away from the traditional West Midlands and South-East regions. But it is doubtful that the controls on building in non-development districts would have been harshly exercised against car firms if they had insisted on expanding in traditional areas, and investment in traditional areas for *modernising existing factories* was also falling off seriously during the 1960s.[33]

As Beynon puts it:

The reasons which influenced the Ford Motor Company's move to Halewood were the same as those that led it to establish a plant at Genk in the underdeveloped Linsburg region of Belgium. Unemployment means low wages and a vulnerable labour force. . . . In Britain expansion away from traditional areas of manufacture created the possibility for the motor employers to organise the production of motor cars free from the job control that had built up in the old factories (1973, p. 65).[34]

While wages in Ford and Vauxhall's large new factories were quickly brought into line with those in their older factories in the South East, Rootes, B.M.C. and Leyland continued to pay far lower rates than in their Midlands factories. The difference in approach among the firms reflected wide pay differences between Midlands factories (especially those in Coventry) and those of the South East.[35]

Increasingly, from the mid-1960s, disputes for parity between factories of a single firm and between firms replaced disputes over differentials within factories as the major source of wage grievances in the motor industry. A six-week long strike involving 4000 workers at Leyland's Bathgate factory in Scotland for parity with its Standard-Triumph factory in 1966 was the first of a series of major parity strikes of the late 1960s and early 1970s in which

TABLE 14.6

Percentage of Persons Employed in Each Occupational Group, England and Wales, Coventry C.B.; 1951, 1961 and 1966

		1951			1961			1966		
		Male	Female	Total	Male	Female	Total	Male	Female	Total
England and Wales										
Higher professionals	1A	2.57	0.51	1.93	3.40	0.55	2.48	3.92	0.50	2.70
Lower professionals	1B	2.85	8.03	4.45	4.15	9.09	5.75	4.64	9.12	6.23
Employers and proprietors	2A	5.64	4.46	5.28	2.61	3.32	2.84	2.31	3.00	2.56
Managers and administrators	2B	5.02	1.15	3.83	9.13	4.00	7.46	9.70	4.07	7.70
Clerical workers	3	7.46	20.43	11.46	8.70	25.83	14.26	8.49	26.31	14.82
Foremen, inspectors and supervisors	4	4.16	1.25	3.26	4.68	1.41	3.63	7.89	1.43	3.75
Skilled manual	5	35.07	15.42	29.01	37.53	17.05	30.33	37.12	14.63	29.03
Semi-skilled manual	6	23.68	38.19	28.15	19.23	31.38	23.17	18.67	32.79	23.69
Unskilled manual	7	13.55	10.57	12.63	10.57	7.37	9.48	10.26	8.14	9.52
Total		100.00	100.00	100.00	100.00	100.00	100.00	100.00	100.00	100.00
		14,063,542	6,272,876	20,336,418	1,441,766	691,646	2,133,412	1,441,029	794,401	2,235,430

TABLE 14.6 (*Continued*)

Coventry C.B.

Higher professionals	1A	2.46	0.57	1.92	4.12	0.17	2.86	3.85	0.32	2.63
Lower professionals	1B	3.45	6.85	4.43	5.04	7.68	5.88	5.26	7.74	6.11
Employers and proprietors	2A	2.84	4.12	3.21	0.56	5.31	2.06	0.46	2.23	1.08
Managers and administrators	2B	3.84	0.68	2.93	5.65	3.75	5.05	6.41	5.95	6.25
Clerical workers	3	5.98	25.25	11.52	6.42	29.36	13.71	6.94	26.49	13.69
Foremen, inspectors and supervisors	4	6.83	3.86	5.98	7.51	4.98	6.58	8.26	5.48	7.24
Skilled manual	5	43.76	12.38	34.73	43.94	12.16	34.91	41.89	10.59	31.58
Semi-skilled manual	6	19.40	37.76	24.68	18.67	28.45	21.77	17.93	31.93	22.76
Unskilled manual	7	11.44	8.53	10.60	8.09	7.24	7.18	8.00	9.27	8.66
Total		100.00	100.00	100.00	100.00	100.00	100.00	100.00	100.00	100.00
		90,834	36,662	127,496	10,366	4,823	15,189	10,784	5,685	16,469

NOTE: 10 per cent sample used in 1961 and 1966 Censuses
SOURCE: Relevant *Censuses of Population*; Occupational Classification following Routh [1965].

Coventry's high wages, made more visible because of the Coventry Toolroom Agreement, were held up to employers as a standard for the whole industry in Britain. Also, while workers in the new centres began as more docile 'green' labour, they soon developed strong shop steward organisations. Remember the 'new' car factory areas themselves were strong 'old' centres of worker resistance. Thus the strategy of building a periphery of workers within car firms in this country, separated from Coventry and other traditional motor areas, began to crumble during the late 1960s.

Table 14.6 compares the occupation distribution between Coventry and England and Wales for 1951, 1961 and 1966. Again the proportion of skilled manual workers compared with semi-skilled workers has been consistently higher for Coventry, but this difference declined seriously during the early 1960s. The proportion of foremen, inspectors and supervisors in Coventry continued at almost double that of England and Wales, and this differential grew somewhat between 1961 and 1966, reflecting an intensification of Direct Control strategies in Coventry.

5   Period of Declining Ownership Growth 1966 – ?

During the ten years from 1966 to 1975 profits of British car firms collapsed. Failing Rootes was taken over by Chrysler in 1967. In October 1975 Chrysler announced they would begin liquidating their U.K. operations. As a result, the U.K. Government agreed to prop up the firm with £162.5 million. British Leyland Motor Corporation was formed in 1968 in recognition of the need to consolidate British-owned car factories to meet increasingly severe foreign competition. The Government began supporting B.L.M.C. from the start with a £25 million loan in 1968. The firm lost more than £100 million in 1973 and again in 1974. In 1975 B.L.M.C. was nationalised and the Government accepted that the firm would probably need £2800 million to the end of 1982 simply to remain viable.

The near-collapse of Chrysler and British Leyland (car firms highly concentrated in Coventry) also meant distress for car firm suppliers. Several small Coventry supplier firms have gone bankrupt and Alfred Herbert, Coventry's largest machine tool employer, was nationalised. Also Rolls Royce, making aircraft engines in Coventry, was nationalised in 1971. Thus in the four years to 1975, four out of Coventry's ten largest firms by employment, representing more than one in four of Coventry's working men came to be state owned or heavily state supported.

Intensified competition encouraged the intensification of work (speeding up lines), the intensification of worker resistance and the imposition of Direct Control strategies (Measured Daywork). Intensified competition also encouraged firms to shift more of their new investment out of the U.K., both reducing the proportion of troublesome British workers and increasing firms' ability to maintain production during strikes in Britain by using *duplicate* facilities abroad.

Monopoly Power

Since 1964 output has virtually stagnated. Since 1966 the percentage of Coventry's labour force employed in motor manufacturing has declined regularly and Coventry's level of male unemployment has shot up significantly, (Graph 13.2). Exports recovered somewhat between 1967 and 1969, but home demand for *British cars* has not provided the stimulus to U.K. production which it did during the previous decade. Instead imports have soared.

Between 1968 and 1972, as part of the 'Kennedy Round', the general tariff on cars and parts was reduced from 22 per cent to 11 per cent. Since then, the share of U.K. new car registrations which were imported has risen significantly. In 1966 imports accounted for 6 per cent of new car registrations. By 1968 their share was 9 per cent, by 1972, 24 per cent. The figure for 1976 was 38 per cent.

TABLE 14.7

Pre-tax Profits (Losses) of Major Car Firms in Britain (£m), 1964–75

	Ford	B.L.M.C.	Vauxhall	Chrysler
1964	24.0	54	17.9	1.5
1965	8.9	50	17.7	(2.5)
1966	7.4	44	3.6	(3.4)
1967	2.6	16	5.7	(10.8)
1968	43.0	38	9.0	(3.7)
1969	38.1	40	(1.9)	(0.7)
1970	25.2	4	(9.7)	(10.7)
1971	(30.7)	32	1.8	0.4
1972	46.8	32	(4.3)	1.6
1973	65.4	51	(4.1)	3.7
1974	8.7	2.3	(17.8)	(17.7)
1975	14.1	(76)	(13.0)	(35.5)

NOTE: B.L.M.C. figures before 1968 are the aggregated pre-tax profits at all the constituent firms. The British Leyland figures are somewhat inflated because of insufficient depreciation allowances, while the Chrysler figures (and perhaps those of Vauxhall and Ford) are understated because of transfer pricing manipulation. I will discuss these two points in a moment. Note also that prices had almost doubled between 1964 and 1973. Ford's figures are for Ford Motor Company (U.K.) and subsidiaries. The subsidiaries are finance, banking, sales and property companies in the main. Taking Ford Motor Company (U.K.) alone the comparable figures for 1974 and 1975 were 5.7 and (2.2) respectively.

SOURCE: Expenditure Committee [1975], p. 24; *Annual Reports.*

Since the import boom market shares in terms of output have been much less significant than market shares in terms of U.K. sales. In the home market British Leyland's share fell from 48 per cent in 1968 to 31 per cent in 1972. Market shares for U.K. production and sales in 1975 are shown on Table 14.2.

Declining ownership growth, rising imports and falling export shares, combined with rising wage costs, increasing inflexibility for moving workers around within plants, steadily rising numbers of disputes and the harvest of years of underinvestment, have wrought a heavy toll on the profitability of car firms in Britain. This may be seen from Table 14.7.

The major changes in market structure among U.K. firms during the past ten years have been Chrysler's take-over of the Rootes empire and the formation of B.L.M.C.

Chrysler and Coventry

Chrysler's international expansion came very late compared with Ford and General Motors. Ford began production in the United Kingdom in 1909 and General Motors bought Vauxhall in 1928.

Chrysler had been fishing around the British car market for some time. In 1956 Standard was approached by Chrysler to develop a new small car for the European market for Chrysler. In 1961 Chrysler made overtures to both Standard and Leyland. According to Turner this provided an impetus for the two British firms to merge—to avoid the Americans (1971, pp. 49–50). Again in 1962 Chrysler tried to buy a stake in Leyland. Finally, in 1964, Chrysler managed to buy into a major British car manufacturer – Rootes.

Rootes earned good profits until 1962, but in 1962 and 1963 Rootes was the only major car firm to lose money. In 1964 Chrysler took only a minority of Rootes' voting shares, but in 1967 it acquired the majority interest. Since then rumours have regularly circulated around Coventry that Chrysler was planning to pull out of the United Kingdom. Company threats to leave Britain indicate the move from Responsible Autonomy strategies to Direct Control strategies and the change in position of Coventry's workers at Stoke and Ryton[36] from central workers within Rootes, to be protected from unemployment, to peripheral workers within Chrysler, continually under the shadow of redundancy.[37]

From 1967 to 1975 Chrysler U.K. made a cumulative trading loss of £80 million. While the Government was considering what to do about Chrysler's liquidation announcement in October 1975, some of Chrysler's shop stewards produced a report which accused the firm of deliberately running down its U.K. operations, particularly since 1970, and of deliberately understating earnings on the U.K. operations (Joint Union delegation of Chrysler shop stewards and Staff Representatives – Chrysler Stewards [1975]).

According to the Chrysler stewards the Stoke plant 'has been allowed to become a museum of antiquated machinery', with most of the machines over

14 years old and several over 33 years old. (1975, Synopsis, p. 2). In 1972 Chrysler U.K. had the lowest fixed capital assets per man of any of Chrysler's subsidiaries (United Kingdom, £1550; France, £2274; Spain, £2836 and the United States, £3377; Expenditure Committee [1975]), and by 1974 the gap between the French and U.K. operations had widened still further (United Kingdom, £1600; France, £3400). Machine tools and machines had been physically transferred from Coventry to Chrysler operations in France, Spain and South America. The design centre at Whitley had been working primarily on models destined to be produced elsewhere and the Chrysler stewards doubted that adequate payment had been credited to the U.K. operations for this work. In the U.K. Chrysler was offering far better advertising allowances and dealers' trade allowances on cars coming from France than those produced in the U.K., while these promotion awards were costed against the U.K. budget (p. 4). Finally the stewards cited evidence produced by the Labour Research Department that Chrysler U.K. was selling cars to a Chrysler export agency in Switzerland (transfer pricing) at less than economic prices. The Swiss agency would then sell the cars to foreign customers at economic prices and realise the profits (26 June 1975).[38]

In spite of doubts concerning some minor details of the allegations, it is clear that Chrysler Corporation (U.S.) have shifted the centre of their overseas investment programme away from the United Kingdom and towards France and South America. Chrysler had not been alone among the American multinational car firms in this respect. In 1960 top managers at Ford in America decided to use the United Kingdom as the spring-board for their operations in Europe. Ford began major investments at Halewood and Swansea. But since 1967 it has been Ford's German operations rather than those in Britain which have increasingly become the centre of Ford Europe (Beynon [1973], pp. 52, 183).

Faced with the prospect of 25,000 redundancies at Chrysler if the liquidation went ahead, as well as at least another 30,000 redundancies among Chrysler's suppliers and distributors, the Government decided to 'rescue' Chrysler by giving the firm £162.5 million in loans, grants and losses underwritten to 1977.

While 162.5 million seemed a lot of money, the 55,000 redundancies would have cost the State something like £150 million in unemployment and other public benefits (assuming they remained unemployed for one year on average). Also the redundancies would have been heavily concentrated in Coventry and in politically sensitive Scotland. Chrysler's demise in the United Kingdom would have left more room for car imports and Chrysler's important export contract with Iran would probably have been transferred elsewhere.

The rescue plan involved 8200 redundancies in February and June 1976, primarily in Coventry (4600 at Stoke and Ryton and 400 in other Coventry sites, compared with only 1500 at Linwood in Scotland). Because of the world-wide resurgence of car demand in 1976 Chrysler began recruiting again during the summer of 1976.

B.L.M.C. and Coventry

The other major car firm heavily concentrated in Coventry, British Leyland Motor Corporation, employed 167,670 people in the United Kingdom and represented the largest private company in the country by employment. Around 1971 British Leyland employed about 25,000 people from Coventry.[39] In mid-1976 there were about 23,000 (most of the losses were at Triumph and B.M.C. with Jaguar's employment rising by about 2000).

The merger itself was a long-drawn-out affair in which government ministers and agencies played an active role. In November 1967 the pound was devalued. The Government was anxious that the full benefit of the cheapening of British exports caused by the devaluation should be realised. The Leyland – B.M.H. merger was seen as crucial to gaining this competitive advantage (Young and Lowe [1974], p. 60). By late 1967 it had become obvious that B.M.H. was losing money. That this company might go under, or that it may be taken over by a foreign firm, was also of great concern to the Government. In January 1968 the Government's Industrial Reorganisation Corporation (I.R.C.) provided a loan of £25 million to support the merger. In June 1970, quite separately from its other loan to B.L.M.C, the I.R.C. lent the firm £10 million to buy machine tools.

From the start B.L.M.C. suffered from undercapitalisation and this was exacerbated by years of underinvestment following the merger. Too much should not be made of the relative difference between firms in the United Kingdom. The whole U.K. motor industry has suffered from underinvestment.

Firms take in a certain amount from sales each year. After deductions for operating expenses (wages, raw materials and other supplies) firms are left with a certain amount representing their gross earnings. Out of this must come taxes, interest payments and depreciation. The money left over may then be used for dividends, new investment and additions to cash balances. At least this is how it ought to work. The problem is that the amount that a firm sets aside for depreciation of assets is, to some extent, discretionary. Assuming that a firm's assets last about ten years on average, if the firm simply sets aside 10 per cent of what it originally paid for any asset in a year, the firm will probably *not* be able to replace the asset with the accumulated funds at the end of ten years, when the asset has theoretically worn out, because of price rises. Since the early 1960s this problem has become acute due to accelerating inflation. Also, if a firm carries out relatively little net investment over a few years, the amount *theoretically* necessary to put aside for depreciation will fall. If the amounts put aside for depreciation are inadequate then profits declared after depreciation allowances are taken off will be inflated.

It is possible for a firm to run down its assets and continue to pay high dividends for some time – especially if the firm is large. But eventually it will run out of assets to run down *and* it will run out of cash – run out of cash to pay dividends and, more important, run out of cash to pay its operating expenses. Low net investment will mean that the firm is not keeping up with new designs and models, causing sales to fall and less money to come into the firm. Low net investment will also mean that the firm is not keeping up with new techniques of production or economies of scale. Operating expenses will be relatively high compared with competitors, causing more money to flow out of the firm. Squeezed between falling sales and rising operating expenses, and unable to cut down any more on cash set aside for depreciation, the firm will be unable to pay its recurring bills – for labour power and materials. This is the cash-flow problem which faced British Leyland in 1974 and 1975 and which was the inheritance of asset squeezing and dividend overpayment by the constituent companies both before the merger *and* afterwards.

Graph 14.3 compares major European producers with respect to net value added per man and assets per man for 1969. [40] As can be seen from the graph these variables are highly correlated. All four major U.K. producers compare unfavourably with the Continental firms, except perhaps Ford (U.K.). British Leyland and Chrysler (U.K.) compare very poorly.

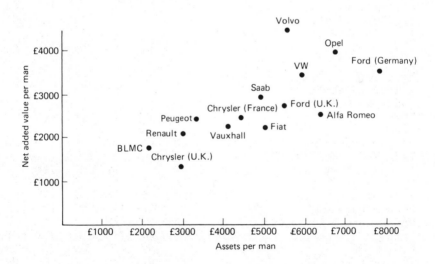

GRAPH 14.3 Assets and Net Added Value per Man for Major Car Firms in Europe, 1969

In spite of British Leyland's relatively weak position at its creation, the low investment and high dividends policy has continued. Comparing two entries in Table 14.8, Profit/ (loss) after all items except dividends, and Dividends, one can see that British Leyland paid out the major portion of its profits in dividends. During its first seven years the company made £74 million in profits, but paid out £70 million in dividends. According to the Ryder Report,

TABLE 14.8

British Leyland in Brief, 1968–75

	Years ended September 30							
	1968	1969	1970	1971	1972	1973	1974	1975
Vehicles sold (000s)	1,050	1,083	984	1,057	1,127	1,161	1,020	845
Sales (£m)	974	970	1,021	1,177	1,281	1,564	1,595	1,868
Profit before tax, interest, depreciation and dividends (£m)	86	87	56	93	84	102	61	12
Interest (£m)	7	5	10	14	9	7	17	38
Depreciation (£m)								
— properties and plant	27	27	27	28	27	29	31	33
— tooling amortisation	14	14	15	19	16	15	11	17
— total	41	41	42	47	43	44	42	50
Profit before tax and dividends (£m)	38	41	4	32	32	51	2	(76)
As a percentage of sales	3.9	4.2	0.4	2.7	2.5	3.3	0.1	(4.1)
Tax (£m) — deferred	–	–	–	–	4	12	15	(22)
— payable	18	20	2	14	7	11	(6)	9
— total	18	20	2	14	11	23	9	(13)
Profit/(loss) after tax and before dividends, minority, extraordinary items (£m)	20	21	2	18	21	28	(7)	(63.2)
Minority interest and extraordinary items (£m)	(1)	(3)	(8)	(2)	3	(1)	(17)	(60)
Profit/(loss) after all items except dividends (£m)	19	18	(6)	16	24	27	(24)	(124)
Dividends (£m)	15	15	5	11	12	9	3	–
Retentions (£m)	4	3	(11)	5	12	18	(27)	(124)
Net operating assets (£m)	98	125	176	221	150	122	139	185
Creditors and bills payable (£m)	(201)	(222)	(245)	(240)	(262)	(363)	(479)	(576)
Debtors (£m)	131	148	167	165	160	189	192	254
Employees (000)	188	196	199	194	191	204	208	191
U.K. employees (000)	168	175	176	169	164	171	173	164

NOTE: British Leyland's loss of £15.7 million on its Australian operations in 1974 was called an extraordinary item to make its profit (loss) look better. Losses in Australia (£5.7m), Spain (£19.0m) and Italy (£33.9), comprised the bulk of the extraordinary item in 1975.

SOURCE: British Leyland Annual Reports.

'Even if all the profits of £74 million had been retained, together with the £49 million of new funds raised by a rights issue in 1972, this would have been inadequate to meet British Leyland's capital needs' (1975, p. 19).

Going on to the inadequate amounts set aside for depreciation, Ryder notes that this is partly because much of the company's long-term assets are so old that they have already been fully depreciated; that is, after the eight to ten years or so that money had been put aside to replace certain plants, in many cases new plants should have been built but were not. With little extra money set aside for depreciation of recent plant because of little plant erected, and with old plant already fully depreciated, the profits declared after depreciation allowances were severely inflated.

Since 1971 British Leyland has also declared inflated profits by running down the working capital necessary to finance stocks and day-to-day trading (Net operating assets on Table 14.8). From 1968 to 1971 the overall proportion of sales set aside as net operating assets was 15 per cent. The £150 million set aside in 1972 was only 11.7 per cent of sales, and in 1973 and 1974 only 7.8 per cent and 8.7 per cent of sales were set aside. Profits in 1972, 1973 and 1974 should have been further reduced by £42 million, £113 million and £100 million respectively to maintain net operating assets at 15 per cent (assuming this to be roughly adequate).[41] It has been estimated that the extra depreciation allowances needed to cover the replacement of fixed assets at current costs, rather than the costs prevailing at the time when the assets were accumulated, would have been £13 million, £18 million and £20 million for 1972, 1973 and 1974 (Harrison and Sutcliffe, [1975]). Subtracting these two factors from British Leyland's declared profits before dividends leaves *losses* of £31 million in 1972, £106 million in 1973 and £154 million in 1974.

During the early 1970s one way the firm had been able to survive while making losses and paying dividends was by not paying its bills. British Leyland had become notorious for not paying its bills. The difference between what British Leyland owed its creditors and what was owed to it by its debtors had risen every year since the firm's creation (difference between rows titled 'Creditors' and 'Debtors' in Table 14.8).

How was this possible?

It was possible, at least in the short run, by forcing suppliers to wait for payment (three to four months) and by forcing purchasers to pay up quickly (within a month). The result was a tight squeeze on small components manufacturers and on general engineering firms supplying machine tools. Sometimes British Leyland got away without ever paying bills because in some cases its suppliers were squeezed into bankruptcy. In October 1974 the Birmingham-based Smaller Businesses Advisory Service was lobbying the Government to guarantee bank loans to small companies because of the cash-flow squeeze imposed, particularly on small Birmingham engineering firms, by larger materials suppliers and the larger car firms (*Financial Times*, 15 October 1974).

The number of Coventry men working at British Leyland and Chrysler rose slightly during the early 1970s (until 1974), but firms producing machine tools and smaller metal products had been laying men off during those years. Between 1970 and 1973 1800 fewer men were employed in Coventry's machine tool industry (MLH 332), 1100 fewer in Coventry's general mechanical engineering industry (MLH 349), and almost 1000 fewer in small metal products (SIC 9), while Coventry's motor vehicles industry (MLH 381) took on another 1700 men (Coventry Employment Exchange Records). Alfred Herbert, Coventry's major employer in the machine tools industry, laid off several thousand men between 1970 and 1972, and the firm is still floundering after being taken over by the State.

State aid to British Leyland during the early 1970s was not confined to I.R.C. loans. As well as not paying its bills to suppliers British Leyland has not been paying its taxes. In 1972 the firm deferred paying £4 million in taxes. In 1973 it deferred £12 million, in 1974, £15 million.

On 18 December 1974 the Government appointed Don Ryder to assess British Leyland. The Ryder Report stated that the firm would need £2,090 million for capital expenditure and £750 million for working capital restoration in the eight years to September 1982. B.L.M.C. was taken over by the National Enterprise Board in 1975 and the first tranche of £200 million was paid out. Since then the Government has been using the threat of withholding further payments to the firm if productivity is not increased and if stoppages due to disputes are not reduced.

One should remember that British Leyland's position is not particularly outstanding. The history of the motor industry is flooded with firms which went under or were taken over. That this should happen to so large a firm as British Leyland is a symptom of the stage of the motor-car product cycle in the 1970s. Takeovers and rationalisation on an international scale at present are, in many ways, simply a progression from the take-overs and rationalisations which have occurred during the past seventy years in the British motor industry.[42] What distinguishes the crisis in British Leyland is that the firm is so large an employer, so large a producer and so large an exporter, plus the fact that there are no other British car firms which could take it over.

Worker Resistance and Management

A concerted effort to extend direct control over all British car workers, though particularly over those in Coventry, has been exerted by car firm top managers during the past decade. Along with strikes over parity with Coventry the major issues causing disputes during the late 1960s and early 1970s have been the introduction of Measured Daywork, the ending of the Coventry Toolroom Agreement and redundancies.

The major change in managerial strategy toward Coventry's car workers, which began in the late 1960s, must be understood in the context of their

central position within the British car industry and the Responsible Autonomy strategies which were pursued towards them during the three previous
decades. During that time Coventry workers had built up strong shop-floor
organisations to protect their central position. In part these organisations
were based on the shop stewards. But in part the organisations were even more
informal, based on the small work groups themselves and encouraged by the
gang system. The sharp rise in disputes during the early 1960s was due
primarily to a rise in what Turner called 'unofficial unofficial' strikes (1967,
p. 223). That is, strikes which began, unsanctioned by either the official trade
unions concerned or the relevant shop stewards.

With shop stewards included in mutuality clauses since 1922, stewards in
many cases have become increasingly separated from ordinary workers,
spending more of their time negotiating rather than doing manual work.
Often negotiation at any level is seen by workers as a stalling tactic,
particularly when grievances concern arbitrary dismissals, or small changes in
work organisation or work speed, implemented by managers. Once a man is
out of the factory, once work arrangements have changed, it is harder to get
such actions reversed than if industrial action is taken at the moment of the
grievance. Furthermore the essence of negotiation is compromise, and
workers have often believed that even ordinary stewards regularly compromise their interests.[43]

Ryton was particularly known for strong shop-floor organisation, somewhat separate from the stewards. 'At Ryton it's the men that make the
running, and the stewards are pushed to do what the workers want' (see Jones
[1973], p. 11).

In these conditions strategies which involve bringing senior shop stewards
into lower-level management decision-making (participation) must be seen as
a *retreat* from Responsible Autonomy strategies if accompanied, as they have
been in the 1970s, by a reduction of the role of ordinary shop stewards in
negotiations and a reduction in direct control by workers over the order and
timing of the particular tasks they perform (Measured Daywork). This was
certainly recognised by Chrysler workers, who strongly rejected the Chrysler
participation plan when it was first 'offered' in 1975.

It would be a serious mistake to separate current industrial democracy or
participation plans, as well as British Leyland's limited introduction of
autonomous assembly techniques at its new Rover complex in Birmingham,
from the significant loss of autonomy suffered by car workers during the late
1960s and early 1970s.

During the 1950s and most of the 1960s bargaining over wages was carried
out between ordinary stewards or gangers and low-grade managers in
Coventry and Birmingham car factories. The managers, often anxious to
avoid a dispute, allowed piece-rates to rise in proportion to the militancy of
the workers involved. This caused innumerable differentials and parity
disputes and made it difficult for top managers to assess their labour power

costs. Also, under money piece-working the actual manner of work execution was left to individuals or gangs themselves, making it difficult to get workers to work harder. Earnings could be significantly improved by negotiating for higher rates instead of producing more pieces per day.

Workers often established 'float' patterns, even when they were not formally paid as gangs. A float worker is *supposed* to be available to fill in for absent workers, but float workers (won through negotiation) may also fill in for workers going to the toilet, going for a cigarette, or taking any other form of relief from work while still formally on the job.

During the late 1960s and early 1970s Measured Daywork was seen as a method of avoiding all these problems; of allowing greater direct control over costs and work methods, easier intensification of work, reducing differentials disputes within factories and increasing the power and status of rate-fixers.

Measured Daywork and the End of the Coventry Toolroom Agreement

With Measured Daywork pay rates per day are negotiated factory-wide. Work tasks are measured closely and the shop-floor struggle shifts to how much time specific tasks 'ought' to take, rather than how much workers 'ought' to be paid for the job. Managers try to convince workers that the former is a scientific matter, while the latter had long been treated by both as a moral, political and economic matter in Coventry.[44]

Work measurement was as old as the car industry itself, but during the period of Declining Ownership Growth firms began to intensify Direct Control strategies involving systematic work measurement with vigour. In Coventry and Birmingham the shift in strategy was most noticeable and provoked the most serious resistance. The introduction of Measured Daywork has also meant the end of Coventry's gang system.[45]

Ford had never paid wages by the piece in the United Kingdom. They had a day-rate system of payment with the company formally maintaining responsibility for work-loads. In 1967 the firm decided that this was insufficient and introduced a system of work measurement to help control work loads. Ford's simple system of job classification (skilled, semi-skilled, unskilled and women) was replaced by a complex system of job grading based on twenty-eight characteristics of jobs.[46] The switch-over was accompanied by a fairly large wage increase and Ford managed the affair with a few disruptions, though the new system contributed to a series of strikes in 1968, 1969 and 1971.

In 1969 Chrysler began replacing their piece-work systems with Measured Daywork. This provoked a series of short disputes at Linwood, Ryton and Stoke during 1969 by inspectors and progress chasers as well as manual workers. Measured Daywork meant the hiring of many new supervisors and measurement 'experts' into authoritative positions above many existing white-collar workers.

Chrysler workers were able to extract high wage rises and easy manning levels in return for accepting Measured Daywork. Nevertheless the system has made it easier for managers to control work-loads directly, and to speed up work during periods of relatively high unemployment when workers are in a much weaker position (as in 1971 and in 1974–5).[47]

By 1970 top managers at British Leyland considered their major industrial relations problem to centre around piece-work (Ryder [1975], p. 34). Measured Daywork was introduced at Cowley, Oxford, with relatively little resistance early in 1971. Later in the year attempts to introduce the system at the Standard Triumph factory in Coventry and at Longbridge, Birmingham, resulted in protracted strikes. The system was finally assured after a long and bitter strike at Jaguar in 1972. By September 1974 94 per cent of British Leyland's manual workers were on Measured Daywork. The price B.L.M.C. had to pay, as with Chrysler, was significant wage rises and high manning levels.

For top managers at British Leyland 1971 and 1972 were particularly bad years for disputes (Ryder [1975], p. 32). This reflected strikes over the abolition of the Coventry Toolroom Agreement as well as Measured Daywork disputes.

One of the main purposes of Measured Daywork systems was to avoid comparisons of earnings leading to wage leap-frogging and disputes by negotiating factory-wide pay scales. The Coventry Toolroom rate stood like a beacon inviting comparability on the basis of earnings levels *between* factories. Coventry employers belonging to the C.D.E.E.A. unilaterally abolished the agreement by announcing their intentions in March 1971, and by not publishing the Toolroom rate from September 1971. A series of weekly, one-day toolroom strikes all over Coventry began in September. Top managers responded by laying off related workers and by locking out toolroom workers for one day on the day when they returned to work. This continued until 22 November. On 22 November an all-out strike of Coventry's toolroom workers began. For three days 7,000 Coventry workers were on strike and another 18,000 were laid off.

The workers returned with a £2 per week rise in basic rates for toolroom and toolroom-related workers, a lump sum of £7 as compensation for rises lost through the employers' termination of the agreement in September, and a committee of the A.E.U.W. and the C.D.E.E.A. which would (discreetly) ensure that no firm fell behind wage levels in the district.

Participation, Redundancies and Green Labour

Top managers in Chrysler and British Leyland have attempted to impose a *limited* Responsible Autonomy strategy of participation by senior shop stewards in some decision-making bodies within the firms. Recent participation schemes are a far cry from the extensive Responsible Autonomy schemes represented by the gang system in Coventry. In effect participation has meant the withdrawal of Responsible Autonomy strategies from shop-floor workers and ordinary shop stewards, and concentration of co-option strategies on the senior shop stewards, particularly the conveners.[48]

Such schemes involve an advance in workers' direct control compared with co-option schemes concentrating on official trade unions at the national level as were tried in the 1920s (Mond–Turner). But in the 1970s they represent an attempt to bottle up the power of shop stewards and rank and file, established during the 1940s and 1950s, by cutting off senior stewards from the rank and file, and by making them a party to difficult managerial decisions.

Senior stewards were a party to the Ryder committee managing British Leyland under the National Enterprise Board during its initial stages in 1975. Since then suspicion of these senior stewards from the shop floor has grown. (In December 1976 the senior stewards endorsed an overall earnings policy for hourly paid workers of Leyland Cars which was subsequently rejected by the rank and file.) In effect 'industrial democracy' in nationalised British Leyland has made information, hitherto unavailable to workers, available to the conveners. It has also bound those conveners to secrecy in relation to those they represent concerning future plans for investment and redundancy. The Chrysler conveners have also withheld information made available to them during negotiations with top managers and state representatives during the Chrysler crisis of 1975–6.

The shift in managerial strategy toward British Leyland workers away from Responsible Autonomy and the contribution of the government to that shift may be seen in repeated threats by government officials to withhold further funds earmarked for British Leyland, thereby 'allowing' widespread re-dundancies in response to worker resistance. The toolroom workers strike of March 1977 clearly demonstrated this (*Financial Times*, 7 March 1977 to 25 March 1977).

Two further aspects of the fall in status of U.K. car workers from central workers enjoying 'Responsible Autonomy' as individuals and small groups are important. The first is the use of redundancy and green labour *within Coventry* and other traditional car-worker areas to discipline workers and to weaken their organisation. The second is the increased integration of the American-owned car firms involving multisourcing at an international level.

During 1971 and again in 1974–5 both Chrysler and British Leyland laid off considerable numbers of car workers, ostensibly because of strikes. In 1971 in particular workers did not have to be laid off due to the technical unavailability of work. They were laid off as a disciplinary measure. Top managers' actions were clearly recognised as a lock-out by the Press (*The Times*, 28 October 1971; 2 November 1971). Also, with impending re-dundancies weakening workers' resistance at Chrysler in late 1975 and early 1976, top managers began to disregard procedure concerning moving workers within and between factories. This led to what appeared to be a reckless strike on the part of Linwood workers during 1976 (the issue was called 'inconsequential' by the *Financial Times*, 2 February 1976).

After lay-offs at Ryton during 1971, when Chrysler began recruiting again, men were brought in from the dying hosiery industry around Hinckley, Leicestershire in spite of high unemployment in Coventry at the time. These workers had little tradition of militancy and were used to working very long hours. At first they meant a weakening of worker solidarity at Ryton. Called 'knickerstitchers' and 'woolybacks' in abuse, they were, at first, reluctant to go on strike. Gradually this 'green' labour adjusted to working conditions and worker organisation at Ryton.[49]

Multisourcing Internationally

Multisourcing internationally represents an extremely important development within the capitalist mode of production. As is pointed out in Chapter 8, multisourcing gives firms several advantages in terms of flexibility. Sourcing the same parts both from within the firm and from outside allows top managers to treat more of their own workers as central, offering them relative employment security during poor car demand in order to stave off resistance and to encourage them to behave responsibly.

It also allows top managers to bypass disruptions due to disputes or poor co-ordination within their own firm, (or in their outside suppliers). Thus multisourcing may increase a firm's discretion to apply more Direct Control strategies as well as Responsible Autonomy strategies. This is particularly true if alternative sources exist *within* the firm. Top managers will be less fearful of provoking sections of their own workers with Direct Control strategies, disciplinary action, redundancies, etc., if they can get the work performed by those workers done elsewhere within the firm. The problem with multisourcing within the firm, within a single country, is that it is difficult to treat some workers as central and others as peripheral when they both perform precisely the same tasks. The Parity disputes of the late 1960s and early 1970s have demonstrated this difficulty. Also, when there is a dispute at one factory, pickets against work performed in other factories, parallel strikes and sympathy strikes in other factories are more likely if it is precisely the same work being performed in the other factories. It is easier to view this as scab labour when the work performed is the same. For example, in June 1968 180 women employed as sewing machinists on seat covers at Dagenham went on strike over a pay claim. While there was little solidarity with them among other Ford workers, soon the 200 women sewing-machinists at Halewood were also on strike in support of the claim.

These difficulties may be largely overcome if multisourcing occurs internationally. Setting up new facilities in another country, rather than in a new region of the same country, allows top managers to separate workers in terms of wages, conditions of working and employment security with less fear of parity disputes. If work carried out abroad parallels that in the United Kingdom, there is less danger of picketing, parallel strikes and sympathy strikes.

Recently all four major car firms in the United Kingdom have built up facilities in several European countries which have become increasingly 'integrated' with each other within each firm.[50] Originally operations in different European countries were responsible for entire and separate cars with few interchangeable parts and components. Beginning in 1960 with Ford Europe, followed first by other American-owned firms and then by the Europeans, firms have been producing essentially the same models in several countries. Some operations link to each other vertically (such as engine machinery from Valencia, engine blocks from Dagenham, transmissions and axles from Bordeaux for Ford's most integrated car to date – the Fiesta), but others, usually the most strike-prone operations, run parallel to each other between countries (the Fiesta will be assembled at *three* centres, Saarlouis, Valencia and Dagenham; *Financial Times*, 16 July 1976).[51]

The ability to maintain production of their full model range using little of their U.K. operations has increased the power of top managers in car firms to impose Direct Control strategies and to counteract worker resistance in this country. On the one hand the faster pace in Continental firms is used as a yardstick and a driving stick for workers in this country. Referring to the situation at Ford, Beynon states:

> The company owned another assembly plant in Cologne manned mainly by Spanish and Turkish workers, whose immigrant status made them extremely vulnerable. The sack could mean deportation. The 'Cologne Yardstick' was increasingly applied to the Dagenham PTA plant in the 1960s. Supervisors were frequently taken to the Cologne plant to compare the ways in which the job was run in the two plants. . . . By establishing work-rate standards in one place, like Cologne, the company can make this rate reverberate throughout its other operations (Beynon [1973], pp. 52–3, 291–2).

On the other hand top managers in large firms develop a weapon similar to a lock-out, the threat to withdraw employment permanently. One of the most significant features of industrial relations in the U.K. motor industry from the mid-1960s has been the ever-present threat, particularly coming from Chrysler and Ford, to shift operations to other countries.

Given the traditional lack of solidarity among workers in different countries, international multisourcing within car firms appears to answer top managers' problems with 'difficult' workers in any one country. But citing work standards in one country to measure the performance of those in other countries, intimidating workers with the threat of shifting operations to other countries and bypassing worker resistance by carrying out that work in other countries, all encourage international solidarity. They come to raise the level of worker resistance to an international level. While this most recent change will take some time to develop, signs of this shift are already apparent. For example, in 1968, during a strike in the Ford assembly plant at Genk (in the underdeveloped Linsburg region of Belgium) workers at Ford plants in Cologne, Germany and in Britain pledged not to accept work transferred from Genk or to increase production. National prejudices are extremely difficult to break down, but Ford's multinational strategies have encouraged some softening of these prejudices. However increased solidarity among workers in Europe will push car firms into more distant underdeveloped countries more quickly.

CHAPTER FIFTEEN

Centre–Periphery Patterns in the U.K. Car Industry

1 Centre–Periphery Patterns within Car Firms in the United Kingdom

Centre–periphery relations between firms in the U.K. car industry have been more noticeable than those within firms. Both sorts of relations are discussed in this chapter, though both have been examined earlier (Chapter 8, Section 4 and Chapter 14, Sections 4 and 5).

From the Experimental Period, particularly in Coventry, the concentration of growing firms requiring more semi-skilled as well as skilled workers than were available within the employment catchment area enhanced the bargaining position of semi-skilled workers as individuals. Already by 1913 many grades of semi-skilled workers in Coventry's engineering industries were earning the full district craft rate. State encouragement of Responsible Autonomy strategies to ensure steady supplies during wartime and the long Peak Period, when top managers of major car firms themselves were willing and able to pursue Responsible Autonomy strategies, combined to encourage strong local shop-floor organisation, particularly among Coventry's semi-skilled car workers.[1] Not only has the entire pay structure of car firms been raised well above that for other engineering industries, but also the differential between semi-skilled and skilled workers has almost disappeared.

This is shown in Table 15.1. Note that within the motor industry workers on payment-by-results were primarily those in Coventry and Birmingham.

Unskilled car workers, while receiving more than those in other engineering industries, receive much less than skilled or semi-skilled car workers.[2] Unskilled workers form a rather small proportion of car workers (17 per cent in 1963; N.E.D.O. [1969], p. 37) compared with skilled and semi-skilled manual workers (29.1 per cent and 33.3 per cent respectively).

The difference between skilled and semi-skilled car workers in terms of employment security has also been quite small, particularly from 1940. During the interwar years, when large numbers of car workers were laid off

TABLE 15.1

Percentage Ratio of Average Hourly Earnings (including overtime),
Average of January and June 1963

	Time-Workers			Payment-by-results workers		
	Skilled to labourer	Semi-skilled to labourer	Skilled to Semi-skilled	Skilled to labourer	Semi-skilled to labourer	Skilled to Semi-skilled
All engineering:	142	126	113	143	132	108
Motor vehicles:	142	130	109	153	150	102

NOTE: In 1965 semi-skilled workers on payment-by-results received on average 1.5 per cent *more* than skilled workers. Also in 1963 skilled workers on payment-by-results in the motor industry were getting 10 per cent more than those on time rates; N.E.D.O. [1969], p. 41.

SOURCE Turner [1967], p. 158.

during the summer slack season, it appears that car firms did try to protect skilled workers compared with other manual workers. At Daimler, for example, skilled workers were employed on buses and commercial vehicles during the 1920s and 1930s when demand for Daimler cars was slack (Richardson [1972], p. 54). During the slump in 1966–7 employment in the motor vehicle industry fell by 50,000. Between 1964 and 1967 the number of semi-skilled manual workers fell by 13.1 per cent, and the number of skilled manual workers fell by 10.4 per cent.

While differences among workers according to manual skills do not follow a strong centre – periphery pattern, the division between manual and non-manual workers (particularly managerial and technical workers) has (until very recently) followed a clear centre – periphery pattern. In 1964, the peak output year for the industry, 80.1 per cent of the British car industry's 465,300 employees were manual workers. In 1967, after major lay-offs, only 77.1 per cent were manual workers, (N.E.D.O. [1969], p. 37). As Rhys notes, 'as demand falls it is easier to lay-off production workers quickly but more difficult to cut down on the "fixed" labour content such as managerial and technical staff' (1972, p. 442). The number of managers fell by only 0.5 per cent between 1964 and 1967. The number of technical workers *rose* by 36.8 per cent. The other major group of workers, clerical and administrative workers, also *rose* in numbers between 1964 and 1967 (by 6 per cent).[3]

The greater stability of employment for clerical and administrative workers in particular (about 50 per cent of workers in this category are women representing about 50 per cent of all women employed in the car firms) stems from their close connection with the exercise of managerial authority and co-ordination, not from the strength of their resistance. Earnings of male administrative, technical and clerical workers in the motor industry were only 4 per cent higher than those in all manufacturing industries compared with a differential of 22 per cent for male manual workers in 1963.[4]

During the major lay-offs of 1975–6 the difference between manual and non-manual workers has been even less pronounced. Williamson's studies showed that significant white-collar lay-offs in America during the early 1960s *followed* even *more drastic* lay-offs of manual workers. The Chrysler 'rescue' plan specified 8200 redundancies out of about 25,000 workers, or about a 25 per cent reduction in labour force during 1976, 6300 to be laid off in February 1976 and another 1400 to be laid off in June 1976. Of the 6300 to be laid off in February, 900 would be from central staffs and 100 from the Whitley design centre, making *at minimum* 1000 or 16 per cent of lay-offs to be white-collar workers (Chrysler U.K. [1976], p. 2). Thus the number of white-collar lay-offs was, from the outset, something close to the percentage of manual workers laid off.[5]

An indication of the weight of the white-collar redundancies proposed is that the only union to oppose Chrysler's redundancy plan in Coventry was the Association of Scientific, Technical, and Managerial Staffs (A.S.T.M.S.), whose members are primarily supervisors and foremen (*Coventry Evening Telegraph*, 19 December 1975; 2 January 1976; 22 January 1976).[6] One must remember that the rescue plan represented a situation of severe crisis in Chrysler when strong state and national trade union pressure was brought to bear on Chrysler workers to accept the plan (*Financial Times*, 31 January 1976; 6 February 1976). In these circumstances Chrysler was willing to risk the weakening of managerial authority which major staff lay-offs might involve because of pressure outside the firm to ensure the maintenance of managerial authority. In less critical times the company might be expected to give white-collar workers somewhat more protection (as during 1964–7). Nevertheless the centre – periphery pattern between white-collar and manual workers within large car firms is less strong than in firms where skilled and semi-skilled manual workers are less well organised.

Those working at the major car firms are overwhelmingly white and male.[7] The only major car firm which is known to have a significant number of blacks is Ford. In 1972 about 20 per cent of the 28,000 workers at Ford Dagenham, and about 75 per cent of the 2,500 workers at Ford's Langley plant (near Slough) were West Indians and Africans (Gambino [1972], pp.9–12). It is no mere chance that the car firm with the highest number of black workers has also traditionally paid the lowest wages among the major firms and appears to have the most intense working conditions (see Beynon [1973], and Gambino [1972]).

Gambino shows how the strength of worker resistance at Ford is weakened by tensions between white and black workers. This is exacerbated by union policies. For example the unions sanction an unfair distribution of overtime between whites and blacks. Overtime represents a significant proportion of a worker's take-home pay (1972, p. 12). Until 1967 none of the 75 per cent black union members at Langley had ever been elected shop stewards (1972, p. 13). As I shall point out in Chapter 16 it has been a policy of Ford to employ immigrant or migrant labour world-wide in all its operations. Also Ford was the first firm to introduce Measured Daywork in this country and one of the last to recognise unions.

The wage differential between men and women in car firms is slightly less than the differential in other industries, but it is still significant. In part this parallels the separation between unskilled manual workers and other manual workers. A high proportion of women are employed as canteen workers and cleaners, and are paid at unskilled workers' rates. Until the Equal Pay Act there were also special women's categories of pay which were even lower. Between 1959 and 1968 women in the vehicles industry (SIC) earned between 50 and 51.6 per cent of what men earned, while the comparable figures for all manufacturing industries were between 47.6 and 49.7 per cent (Department of Employment [1971]).

During the first half of the twentieth century people came pouring into Coventry's car firms from the northern and western edges of the United Kingdom in search of high wages. But during the early 1960s the car firms began to concentrate their new British investments in the northern and western parts of the country in search of a pool of workers who would accept relatively low wages. In 1959 11.8 per cent of those employed in the motor vehicle industry worked in Scotland, Wales, and the North and North-West of England. By 1968 22.4 per cent were working in these 'depressed' areas (N.E.D.O. [1969], p. 36). Originally top managers hoped workers in these new car plants would accept lower wages than Midlands workers and that they would be more amenable to managerial initiatives.[8] By the late 1960s car workers in Liverpool and in Scotland had earned a reputation for being the most militant in the industry. In recognition of the difficulty of maintaining a centre – periphery pattern along location lines *within a single country*, the major car firms, led by Ford, began to shift their new investment out of Britain, first to continental Europe and then to more underdeveloped countries, particularly in South America.

Thus, while important differentials in wages and employment security exist within car firms within single countries, these differences are somewhat less marked than for other industries. This may change significantly in future as Direct Control strategies come to be applied to skilled and semi-skilled manual workers more and more. In the past top managers in large car firms were able to view the majority of their workers as central, and to pursue Responsible Autonomy strategies towards them, because of their strong monopoly power and because of their relations with smaller firms in the industry. In future, as large firms adjust to increased competition, particularly by shifting the centre of their operations out of this country, manual workers in large car firms are likely to fall in status from central to peripheral workers (in the absence of major structural and political changes).

2   Centre–Periphery between Firms and between Countries in the Car Industry

The large car firms are primarily assemblers of parts and components. Some of these they produce themselves, but much is brought out from outside suppliers. Large car firms in Britain buy out a relatively high proportion of the value of the cars they assemble (see Chapter 8, Section 4). In part this reflects the relative militancy of car workers in this country; in part it reflects the attendant difficulty of creating a strong centre – periphery pattern within firms in Britain compared with other countries (where immigrants in particular allow a strong centre–periphery pattern within firms).[9]

In the U.K. car industry top managers of large car firms are able to treat a high proportion of their workers as central, and to pursue Responsible Autonomy strategies toward them, because of a large periphery of small suppliers. As pointed out in Section 4 of Chapter 8, *not taking over* these small suppliers is part of a rational managerial strategy in spite of economies of scale foregone, out-of-date technology tolerated and increased difficulties with co-ordination.

The possible advantages to top managers of large car firms from centre – periphery relations between firms may be divided into three types. First is the possible advantage concerning the price of goods transferred to the larger firms. Second is the advantage concerning the conditions under which those goods may be transferred (flexibility in co-ordination because of the ease and speed of commencement or termination of the transfer). Third is the added flexibility in maintaining managerial authority over workers. Disruptions due to worker resistance (or poor co-ordination) may be bypassed and groups of disruptive workers may be laid off more easily if alternative sources are available for the work they perform.

Maintaining subcontracting relations *may* raise the cost of goods transferred to a car assembly firm above the cost at which the firm could have produced the goods itself, for technical reasons, in the short run. But parity struggles within car firms from the late 1960s and significant differences in wage levels between the large car firms and smaller supplier firms suggest that the loss of economies of scale may be outweighed by cheaper labour costs when maintaining subcontracting relations. From the 1920s at least, wages in smaller supplier firms have been significantly lower than in the larger car assembly firms. Table 15.2 demonstrates this difference for the inter-war period.

Wages in the larger car and cycle firms were from 22 per cent to 32 per cent

TABLE 15.2

Average Weekly Earnings in Certain Branches of Engineering, 1924–31

	1924 (shillings)	1928 (shillings)	1931 (shillings)
Motor vehicle and cycle manufacture and repair			
(a) Larger firms	58.2	62.1	57.5
(b) Smaller firms	46.3	47.0	47.0
General engineering	51.1	53.7	49.0

NOTE: Larger firms employ 25 and over and smaller firms employ under 25. The category Motor Vehicle and Cycle Manufacture and Repair includes some small component manufacturers supplying spare parts and carrying out repairs.
SOURCE: Ministry of Labour Enquiries; see *Ministry of Labour Gazette*, September 1926; November 1929; January 1933.

higher than in the smaller firms, and between 14 per cent and 17 per cent higher than in firms in general engineering.

One of the main reasons for the wage differential has been the higher proportion of women employed in the supplier firms. In 1921 8 per cent of those employed in the construction of motor vehicles and cycles were women, while 41.1 per cent of those employed in the cycle and motor accessories industry were women. Comparable figures for 1931 were 9.7 per cent and 44 per cent.[10] Women's wages were about 50 per cent of men's wages in both industries.

There is evidence that more Direct Control strategies have been pursued among suppliers. During the 1930s the Bedaux system was introduced more readily into supplier factories, largely because they had a high proportion of women workers, who have traditionally been poorly organised (such as at Lucas in Birmingham), compared with the car factories (Branson and Heinemann [1971], pp. 81–2).

After the war these wage differentials remained. Table 3.1 shows that in 1973 semi-skilled manual workers in engineering firms employing more than 500 people earned 28 per cent more than those in firms employing 25 to 99 people. Birmingham and the Black Country have had a much higher ratio of. supplier firms to car firms among their engineering industries than Coventry. This has been reflected in the substantial earnings differential between Coventry and the rest of the West Midlands. For example, earnings for male manual workers in 1969 were 16 per cent higher among engineers in Coventry than those in the West Midlands as a whole (Brown [1971], p. 7). Between 1948 and 1959 the proportion of women employed in making parts and accessories for motor vehicles was roughly twice as great as the number in motor vehicle manufacture (12 to 15 per cent for motor vehicle manufacture and 21 per cent to 28 per cent for parts and accessories).[11] The proportion of women in other industries supplying parts and materials to the car firms was also higher than in the car firms themselves (around 20 per cent for other engineering industries and around 34 per cent for small metal goods such as screws, nuts, wires, etc.)[12]

The third sort of advantage to top managers in large car firms, flexibility in maintaining authority over workers, has become particularly important since the Deceleration Part of the Peak Period. Car firms have been particularly concerned with establishing multiple sources for as many materials, parts and components as possible.

Ford in particular has pursued this policy.[13] Also a recent trend among the American-owned firms has been the establishment of international multi-sourcing of supplies *both* from their own factories and from outside firms. Ford U.K., for example, buys most of its steel from British Steel Corporation, but also has a policy of keeping open alternative supplies from Continental Europe 'as a self-protecting measure against possible "shortages" resulting from the frequent strikes in the U.K. steel sector' (Gambino [1972], p. 3).

CHAPTER SIXTEEN

Hillfields, Coventry and the Car Industry

Coventry was a showpiece of British capitalism from the late 1880s until the late 1960s. First with bicycles and motor cycles, and most important with cars, Coventry workers have enjoyed a central position within fast-growing major industries. They have had central status within powerful firms which have for decades enjoyed the discretion of being able to use Responsible Autonomy strategies toward most of their workers. In consequence Coventry had been the fastest growing and richest major city in Great Britain for seventy-five years (see Graph 16.1).

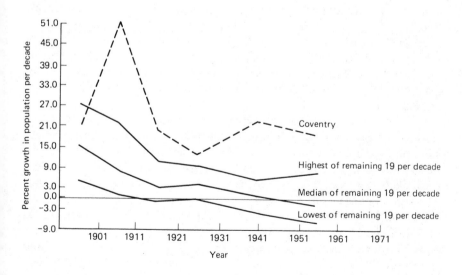

GRAPH 16.1 Coventry Population Growth Compared with other Major British Cities, 1891–1971.

Throughout this century, until the 1970s, average wages in Coventry's car firms have been considerably higher than those in other car firms and in other metal-working industries in Britain. Unemployment levels have been considerably below average, and Coventry workers have acquired a proud tradition for a high degree of direct control within productive activity.[1] Car ownership and house ownership among workers is much higher in Coventry than elsewhere.[2]

Nevertheless two other features also stand out when taking a long-run view of Coventry. First, Coventry has contained pockets of deprivation like Hillfields throughout this long period of overall prosperity (discussed in Section 1). Second, Coventry in the 1970s has suffered a severe reversal of its 'normally' prosperous condition. The city is now under the threat of a long depression, due to the decline of the U.K. car industry, such as occurred after 1860 due to the decline of the silk ribbon-weaving trade in Britain (discussed in Section 2).

1   Hillfields and Coventry

I left off the discussion of Hillfields in Chapter 11 with the decline of the silk ribbon-weaving trade from 1860 and the attendant collapse of prosperity in the entire Coventry area. With the coming of the bicycle boom in the late 1880s, almost thirty years later, Coventry's fortunes revived, but Hillfields was no longer the most prosperous area of the city. The weaving skills which had been concentrated in Hillfields when it was the preserve of first-hand journeymen were inappropriate for the new engineering and metal-working trades.

People who moved into Coventry after the 1880s moved to the newer suburbs if they could afford it (Chapelfields and particularly Earlsdon before the First World War). As bicycles and cars allowed workers to live fairly far from the factories, Hillfields' central location no longer represented an attraction, (see Map 16.1).

Map 16.2 shows that most firms situated in Hillfields at the beginning of the car product cycle were bicycle component manufacturers, except for Singer and Humber, and Humber's main factories were moved to Stoke area. All sites in Hillfields were relatively small and cramped. By 1968, most sites had been taken over by G.E.C., employing mainly women making telephones and telegraph apparatus.

New car factories built during the inter-war period and the shadow factories built during the Second World War were located far from the city centre area; primarily in the south-east (numbers 15, 16, 19 on Map 16.3, comprising almost all Chrysler's present sites), the south-west (number 4 on Map 16.3, where Standard Triumph is located), and the western edges of Coventry (Massey Ferguson, formerly Standard's tractor factory, at number 6 and Jaguar at number 7).

MAP 16.1 The Location of the Hillfields Area within the City of Coventry

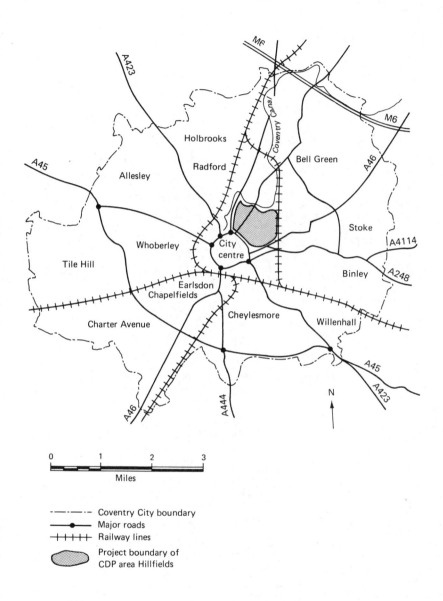

SOURCE: Coventry Community Development Project.

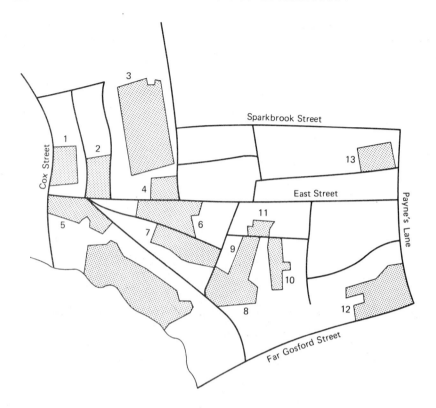

M AP 16.2 Changing Use of Industrial Sites in Hillfields, 1896–1968

site	use in 1896	use in 1906	use in 1951	use in 1968
1	—	chemical works	chemical works	electrical wholesaler
2	Taylor, Cooper & Bednell	?	Coventry Glass	Coventry Glass
3	Singer & Co.	Singer & Co.	Singer & Co.	Hills, Precision
4	Antifriction Ball Co.	Raglan Cycles	—	printer, bookbinder
5a	Bayless, Thomas & Co.	Excelsior Cycles	—	G.E.C.
b	Bayless, Thomas & Co.	Stevengraph Silk Works		
			—	G.E.C.
6	Cycle Components Manufacturing Co.	?	Singer & Co.	G.E.C.
7	Pneumatic Tyre Co.	Dunlop	electrical engineer	G.E.C.
8	Humber & Co.	Humber & Co.	electrical engineer	G.E.C.
9	Auto Machinery Co.	?	electrical engineer	G.E.C.
10	Premier Cycle Co.	Premier Cycle Co.	?	G.E.C.
11	Coventry Plating Co.	Coventry Plating Co.	?	G.E.C.
12	Townend Bros.	Coronet Motor Works	engineering works	—
13	—	Sparkbrook Cycle Works	Singer Motors	Coventry Tubes

NOTE: All the concerns listed in 1896 were engaged in the bicycle industry.
SOURCE: Geographical Association, Coventry Branch [1970], 'Urban Field Studies for Coventry Schools'.

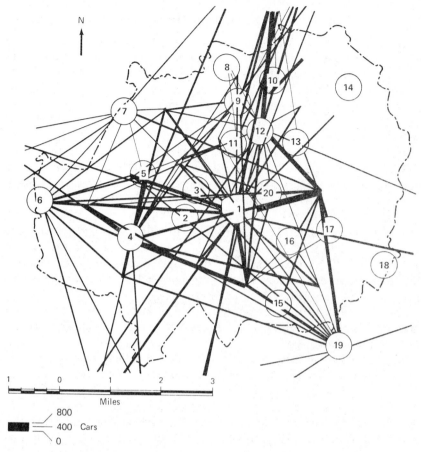

N

MAP 16.3 Desire Lines 1961—Journey-to-Work Trips by Car

800
400 Cars
0

Miles

1. Central Area
2. Chapelfields – small-scale engineering
3. Holyhead Road – B.L.M.C. (Alvis – military) Renolds chain, B.S.A. Carbodies
4. *Canley/ Torrington Ave – B.L.M.C. (Standard-Triumph), several engineering firms*
5. Allesley – B.L.M.C. (Daimler)
6. Banner Lane – Massey-Ferguson (Formerly Standard's Ferguson plant), Wickman Machine Tools
7. *Brown Lane – B.L.M.C. (Jaguar)*
8. Rowley Green – Gasworks
9. Holbrooks – Dunlop (rim & wheel, Umbrako car brakes)
10. Little Heath – Courtaulds (artificial silk)
11. Radford – Courtaulds (artificial silk)
12. Foleshill – Alfred Herbert (machine tools)
13. *Courthouse Green – B.L.M.C. (B.M.C. engines)*
14. Aldermans Green – proposed future industry
15. Whitley – Chrysler (Whitley design centre)
16. *Humber Road – Chrysler (Stoke engines), Smiths Stamping*
17. Copsewood – G.E.C. (telephone and telegraph apparatus)
18. Binley – old colliery, proposed future industry
19. *Ryton/ Bagington – Chrysler (Ryton assembly)*
20. Hillfields – G.E.C. (telephone and telegraph apparatus)

SOURCE: Coventry City Council [1967], p. 87.

The wealthier people who worked in Coventry began to move to out-lying villages to the south of Coventry. Also, from the 1920s, new housing estates were specifically built in suburbs close to the car factories, for example: the Bell Green estate near the B.M.C. engine works, built privately between the wars and by the council after the war; Whoberley and Tile Hill near Standard Triumph; Allesley near Jaguar, built between the wars; and Willenhall near Chrysler, built since the war (Map 16.1).

As first-hand journeymen moved out of the city centre in the 1830s, so in the 1920s and 1930s those who were able to get out of Hillfields, with its old housing stock and relatively cramped streets, moved to outlying suburbs. If rich enough, they moved to the more pleasant nearby villages of Leamington Spa, Kenilworth and Warwick.

Those who remained in Hillfields, along with those who remained in Coventry, had to meet the high costs of providing basic infrastructure to satisfy industry's needs and their own housing and community services, plus the commuter needs (such as car parking and roads) of the managerial and professional groups who moved to the villages.

Hillfields tended to attract poorer, unskilled immigrants. Some of these managed to increase their earnings to the point where they were able to move out of Hillfields to one of the more attractive, newer suburbs. This was easier during the 1940s and 1950s. Since then the number of the highest paying jobs, those in the car factories, have hardly expanded.

During the Second World War Hillfields suffered considerable bomb damage. In 1951 a Development Plan was produced by Coventry Corporation designating Hillfields among three comprehensive development areas (Coventry City Council [1952]). While Hillfields did receive aid, top priorities were given to reconstruction of the city centre and new housing estates. This resulted in twenty years of delay in implementing the redevelopment plans for Hillfields, (see Coventry C.D.P. [1975]).

In 1951 only 2.5 per cent of the property in Hillfields was judged 'unfit', but by 1961 more than 25 per cent of houses in Hillfields were declared unfit by the Chief Public Health Inspector. It was estimated that 53 per cent of the housing in Hillfields would become unfit over the next five years (Ling [1961]). By 1970 the Coventry City Council had managed to convince the Home Office that Hillfields was sufficiently blighted for one of the two first Community Development Projects to be set up, not in the slums of Manchester or Leeds, but in Coventry, the country's boom city.[3] In 1971 52.5 per cent of private households in Hillfields were without the exclusive use of hot water, bath and w.c., compared with 20.2 per cent for Great Britain and 15.9 per cent for all of Coventry, (Coventry C.D.P. [1975], p. 9). The income of about half of household heads (earned or unearned) was less than £25 a week in Hillfields and 15 per cent of the local population, with an unknown number of dependants, were claiming supplementary benefits.

The deterioration of Hillfields' housing stock over the past thirty years has

TABLE 16.1

Hillfields Employment from 1-in-6 Survey, 1971, Occupation by Firm Type (Males and Females)

	Large car firms		G.E.C.	Rest of 15 largest firms	Other engineering firms	Coventry Corporation	Small shops	Others	Percentage of grand total
	B.L.M.C.	Chrysler							
Higher professionals 1A	0.0	0.0	0.0	0.9	0.0	0.0	0.0	0.4	0.25
Lower professionals 1B	2.9	2.1	1.4	1.8	1.1	1.3	0.0	5.6	3.02
Employers and proprietors 2A	0.0	0.0	0.0	0.0	0.0	0.0	1.9	1.2	0.50
Managers and administrators 2B	2.9	0.0	2.7	1.8	2.2	2.5	44.2	3.6	5.28
Clerical workers 3	5.9	6.3	9.6	13.5	4.4	2.5	3.8	12.4	8.79
Foremen, inspectors, supervisors 4	10.3	6.3	8.2	12.6	6.6	1.3	0.0	0.8	4.90
Skilled manual 5	36.8	54.2	16.4	24.3	30.8	28.7	9.6	30.0	28.77
Semi-skilled manual 6	14.7	12.5	54.8	25.2	25.3	27.5	38.5	28.0	28.02
Unskilled manual 7	26.5	18.7	6.8	19.8	29.7	36.3	1.9	17.6	20.48
Total	100.0	100.1	99.9	99.9	100.1	100.1	99.9	100.0	100.01
Percentage of Grand Total	9.26	6.58	9.62	14.38	12.06	10.23	6.33	31.55	100.01

NOTE: (a) The other 12 of the 15 largest firms in Coventry are Rolls Royce (1971), Dunlop, Massey Ferguson, Associated Engineering, Tube Investments, Torrington, Renold Chain, Alfred Herbert, Birmingham Small Arms, Courtaulds, John Brown, Lucas.
(b) Sample size, 861.
SOURCE: Coventry Community Development Project [1971]

TABLE 16.2

Hilfields Employment from 1-in-6 Survey, 1971, Occupation by Firm Type (Males)

		Large car firms		G.E.C.	Rest of 15 largest firms	Other engineering firms	Coventry Corporation	Small shops	Others	Percentage of grand total
		B.L.M.C.	Chrysler							
Higher professionals	1A	0.0	0.0	0.0	1.2	0.0	0.0	0.0	0.7	0.39
Lower professionals	1B	3.2	0.0	0.0	2.4	1.4	2.2	0.0	4.9	2.74
Employers and proprietors	2A	0.0	0.0	0.0	0.0	0.0	0.0	4.5	0.7	0.39
Managers and administrators	2B	3.2	0.0	6.9	2.4	0.0	2.2	54.5	5.6	5.28
Clerical workers	3	3.2	2.8	6.9	8.3	1.4	0.0	0.0	3.5	3.72
Foremen, inspectors, supervisors	4	11.3	8.3	10.3	14.3	5.6	2.2	0.0	1.4	6.26
Skilled manual	5	37.1	52.8	34.5	25.0	35.2	46.7	22.7	45.5	38.36
Semi-skilled manual	6	12.9	16.7	31.0	26.2	23.9	31.0	18.2	21.0	22.31
Unskilled manual	7	29.0	19.4	10.3	20.2	32.4	15.8	0.0	16.8	20.54
Total		99.9	100.0	99.9	100.0	99.9	100.1	99.9	100.1	99.99
Percentage of grand total		12.99	7.91	6.21	16.76	14.88	8.85	4.14	28.25	99.99

NOTE: Sample size, 561.
SOURCE: Coventry Community Development Project [1971]

TABLE 16.3

Hillfields Employment from 1-in-6 Survey, 1971, Occupation by Firm Type (Females)

	Large car firms		G.E.C.	Rest of 15 largest firms	Other engineering firms	Coventry Corporation	Small shops	Others	Percentage of Grand Total
	B.L.M.C.	Chrysler							
Higher professionals 1A	0.0	0.0	0.0	0.0	0.0	0.0	0.0	0.0	0.00
Lower professionals 1B	0.0	8.3	2.3	0.0	0.0	0.0	0.0	7.4	3.50
Employers and proprietors 2A	0.0	0.0	0.0	0.0	0.0	0.0	0.0	1.9	0.70
Managers and administrators 2B	0.0	0.0	0.0	0.0	10.0	2.9	36.7	1.9	5.59
Clerical workers 3	33.3	16.7	11.4	29.6	15.0	5.7	6.7	24.1	17.83
Foremen, inspectors, supervisors 4	0.0	0.0	6.8	7.4	10.0	0.0	0.0	0.0	2.45
Skilled manual 5	33.3	58.3	4.5	22.2	15.0	5.7	0.0	9.3	11.54
Semi-skilled manual 6	33.3	0.0	70.5	22.2	30.0	22.9	53.3	37.0	38.11
Unskilled manual 7	0.0	16.7	4.5	18.5	20.0	62.9	3.3	18.5	20.28
Total	99.9	100.0	100.0	99.9	100.0	100.1	100.0	100.1	100.00
Percentage of grand total	2.41	4.12	15.81	9.97	6.87	12.71	10.31	37.80	100.00

NOTE: Sample size, 302
SOURCE: Coventry Community Development Project [1971]

reflected the poverty and unemployment of those who live there. The car industry has been important for Hillfields as well as the rest of Coventry, but Hillfields' workers have been more concentrated in peripheral jobs and among peripheral firms compared with other Coventry workers. Herein lies the Hillfields 'problem'.

In 1971, of Coventry's 190,000 workers, about 25,000 were employed by B.L.M.C. and a further 13,000 were employed by Chrysler.[4] Thus the two major car firms employed 20 per cent of Coventry's workers. Of the 38,000 large car firm employees about 34,000 were men representing 26 per cent of Coventry's 129,000 male workers. As may be seen from Tables 16.1, 16.2 and 16.3, B.L.M.C. and Chrysler accounted for a substantial, but somewhat smaller proportion of Hillfields' workers, 15.8 per cent of total employment and 20.9 per cent of male workers.

The proportion of Hillfields' people at B.L.M.C. and Chrysler who were unskilled manual workers was particularly high – 23.3 per cent compared with 16.4 per cent to 18.8 per cent between 1963 and 1968 for MLH 381 for all Great Britain (N.E.D.O. [1969], p. 37).[5] Also the proportion of Hillfields people employed by small firms in the metal-working industries is particularly high. In 1971 7.2 per cent of Coventry's workers were employed by firms in the metal-working industries (SIC 6 to 12) other than in the fifteen largest firms in Coventry (Coventry Employment Exchange). Table 16.1 shows that 12.1 per cent of those living in Hillfields were so employed. Also the proportion of Hillfields people who worked as unskilled manual labourers within these firms was very high, 29.7 per cent.[6]

TABLE 16.4

Employment in Hillfields and Coventry by Socioeconomic Groups, 1971

| | Hillfields | | Coventry | |
	Male (per cent)	*Female* (per cent)	*Male* (per cent)	*Female* (per cent)
Professional, employers, managers	4.7	4.6	12.1	4.1
Non-manual intermediate and junior workers	7.6	30.8	15.3	48.5
Personal service workers	0.4	14.1	0.4	12.3
Foremen and supervisors	1.9	1.0	3.6	0.8
Skilled manual workers	33.8	5.0	36.3	6.3
Semi-skilled manual workers	23.4	19.0	21.3	13.1
Unskilled manual workers	20.6	15.0	5.8	9.2
Others	7.6	10.5	5.2	5.7
	100.0	100.0	100.0	100.0

SOURCE: 1971 *Census of Population*

Table 16.4, constructed from the Ward Tables of the 1971 Census, shows the skill distribution of Hillfields compared with Coventry.[7]

While Hillfields has slightly fewer skilled workers than the rest of Coventry, Hillfields is primarily distinguished by a much higher proportion of unskilled manual workers and a much lower proportion of technical, administrative and clerical workers. But the poverty of Hillfields cannot be explained by the high proportion of Hillfields' workers employed in *peripheral occupations* alone. Relatively high employment in *peripheral firms* also contributes to Hillfields' impoverished state. The average weekly wage in 1971 for male manual workers was £33 in Great Britain, £40 in Coventry, but only £24 in Hillfields (Hill, [1973], p. 60; Coventry C.D.P., [1971]). The majority of Hillfields' male manual workers were skilled or semi-skilled and the proportion of workers in these categories was similar to the overall Coventry proportion (Table 16.4). Unless these workers (and Hillfields' unskilled male manual workers) were receiving less pay than Coventry workers in the same occupation groups, it is unlikely that the average Hillfields wage would be so much lower than the average Coventry wage.

Peripheral occupations and employment in peripheral firms mean more insecure employment as well as lower wages for those living in Hillfields. In December 1971, with the proportion of people unemployed and actively seeking employment at 3.8 per cent for Great Britain and 3.7 per cent for Coventry, 7.4 per cent of those in Hillfields were so classified (Census [1971]). Relative deprivation in Hillfields is indicated by the lower level of car and house ownership compared with Coventry. Average car ownership per household was 0.24 in Hillfields and 0.56 in Coventry for 1966 (Census [1966]). In 1966 57.7 per cent of households were owner-occupiers in Coventry compared with 36.4 per cent in Hillfields. Comparable figures for 1971 were 59.7 per cent for Coventry and 36 per cent for Hillfields.

Deprivation in a peripheral area like Hillfields is not likely to be reversed. Whenever car demand picks up, top managers will be anxious to refill their Coventry factories with younger men, preferably from outside Coventry (as Chrysler has during the 1970s, see Chapter 14, Section 5). Those unemployed in Coventry and Hillfields are likely to take jobs outside car factories and even outside the metal-working industries altogether, if they can find jobs at all.

Unemployment often means deskilling. In Coventry, in 1971, most unemployed workers left their jobs because of redundancy or dismissal (61 per cent). Only 13 per cent left work to better themselves or because they thought their jobs were unsatisfactory (Hill [1973], p. 73). In December 1971 21 per cent of Coventry men unemployed had left unskilled manual work, *four* times higher than the proportion of Coventry men who were classed as unskilled manual workers (5.2 per cent). But 36 per cent of those who were unemployed were registered for unskilled manual jobs.[8]

The legacy of past unemployment continues to mark Hillfields. It appears in the industrial and occupational distribution of Hillfields as well as in

Hillfields' higher level of unemployment. Unemployment increases the likelihood of future unemployment because of deskilling through the necessity to take an 'inappropriate' job (as well as the loss of self-confidence).[9] Also there is one job category which acts as a last stop before 'permanent' unemployment; that is working for the local authority. In 1971, 2.3 per cent of Coventry workers were employed by Coventry Corporation, but 10.2 per cent of those living in Hillfields' worked for the corporation. Most did not work as administrators, clerks or school-teachers. In fact 92.5 per cent were manual workers and 36.3 per cent were unskilled manual workers (Table 16.1).

In the future, as Coventry's overall unemployment rates climb, the proportion of Hillfields people doing unskilled jobs and unemployed may be expected to rise quickly.

While Hillfields is the site of relative deprivation in Coventry, the causes are not to be found by examining Hillfields in isolation. Centre – periphery patterns exist independently of poor housing. People in peripheral occupations or working for peripheral firms congregate in places like Hillfields because houses are old and because relatively cheap rented accommodation is available. There are other areas in Coventry which are also marked by serious deprivation, such as the post-war cheap council estate at Wood End near Bell Green. Areas like Hillfields and Wood End exist in all major cities, as they do in what has been Britain's most prosperous city, Coventry.

2   Shifting Centre for the Car Industry and Coventry's Future

From the late 1960s the American-owned car firms have been concentrating their new investments in Europe outside the United Kingdom. Why? I have already pointed out the advantages of multisourcing internationally within and between firms. But during the last few years it has become obvious that the large American car firms have not been building a periphery around central U.K. factories and workers. Top managers in the American car firms now view workers in their continental European car factories (at least the native, white ones), particularly those in Germany (Ford, General Motors) and France (Chrysler) as central to their European operations. Car firms in Germany and France, as well as those in Belgium and Italy, now pay higher average wages than are paid in the United Kingdom.[10] Productivity (output per man) is higher there[11] because of greater investment per man and because of relatively weak worker resistance. Weak worker resistance (plus close state co-operation) is the reason for the firms shifting their operations to the Continent. Higher investment by car firms on the Continent reflects this shift.

Perhaps the major advantage which the German, French, Belgian and Swedish motor industries have over the British is the high proportion of underpaid and overworked immigrant and migrant workers employed there. These workers are given semi-skilled and unskilled jobs in Continental car firms thereby deepening divisions in the labour force.

One of the most remarkable things about the German and Swedish motor industry is the increasing reluctance of the Germans and Swedes to work in them; more than half of the places on the production line are filled by 'guest workers' or 'immigrants' respectively (*The Times*, 8 November 1972).

The use of guest and immigrant workers is important to the firm in the external labour power market in that these workers have been both readily available for hire in quantities desired by the firm and easily dischargable in desired quantities – an excellent periphery. The use of immigrant workers on the Continent reminds one of the silk ribbon weavers in the villages around Coventry in the early nineteenth century. According to Castles and Kosack [1973]:

> The idea is that foreigners should be used as the regulators of the labour market: in times of labour shortage they should be brought in; if there is a recession they should simply be dismissed and expelled from the country with no consideration of their needs.

This weakens overall worker resistance. Native-dominated trade unions have given little support to immigrants when they go on strike for their own interests (Castles and Kosack [1973], p. 177). Employers have encouraged this split by separating natives from immigrants according to the jobs they do.[12] 'In addition, employers and authorities have carried out propaganda campaigns in which chauvinist attitudes toward immigrants have been encouraged in order to weaken the labour movement and counter its demands' (Castles and Kosack [1973], p. 177).

Immigrant workers also offer top managers greater flexibility and control in internal labour markets. Because the legal rights of immigrants are limited, the danger to top managers of disputes involving immigrants is reduced.

> They are granted labour permits for a specific job in a certain firm for a limited period. They do not have the right to move to better paid or more highly-qualified positions, at least for some years. Workers who change jobs without permission are often deported (Castles and Kosack [1973], p. 113).

As a result the pace of work is much faster in Continental firms, and this faster pace is used as a yardstick and a driving stick for workers in the United Kingdom (such as Ford's application of the 'Cologne Yardstick' to Dagenham; Beynon [1973], pp. 52–3).

The standard reason for companies becoming multinational is to jump tariff barriers. Firms wishing to expand into a new market may find it impossible to compete while importing into that market because of their disadvantage when the tariff is added to their product's price. This problem may be avoided by directly investing in manufacturing capacity in foreign countries. But within Europe this problem is insignificant. Tariffs on imported cars are generally around 10 per cent or less. The major reason for multinationalisation within Europe is the flexibility gained by firms in dealing with their workers by having duplicate facilities in different countries. For example, the *Financial Times* reported:

> Leyland is now building up its production of cars at Continental plants. Most of the cars which it sells on the Continent are now being assembled in Belgium, Italy or Spain from British engines and components. Increased supplies from these plants will protect the company from industrial problems at its British plants and enable it to continue its drive for a larger share of the total European market (15 March 1973).

While the centre of European car production has shifted to areas where a high proportion of immigrants are available, car firms have been expanding in underdeveloped countries even more quickly. The main process to be set up in underdeveloped countries has been the relatively labour intensive and strike-prone final assembly operation, but gradually other processes have been set up as well.

The main advantages of producing in less developed countries such as Spain, Brazil and Argentina are low wages and the underdeveloped state of worker organisation in those countries. Besides tax rebates and access to official credits which the Spanish Government offers to major car manufac- turers setting up in the country (*Financial Times*, 29 January 1973), unions independent of employers have been illegal in Spain as well as virtually all strikes (Counter Information Services [1974], pp. 32–3). Deliberate slacking at work is a punishable offence. Brazil, the main car manufacturing country in Latin America, is notorious for its suppression of unions and wages (Counter Information Services [1974], p. 43).

After 1860 the centre – periphery relation between Hillfields and the neighbouring villages paled into insignificance with the general depression caused by the maturation of the silk ribbon product cycle and competition from technically more advanced firms in Switzerland and France. After a full thirty years of depression Coventry re-emerged as the centre of prosperity, but the precise centre shifted from Hillfields to the bicycle firms in the south of the city. Hillfields firms did subcontracting work for the larger bicycle assembly firms. Hillfields became part of the periphery for the new industry and a depressed area.

Many of the distressing omens for Coventry which were barely discernible during the deceleration part of the peak period have become all too obvious during the 1970s. In January 1975 Coventry's rate of male unemployment was 8 per cent, with another 12 per cent of the city's male labour force on short time. At Jaguar more than 7000 workers were on short time, and at Chrysler

5000 workers were on short time, with 4000 on a two-day week. In all, more than 27,000 of Coventry's male workers were unemployed or on short time (*Coventry Evening Telegraph*, 23 and 29 January 1975). The region's coalmines reported no problems in finding recruits.[13]

As the bicycle product cycle approached maturity just before the First World War, the danger to Coventry was thwarted by the overlapping motor-car product cycle. In the 1900s, 1910s and 1920s Coventry's bicycle firms were switching to cars, but in the 1960s and 1970s there have been no product shifts within Coventry's major firms. The firms have been expanding their operations elsewhere while Coventry plants use old, outmoded equipment. The centre – periphery relation between Coventry and areas like Hillfields or parts of Birmingham (where many are employed in smaller supplier firms) may well pale into insignificance as the whole of the West Midlands becomes the periphery to a world motor industry, dominated by perhaps a half dozen or even fewer firms.

PART SIX
ARGUMENT AND CONSEQUENCE

CHAPTER SEVENTEEN

Argument and Consequence

In Chapter 1, I suggested that the main theoretical barrier against analysis of concrete micro situations within the Marxian framework has been the absence of explicit consideration of class struggle, particularly struggle within productive activity. Once class struggle is incorporated fundamentally and explicitly into a Marxian framework, two types of consequences follow. First, it becomes clear that a number of new categories and concepts should be incorporated into the analysis. Second, alterations to a number of Marx's categories are suggested. The first set of consequences are examined briefly in Section 1. The value of labour power is discussed in Section 2. Discretion, class struggle and other Marxian categories are examined in Section 3, and Section 4 deals briefly with general aspects of micro analysis and industry-area links.

1 New Concepts

The main new subject required of an analysis explicitly dealing with class struggle is managerial strategy for maintaining and augmenting authority over workers. Once we recognise that workers are able to exert a degree of direct control within the labour process and bargaining power within the valorisation process (Chapter 6, Section 3), we must accept (as did top managers) that the job of maintaining managerial authority over workers is not automatic and it is not straightforward. Marxists have generally ignored the problem (Lenin), or they have presumed managerial control to grow smoothly via coercive Direct Control strategies alone, unopposed and uninfluenced by worker resistance (Braverman).

In fact Responsible Autonomy strategies have been used by top managers towards certain groups of workers throughout the history of capitalism. Similarly top managers have always tried to limit the power of their entire labour force to resist exploitation by treating the most powerful groups of workers differently from the rest; by giving them status, security, responsibility. Workers have always been divided into those with central status and those treated as peripheral to the firm.

Top managers consciously forgo a degree of direct control over productive activity in these cases. This should not be surprising. That some things must change so that the more fundamental relations of production may remain the same, that capitalism can and does accommodate its contradictions (up to a point), becomes clear from historical examination of class struggle. This accommodation is not automatic. It requires careful and complex strategic manoeuvring by top managers.

Another 'new' concept concerns institutionalised power relations during productive activity and the importance of internal labour markets. Marx concentrates almost exclusively on the consequences of the unequal situations of capitalists and workers when they enter productive activity. After the exchange of labour power for means of subsistence, the capitalist, who retains ownership over the means of production, 'now strides in front', while the worker 'follows'. 'The one with an air of importance, smirking, intent on business; the other timid and holding back, like one who is bringing his own hide to market and has nothing to expect but – a hiding.' But after productive activity had begun, in internal labour markets, groups of workers threw off much of their 'timidity' through collective resistance.

Many battles won through collective resistance have to be refought again and again (such as disputes over work pace), but other victories become institutionalised in customs, rules or procedures (such as shop stewards' privileges). Workers who exchange their labour power for means of sub-sistence after such changes in productive activity have occurred are able to begin their work experiences less 'timidly'. The consequences of the exchange itself have altered due to the development of struggle during productive activity.

When the worker sells his labour power for a fixed period of time he has actually exchanged his capacity to work over a period of time for money, *and* for some degree of hardship during that period of time. The degree of hardship which the worker may expect on giving up his labour power *and his time* is limited broadly by laws and customs. These are established through class struggle in the society as a whole, and by institutions established within productive activity as a result of struggle in individual firms and industries.

Top managers often accept and encourage institutionalisation of the results of disputes, (even if those disputes resulted in worker victories), because they are anxious to avoid further disruptions of productive activity. Top managers' readiness to encourage this institutionalisation depends critically on competitive conditions. As demonstrated in Chapters 12 and 14, when demand is strong top managers will be anxious to buy off disruptions and to 'stabilise' their relations with workers. In these situations top managers try to limit the power of worker resistance by institutionalising it. In the short run this may achieve the desired results. But in the long run limiting the power of worker resistance by recognising its reality through customs, rules or procedures makes that power harder to break when competitive conditions tighten (see Chapter 14, Sections 4 and 5). Though worker resistance may be limited by strategy or institutions, this accommodation increases inflexibility which may hamper the ease with which resistance may be accommodated in future.

2   The Value of Labour Power

In the previous section I suggested that struggle during productive activity will affect the exchange relation which initiates that activity – the sale of labour power over a period of time for money and for a degree of hardship during that time. Usually the degree of hardship to be endured is not explicitly written into the contract when labour power is sold. Marx did not consider this element of the relations of production in his value framework. But once struggle during productive activity is explicitly recognised, the aspect of the major relation of production which Marx did consider must also be altered: that is, the money which the worker receives in return for his labour power, or what Marx calls the 'value of labour power'.

Marx's model of exchange relations assumes that firms are highly competitive and that the industrial reserve army lowers wages for all groups of workers. The value of labour power is the labour time necessary to produce the subsistence goods socially necessary to maintain and reproduce workers. It is treated as being the same, for analytical purposes, for all workers in a given country and at a given period. Wages tend toward this value of labour power for all workers.[1] At the heart of Marx's value theory is the proposition that labour powers are made comparable with each other through the operation of capitalist competition and the reserve army, both forcing wages for all workers down towards the value of their labour power, the subsistence level.

At the heart of the framework set up in Parts Two and Three is the proposition that the condition of different groups of workers within the same country, in fact within the same firm, depends on the outcome of differential worker resistance (buttressed by custom and different strengths of the reserve army for different categories of jobs) and managerial strategy for counter-pressure. The wage, at base, depends not on need, but on struggle.

I therefore think it is necessary to redefine the value of labour power by removing its connection with the idea of subsistence considered physiologically and by tying it to the idea of struggle.

Marx allowed the value of labour power to depend on socially based needs as well as 'natural' or biological needs.[2] But the idea of need begins to lose any operational value once its connection with the physiological is weakened. By considering the value of labour power in terms of subsistence, its operational content appears to relate to the wage socially necessary to render the workers *capable* of supplying their labour power to capitalists in the long run. This has led Marxists to imply that differences in real wages earned within advanced capitalist countries represent subsistence levels in that they simply provide for needs which are comparably urgent. What is necessary to satisfy psychological needs (such as for televisions), or quasi-technical needs (such as for telephones), can be just as important as what is necessary to satisfy physiological needs. To presume that American wages, at more than double European wages, are still at subsistence levels because Americans may sometimes be undernourished compared with Europeans, or because the scarcity of public housing or shacks in America implies that 'American workers are doomed either to live in elegant and comfortable small houses or else to sleep under bridges' (Emmanuel [1972], pp. 117–18), is to transform the concept of need into a simple enumeration of the *status quo*. It is to borrow the most conservative secular justification that I know of for tolerating the persistence of poverty amidst plenty, rich races or countries beside poor ones – that the poor simply need less than the rich.[3]

The unequal distribution of income within countries and between them does not reflect differing needs, it reflects differing desire *and ability* to resist, plus managerial strategies. While psychological needs may affect the desire to resist exploitation, even the desire to resist will depend on much more than need. It will also depend on consciousness of one's relative position as a consumer compared with other groups within firms, areas or countries,[4] the strength of one's idea of a 'fair' distribution, as well as particular desires and grievances which arise from struggle normally during productive activity.

Once the fact that real long-run wage levels are determined by struggle is accepted, the relation between real wages and the value of labour power must be re-examined. There are some Marxists who suggest that we ought to do away with values altogether and instead deal only with visible categories of exchange such as prices and wages (Hodgson [1976]). But the purpose of dealing primarily with values for Marx was to reveal the essential, class-divided nature of capitalist society. This project continues to require reiteration, particularly once the class-divided nature of capitalist society becomes even more obscured by persistent differentials in economic conditions among working people.

The problem becomes far simpler if the value of labour power is redefined slightly to mean the labour time necessary to produce the goods which are politically and socially necessary to keep workers' labour power (as a class) available to capitalists.

It is not what is necessary to ensure that workers will be *capable* of maintaining and reproducing labour power; rather it is what is necessary to ensure that workers will be *willing to accept* exploitation in the capitalist mode of production.[5] Sections of workers may resist the *degree* of their exploitation compared with others, but it is only the class as a whole, or at least a majority of that class, which could resist, with any hope of success, the existence of exploitation as such.

I think that the value of labour power so expressed can only be defined separately for each country at the moment for two reasons. First, in the past all revolutions have been confined within national boundaries. Second, even now workers generally are concerned only with their position in relation to others in their own country, both in sectional terms, concerning relative wages, and in collective terms concerning social dividends (social security, unemployment insurance, pensions, etc.) and state-imposed restraints on employers (hours of work, health and safety at work, etc.). Workers are relatively unconcerned with the situation of those in other countries. Their wages and conditions of work do not enter into calculations of distributive justice or the 'proper' average standard of living. This may change with the internationalisation of capital. If worker resistance became internationalised the value of labour power would have to be defined globally. At the moment, however, separate national levels are more appropriate.

As the reserve army has dried up and organised worker resistance has grown in strength, the value of labour power in advanced capitalist countries has been rising. In the short run, as wages and conditions improve, many groups of workers within advanced capitalist countries receive more than the current long-run value of their labour power.[6] This short-run differential slowly becomes incorporated into the long-run value of labour power. As long as wages are rising, this differential will remain. It provides a cushion against revolution in those countries. Furthermore central workers within advanced capitalist countries have gained more than the value of their labour power in the long-run sense that as long as any particular group of workers remains central their wages (and conditions) will be significantly above the national average. This represents a particularly thick cushion against their disaffection with the system and with their individual employers.

While the value of labour power is different between countries, it is not different for different groups within a country. If one group of workers' standard of living is threatened, they will only be able to challenge the system itself if they can generate solidarity among other groups of workers. If those other workers think the first group's wages are too high, the disruption caused by their resistance will breed hostility among the other groups of workers rather than solidarity.[7] The availability of workers' labour power to the capitalist mode of production will therefore depend on a standard of wages which roughly corresponds to most workers' notions of distributive justice and a 'decent' wage. That central workers may find themselves out of work because of the unplanned nature of the system will also encourage a majority view of the adequacy of unemployment benefit, social security and pensions, in spite of only a minority relying on these payments at any point in time.

3 Discretion, Class Struggle and other Marxian Categories

The Marxian framework outlined here suggests that the rate of exploitation will depend critically on class struggle on two counts. First, the value of labour power should be thought of as the outcome of struggle rather than a reflection of need. Second, the rate of surplus value will depend on how intensively people can be made to work, which will of course depend on class struggle. But there are other Marxian categories which should be altered somewhat in the light of the framework set out above.

The reserve army ought to be thought of as divided or stratified on the basis of availability to the capital *which requires it* (that is, expanding capital). The balkanization of the reserve army on the basis of skills or other educational attributes, sex, race, nationality or location is the outcome of social divisions which pre-dated capitalism. It is also the result of those divisions which are encouraged during capitalism by the interplay of worker resistance and managerial counter-pressure at the level of individual production units, industries and the social formation as a whole. In turn these divisions in the reserve army will affect the location of capital, types of managerial strategies used, the rate of exploitation and the direction of technical change.

One of the major themes of this book, outlined in Chapter 6, is that the direction of technical change is not predetermined. It too is the outcome of class struggle and depends on whether top managers are pursuing Direct Control or Responsible Autonomy strategies as well as on the relative ability of particular groups of workers to resist authority.

Finally, all of these categories will depend in part on the degree of monopoly power enjoyed by the firms involved. If one takes Marx's Law of Value as a description of the way capital is allocated (according to relative profit rates), arising out of the definition of the capitalist mode of production, then one would expect the degree to which the Law of Value acts to depend on the degree to which elements of the definition are satisfied (see Chapter 2, Section 1). One may think of the degree to which firms enjoy monopoly power as an indicator of the degree to which allocation based on the Law of Value will be relaxed.

4 The Framework and Micro Analysis of Industries and Areas

The analysis presented in this book is intended to guide further work in Marxian political economy in a particular direction. While I think a Marxian framework is capable of illuminating micro situations and industry-area links better than the neo-classical economic framework, most Marxist analysis has been confined to macro analysis, often never coming to grips with concrete situations even at the macro level. Alterations and additions to Marx's categories which require one to analyse concrete situations were outlined in the previous three sections. The value of the amended framework for illuminating concrete micro situations and industry-area links was illustrated in Parts Four and Five.

To demonstrate that micro situations arise out of the interplay between capitalist social relations of production which give rise to the Law of Value, managerial discretion and class struggle has been the primary aim of this book. The persistence of areas of deprivation near areas of prosperity is primarily a reflection of the interplay of those forces and cannot be understood unless those forces are examined in concrete situations.

Notes and References

Chapter 1

1. This view underlies the Cycle of Deprivation Studies which were set up jointly between the Department of Health and Social Services and the Social Sciences Research Council, encouraged by the Secretary of State for social services, Sir Keith Joseph, in 1972.

2. This view underlies the Six Towns Studies set up by the Department of the Environment in 1973 and the Comprehensive Community Programmes set up by the Home Office in 1974.

3. This is the standard pluralist view underlying most liberal academic treatments of the poverty 'problem'.

4. With Liverpool, the Coventry Community Development Project was the first of the twelve Community Development Projects set up by the Home Office from 1969. The Coventry project submitted its final report, which contained a summary of the Coventry Industry – Hillfields study, in March 1975.

5. The Marxian critique of neo-classical economic theory is now well known. As it does not add to the analysis developed in this book it will not be repeated here. Those interested may look at Rowthorn [1974] or Hollis and Nell [1975] for recent contributions to that critique.

6. For an interesting explanation of this lack of concreteness in most Marxist analysis during the past fifty years, see Anderson, [1976].

Chapter 2

1. 'In broad outline, the Asiatic, ancient, feudal and modern bourgeois [capitalist] modes of production may be designated as epochs marking progress in the economic development of society.' (*A Contribution to the Critique of Political Economy*, p. 21.) Note that all Marx's writings will be cited by title alone, rather than author and date of publication as for other writers. All page numbers refer to Lawrence and Wishart editions unless otherwise stated.

2. A use-value is something which has utility; that is, something which is capable of serving human needs or wants (*Capital*, vol. 1, p. 45).

3. Marx recognises that the capitalist mode of production as defined above does not characterise every productive relationship in a capitalist society. For example, in a capitalist society there are still what Marx calls 'simple commodity producers', people who themselves produce commodities directly for sale on the market without the use of wage labour. Capitalist

society or a capitalist social formation is one where the capitalist mode of production dominates. The term 'social formation' is used to describe the whole set of social relations which characterise a society at a given point in time.

4. Alienation was a more specific concept for Marx than the notion of alienation which is popular today. Following Durkheim [1933], many think alienation means a deviation from the 'natural' human condition in individuals caused by the manner in which society controls them. For Marx human beings are naturally social animals and the alienation which most suffer in capitalist society is specifically related to the relations of production. For Marx alienation refers to the sale of workers' labour power. This act implies the legal or formal loss of control over the fruits of the workers' labour and the disposition of that labour power. The matter is not quite so simple because the formal or legal loss of control over workers' labour power which the act of sale implies, must be enforced during the employment period by the capitalist through disciplinary codes and other managerial strategies. Therefore alienation is both an act, the sale of labour power, and a process in which control over what workers do during the time they are employed is captured in practice by the capitalist.

5. 'The fact that half a day's labour is necessary to keep the labourer alive during 24 hours, does not in any way prevent him from working a whole day. Therefore, the value of labour-power, and the value which that labour-power creates in the labour-processes, are two entirely different magnitudes; and this difference of the two values was what the capitalist had in view, when he was purchasing the labour-power' (*Capital*, vol. 1, p. 188). Productive activity is the unity of two processes, the *labour process* through which labour power produces use-values, and the *valorisation process* through which labour power produces surplus value.

6. This then means that the value of any particular physical quantity of commodities will fall, that is, the amount of socially necessary labour time embodied in a fixed amount of commodities will be reduced. See following paragraph.

7. Marx distinguishes the manufacturing division of labour from the social division of labour. The social division of labour is the division of employments or branches of production. As the capitalist mode of production develops this becomes more relevant for capitalists than for workers. Under simple commodity production the social division of labour meant that the butcher, the baker and the candlestick-maker were all different people and that each produced only one type of commodity. The social division of labour is based on exchange relations, that is, that people bring different commodities to market. As the worker brings only his labour power to market the social division of labour characterises his position less and less; see *Capital*, vol. 1, chap. 11, sect. 4.

8. Marx distinguishes machines from tools in that for tools the motive force behind the instrument of labour is human, while for machines it is some other natural force (*Capital*, vol. 1, p. 352).

9. 'Modern Industry' is the term used in the Lawrence and Wishart edition. In some ways the term 'Machinofacture', used in the Everyman

edition, is better, particularly because a succeeding stage of the capitalist mode of production is often distinguished thereby making the term 'Modern Industry' somewhat contradictory. The most recent English edition of Capital, the Penguin edition, uses the term 'large-scale industry'. For me this term is not much better than Modern Industry because for me the succeeding stage of the capitalist mode of production, Monopoly Capitalism, is distinguished by widespread monopoly power enjoyed by large-scale firms.

10. A higher rate of exploitation of living labour will discourage the replacement of that labour by machinery. Similarly the replacement of adult men by women and children, which actually reduced wages below the value of labour power, slowed down the spread of machinery in early industrialising England (Capital, vol. 1, pp. 365–72).

11. Marx distinguishes four layers to the reserve army – floating, latent, stagnant and the sediment (Capital, vol. 1, pp. 600–3). The floating layer consists of those temporarily thrown out of work by technical change or slumps in demand. The latent layer comprises those thrown out of agriculture. The stagnant is those irregularly employed, coming from decaying domestic industry and manufacture sectors. The sediment is the paupers, the sick, the old and the mutilated. For the purposes of this book it will be sufficient to divide the reserve army into only two categories–active and latent. The active reserve army will include all those immediately available to work for capitalists in the modern industry, and later the monopoly capitalism, sector. The latent reserve army is all the rest, including those underemployed in agriculture, petty commodity producers going bankrupt and those working in domestic industry. Marx's divisions are based on the social conditions of people, while mine is based on their availability to capitalists. The latent reserve army will compete directly with the active reserve army for jobs in the medium term if relative wages rise in factories or if conditions deteriorate further in their current pursuits.

12. If c/v, the organic composition at capital, rises and if s/v, the rate of exploitation remains the same, then

$$\frac{s}{c+v}$$ will fall since:

$$\frac{s}{c+v} = \frac{(s/v)}{(c/v)+1}$$

See Capital, vol. 3, pt 3.

Chapter 3

1. In so doing I have rejected the term 'Imperialism'. In part this is because the word has come to represent a relation between advanced capitalist countries (or capital emanating from those countries), and less developed countries, rather than a stage of the capitalist mode of production (in spite of Lenin's clear insistence on the latter interpretation; Lenin [1916]). Also my

interpretation of this stage is quite different from Lenin's, as will become clear. I have also rejected the Communist Party's label, State Monopoly Capitalism. While the rise in monopoly power among certain firms has proceeded to the stage where a qualitative change in the mode of production may be discerned, the State has always crucially affected capitalist accumulation. The term 'Monopoly Capitalism' therefore distinguishes more precisely the stage of the capitalist mode of production from the end of the nineteenth century (see Baran and Sweezy [1966], pp. 75–6).

2. '. . . those who, as participants, contribute information to group decisions. This latter group is very large; it extends from the most senior officials of the corporation to where it meets, at the outer perimeter, the white and blue collar workers whose function is to conform more or less mechanically to instruction or routine. It embraces all who bring specialized knowledge, talent or experience to group decision-making. This, not the management, is the guiding intelligence – the brain – of the enterprise. There is no name for all who participate in group decision-making or the organisation which they form. I propose to call this organisation the Technostructure' (Galbraith [1967], p. 80).

3. Baran and Sweezy recognise that smaller firms are also part of Monopoly Capitalism, but for Baran and Sweezy their role is secondary. 'From the point of view of a theory of monopoly capitalism, smaller business should properly be treated as part of the environment within which Big Business operates rather than as an actor on the stage' (Baran and Sweezy [1966], p. 62). Baran and Sweezy then largely ignore this environmental factor. But the links between large and small firms are central aspects of Monopoly Capitalism as can be seen from the historical sections of this chapter, and they are especially important for linking industrial to area developments.

4. The literature on alternative goals and satisficing is large and growing quickly. The three best known theories of the firm suggesting alternative goals are Baumol [1959]; Marris [1964]; and Williamson [1964]. On satisficing see Simon [1957]; and Cyret and March [1963].

5. Thus modern industry (an *analytical* concept) may be thought of as an industry characterised by a significant number of firms using complex machines which is highly competitive; while Modern Industry (the *stage*) would be the time when modern industry characterises most industries in a particular country. Marx's definition of a machine is an instrument of labour powered by some non-human force. A complex machine was distinguished as a mechanism which operated simultaneously a number of identical or similar tools (*Capital*, vol. 1, chap. 15).

6. Presumably because industry has become more constant capital intensive in developed countries, though Lenin simply says capitalism had become 'overripe' in the advanced capitalist countries.

7. Marxist interest in the theory of Imperialism all but disappeared after around 1925. It revived during the late 1950s and 1960s encouraged by the Algerian revolution, 1954–64, and the Cuban revolution, 1961. Baran and Sweezy's distinctive contribution began with Baran's book *The Political Economy of Growth* [1957]. Since then, and particularly after their most

famous book *Monopoly Capital* [1966] was published, their ideas have been very influential among Marxists. They exerted considerable influence through the journal *Monthly Review*, which they edited jointly until Baran's death in 1964.

8. Primarily what is spent on distribution, including the expenses of employing people in marketing, the maintenance of excessive numbers of sales outlets, public relations activities, lobbying, the maintenance of showy office buildings, etc. Also costs associated with finance, insurance, real estate and legal service industries are included (pp. 365–6).

9. Between 1911 and 1966 the number of managers and administrators grew by 240 per cent in Great Britain while the number of foremen and inspectors grew by 311 per cent (Halsey [1972], p. 113).

10. Perhaps the strength of dividing the epochs into transitional and proper stage periods – periods when *some* industries are characterised by modern industry or monopoly capitalism (the *analytic* concepts), and periods when *most* industries are characterised by modern industry or monopoly capitalism – would have been clearer if I had divided the time between the 1870s and the 1970s into only two periods, probably dividing at the 1930s for Britain. But the wartime experiences and the inter-war period were so distinctive that I have considered the expositional advantages of treating them separately to outweigh the clumsiness of the asymmetry.

11. Marx is very sensitive to this. In introducing the Modern Industry stage he says, 'epochs in the history of society are no more separated from each other by hard and fast lines of demarcation, than are geological epochs' (*Capital*, vol. 1, p. 351).

12. 'The steam-engine itself, such as it was at its invention, during the manufacturing period at the close of the 17th century, and such as it continued to be down to 1780, did not give rise to any industrial revolution' (*Capital*, vol. 1, p. 355).

13. Even in the cotton industry the number of factory workers only exceeded domestic workers from the mid-1830s.

14. '. . . outwork became the predominant – though never the sole – form of capitalistic industrial organisation in Britain. Probably it was still the predominant form in the reign of George IV [1820–1830]; for though it was losing ground on one side to great works and factories, it was always gaining on the other at the expense of household production and handicraft' (Clapham [1926], pp. 178–9). Clapham was referring to industrial organisation in general. In cotton weaving there were 224,000 power looms by 1850, but little more than 50,000 hand-loom weavers by the middle 1850s.

15. For information on the growth of iron foundries see Dobb [1969], pp. 263–4; for other textiles see Wood [1910], p. 607; and Clapham [1972], pp. 70–80.

16. In 1851 cotton textiles accounted for 16.5 per cent of those occupied in manufacturing in the United Kingdom and all textiles together accounted for 33 per cent.

17. 'From the Metropolis the demand for labour pushes outwards over the country. Recourse is had to "inferior soils". Old weavers in the villages get work, together with their wives and families. Even farm labourers are

impressed' (Fay [1920], p. 175).

18. The sewing machine gave outworking new life from the 1860s. There are about 250,000 outworkers in Britain today.

19. This argument about relations between stages of the capitalist mode of production in one country also holds for relations between more and less developed countries, though with important qualifications which are discussed in Chapters 8 and 9.

20. Such as dyes for the textile industry from coal tar which was a by-product of steel making; new steel alloys to fix to machine tools to cut steel and for arms; photography; and the design of equipment to take advantage of electrical power in most factories.

21. Such as Krupp's industrial research laboratories at Essen. By 1900 the six largest German chemical works employed more than 650 chemists and engineers (Braverman [1974], p. 162).

22. Compared with the 10 per cent to 50 per cent of workers in factories who would have been classed as skilled around the mid-nineteenth century, only 7 per cent of all occupied people were classed as professionals (and almost one-third of them were teachers or in the Church, Law or Medicine in 1951); (Hobsbawm [1969]; Routh [1965]).

23. The Salt Union, created in 1888, was formed by the merging of 64 separate firms, the United Alkali Company of 1890 by the merging of 48 firms, the Bleachers' Association of 1900 by the merging of 53 firms (Utton [1972], p. 53).

24. The new British Iron and Steel Federation, so intent on reducing output from outlying areas, successfully opposed an outside syndicate's plan for a new integrated steel plant at Jarrow with 80 per cent of Jarrow's entire work-force out of work in 1933 after the closure of Palmers' shipyard. Protest at this decision helped to touch off the famous Jarrow unemployed march to London (Wilkinson [1939]).

25. George [1972] compared 208 industries between the 1958 and 1963 censuses. He found that 141 showed an increase in concentration and 67 showed a decrease.

26. Trades other than Building and Contracting, Mines and Quarries, Public Utility Services and Government Departments, *Census of Production* [1935], summary tables pp. 1–4.

27. The conditions which Robson suggests would make the partially integrated structure less desirable, disappeared after Robson wrote his book.

Chapter 4

1. For a discussion of the weak economic role within the capitalist mode of production which Marx and Engels attributed to trade unions, see Hyman [1971]; and Engels [1892], pp. 216–17.

2. Braverman's important work on the labour process will be discussed more fully in Chapter 6.

Chapter 5

1. Depressions generally began with bad harvests in the early nineteenth century. This affected industry through a fall in the primarily rural home demand for industrial goods. Thus high unemployment and savage wage cuts for non-artisans (in the absence of well-organised worker resistance which was to come later in the century), coincided with famine prices.

2. In the textile industry the strongest societies were among bleachers, dyers and calico printers. These were the highest paid workers. Their societies did not admit women. In fact the only important group of women trade unionists in the whole country until the 1880s were the local societies of weavers, cardroom operatives, and 'beamers' and 'twisters' of the textile industry. These were jobs which had become deskilled during the early days of Modern Industry, though they were still sufficiently skilled to allow discernible separate local societies to be formed in each (Clapham [1932], p. 167).

3. The Ten Hours Act was evaded by a system of relay working until the supplementary act of 1850 ordered that women and young people should work only between 6.00 a.m. and 6.00 p.m., or between 7.00 a.m. and 7.00 p.m., with an hour and a half for meals. The Factory Acts officially protected the health and safety of women and children and thereby raised their cost to employers.

4. Many craftsmen opposed subcontracting as they saw in the relation with the piece-master a system by which they could be driven as well as their labourers. This was particularly true of engineers who also bitterly opposed all forms of piecework (J. and M. Jefferys [1947] p. 437).

5. Dilution meant bringing unskilled workers, usually women, into factories to do jobs traditionally reserved for skilled workers.

6. This is a necessary but insufficient condition. Existing employees may be able to keep their own numbers intact and ensure that excess workers are paid at the going rate through the threat of industrial action.

7. The proportion of engineers on piece-work increased from 5 per cent to 28 per cent between 1886 and 1906 (Jefferys [1945], p. 219).

8. The trades councils, representing city-wide trade unionists, were first established during the Modern Industry period by privileged craftsmen to co-ordinate negotiations. With the rise of new unionism the numbers of trades councils doubled in the few years between 1889 and 1891. The London Trades Council was established in 1860 and the Glasgow Trades Council in 1858 (Pelling [1971], pp. 54, 63, 103). During the war shop steward committees began to use the trades councils to co-ordinate their own local activities.

9. Which meant industrial action of a nature not very clearly defined, but which could include a general strike.

10. Average weekly money wage-rates fell by 17 per cent and average weekly real wages of fully employed workers fell by 11 per cent between 1921 and 1922.

11. The National Minority Movement was formed on the initiative of the Communist Party.

12. The Triple Alliance was negotiated between the Miners' Federation,

the National Union of Railwaymen and the Transport Workers' Federation in 1914, but it was suspended due to the Treasury Agreement. In October 1920 the government capitulated to the miners, granting a temporary six-month wage increase at the threat of support for their claim from the rest of the Triple Alliance.

13. The N.U.M.G.W. had 269,000 members in 1934 and 467,000 in 1939.

14. Routh estimated unskilled manual workers wages to be 64 per cent of skilled workers in 1913/14, 71 per cent in 1922/24 and 66 per cent in 1935/36 for men. The comparable figures for women were 64 per cent, 84 per cent and 85 per cent (1965, p. 107).

15. While the organisational strength of unskilled workers grew it has remained much weaker than that of skilled workers. In 1939 Cole listed five categories of employed workers which were still largely unorganised. These were: domestic servants, clerks and typists, agricultural workers, the distributive trades and unskilled and general labourers. Women were poorly organised in general (Pelling [1971], p. 205).

16. Trade union membership rose as a proportion of the labour force up to a peak of 45.2 per cent in 1948, it then declined to a low of 41.9 per cent in 1967. Since then it has risen, largely on the strength of the progress of white-collar unions.

17. Nevertheless women in the cotton industry were paid much more than women in other industries in consequence of their strong unionisation. In 1906 women cotton workers earned about 18s. 8d. (18 shillings and 8 pence), while the median manual wage for women was only 13s. 4d., and the median of men's wages was 26s. 7d. (Rowbotham [1973], p. 108; and Routh [1965], p. 57).

18. The Equal Pay Act of 1970, which came into effect on 29 December 1975, is directed at women who are engaged in:

(a) the same or broadly similar work,

(b) work rated as equivalent with that of any men, if, and only if, her job and their job have been given an equal value.

This has caused a flurry of grading and job evaluation schemes by managers, often with more-or-less tacit union support, to segregate women's jobs from men's to comply with the law. In the first six months of operation of the industrial tribunals (January – June 1976) 79 of 110 cases were dismissed including such clear violations of the spirit of equal pay as the case of a Leicester community worker who was refused equal pay because she had *greater* responsibility and seniority than a man (Boston [1974], pp. 289–98, and *Financial Times*, 6 August, 1976, p. 11).

Chapter 6

1. Management is taken to mean the process or activity of managing economic enterprises or firms, rather than the group of top managers who direct those enterprises. To manage originally meant to handle or to train a horse in its paces.

2. While it may seem confusing to enumerate these different categories,

the value of the distinctions stems from the different approaches which top managers take toward different groups of workers at different times, largely in response to different forms and strengths of their resistance. Also the distinction will help to clear up what I believe to be a major error of Marxist analysis of the labour process, discussed in Section 2 of this chapter.

3. Scientific method is taken to mean the formulation of general laws or hypotheses based on systematic observations.

4. This ignores more than simply managerial mistakes. I am not dealing explicitly with the general contradiction of capitalism at the moment: that the basic interests of capitalists and workers are opposed to each other because of exploitation, and that masking that opposition or dampening worker resistance by financial concessions, more pleasant working conditions or ideological persuasion all create expectations of the system which become increasingly difficult to satisfy – particularly as safety valves outside the capitalist mode of production come to be incorporated. The problem with leaving the story at this highly abstract level is that the growth of worker resistance tends to be treated as a homogeneous development in which one strategy or tactic appears to be as good as another and all developments appear progressive because progress towards 'the revolution' is assumed to be inevitable and inexorable. Once we admit that the world's date for changing the mode of production is not fixed for some particular future moment, we must accept that some moves by workers can be regressive *and* that some moves by top managers may successfully forestall fundamental change (see Amin [1975]). The managerial strategies described in this chapter are concerned with attempts to forestall fundamental change and get on with the business of accumulation, not with affecting the probability of revolution in some ultimate sense. I am avoiding dealing with the latter issue.

Chapter 7

1. Though I discuss inflexibility of firms due to worker resistance, Taylorism and Procedure in the 1870s to 1914 section below, these features of Monopoly Capitalism are not confined to this period. They simply became particularly important at that time.

2. Differential piece-rates meant that workers had a target 'fair day's work' to perform and that the rate structure of penalties for not achieving the target was different from the rate structure of bonuses for exceeding the target. The loss function for underachieving was steeper and bonus payments would reach a ceiling at 30 per cent to 100 per cent above normal. 'The ceiling was advocated,' Taylor claimed, 'for the benefit of the worker, since if men "got rich too quick" dissipation, drunkenness and absenteeism would increase' (Rose [1975], p. 37).

3. Only 20 per cent of the 887,000 clerical workers and only 16 per cent of the 865,000 managers, administrators, foremen, inspectors and supervisors in 1911 were women (Routh [1965], pp. 4–5).

4. Nevertheless, unions are used to soften the blow of redundancies and

they do help top managers to achieve smoother rationalisations (see Part Five below).

Chapter 8

1. For expositional purposes only two groups of workers are distinguished here – privileged and unprivileged. In fact within any particular firm a complex system of status and privilege levels, depending on such factors as age, sex, race, country of origin, seniority, skill, nepotism and education levels, will be used to discourage resonance and solidarity.

2. Domestic Industry, on the other hand, was far more flexible because an individual merchant or factor would have many workers generally performing the same operations in parallel. Privileged workers still existed (i.e. those most concentrated geographically, who represent lower transport cost workers), but operations could always be reduced quickly, with no technical disruption to the rest of the operation and little disruption due to worker resistance, by simply not giving out work to the outlying domestic workers. Outlying domestic workers were generally just as skilled as town domestic workers, though they sometimes used less advanced tools (see Chapter 11).

3. The Fiat case is somewhat atypical as the changed work organisation came from the initiatives of the workers rather than top managers – see Chapter 6, Section 3.

4. The category of skilled manual workers during Monopoly Capitalism is particularly troublesome. While many manual workers are classified as skilled, their position is unlike pre-twentieth-century craftsmen who served five-or seven-year apprenticeships. Often the label 'skilled' reflects the power of a category of workers' organisation or mere custom, rather than the training necessary to perform the work they do (see Braverman [1974], chap. 20; and consider the technical ease with which wartime dilution was achieved during this century).

5. Differences in male versus female unemployment rates are very difficult to interpret because married women are often classified as unoccupied when they ought to be considered unemployed. They cannot claim supplementary benefits if they are living with their husbands, nor can they claim unemployment benefit unless they are paying a full contribution to the National Insurance Scheme (as opposed to the reduced married women's rate).

6. Workers with unstable earnings will find it difficult to get credit for consumer durables purchase – particularly houses. They will therefore have to pay cash more often or have to rent at what generally turns out to be higher rates than for those with stronger financial backing.

7. This will be mitigated somewhat in the very short run by redundancy payments, but these payments do not amount to much for younger workers, and older workers have much poorer chances of finding alternative employment (Martin and Fryer [1973]).

8. They are Lucas, Birmid, G.K.N., Dunlop, Smiths and Automative Products.

9. This need not imply perfect competition. In oligopolistic markets prices

are normally stable in the short run. Changes in output may then be expected to be due primarily to changes in demand for the industry's product, (say due to changing tastes or income levels), rather than market shares. Also market shares may change due to non-price competition. *Note* that *OR* is not a locus of output choice points as for a standard total revenue curve. It is the locus of expected total revenue given levels of output achieved due to uncontrollable fluctuations in demand. Only OQ_t in Graph 8.1 and 01 in Graph 8.2 represent chosen levels of output.

10. In spite of a very poor response to this question over half who answered it in MLHs 332 and 342/349 stated that some of their work was carried out on a subcontract basis.

Chapter 9

1. See Chapter 3, Section 2 for a critique of the theory on which Baran and Frank's analyses are based; see Chapter 17 for criticisms of Emmanuel.

2. Labour power was unlimited in supply for unskilled work only, and this required breaking down old modes of production (it was a latent rather than an active reserve army being drawn upon). Generally conditions of labour power supply for skilled jobs and jobs involving the exercise of authority were even more limited than in the homelands because those jobs were reserved for white colonists. Nevertheless these white colonists formed a small minority of the labour force in the export industries of the colonies. Vast latent reserve armies in underdeveloped countries continue to depress native wages there.

3. This situation of unequal exchange has been formally examined by Emmanuel in *Unequal Exchange* (1972), with illustrations using Marx's value categories: $c + v + s$.

4. The British terms of trade have deteriorated since then, but this was primarily due to the war and the period from 1948 to 1951 when Britain decided to expand exports and maintain extremely low levels of unemployment with an undervalued exchange rate. This has been reversed somewhat since 1951. Taking 1964 as 100, the British terms of trade were 114 in 1951, though they were 88 in 1956.

5. There are also the balance of payments problems of underdeveloped countries; such as when their export goods prices fall while their import goods prices remain relatively constant because their demand for these import goods is relatively inelastic. While some of the fluctuations in demand for commodities from underdeveloped countries are absorbed by price changes *instead of* quantity adjustments, I suspect the wide price changes also indicate wide fluctuations in employment in export industries.

6. The ease with which British colonies gained independence in the early 1960s, the intensifying competition among 'great' powers for spheres of influence among underdeveloped countries, the growth of left-wing movements in these countries and the collusion of governments from underdeveloped countries concerning the maintenance of certain raw material prices (notably oil) indicate the probability of a re-examination of the peripheral status of workers in certain underdeveloped countries. Nevertheless this is

likely to be an extremely slow process and very selective among underdeveloped countries (see Warren [1973]).

7. While the advantages will be greater for setting up more labour-intensive processes in underdeveloped countries, this does not prevent underdeveloped countries from using the 'optimal' combination of capital goods and labour power, while continuing to produce more cheaply due to cheaper labour power. Factories producing textiles or assembling motor cars in underdeveloped countries (relatively labour-intensive processes), use the most up-to-date equipment with increasingly disastrous results for British car and textile workers. Thus the growing call for 'selective' import controls (as at the 1976 annual conference of the T.U.C.). This also implies that one cannot attribute lower wages in underdeveloped countries simply to lower productivity; see Emmanuel [1972], p. 158.

Chapter 10

1. If the industry is important enough nationally, and if the shift in location is out of an advanced capitalist country, worker resistance combined with national considerations (balance of payments effects) may result in state aid for the industry; see Chapter 14.

2. While the sample sizes for *white-collar* workers were small, Daniel's data (see Chapter 8 Section 3) clearly shows a significant loss in status for those who had been unemployed. Of the 16 who had been managerial and professional workers only half found new jobs in this category, while 5 found jobs as clerks or technical workers, one as a supervisor and two as unskilled manual workers. Of the 46 clerical and technical workers, only four moved up to managerial or professional categories, while 15 took manual jobs (six unskilled and six semi-skilled); (1974, p. 99).

3. This applies to the position of immigrant works in most developed countries as well as workers in underdeveloped countries; see Castles and Kosack [1973].

4. Though I shall be particularly concerned with changes in expendability of workers distinguished by their geographic location in the industry-area studies, it should be clear from the earlier chapters that the other main characteristic which often separates central from peripheral workers, their skills, is not sacred. Braverman (1972, chap. 15) clearly shows how male, white-collar, high status, clerical jobs have been deskilled during the twentieth century in a manner similar to the deskilling of craftsmen's jobs throughout the nineteenth century.

5. This general shift is reflected in the movement of the hosiery industry from London to the East Midlands (Chapter 12).

6. By 1907 iron and steel exports reached 50 per cent of gross product for the first time; the proportion of coal output exported rose from under 20 per cent before the late 1880s to 26 per cent in 1900 to 33 per cent in 1913; by the turn of the century 79 per cent of cotton output was exported (Deane and Cole [1967]).

Chapter 11

1. They were called factory hands, but they were properly workshop hands until 1837, when the first permanent steam factory was built in Coventry.

2. The largest of these employed over 400 looms (Prest [1960], pp. 50–51).

3. Which in the early nineteenth century meant paying domestic weavers enough to allow them to live comfortably without being pressed into the workshops or factories.

4. The list had completely broken down in the nearby Nottingham and Leicester hosiery trades by 1820.

5. In 1840, for example, the register of electors contained 3200 freemen and only 589 others. These lands were finally enclosed under the Health of Towns Act in the 1850s.

6. In 1838, of the 27 masters with workshops, only two had factories using steam power.

7. Of course it was not the city which exploited the village weavers. Coventry weavers and village weavers were both exploited by the masters. The centre – periphery pattern arose from their different abilities to resist that exploitation (see Chapter 8, Section 5).

8. Unfortunately there are no figures for Hillfields' population separate from Coventry in the Censuses.

Chapter 12

1. In 1664, of 650 frames in the United Kingdom, 400–500 were in London. About 100 were in Nottingham and 50 in Leicester (Wells [1935], pp. 27–8).

2. By 1727, of 8000 frames in England, there were only 2500 in London, but 4650 in the East Midlands counties. In Leicester there were 500 frames, in Nottingham, 400 (Wells [1935], p. 56).

3. See Map 12.1 for the distribution of frames throughout the United Kingdom for 1844.

4. While frames were expensive, not less that £50 or £60 in the seventeenth century, cheap second-hand frames became increasingly available during the eighteenth century. These could be had for under £10 by the 1770s. While some stockingers did buy second-hand frames, this often put them into debt. Knowledge of this allowed some masters to force down prices even further. Often masters would not employ a man without his taking a frame; or, if a man used his own frame, he was charged half-rent.

5. Often when the stockinger could not get work from the master who supplied his frame he would be forced to seek work elsewhere. While the stockinger could exchange his frame for one from a new master, it was difficult to adapt to a new frame. Often this required three to four months during which the stockinger's earnings would be reduced due to lower productivity (Select Committee [1812], p. 17).

6. Frames were extremely durable, generally lasting from 100 to 150 years (Nelson [1930], p. 475).

7. It was also easier for the bagman to pay lower prices to villagers because many could rely, in early years, on their gardens and on grazing rights on the commons.

8. A large power frame of the early type available in the 1850s cost between £100 and £200 (Wells, [1935], p. 146).

9. In 1851 there were 1722 people employed in the boot and shoe industry in Leicester or 5.1 per cent of the occupied population. The number had risen to 3206 in 1861, 13,055 in 1881, and 24,159 in 1891, or 25 per cent of Leicester's occupied population. The number rose to 30,686 in 1901, but fell off drastically by 1911 to 18,523. The industry declined even further in Leicester after 1931, and by 1971 employed only 5410 people.

10. Church cites examples of hosiers in the 1870s and 1880s whose businesses were worth well under £1000 according to initial financial resources employed and values of businesses on bankruptcy (1966, p. 263).

11. The average annual value of cotton hosiery fell from £590,000 between 1814 and 1816 to £181,000 between 1834 and 1843. Comparable figures for silk hosiery were £209,000 and £103,000 and for wool £357,000 and £125,000 (Wells [1935], p. 133).

12. Average earnings for male domestic workers had fallen to between 5s (shillings) and 7s by the mid-1840s (from 12s to 14s in the 1780s), by 1862 men were getting 12s to 15s in factories and by the late 1880s they were getting 25s 4d (pence) on average (Nelson [1930], p. 487; Wells [1935], p. 148; Ashworth [1958], p. 311).

13. The Nottingham Board of Conciliation and Arbitration was set up first in 1860. It served the districts surrounding Nottingham, Derby, Belper and Loughborough. The Leicester Board covered the districts surrounding Leicester and Hinckley (see Map 12.3 for a rough view of the districts involved).

14. The federation was set up in 1889. The L.L.A.H.U. comprised over half the total membership of the federation. In 1892 the L.L.A.H.U. had 3000 members while the Nottingham and Derby Union had 1900 members.

15. As in Coventry, the larger manufacturers, those with more highly developed internal labour markets and more expensive equipment, were most anxious to pursue Responsible Autonomy strategies.

16. Taking 13s 6d as the average male wage and 9s as the average female wage in 1861, it appeared as though wages had risen tremendously to 25s 4d for men and 11s 6d for women. But the rise of 87 per cent for males was overshadowed by the substitution of women for men. Overall average wages in Leicester's hosiery industry rose from 11s 11d in 1861 to only 16s 3d in 1891, taking the census proportions for males and females to be accurate. Thus wages only rose by 36 per cent over the thirty years. Average money wages in the United Kingdom rose by 46 per cent between 1861 and 1891 (Mitchell and Deane [1971], pp. 343–4).

17. While men were concerned about their own earnings they were also extremely concerned about employment prospects. Generally firms increased their proportion of women to men workers by moving to a village. Thus all the men (except for a few who moved with the factory) lost their jobs. Unable to

stop firms from moving, trade unionists did try to discourage these moves by forming Midlands-wide organisations (1889) and recruiting women (from 1890) to narrow the tempting differential. But conventional social prejudices against women and animosity encouraged by managerial strategies weakened their resolve, and unemployment in the 1890s weakened their strength. Between the Censuses of 1891 and 1901 the number of males employed in Leicester's hosiery trade fell by 1004 while the number of women employed rose by 726.

18. This particular incident concerned competition fostered between town and country hand-frame knitters. Nevertheless within factories workers in the countryside accepted wage rates at 30 per cent to 50 per cent below rates negotiated by trade unions in Leicester during the 1880s and 1890s. In spite of the relative inefficiency of village factories, savings of 25 per cent on manufacturing costs were possible with a move to the villages (Wells, [1935], pp. 193–4).

19. Firms employing 100 men in 1851 would have employed roughly 50 women or 150 people in all taking the 1851 ratio between males and females in Leicester (Table 12.2). The 1930 Census of Production lists 801 firms, of which 545 employed less than 100 and more than 10 people, and 691 employed less than 200 and more than 10. The Census only states that firms employing 10 people or less accounted for 2332 hosiery works. Assuming these to employ five people on average, I have added 466 firms. This is likely to be an *underestimate*, because of the number of firms excluded for giving inadequate information (96), a higher proportion are likely to be small than those which gave adequate information. Note that I am comparing Leicester firms in 1851 with firms in the whole country in 1930.

20. In 1851 29.4 per cent of Leicester's occupied males were hosiery workers compared with 18.4 per cent of the Leicestershire countryside's occupied males. Of Leicester's occupied females, 20.9 per cent were classed as hosiery workers compared with 30.6 per cent of countryside women. Both figures for women, though particularly the countryside one, are likely to be underestimates because of the large number of part-time workers who were not enumerated.

21. What allowed Leicester workers to enjoy significant improvements from the late 1860s to the early 1880s was the vast growth in the boot and shoe industry (mainly employing men) from the 1860s to the end of the century, and especially during the 1870s and 1880s. In 1861 hosiery workers out-numbered those in the boot and shoe industry by two to one in Leicester. By 1881 there were about 50 per cent more boot and shoe workers than hosiery workers and by 1901 they outnumbered hosiery workers by two to one.

22. Also the growth in boot and shoe employment in Leicester slowed down considerably in the 1890s. The number of boot and shoe workers rose by 8104 between 1881 and 1891, but by only 3503 between 1891 and 1901.

23. According to Tabberer the company first tried a few new machines in Foleshill (an area with a large number of unemployed female silk ribbon weavers). This provoked union leaders in Leicester to ask that the machines be brought back to Leicester. Top managers refused to meet trade union leaders, provoking a strike which, according to Tabberer, was the immediate cause of

the removal of the entire factory to Foleshill. Nevertheless Tabberer maintained that Leicester factory workers had always strongly resisted their attempts to put women on to frames in Leicester. By moving to Foleshill the majority of the firm's factory workers were now women paid at 10s to 15s a week instead of mainly men in Leicester earning as much as 50s a week. Even the men in Foleshill were getting less than those in Leicester, 20s to 40s. A further consequence of the move was that the top managers were able to rule that none of their employees in Foleshill *or Leicester* could belong to a trade union (Royal Commission [1892], pp. 93–101).

24. Though workers in the countryside were somewhat less efficient they were paid 30 per cent to 50 per cent less than trade union prices in Leicester. Also the late nineteenth century practice of selling to merchants by offering samples meant the location in the trading centre was no longer a great advantage (Wells, [1935], pp. 193–4).

25. The latter figure is lower due to the war deaths which were estimated to have amounted to 3.1 per cent of the 1921 male population. The natural increase for the United Kingdom between 1901 and 1911 was 11.7 per cent. It would have been somewhat lower for a depressed region such as Leicester. In the 1921 Census the natural increase between 1911 and 1921 for Leicester was estimated at 6.9 per cent.

Chapter 13

1. British car exports were very minor before the Second World War and since 1950 they have grown very slowly (see Graph 13.2). Car imports had been negligible due to the 33.3 per cent *ad valorem* tariff which remained in force from 1915 to 1956. The tariff was slowly reduced until 1968 when it stood at 22 per cent. By 1972 it had been cut to 11 per cent. Car imports accounted for only 6 per cent of the market in 1966 and 9 per cent in 1968.

2. New registrations may also rise with rising numbers of households, but this is highly unlikely in Britain considering her extremely slow population growth during this century.

3. For a detailed discussion of car demand see Roos and von Szeliski [1939]; Chow [1957]; Cramer [1962]; Bonus [1973]; and Smith [1975].

4. Note that these idealised curves are intended to show the general shape of the long-run car purchase pattern. Their height is not significant. While formula S-shaped curves (such as the logistic, gompertz or lognormal curves – see Aitchison and Brown [1969]) have been used extensively for forecasting car demand, what is of concern here is simply the basic S-shape, making the very broad prediction that market conditions during the peak period may be clearly distinguished both from those which preceded it and from those which will succeed it. Spotting exactly when this peak period begins and ends is difficult, but a reasonable estimate can be made if an idea of the long-term pattern is all that is required.

5. In addition 1.5 per cent of occupied males and 3.6 per cent of occupied females were employed in the motor vehicle accessories industry in Coventry.

Note the higher proportion of women to men in accessories compared with those in the firms producing whole cars.

6. The 1971 figures were from the Employment Record of the Coventry Employment Exchange while earlier figures were from the Censuses. The discrepancy between the two sources was minor for 1961 when both sources were available. The 1961 and 1971 figures refer to MLH 381.

7. Not all metals and mechanical engineering is affected by the car industry: the aircraft industry is also significant in Coventry (8.2 per cent of males and 2.4 per cent of females), but I have not included retail and transport industries dealing with cars and of course the effect of car-worker purchasing power on general service industries.

Chapter 14

1. 'Several hundred Benz cars were produced in 1883' (Political and Economic Planning [1948], p. 18).

2. Watch-making was a male occupation. The 2704 people occupied in the trade represented 11.2 per cent of Coventry's occupied population in 1861. Of these, 2637 were males, representing 20.2 per cent of all occupied males. In 1851 only 1700 were employed in the trade in Coventry.

3. The only other important centres for bicycle production in England during the nineteenth century were Birmingham and Wolverhampton. In 1881 these two cities employed 300 bicycle workers, and in 1891, 3,300.

4. In 1891 there were over 100 bicycle firms in Coventry employing 12–500 workers in each (Stephens [1969], pp. 177–83).

5. Car and cycle workers accounted for 25.8 per cent of Coventry's labour force and 31.8 per cent of its male workers in 1911.

6. First by limiting the ratio of apprentices to journeymen, and second by restricting skilled jobs to 'legal men' – either qualified journeymen, or men who had worked five years at the trade and were paid at the standard craft rate (Hinton [1973], p. 56).

7. The engineering employers tried to smash the A.S.E. with the engineering lock-out of 1852. Though the employers won this battle in that they won the right to force workers to sign a declaration that they did not belong to a union and would not join one, people continued to belong to the union in secret and within a few years the union's pre-lock-out strength was restored (Wigham [1973], pp. 3–5).

8. This may be seen from the proportion of women employed in bicycle factories compared with car factories. In 1911, 16 per cent of those in bicycle factories in Coventry were women; only 2.7 per cent in car factories were women.

9. There were still 2625 watch-makers in Coventry in 1901. Their numbers declined by 1179 during the decade to 1911 and it is likely that most went into car factories.

10. The Workers' Union was established in 1898. In 1929 it was taken over by the Transport and General Workers' Union. For an excellent account of

the union's history see Hyman [1971].

11. In 1901 and 1912 the A.S.E. formally agreed to admit semi-skilled workers into a special section of its own union, but in practice little effort went into recruitment.

12. Hotchkiss et Cie, a French machine-gun firm, was set up in Coventry in 1915. In 1923 Morris took over the works in order to produce car engines there.

13. See Table 14.2 for changes in the structure of the car market producers between each of the periods of the product cycle.

14. Top managers knew about this system, but given wartime conditions of demand and the Ministry of Munitions' policy of maintaining supply, top managers chose not to recognise the nascent gang system.

15. The division within engineering paralleled the division within British industry, in general based on age and dependence on home markets (discussed in Chapter 10).

16. The remainder was accounted for by constructional engineering which grew, but not so quickly as the latter group (Yates [1937], pp. 9, 11).

17. Figures are from earnings returns compiled by the E.E.F. in 28 major towns, cities and labour market areas in Great Britain. In the early 1930s the Coventry differentials fell to 13 per cent for fitters (1933) and 8 per cent for labourers (1934), but the differentials quickly grew after 1934.

18. In 1921 30 per cent of Coventry's occupied population was employed in the motor vehicle industry and in 1931 28.3 per cent. An additional 9.5 per cent in 1921 and 11.2 per cent in 1931 were employed making machines, tools and implements. (In 1921, 36.8 per cent of men were in the motor vehicle industry and 11.6 per cent in machines, tools and implements. The figures for 1931 were 34.1 per cent and 13.8 per cent.)

19. The 1911 figures are not strictly comparable as they refer only to general engineering in Coventry; nevertheless the direction of change may be trusted.

20. The only major price change was Ford's reduction of the Ford Eight's price in 1935 by 13 per cent, which resulted in doubled sales of the model in 1936. In 1937 and 1938 Ford raised the price of the Ford Eight, bringing it back into line with competing firms' models of similar size.

21. Unemployment approached 1 per cent in Coventry in 1953 when many car workers were laid off. Figures from Ministry of Labour and quoted in Ling [1963], p. 17.

22. Maxcy and Silberston [1959], p. 229. Net profits before tax meaning trading profits plus other income, less depreciation, directors' salaries, minority interests, debenture interest, etc., before deductions of preference and ordinary dividends and before deduction of tax.

23. Of course much of this was invested in the firm, but the firm's investment rate on profits earned remained significantly lower than Ford and Vauxhall's.

24. Primarily the Amalgamated Engineering Union, (A.E.U. — formed in 1920 when the A.S.E. took over several smaller craft unions), and also the National Union of Vehicle Builders (N.U.V.B.).

25. The dominance of the A.E.U. and the T.G.W.U. was even more

marked in Coventry's car firms compared with the rest (Turner [1967], pp. 194–5).

26. Nevertheless Drayton (an enthusiastic supporter of the gang system from the workers' point of view) points out that gangers sometimes became secretive with the members, becoming 'Gaffers' Men'. In consequence 'gang stewards' were sometimes elected.

27. The organisation of work is not set by technical conditions (see Chapters 6 and 7 above and a strong statement of this position by Melman following from his detailed investigation at Standard [1958], pp. 3–20), but firms must adapt their organisation to new machines available, within limits.

28. Of course the obvious question is – what new product could the car firms have been experimenting with? The answer is difficult, but products such as Hovercraft, Hovertrain, electric or non-petrol-using cars come to mind. Also the productive facilities and labour may have been used for machine tools, electrical equipment or electronic equipment. While it is difficult to imagine such great product changes undertaken by car firms by themselves, the imaginative leap is not so great if such a switch-over were nationally supervised with a certain level of initial demand guaranteed by the government. Such events occur in the military sector of most economies.

29. Ford never used piece-work wage systems. They had a day-rate system of payment with the company formally responsible for work loads. Vauxhall consolidated its piece-rates into time-rates in 1956.

30. Note (Table 14.5) the rise in proportion of strikes over individual dismissals after 1960. These were usually concerning dismissal of more active shop stewards as firms began to try to break the strength of the stewards.

31. Very few women or black immigrants were employed by the car assemblers during this period. The main centre – periphery pattern during these years was *between* firms; see Chapter 15.

32. These acts provided grants for the first time for buildings (25 per cent of cost) and machinery (10 per cent of cost) set up in Development Districts.

33. Low investment in plant and machinery in British car firms' pre-1960s factories during the 1960s was revealed by the Ryder Report on British Leyland [1975] and the Expenditure Committee Report on the U.K. Motor Vehicle Industry [1975].

34. The term job control is misleading. The 'control' which workers achieved at Dagenham should be interpreted in the relative sense as a rise in direct control.

35. In 1969 the net pay rate for an industrial task (installation of door-lock with door-handle and connecting rods) was 9s. 10d. at Vauxhall (Luton) and 10s. 6d. at Ford (Dagenham), but 15s. 8d. at B.M.C. (Longbridge in Birmingham) and 17s. 4d. at Rootes (Ryton in Coventry); (*Sunday Times*, 21 December 1969).

36. By the end of 1975 Chrysler employed about 25,000 workers in the United Kingdom, (compared with 28,000 in 1974); 7000 at Linwood, in Scotland; 6000 at Stoke and 5000 at Ryton, both in Coventry. The remaining 7000 were employed in about eight different sites including 2000 at Whitley, Coventry, and 1000 in two components factories in Coventry.

37. In 1969, for example, a Chrysler spokesman in Geneva said, 'Labour

troubles at Coventry and Linwood could jeopardise the long-term investment program in the U.K.' (*Coventry Evening Telegraph*, 20 December 1969).

38. Chrysler answered the allegation of inappropriate transfer pricing (Chrysler U.K., 1 July 1975) and the Labour Research Department following with a counter-claim (15 July 1975). The issue remains in doubt because the Labour Research Department were unable to produce figures in sufficient detail (prices by models sold) to prove their case, and Chrysler refused to publish such figures in order to refute the case.

39. This included 6500 at two Jaguar plants; 4800 at two B.M.C. plants; 1500 at three Coventry Climax engine plants; 500 at a gear manufacturing plant; 11,400 at three Standard Triumph plants; and 700 at a Range Rover plant.

40. Assets per man include all capital assets, e.g. fixed assets, stocks, work in progress, cash, etc (Rhys [1972], pp. 370, 371).

41. Profits in 1975 should have been reduced by £95 million according to this criterion as well.

42. Volvo recently took over DAF, i.e. the entire Dutch motor industry.

43. Of course *some* stewards are much more militant than the workers they represent.

44. Of course science has nothing to do with how much people 'should' work. Even how much workers are capable of doing is an unresolved scientific issue as Meyers showed in the inter-war period (Rose [1975], pt 2).

45. The gang system was dealt a severe blow with the 1956 lay-offs and strikes at Standard. From then on gangs were mostly smaller groups of workers and the trend towards more gangs as a proportion of manual workers in other Coventry firms was reversed.

46. Characteristics such as responsibility, level of fatigue, working conditions were used (see Beynon [1973], p. 160).

47. Chrysler workers won a mutuality clause over either manning levels or line speeds. They chose manning levels. Thus manning levels are negotiated, primarily through ordinary shop stewards, while line speeds are the cause of most 'unofficial unofficial' disputes.

48. In a well-organised factory there will usually be one shop steward per five to five hundred workers. An individual factory of thousands of workers will generally have only one convener and perhaps a few deputy conveners.

49. Their absorption was made easier because they were, on the whole, white and male.

50. Though British Leyland have had to liquidate facilities on the Continent (their Italian operation, Innocenti, and their Spanish operation) to economise.

51. Chrysler's latest model, the Alpine, is produced with similar 'integration' between Chrysler France and Chrysler U.K. Multisourcing internationally by large car firms has also pushed component manufacturers to follow suit; see *Financial Times* 23 May 1974 and 27 May 1976.

Chapter 15

1. Local organisation was also encouraged by piece-working, mutuality and the gang system, as well as the fact that the major unions in car firms have a majority of their members in other unions.

2. In an agreement between Chrysler and the unions for the Ryton factory in 1971, the highest-paid groups of skilled workers were to get only 1.5 per cent more than direct production workers (semi-skilled workers on the lines) per hour. Direct production workers were to get 36.1 per cent more than cleaners and other unskilled workers; Chrysler U.K. [1971], pp. 6–7.

3. The numbers of these last two categories rose between 1964 and 1966, and then fell significantly in 1967, by 7.6 per cent for technical workers and 7.4 per cent for administrative and clerical workers.

4. Male white-collar workers earned only 10 per cent more than male manual workers in the car industry on average compared with 28.9 per cent for all manufacturing in 1963 (N.E.D.O. [1969], p. 40).

5. Assuming white-collar workers to comprise about 20–25 per cent of Chrysler workers.

6. The main reason for the company's drastic cuts in white-collar workers stems from the extra supervisors and foremen hired by Chrysler during the transition to Measured Daywork in 1969–70. With the strong mutuality clauses won on manning levels and strong shop-floor power to resist increased line speeds, many of the extra staff who were to provide a veil of science became superfluous as work intensity continued to be an issue of power and struggle rather than expertise.

7. The proportion of women in motor vehicles (MLH 381) varied between 12 per cent and 14 per cent between 1959 and 1968, while the proportion in engineering and electrical goods varied between 21 per cent and 26 per cent and for all manufacturing the proportion varied between 31 per cent and 32 per cent (Department of Employment [1971]).

8. For example, Chrysler first tried to introduce Measured Daywork at Linwood in 1967–8; see Weller [1968], pp. 3–12.

9. Though it also reflects the relatively strong components industry of this country; this itself reflects the strategy of large car firms.

10. Census figures cited in Yates [1937], pp. 5–6.

11. After 1959 'Parts and Accessories' was not available as a separate item for the motor vehicle industry because of a change in methods of classification.

12. Though the proportion in metal manufacture (primarily iron and steel) was slightly lower at around 12 per cent (Department of Employment [1971]).

13. Multiple sourcing may actually involve increased vertical integration in the case of supplies which traditionally come from a few large sources. Ford used to get virtually all its supplies of gears from only eleven suppliers. In order to reduce this dependence Ford now supplies close to 50 per cent of its own needs from its own plants at Halewood and Antwerp (Gambino [1972], p. 5). It appears that *internal* international multisourcing is growing rapidly, in

part reflecting top managers in large car firms' confidence in their ability to maintain authority over their own workers better than top managers in supplier firms can over theirs. They may well be mistaken and this trend *may* soon be reversed.

Chapter 16

1. '*We* ran the place,' is a common judgement of Coventry car workers on the slack managerial authority maintained in car firms, particularly from the 1940s to the 1960s.

2. In 1966 there were 0.56 cars per household in Coventry compared with 0.51 for Great Britain and 57.7 per cent of households were owner-occupiers compared with 46.7 per cent for Great Britain.

3. The choice of Coventry for a national experiment into multiple-deprivation was criticised publicly at the time (Holman [1970]).

4. Chrysler employed about 16,000 workers on its five Coventry sites (Ryton, Stoke, Whitley and two component factories), but as can be seen from Map 16.3, some workers came from outside Coventry. Similarly B.L.M.C. employed over 29,000 in factories around Coventry, but several thousand came from outside the Coventry Employment Exchange area.

5. The comparable figure for unskilled manual workers in Coventry's major car firms is likely to be something far lower than 16 per cent—probably around 10 per cent – given the fact that the four major car firms only accounted for about two-thirds of employment in MLH 381 for Great Britain in the late 1960s and early 1970s, and given the low proportion of unskilled manual workers in Coventry in 1971–7 per cent. (Minimum List Heading – MLH – 381 stands for Motor Vehicle Manufacture in the Census classification system.)

6. The 15 largest firms in Coventry employed 54 per cent of Coventry's workers, but only 40 per cent of Hillfields' workers. For example, Alfred Herbert, John Brown and Massey Ferguson employed 8.1 per cent of Coventry's workers, but only 3.4 per cent of those from Hillfields.

7. Discrepancies between Table 16.4 and the figures in Tables 16.2 and 16.3 are due to slight differences in the area defined as Hillfields and sampling errors.

8. Also, only 18 per cent of those unemployed stated that their usual job was unskilled manual work.

9. Unemployment increases the likelihood of future unemployment, and the longer unemployment has lasted the more vulnerable to unemployment one becomes. See references and evidence in Hill [1973], pp. 72–75.

10. 'Total labour costs' including basic wage rate plus fringe benefits or social security contributions paid by the car firms were surveyed across Europe for assembly line workers. Using exchange rates at 1 September 1975, it was estimated that with U.K. costs at 100, comparable levels for other countries would be France, 120; West Germany, 180; Belgium, 180; and Italy, 130; Central Policy Review Staff (C.P.R.S.) [1975], p. 78.

11. Comparing productivity across countries is extremely difficult. That

output per man in car firms is higher on the Continent compared with the United Kingdom is clear from the C.P.R.S. report. By 1965 Germany, France and Italy were producing 7.1 per cent, 6.1 per cent and 7.4 per cent more vehicles per employee per year than in the United Kingdom (Pratten and Silberston [1967]).

12. At Ford Cologne, Turks make up 34 per cent of the work-force, but 90 per cent of assembly-line workers (*Der Spiegel*, 10 September 1973).

13. These short weeks and lay-offs were *not* due to strikes in the firms concerned or elsewhere in the industry. They were due to poor car demand.

Chapter 17

1. While Marx recognises wage differentials, for him they are in the long run based only on skills. The differentials merely represent the expenses of educating the skilled worker (*Capital*, vol. 1, pp. 168–9).

2. 'His means of subsistence must therefore be sufficient to maintain him in his normal state as a labouring individual. His natural wants, such as food, clothing, fuel and housing, vary according to the climatic and other physical conditions of his country. On the other hand, the number and extent of his so-called necessary wants, as also the modes of satisfying them, are themselves the product of historical development, . . . there enters into the determination of the value of labour power a historical and moral element' (*Capital*, vol. 1, p. 168).

3. The tangle created by tying the value of labour power to the idea of need and subsistence is clearly demonstrated by the statements of an eminent Marxist, Arghiri Emmanuel, on wage differences between whites and blacks in South Africa and between natives and immigrants in America. He says,

The very fact, however, that in countries where several communities live side by side, with ways of life and needs that are very different from each other, as in South Africa, and in more or less all the former colonies, even if there is no legislative discrimination, a rate of wages appropriate to each of these communities is established. . . . In a country like the United States, these immigrants feel the need for an automobile less than they would if they had remained in their country of origin. There, however poor the country might be, and despite the relative scarcity of cars, there would always have been some friend or some relative luckier than themselves, who would have owned a car and so aroused in them a feeling of envy or a tendency to imitation. In the country where cars are more plentiful, however, this does not happen to them, for the cars that pass them in the street are too anonymous, too unknown, too remote from them to provide them with either a stimulus or an example (1972, pp. 122–3).

4. Which will involve consuming goods which individual workers may never have consumed before.

5. Actually this is too crude. Conditions of work as well as wages are objects of struggle. For example, central workers are distinguished by their

greater direct control over the labour process (or their 'autonomy' within it), and by their relative employment security. Therefore the overall value of labour power is more than simply the amount of labour time necessary to produce a quantity of goods and services *at an instant of time*. It will also include labour time necessary to pay for all the paraphernalia of Responsible Autonomy strategies used for dealing with central workers – such as industrial relations officers, the cost of giving up some economies of scale due to finer division of labour forgone with autonomous work groups, as well as the cost of keeping central workers employed during recessions.

6. The value of labour power considered here is an average of a distribution with a limited range. The position of any group along that range depends on their expendability within productive activity and their disruptive potential generally within the society. Nevertheless the range is limited because those who are strong have an interest in not allowing the differential to become too great. This occurs in part because well-organised workers fear that top managers' temptation to substitute cheap workers will become so great as to undermine their own position; in part because the vagaries of fortune within capitalist society can easily cause any central worker to tumble into a peripheral category through unemployment or disability, (and all will fall into the old-age pensioner category); and in part through solidarity with fellow-workers when all are challenged (as in a deep recession), which the concentration of capital and the growth of large factory units encourage.

7. The widespread lack of solidarity or sympathy with many car-worker strikes during the 1970s in Britain reflects this differential as well as strong propaganda on the part of the companies and the State against worker-stimulated disruption to car production.

Bibliography

J. AITCHISON and J. A. C. BROWN [1969], *The Lognormal Distribution* (Cambridge: Cambridge University Press).

G. C. ALLEN [1929], *Industrial Development of Birmingham and the Black Country 1860–1927* (London: Allen & Unwin).

S. AMIN [1975], 'Toward a Structured Crisis of World Capitalism', *Socialist Revolution*, 38 (2) (June).

P. ANDERSON [1976], *Considerations on Western Marxism* (London: New Left Books).

A. ARMSTRONG and A. SILBERSTON [1967] 'Size of Plant, Size of Enterprise and Concentration in British Manufacturing Industry 1915–58', *Journal of the Royal Statistical Society*, Series A 128.

T. S. ASHTON and J. SYKES [1929], *The Coal Industry of the Eighteenth Century* (Manchester: University of Manchester).

C. ASHWORTH [1958], 'Hosiery Manufacture', in R. A. McKinley *A History of the County of Leicester*, vol. 4, ed. (London: Oxford University Press).

P. BARAN [1957], *The Political Economy of Growth* (New York: Monthly Review Press).

— and P. SWEEZY [1966], *Monopoly Capital* (New York: Monthly Review Press).

W. J. BAUMOL [1964], *Business Behavior, Value and Growth* (London: Macmillan).

A. A. BERLE and G. C. MEANS [1932], *The Modern Corporation and Private Property* (New York: Harcourt, Brace and World).

H. BEYNON [1973], *Working For Ford* (Harmondsworth, Middlesex: Penguin).

J. E. BOLTON [1971], *Small Firms: Report of the Committee of Inquiry on Small Firms* (London: A0fCurves, H.M.S.O.).

H. BONUS [1973], 'Quasi-Engel Curve's, Diffusion and the Ownership of Major Consumer Durables', *Journal of Political Economy*, 81.

N. BOSANQUET and G. STANDING [1972], 'Government and Unemployment, 1966–70: A Study of Policy and Evidence', *British Journal of Industrial Relations*, 10 (2).

S. BOSTON [1974], 'Equal Pay', in *Conditions of Illusions*, ed. S. Allen *et al.*, (Leeds: Feminist Books).

A. L. BOWLEY [1921], *Prices and Wages in the United Kingdom 1914–1920* (London: Oxford University Press).

N. BRANSON [1975], *Britain in the Nineteen Twenties* (London: Weidenfeld & Nicholson).

— and M. HEINEMANN [1971], *Britain in the Nineteen Thirties* (London: Weidenfeld & Nicholson).

H. BRAVERMAN [1974], *Labor and Monopoly Capital* (New York: Monthly Review Press).

British Leyland Motor Corporation, *Annual Reports* (various years).

W. BROWN [1971], 'Piecework Wage Determination in Coventry', *Scottish Journal of Political Economy*, 18 (Feb).

S. CASTLES and O. KOSACK [1973], *Immigrant Workers and Class Structures in Western Europe* (London: Oxford University Press).

Census of Population, England and Wales (various years) (London: H.M.S.O.).

Census of Production (various years) (London: H.M.S.O.).

Central Policy Review Staff [1975], *The Future of the British Car Industry*, (London: H.M.S.O.).

D. CHADWICK [1860], 'On the Rate of Wages in Manchester and Salford and the Manufacturing Districts of Lancashire 1839–59', *Journal of the Royal Statistical Society*, 23.

S. D. CHAPMAN [1972], *The Cotton Industry in the Industrial Revolution* (London: Macmillan).

— and T. S. ASTON [1913–14], 'The Sizes of Business, Mainly in the Textile Industries', *Journal of the Royal Statistical Society*. New series 77 (April).

G. C. CHOW [1957], *Demand for Automobiles in the United States* (Amsterdam: North Holland).

Chrysler Corporation, *Annual Reports* (various years).

Chrysler U.K. [1971], *Agreement on Pay and Associated Conditions* (Coventry: Chrysler U.K.).

Chrysler U.K., *Annual Report* (various years).

Chrysler U.K. [1975], 'Chrysler Refute Allegations in Labour Research Department Report' (press release, 1 July).

R. A. CHURCH, [1966], *Economic and Social Change in a Midland Town: Victorian Nottingham 1815–1900* (London: Cass).

J. H. CLAPHAM [1926], *An Economic History of Modern Britain: The Early Railway Age 1820–1850* (Cambridge: Cambridge University Press).

—[1932], *An Economic History of Modern Britain: Free Trade and Steel 1850–1886* (Cambridge: Cambridge University Press).

— [1938], *An Economic History of Modern Britain: Machines and National Rivalries 1887–1914* (Cambridge: Cambridge University Press).

H. A. CLEGG, A. FOX and A. F. THOMPSON [1964], *A History of British Trade Unions since 1889* (London: Oxford University Press).

G. D. H. COLE [1948], *A Short History of the British Working Class Movement 1789–1947* (London: Allen & Unwin).

Commission on Framework Knitters [1845], *Report* (London: H.M.S.O.)

Counter Information Services [1974], *British Leyland: The Beginning of the End?* (London: Counter Information Services).

Coventry City Council [1967], *City of Coventry: 1966 Review of the Development Plan* (Coventry: Coventry City Council).

— [1952], *Coventry: The Development Plan 1951* (Coventry: Coventry City Council).

Coventry Community Development Project [1975], *Final Report: Part I* (London: Community Development Project Information and Intelligence Unit).

Coventry Community Development Project [1971], *One-in-Six Household Survey of Hillfields*, carried out in May-June 1971.

Coventry and District Engineering Employers' Association (C.D.E.E.A.) [1968], *Wage Drift, Work Measurement and Systems of Payment* (Coventry: C.D.E.E.A.).

Coventry Employment Exchange *Reports* (various years).

Coventry Evening Telegraph (various dates).

J. S. CRAMER [1962], *The Ownership of Major Consumer Durables* (Cambridge: Cambridge University Press).

R. M. CYERT and J. G. MARSH [1963], *A Behavioral Theory of the Firm* (Englewood Cliffs, N.Y.: Prentice-Hall).

W. W. DANIEL [1974], *A National Survey of the Unemployed* (London: Political and Economic Planning).

R. B. DAVIDSON [1964], *Commonwealth Immigrants* (London: Oxford University Press).

P. Deane and W. A. Cole [1967], *British Economic Growth 1688–1959* (Cambridge: Cambridge University Press).

Department of Employment [1971], *British Labour Statistics: Historical Abstract 1886–1968* (London: H.M.S.O.).

Department of Employment, *Labour Gazette* (various dates).

J. B. D. Derksen and A. Rombouts [1937], The Demand for Bicycles in the Netherlands', *Econometrica*, 5 (July).

Der Spiegel (10 September 1973).

M. Desai [1974], *Marxian Economic Theory* (London: Gray-Mills).

M. Dobb [1963], *Studies in the Development of Capitalism* (London: Routledge & Kegan Paul).

P. B. Doeringer and M. J. Piore [1971], *Internal Labor Markets and Manpower Analysis* (Lexington, Mass.: D. C. Heath).

D. Drayton [1972], *Shop Floor Democracy in Action* (Nottingham: Russell Press).

E. Durkheim [1933], *The Division of Labour in Society* (New York: Macmillan).

J. Eatwell [1971], 'Growth, Profitability and Size: The Empirical Evidence', in *The Corporate Economy* ed. R. Harris and A. Wood (London: Macmillan).

M. Edney and D. Phillips [1974], 'Striking Progress', in *Conditions of Illusion*, ed. S. Allen *et al.*, (Leeds: Feminist Books).

R. C. Edwards, M. Reich, and D. M. Gordon [1975], *Labor Market Segmentation* (London: D. C. Heath).

A. Emmanuel [1972], *Unequal Exchange* (New York: Monthly Review Press).

F. Engels [1892], *The Condition of the Working Class in England in 1844* (London: Allen & Unwin).

R. Evely and I. M. D. Little [1960], *Concentration in British Industry* (Cambridge: Cambridge University Press).

Expenditure Committee [1975], *The Motor Vehicle Industry* (London: H.M.S.O.).

C. R. Fay [1920], *Life and Labour in the Nineteenth Century* (Cambridge: Cambridge University Press).

W. Felkin [1867], *A History of the Machine Wrought Hosiery and Lace Manufacturers* (London: Longmans).

Financial Times (various dates).

Ford (U.K.), *Annual Reports* (various years).

J. Foster [1976], 'British Imperialism and the Labour Aristocracy', in *The General Strike 1926*, ed. J. Skelling (London: Lawrence & Wishart).

A. G. Frank [1967], *Capitalism and Underdevelopment in Latin America* (New York: Monthly Review Press).

A. L. Friedman [1977], 'Responsible Autonomy Versus Direct Control Over the Labour Process', *Capital and Class*, 1.

— and L. Carter [1975], 'Industry in Coventry and the Decline of Hillfields', in *Final Report*, part 2, Coventry Community Development Project (London: Community Development Project Information and Intelligence Unit).

J. K. Galbraith [1967], *The New Industrial State* (London: Hamish Hamilton).

F. Gambino [1972], *Workers' Struggles and the Development of Ford in Britain* (London: Big Flame).

J. Gardiner [1974], 'Women's Work in the Industrial Revolution', in *Conditions of Illusion*, (eds) S. Allen *et al.*, (Leeds: Feminist Books).

K. D. George [1974], *Industrial Organisation* (London: Allen & Unwin).

— [1972], 'The Changing Structure of Competitive Industry', *Economic Journal*, 82 (3255).

F. J. Glover [1961], 'The Rise of the Heavy Woollen Trade of the West Riding of Yorkshire in the Nineteenth Century', *Business History*, 4 (1).

A. GLYN and B. SUTCLIFFE [1972], *British Capitalism, Workers and the Profits Squeeze* (Harmondsworth, Middlesex: Penguin).

C. L. GOODRICH [1975], *The Frontier of Control* (London: Pluto).

D. M. GORDON [1972], *Theories of Poverty and Underemployment: Orthodox, Radical, and Dual Labor Market Perspectives* (Lexington, Mass.: D. C. Heath).

A. H. HALSEY [1972], *Trends in British Society Since 1900* (London: Macmillan).

J. L. and B. HAMMOND [1919], *The Skilled Labourer, 1760–1832* (London: Longmans).

L. HANNAH [1974a], 'Mergers in British Manufacturing Industry 1880–1918', *Oxford Economic Papers*, new series 26 (1).

— [1974b], 'Managerial Innovation and the Rise of the Large-scale Company in Inter-war Britain', *Economic History Review*, second series 27 (2).

J. HARRISON and B. SUTCLIFFE [1975], 'Autopsy on British Leyland', *Bulletin of the Conference of Socialist Economists*, 4 (1).

R. A. HART and D. I. MACKAY [1975], 'Engineering Earnings in Britain, 1914–1968', *Journal of the Royal Statistical Society*, series A 138 (1).

P. HIGGS [1969], 'The Convenor', in *Work*, vol. 2, ed. L. Fraser (Harmondsworth, Middlesex: Penguin).

M. HILL, R. M. HARRISON, A. V. SARGEANT and V. TALBOT [1973], *Men Out of Work* (Cambridge: Cambridge University Press).

J. HINTON [1973], *The First Shop Stewards' Movement* (London: Allen & Unwin).

E. J. HOBSBAWM [1969], *Industry and Empire* (Harmondsworth, Middlesex: Penguin).

— [1968], *Labouring Men* (London: Weidenfeld & Nicholson).

— [1974], *Labour's Turning Point 1880–1900* (Brighton, Sussex: Harvester).

G. HODGSON [1976], 'Exploitation and Embodied Labour Time', *Bulletin of the Conference of Socialist Economists*, 5 (1).

M. HOLLIS and E. NELL [1975], *Rational Economic Man* (Cambridge: Cambridge University Press).

R. HOLMAN, *Socially Deprived Families in Britain* (London: Bedford Square Press).

R. HYMAN [1971], *Marxism and the Sociology of Trade Unionism* (London: Pluto Press).

— [1971], *The Workers' Union* (Oxford: Clarendon Press).

International Labour Office (various years), *Yearbook of Labour Statistics* (Geneva: International Labour Office).

J. B. JEFFERYS [1945], *Story of the Engineers*, reprinted 1970 (New York: Johnson).

— and M. JEFFERYS [1947], 'The Wages, Hours and Trade Customs of the Skilled Engineer in 1861', *Economic History Review*, 17 (1).

Joint Union Delegation of Chrysler Shop Stewards and Staff Representatives, (Chrysler Stewards) [1975], 'Chrysler's Crisis: The Workers' Answer, mimeographed.

P. JONES [1973], 'Politics and the Shop Floor', *International Socialism*.

F. KNIGHT [1921], *Risk, Uncertainty and Profit* (Boston: Houghton Mifflin).

K. G. J. C. KNOWLES [1954], ' "Strike-Proneness" and its Determinants', *American Journal of Sociology*, 60 (3).

— and D. ROBINSON [1969], 'Wage Movements in Coventry', *Bulletin of the Oxford University Institute of Economics and Statistics*, 31 (1).

Labour Research Department [1975], *Fact Service* (26 June).

Labour Research Department [1975], Press Release (15 July).

R. J. LARNER [1970], 'The Effect of Management-Control on the Profits of Large Corporations', in *American Society Inc.* ed. M. Zeitlin (Chicago: Markham).

S. J. LATSIS [1972], 'Situational Determinism in Economics', *British Journal for the Philosophy of Science*, 23.

V. I. Lenin [1916], *Imperialism, the Highest Stage of Capitalism* (Moscow: Progress).
— [1918], 'The Immediate Tasks of the Soviet Government', in *Collected Works* (London: Lawrence & Wishart, 1962).
— [1902], 'What Is to Be Done?' in *Selected Works*, (London: Lawrence and Wishart, 1937).
W. G. Lewellen [1969], 'Management and Ownership in the Large Firm', *Journal of Finance* 24 (2).
A. Ling [1961], *Hillfields, C. D. A.* (Coventry: Coventry City Council).
— [1963], *Work in Coventry* (Coventry: Coventry City Council).
D. Lockwood [1958] *The Blackcoated Worker* (London: Allen & Unwin).
E. Mandel [1975], *Late Capitalism* (London: New Left Books).
S. A. Marglin [1974], 'What Do Bosses Do? The Origins and Functions of Hierarchy in Capitalist Production', *The Review of Radical Political Economics*, 6 (2).
R. Marris [1964], *The Economic Theory of 'Managerial' Capitalism* (London: Macmillan).
A. Marshall [1919], *Industry and Trade* (Cambridge: Cambridge University Press).
R. Martin and R. H. Fryer [1973], *Redundancy and Paternalistic Capitalism* (London: Allen & Unwin).
K. Marx [1859], *A Contribution to the Critique of Political Economy* (London: Lawrence and Wishart, 1971).
— [1867], *Capital, vol. 1* (London: Lawrence and Wishart, 1970).
— [1885], *Capital, vol. 2* (London: Lawrence and Wishart, 1970).
— [1895], *Capital, vol. 3* (London: Lawrence and Wishart, 1972).
— and F. Engels [1848] *Manifesto of the Communist Party* (Moscow: Progress).
G. Maxcy [1958], 'The Motor Industry', in *Effects of Mergers*, P. L. Cook (London: Allen & Unwin).
— and A. Silberston [1959], *The Motor Industry* (London: Allen & Unwin).
S. Melman [1958], *Decision-Making and Productivity* (Oxford: Basil Blackwell).
Ministry of Labour, *Labour Gazette* (various years).
B. R. Mitchell and P. Deane [1971], *Abstract of British Historical Statistics* (Cambridge: Cambridge University Press).
D. Moggridge [1969], *The Return to Gold, 1925* (Cambridge: Cambridge University Press).
T. Nairn [1973], *The Left Against Europe?* (Harmondsworth, Middlesex: Penguin).
National Economic Development Office (N.E.D.O.) [1971], *Japan: Its Motor Industry and Market* (London: H.M.S.O.).
— [1969], *Motor Industry Statistics, 1959–1968* (London: H.M.S.O.).
E. G. Nelson [1930], 'The English Framework-Knitting Industry', *Journal of Economic and Business History*, 2 (3).
J. O'Connor [1972], 'Inflation, Fiscal Crisis and the American Working Class', *Socialist Revolution*, 2 (2).
L. A. Parker [1955], 'Hosiery', in *A History of the County of Leicester*, vol. 3, ed. W. G. Hoskins and R. A. McKinley (London: Oxford University Press).
P. L. Payne [1967], 'The Emergence of the Large-scale Company in Great Britain, 1870–1914', *Economic History Review*, second series 20 (3).
H. Pelling [1971], *A History of British Trade Unionism* (Harmondsworth, Middlesex: Penguin).
Political and Economic Planning (PEP) [1948], 'The Motor Industry', *Planning*, 25 (284).
— [1939], *'Report on the Location of Industry in Great Britain'* (London: PEP).
S. Pollard [1954], 'Wages and Earnings in the Sheffield Trades, 1851–1914', *Yorkshire Bulletin of Economic and Social Research*, 6 (1).

N. Poulantzas [1975], *Classes in Contemporary Capitalism* (London: New Left Books).

C. Pratten and A. Silberston [1967], 'International Comparisons of Labour Productivity in the Automobile Industry, 1950–1965', cited in *The Future of the British Car Industry,* Central Policy Review Staff, (London: H.M.S.O., 1975).

J. Prest [1960], *The Industrial Revolution in Coventry* (London: Oxford University Press).

Red Notes [1976], 'Workers' Struggles and the Crisis of the British Motor Industry', mimeographed.

M. Reich, D. M. Gordon and R. C. Edwards [1973], 'A Theory of Labor Market Segmentation', *American Economic Review Papers and Proceedings*, 85.

Report on Factory Inspectors (various years) (London: H.M.S.O.).

Reports of the Commissioners to the Commission on Unemployed Handloom Weavers, (Reports Commissioners) [1840], 24 (London: H.M.S.O.).

— [1860], 34, (London: H.M.S.O.).

D. G. Rhys [1973], *The Motor Industry: An Economic Survey* (London: Butterworth).

A. K. Rice [1963], *The Enterprise and Its Environment* (London: Tavistock Institute).

K. Richardson [1972], *Twentieth-Century Coventry* (London: Macmillan).

R. Robson [1957], *The Cotton Industry in Britain* (London: Macmillan).

C. F. Roos and V. von Szelisk [1939], *Factors Governing Changes in Domestic Automobile Demand* (New York: General Motors).

M. Rose [1975], *Industrial Behaviour* (London: Allen Lane).

W. W. Rostow [1948], *The British Economy of the Nineteenth Century* (London: Oxford University Press).

G. Routh [1965], *Occupation and Pay in Great Britain 1906–1960* (Cambridge: Cambridge University Press).

S. Rowbotham [1973], *Hidden From History* (London: Pluto Press).

J. W. F. Rowe [1928], *Wages, in Theory and Practice* (London: Routledge & Kegan Paul).

B. Rowthorn [1974], 'Neo-Classicism, Neo-Ricardianism and Marxism' *New Left Review*, 86.

Royal Commission on Labour [1892], *Report* (London: H.M.S.O.).

D. Ryder [1975], *British Leyland: The Next Decade* (London: H.M.S.O.).

L. R. Sayles [1958], *The Behavior of Industrial Work Group: Production and Control* (New York: Wiley).

Select Committee on Joint Stock Companies [1844], *Report* (London: H.M.S.O.).

Select Committee on Framework Knitters' Petitions [1812], *Report* (London: H.M.S.O.).

D. Seward [1972], 'The Wool Textile Industry 1750–1960', in *The Wool Textile Industry in Great Britain*, J. G. Jenkins (London: Routledge & Kegan Paul).

H. A. Simon [1957], *Models of Man* (New York: Wiley).

A. Singh [1971], *Takeovers* (Cambridge: Cambridge University Press).

— and G. Whittington [1968], *Growth, Profitability and Valuation* (Cambridge: Cambridge University Press).

A. Smith [1776], *The Wealth of Nations* (Harmondsworth, Middlesex: Penguin, 1974).

D. M. Smith [1963], 'The British Hosiery Industry at the Middle of the Nineteenth Century: An Historical Study in Economic Geography', *Institute of British Geographers Transactions and Papers*.

R. P. Smith [1975], *Consumer Demand for Cars in the U.S.A.* (Cambridge: Cambridge University Press, Cambridge.

Society of Motor Manufacturers and Trades (S.M.M.T.), *The Motor Industry of Great Britain* (London: S.M.M.T., various years).

R. Solow [1967], 'The New Industrial State or Son of Affluence', *Public Interest*.

W. B. Stephens [1969], 'Crafts and Industries', in *A History of the County of Warwick*, vol. 8, ed. W. B. Stephens (London: Oxford University Press).

Sunday Express (various dates).

Sunday Times (various dates).

F. W. Taylor [1903], 'Shop Management', reprinted in *Scientific Management* (New York: Harper, 1947).

— [1911], 'Principles of Scientific Management', reprinted in *Scientific Management* (New York: Harper, 1947).

Terms of Settlement [1898], 'General Principle of Freedom to Employers in the Management of their Works', in *The Power to Manage*, E. Wigham (London: Macmillan, 1973).

The Times (various dates).

E. P. Thompson [1968], *The Making of the English Working Class* (Harmondsworth, Middlesex: Penguin).

E. L. Trist *et al.* [1963], *Organisational Choice* (London: Tavistock Institute).

G. Turner [1971], *The Leyland Papers* (London: Eyre & Spottiswoode).

H. A. Turner, G. Clack and G. Roberts [1967], *Labour Relations in the U. K. Motor Industry* (London: Allen & Unwin).

United Nations [1970], *Economic Bulletin for Europe*.

A. Ure [1863], *Dictionary of Arts, Manufactures and Mines*.

M. A. Utton [1972], 'Some Features of the Early Merger Movements in British Manufacturing Industry', *Business History*.

Vauxhall Motors, *Annual Reports* (various years).

H. M. Wachtel [1975], 'Class Consciousness and Stratification in the Labor Process', in *Labor Market Segmentation*, R. C. Edwards, D. M. Gordon and M. Reich (Lexington, Mass.: D. C. Heath).

A. P. Wadsworth and J. de L. Mann [1931], *The Cotton Trade and Industrial Lancashire* (Manchester: University of Manchester).

I. Wallerstein [1974], *The Modern World-System* (London: Academic Press).

B. Warren [1973], 'Imperialism and Capitalist Industrialization', *New Left Review*.

S. and B. Webb [1894], *History of Trade Unionism* (London: Longmans).

K. Weller [1968], 'Linwood-Rootes and the Motor Industry', *Solidarity*.

F. A. Wells, [1935], *The British Hosiery Trade: Its History and Organisation* (London: Allen & Unwin).

E. Wigham [1973], *The Power to Manage* (London: Macmillan).

E. C. Wilkinson [1939], *The Town That Was Murdered* (London: Gollancz).

G. Williamson [1966], *Wheels within Wheels: The Story of the Life of the Starleys of Coventry* (London: Geoffrey Bles).

O. E. Williamson [1964], *The Economics of Discretionary Behavior: Management Objectives in a Theory of the Firm* (Englewood Cliffs, N.J.: Prentice-Hall).

G. H. Wood [1910], 'The Statistics of Wages in the Nineteenth Century: The Cotton Industry', *Journal of the Royal Statistical Society*, new series 73 (Jan).

P. Wright [1968], *The Coloured Worker In British Industry* (London: Oxford University Press).

M. L. Yates [1937], *Wages and Labour Conditions in British Engineering* (London: Macdonald and Evans).

S. Young and A. V. Lowe [1974], *Intervention in the Mixed Economy* (London: Croom Helm).

Index

NOTES: *See* car industry, hosiery industry *and* silk ribbon industry *for references to several items when they appear in the industry–area studies.*

Formerly independent British car firms now part of British Leyland and Chrysler (U.K.) are listed under the modern firm name.

(def.) = definition.